MILK IT!

MILK IT!

Collected Musings on the
ALTERNATIVE MUSIC
EXPLOSION of the '90s

Da Capo Press
A Member of the Perseus Books Group

Cataloging-in-Publication data for this book
is available from the Library of Congress

First Da Capo Press edition 2003
ISBN 0-306-81271-1
Published by Da Capo Press
A Member of the Perseus Books Group
http://www.dacapopress.com

Da Capo Press books are available at special discounts
for bulk purchases in the U.S. by corporations,
institutions, and other organizations. For more information,
please contact the Special Markets Department at the
Perseus Books Group, 11 Cambridge Center,
Cambridge, MA 02142,
or call (800) 255-1514 or (617) 252-5298, or e-mail
j.mccrary@perseusbooks.com.

Interior book design by Cynthia Young

1 2 3 4 5 6 7 8 9—07 06 05 04 03

For the teachers and editors

who taught me to convey my ideas on the page—

in particular Marisa Pitaro-Minkler, Dorothy Campbell,

John Campion, Jim O'Donnell, Jim Testa,

Mickey Carroll, Steven Newhouse, Pat Donnelly,

Margaret Schmidt, Keith Moerer, Susan Hamre,

and all of my colleagues at the Chicago Sun-Times—

with the caveat that any obstinate opinions and

boneheaded mistakes herein are entirely my own.

Contents

Foreword
by Keith Moerer

LOUD, OBNOXIOUS, FREQUENTLY WRONG—these are just three of the qualities I love about Jim DeRogatis.

You see, I don't want to read rock critics who never rattle me, and I don't need them to guide or confirm my own impeccable taste. I prefer to be challenged, surprised, infuriated, informed, amused, or touched. Yet most of what passes these days for rock criticism—and its even milder cousin, rock journalism—is stultifying in its predictability: timid hacks praising artists more for what they've done in the past than in the present, or lamenting prefab pop as if it had been invented by the Backstreet Boys and will topple for good with the inevitable career decline of Christina Aguilera.

To state what is already obvious or soon will be, Jim doesn't have a problem speaking his mind. Every critic angers artists they pan; Jim is one of the few with an ability to piss off people whose work he generally *admires*, mostly by telling the truth as he sees it on a particular Saturday night or Tuesday afternoon. If not always painful, the truth is often inconvenient, which is why over the years he's earned the grudging respect, corrosive scorn, and rock-star self-pity of Courtney Love, Billy Corgan, Steve Albini, and the cry-baby half of Sonic Youth (Thurston Moore and Lee Ranaldo).

I met Jim in 1990, shortly after he'd left a job covering parking-ticket scams and corrupt politicians as a reporter for *The Jersey Journal*. Within a year of our meeting, an American president named Bush would attack Iraq and *Nevermind* would dominate the pop charts. As this is being written twelve years later, another American president named Bush is preparing to attack Iraq, and Nirvana is back on the charts—this time with a posthumous greatest-hits collection and a best-selling book in Kurt Cobain's haunted *Journals*. During the years in between, alternative rock went boom, followed by a sickening bust (I'm talking about overdoses and suicides, not its misfortunes on the *Billboard Hot 200*). Hip-hop and teen pop took control, much of it formulaic in its calibration of success (Cristal champagne, designer SUVs) and beauty (silicone implants not really optional). Oh, and Jim developed from a reporter covering the Hoboken City Council (with a clip file full of fanzine bylines on the side) to the chief pop music critic at the *Chicago Sun-Times* and a nationally known freelancer who witnessed and documented many of these developments from the third row (the first two being reserved for industry weasels and the holders of scalped tickets).

I hired Jim twice during the first half of the '90s, and the second time he repaid me by getting me fired before I turned into a hopeless wino or, worse, one of those smug New York magazine types—alternative newsweekly graduates who pretend that putting some female celebrity half-naked on a magazine cover qualifies as the satisfying culmination of a long and distinguished career. The first time we worked together we had a blast. It was at a Minneapolis magazine called *Request,* and it was a better publication than it had any right to be (it was owned and distributed by a national chain of mall music stores, but its executives gave us lots of autonomy, and any flaws the magazine had were ours, not theirs). It was at *Request* that I learned firsthand how passionately Jim believes in music, its power to transcend, but also its potential for disappointment or hollow poses. Whenever one of us made a particularly boneheaded pronouncement, the other would yell, "Them's fightin' words!" and off we'd go, arguing as if our jobs, or at least our self-respect, were at stake.

The second time we worked together was at *Rolling Stone,* where we were hired in 1995 to make a publication going through a prolonged identity crisis relevant again, reclaiming its past as a music magazine, covering younger artists sooner and more aggressively. Within months I would be standing in my boss Jann Wenner's office, editing a forty-thousand-word interview he'd done with some up-and-comer named Mick Jagger while a band of snotty upstarts called Fleetwood Mac blared over his office stereo system. Jim was forced to assign a string of news stories about the Grateful Dead, a band for which Jann had rediscovered a passion shortly after Jerry Garcia's death rendered it kaput. In truth, there wasn't much to inspire in the younger musicians we covered, either. Cobain was already dead, replaced on the scene by Nirvana-wannabes Bush and Layne Staley of Alice in Chains, who was well into his own sad, fatal decline.

We didn't last a year at *Rolling Stone,* thanks to all of the above, plus the gall of Jim giving Hootie and the Blowfish one less star than the three Jann felt were guaranteed to any artist who'd previously been on the cover of his magazine. I just checked a few sites on the Internet, and you can now buy that underappreciated classic, *Fairweather Johnson*, for twenty-four cents, or you can join any one of three auctions on eBay, where the starting bid, should someone choose to enter it, is a penny. Which means, of course, that history has proven Jim wrong: He should have taken both of the stars he granted Hootie and given them to Jann for a seven-star review of the next Jagger solo album.

Reading through this collection of Jim's writings from the '90s, I'm struck by a number of things. The first is that his experience as a news reporter has served him well, giving him a good instinct for framing a story and the ability to ask tough, substantive questions. He knows when to hurl a hard question (challenging Tom Morello of Rage Against the Machine on the "righteous" means used by Peru's Shining Path guerrillas, for example) and when to shut up and let his tape recorder do the work (as when Courtney Love freely admits to taking drugs during the first trimester of her pregnancy, but not during the second, dammit, no matter what that writer-bitch Lynn Hirschberg wrote in *Vanity Fair*). He's well-informed enough to talk to Krist Novoselic about the NRA, political action committees, and the Dead Kennedys, but playful enough to pose the following question to Justine Frischmann of Elastica: "You live with Damon Albarn of Blur and two cats. Who's more trouble?" Her answer makes it obvious that their romance will never last.

As might be expected of a collection that covers the '90s, this one includes interviews with Cobain, Love, Corgan, Perry Farrell, the Flaming Lips, and those twin totems of alt-rock, R.E.M. and U2. No book covering the past decade would be complete without them. But Jim also has a keen enough appreciation for history to include the pioneers who preceded them: Lou Reed, John Cale, Wire, Wayne Kramer of the MC5, and David Thomas of Pere Ubu. Yet some of my favorite pieces here are the least obvious ones of all, such as the profile of Ben Weasel, a role model for both Green Day and Blink 182, who ended the century as a recovering agoraphobic, still flying the flag for punk rock, but now driving a new Honda and living in a six-room condo in suburban Chicago.

One of the qualities I appreciate most about Jim is his insistence in following his passions, wherever they might lead. This is why you'll find effusive praise for Julian Cope, Spiritualized, and Wake Ooloo in these pages, but also rare dissenting opinions on such sacred subjects as Guided By Voices, Patti Smith, Alex Chilton, and Lee "Scratch" Perry. When he does tackle an obvious target, he's often able to do so from a fresh perspective.

(Read Jim's piece on Britney Spears toward the end of this collection, wherein he wrestles with his distaste for the teen queen not as a critic defending rock, alt or otherwise, but as the father of a young daughter.)

Jim also has a good eye for telling details. Read in context now, there's something eerie about his description of Cobain having his shoes torn off his feet while crowd-surfing at a Chicago concert, and something touching about Louise Post of Veruca Salt asking for the house lights of a club to be turned up so she can better see the frets on her guitar. It's amusing to read his wry acknowledgment of the long line of rebels at Lollapalooza waiting patiently for wristbands that will permit them to join the mosh pit, or his bold assertion that there wasn't *enough* corporate sponsorship at Woodstock '94, proved by the lack of adequate toilet facilities and sky-high ticket prices.

Much as Jim and I have disagreed about music over the years, reading this book makes me realize that he got most of the big stories of the '90s right, and a lot of the little ones, too. I could give you plenty of examples of what I think he missed or got wrong, but part of the fun of reading this book is nodding in agreement when he strikes a personal chord, or shaking a fist when he hits some particularly sensitive nerve of yours. Contrary to popular opinion, fifty million screaming fans *can* be wrong, and one lone bastard—Jim, me, you—can be right.

As I write this, 2002 is coming to a close, allowing enough perspective on the final decade of the twentieth century for me to state the following: That however great Nirvana's music is, their success didn't "change" the music industry, except on the most superficial level for a couple of years, and Britney Spears won't singlehandedly destroy it, either (although another decade of record executive greed and stupidity just might). That Pearl Jam has never been more admirable, or less interesting, than now. That Courtney Love will probably always be interesting, but never particularly admirable. That Dave Matthews will continue to be more popular than he has any right to be. That PJ Harvey will remain less popular than she deserves to be. That Steve Albini will continue to hate Jim's guts. And, finally, that Jim will carry on as he always has—as loud, obnoxious, and convinced he's right as ever. Don't let him get away without a good fight.

After a five-year stint as Editor-in-Chief of Music and Books at Amazon.com, Keith Moerer is currently working on a book called *Looking for Lewis and Clark,* a social, political, and personal history of his hometown of Great Falls, Montana. In 2004, he plans to launch a magazine for people who appreciate compelling stories and good writing about all kinds of music.

Introduction

IT SEEMS TO BE OBLIGATORY in the introduction to collections such as this one—even my very favorites, like *Psychotic Reactions and Carburetor Dung, A Whore Just Like the Rest: The Music Writings of Richard Meltzer,* and *The Nick Tosches Reader*—to note that the pieces that follow are being presented pretty much as they ran—errors, awkward passages, and snap judgments intact—in the interest of preserving the spirit of the moment, as with dispatches from the front. My guess is that this is a deterrence machine (at least for those rock-writer heroes who are still breathing and compiling themselves), a way to hedge against a charge I make several times herein.

Nostalgia is the most insidious enemy of great art, especially rock 'n' roll, a music that is about living in the moment. That holds for rock writing, too. No writer wants to be accused of dwelling in the past and cannibalizing him- or herself, so he or she puts an ironic, self-deprecating title on their anthology and notes that it's just a bunch of old crap, scribbled in the heat of battle, presented *as is* in the interest of verisimilitude, and collected in the hope of giving the reader some slight sense of what it was like to *be there.*

Well, that holds here, too, for the most part, but I ain't gonna lie to you: Perhaps a quarter of these articles benefited from some correcting, a bit of rewriting, and a touch of synthesizing—especially the daily newspaper pieces, which, after all, are the most immediate and ephemeral kind of criticism or journalism. But I didn't try to turn those newspaper pieces into something they weren't originally—I wanted to preserve the unique feeling of reading an account of a great album published a week before its release, or of a noteworthy show recalled in print a mere five hours after it happened, even if that album or show is now twelve years in the past—and there has been absolutely no revisionism. I change my mind and double back on myself all the time; all of us do. As with lovers and friends, our relationship with the music changes and evolves as we live with it, and I'd advise that you never trust a critic who doesn't admit as much. Still, the opinions and observations here are unaltered because that's what I thought at the time, when I was in the thick of things, and it does seem dishonest to allow hindsight to enter into the picture now.

I cannot imagine the reader who will agree with everything in these pages—as I said, I no longer agree with everything myself!—but that has never been my goal. My approach to rock criticism is that it's best when it's a spirited dialogue between people who care passionately about the music. To that end, I often run my readers' emails and letters in my columns in the *Chicago Sun-Times*; my partner Greg Kot and I encourage listeners to call, voice their thoughts, and challenge us both every Tuesday night on *Sound Opinions*, "the world's only rock 'n' roll talk show"; and as you will soon see, I have no problem accepting and publishing criticism of myself that's as barbed and acerbic as what I've dished out. All of us—critics, artists, and fans—ought to be able to take a little ego bashing if it's in the interest of communicating, exchanging ideas, and growing in our love and under-standing of the music.

How do those of us who love rock 'n' roll interact with it in real life? We sit on the couch and blast the stuff on the stereo, trying to convince each other that the music we love is something that our friends need in their lives, too, while simultaneously railing against the crap that we bought that turned out to be a hype. I can't thank you enough for picking up this book and joining me on my couch, and I'll consider it a compliment if something I've written prompts you to hurl these pages across the room. I'm not try-ing to change your mind. After the fundamental journalistic goal of docu-menting, the slightly more ambitious one of entertaining, and the critical missions of offering context and insight, I was attempting in each of these dispatches to inspire you to question your own reactions, to engage with the music on a deeper and hopefully more fulfilling level, to set your pulse pounding as you race to the record store (or the file-swapping Web site), and most of all to *think for yourself.*

Although I rarely imitate them (not consciously, anyway), Jack Kerouac and Lester Bangs are two writers I love, but the critiques of their work from which I've gained the most are the ones that contend they were charlatans, frauds, and lightweights. Obviously I disagree, but the skeptics forced me to focus my own thoughts and opinions—to question my values and ask *why* I feel as I do—and that is one of the primary joys and affirmations of being alive.

As for what went into this collection, I was trying to fulfill two goals at once, and I'm not sure I completely succeeded at either. *Milk It!* is partly a broad, sweeping overview of the alternative-rock era, an account of the music of the '90s compiled on the fly as it was sprouting, blooming, and withering, but certainly some things are missing. There should probably be more on Seattle, for example, but I spent most of those years in Chicago, and it wasn't only because of homerism that I found its music more interesting. Alt-rock didn't happen in a vacuum, and hip-hop was of course a major force in popular music throughout the decade, but with a handful of exceptions (N.W.A, P.M. Dawn, Arrested Development, Tone-Loc), much of my writing on the subject is absent here because it just didn't seem to fit. There should probably be more on Beck and the riot grrrls and Nine Inch Nails and the Red Hot Chili Peppers. And so on. But all of that had to be balanced with the other goal of this book, which was to stand as a "Best of Jim DeRogatis (So Far)"—or, if you prefer, a bunch of old crap—and I at least wanted to include the stuff that held up the best (or the shit that stank the least).

My own professional odyssey began (as indeed I did) in New Jersey. I was born and raised just across the Hudson River from Manhattan in Jersey City (the armpit of the universe), but I moved up in the world to Hoboken as soon as I was able. I wanted to write about rock 'n' roll from the minute I fell in love with it—like Bangs, I was "a fanatical fan with fanatical opinions that I wanted to inflict on people"—and I scrawled reviews and transcribed interviews for my high school and college newspapers (not the *Washington Square News*, which was the more respectable and dreadfully dull of New York University's two student-run rags, but the far seedier and more subversive *Courier*). The dream of becoming a "professional" rock writer was there all through the time I was pursuing degrees in journalism and sociology (which seemed like the same thing), and my enthusiasm was not dampened by the fact that I was consistently and rather rudely rejected by outlets that should have been open to a precocious and ambitious late teen or early twentysomething at the time.

Shut out of the big leagues, I did what every fanatical fan with fanatical opinions did during the indie-rock heyday of the mid-'80s: I wrote for established fanzines—*Matter, The Bob*, and especially *Jersey Beat*, whose editor, Jim Testa, became a valued mentor and a lifelong friend—and I published my own 'zine, thanks to time stolen on various office copy machines. (It was called *Reasons for Living*; I was nothing if not a ridiculously earnest young thing.) All the while I was playing in bands and hosting college radio shows and going to gigs and reading the rock press and buying and listening to records voraciously—again, like Lester, it all seemed part of the same basic impulse and obsession.

My career proper began at *The Jersey Journal*, a then-sixty-five-thou-sand-circulation daily newspaper in dear old Jersey City, where I rose from a beat reporter to an investigative reporter to a (sub- sub- sub-) Jimmy Breslin–like city columnist. It was exciting stuff. I covered brutal jail riots, I got a councilman indicted for voter fraud, and I saw the Feds fish a mobster's body out of the Hackensack River. (John "Bayonne Butch" DiGilio was a boxer turned mob henchman who "went missing," as they say. After a few months, his mother requested the body so she could bury him, but he'd been gone for quite some time, and he wasn't in the best shape when he resurfaced, as you might imagine. Cop to earnest young reporter at 6 A.M. in the Meadowlands: "Hey, kid, come'n look at dis! They safety-pinned his credit cards to his balls so's we could figger out who he is!" Earnest young reporter to the bushes: "*Blaaahhh!!!*" It was all very *Sopranos*.)

With the exception of a handful of pieces in the final issues of *Creem* (as-signed by my pal and fellow fanziner, David Sprague—we bonded in NYU's magazine editing and production class, where we both got mediocre grades even though we were actually writing, editing, and publishing the "mock magazines" we submitted), I didn't make a dime writing about mu-sic for eleven years, though I probably wrote about it as much then as I do now. After five years at *The Jersey Journal*, I burned out on the day job—I simply could not ask another African-American mother in the projects how she felt after her son had been shot in the street—and I decided to move to Minneapolis in the summer of 1990. I'd visited on tours with various bands through the years, and I realized that all of my slacker friends there (and in places like Cleveland, Portland, Austin, and Seattle) were living better than I was, working fifteen hours a week at Kinko's while playing in a band or publishing a comic book or writing the great American novel. I had no idea what I was going to do, but I needed a change, and I wanted to meet a corn-fed Midwestern farm girl.

As luck would have it, at exactly the point when my savings ran out and the farm girl appeared, my second great mentor and lifelong chum, Keith Moerer, hired me at *Request*. As the assistant editor and junior staffer, my more odious tasks included proofreading, taking out the trash, and fact-checking Chuck Eddy (*ugh*). But I also got to write, and I could never ex-press just how much I learned under Keith and managing editor (later edi-tor) Susan Hamre, who remain two of my dearest friends. Their deft editing and constant prodding to get me to push myself as a journalist, writer, and critic was my version of graduate school.

I'll pick up the pace a bit: Two years at *Request* led to my first stint as the pop music critic at the *Chicago Sun-Times*, starting in the summer of 1992 and ending in the fall of 1995, when I went back to New York to join Keith at *Rolling Stone*. My mercifully brief tenure there lasted eight months (more about that in Chapter Eleven), after which I took my unemployed ass, my Midwestern farm girl, and the baby in her belly back to Minneapolis and square one. There was no guarantee that I'd be able to make it as a free-lancer, and getting by on a Kinko's salary was going to be easier there than in Chicago or New York. I did alright, though, thanks to the faith of editors like Robert Wilonsky at *New Times Los Angeles* and Kiki Yablon at the *Chicago Reader*, whose considerable talents improved many of the pieces collected here, and I was well into writing my second book and labor of love, *Let It Blurt*, when the *Sun-Times* called in the fall of 1997 and asked if I'd like to come back to Chicago.

"Sure," I said, "but I want the deal Roger Ebert has." They rolled their eyes. "No, no, no; I know you're not going to pay me what he makes. But he only comes into the office once a year at Christmas to give everybody a movie-of-the-day calendar. Don't make me work at the paper; I can't sit around and write in my underwear and blast loud music!" They quite rea-sonably agreed. I've been back in Chicago ever since, and I'm never leaving again.

I relate all of this because I'm asked about it fairly often (*Almost Famous* seems to have bred a whole new generation of aspiring rock writers, though I've certainly never met a Kate Hudson doing this, much less a Fairuza Balk), and because it may be helpful to convey the context (or at least the geographic locale) in which some of these pieces were written. If you didn't know already or haven't surmised by now, I took a typically cynical Generation Xer–indie rocker's view of the alternative explosion, amplified by my ingrained journalistic skepticism (that hard-news training) and by the fact that I had already witnessed several times the way music "scenes" are built up and then demolished (the "Hoboken is the new Liverpool!" power-pop craze of the mid-'80s—in which genuinely wonder-ful bands such as the Bongos, the dB's, and the Feelies were briefly anointed as gods, hyped to the high heavens, then just as quickly written off—was similar indeed to what Seattle went through in the early '90s, though the bands of the Pacific Northwest sold a helluva lot more records and won much more mainstream attention).

"Alternative to what?" was a question that cynics asked over and over again through the '90s, and like many punks, my answer was, "Absolutely nothing!" The music business acted like the music business always does (there's plenty of grousing, dirt, and insight about all of that in what's to come, and for even more elucidation, I can't recommend heartily enough *Commodify Your Dissent: The Business of Culture in the New Gilded Age*, an anthology of pieces about the co-option of youth culture during those years culled from the amazingly incisive if sometimes annoyingly Marxist pages of *The Baffler*), but all of that is of secondary interest as far as I'm concerned compared to the actual *sounds*, and those were nothing fundamentally new, either. (Nothing under the sun ever is! It's *all* been done before! So freaking what? If it's good, just turn it up!)

For me the music of the '90s was all a part of the gloriously noisy continuum that stretches from Buddy Holly and Eddie Cochran and Little Richard and Gene Vincent (and some before them, too) through the Thirteenth Floor Elevators and the Troggs and James Brown and the Beatles–Byrds–Rolling Stones Baby Boom canon through the Stooges and Wire and the Sex Pistols and Public Enemy right up to the White Stripes and the Roots and Wilco and the Flaming Lips, *yadda yadda yadda*—the common attitudes and life force shared by all of these rock 'n' rollers being in the end infinitely more enduring and intriguing and vital than their particular genres and personality distinctions (though I spent more than my share of time charting those, too—as I said, I was a sociology-journalism double major).

And yet—and yet, and yet. There *was* something special about the '90s, about a mere seventeen million members of Generation X briefly having their moment in the sun (soon to be eclipsed once again by the seventy-six million Baby Boomers who preceded us and the seventy-two million members of their snot-nosed progeny in Generation Y who followed), seeing *Nevermind* seize No. 1 on the *Billboard* albums chart, enjoying that (illusory, sure, but still fun) sense of community at Lollapalooza, crying together over the death of a hero who never asked to be one, hearing however fleetingly actual *good music* on mainstream radio (three or four songs in a row even!), and feeling like it all really mattered. Which it didn't, not in any sweeping cultural-historical sense (it never does; even the '60s weren't as "important" as the '60s, we all know that), but it made an impact on our lives—mine and yours—and it still can, even if you missed it all, via the best of the music chronicled in the urgent dispatches to come.

In ending this introduction, I'd be remiss if I did not thank some of the other people who assigned, improved, and published these pieces, in addition to those who have already been cited in the dedication and the words above, and with the repeated caveat that anything wrong- or lunkheaded is my fault, not theirs. I also owe particular debts of gratitude to Marc Weingarten at *Request*; P. J. Bednarski, John Barron, Michael Cooke, John Cruickshank, Miriam DiNunzio, Laura Emerick, Darel Jevens, Cristi Kempf, Mark Nadler, Nigel Wade, and Jeff Wisser during various eras at the *Chicago Sun-Times*; Sia Michael, Greg Milner, and Jon Dolan at *Spin*; Bill Holdship and Steve Stolder at *BAM*; Mike Bieber and Doug Hyde at *Audio*; Jim Walsh and Will Hermes at *City Pages*; Keith Goetzman at the *Twin Cities Reader*; Barbara Rice-Thompson at *Penthouse*; Andy Wang at *Ironminds*; John Strausbaugh at the *New York Press*; Bill Wyman and Jeff Stark at *Salon*; Scott Becker and Jason Fine at *Option*; and Keven McAlester at *New Times Los Angeles* (and I apologize to anyone I've omitted).

Thanks are due as well to the (often anonymous to me) copy editors who titled these pieces; with the exception of my daughter, Melody, I have always been lousy at naming things, so very few of these headlines are my own. Additional thanks to Andrea Schulz (who first suggested the idea for this collection before leaving Da Capo) and Ben Schafer (who enthusiastically embraced, encouraged, and shepherded it to completion once he arrived); to production editors Fred Francis and Erica Lawrence, publicist Kate Kazeniac, marketing guru Kevin Hanover, designer Cynthia Young, and copy editor Delia Guzman; to Frank Kozik for the incredible cover image; to my agents, Chris Calhoun and Kassie Evashevski; to *Blurt* editor Gerry Howard (that next book is coming soon, Gerry, I swear!); and to my loyal friends, helpers, volunteer editors, and ever-reliable sounding boards, including Eric Boehlert; my ex-wife Kim DeRogatis; my first writing partner Anthony J. DiMurro; Paula Kamen; Greg Kot; Rob O'Connor; Jay Orff; Erica Roewade; Jason Saldanha; Tom Schraeder, Jr.; Matt Spiegel; Cynthia Taylor-Handrup; my bandmates, Tony Tavano, Chris Martiniano, and Michael Weinstein; my parents, Helene and Harry Reynolds; my brother, his wife, and their son, Michael, Mary Ellen, and Ryan DeRogatis, and *mi corazón verdadero*, Carmél Carrillo.

Finally, thanks again to you, the reader. I hope you enjoy scanning these reviews, reports, features, essays, and asinine opinions as much as I enjoyed writing, living, and spouting them. Try not to break anything if you *do* send this tome flying.

1 RELUCTANT RADIO FRIENDLY UNIT SHIFTERS

ANY ACCOUNT OF THE ALTERNATIVE ERA must begin with the phenomenal success of Nirvana's *Nevermind*, which was released in early 1991 and sold an amazing three million copies within a six-month period during "the year punk broke." The pressures that sudden fame brought to bear on Kurt Cobain have been well-documented (the most riveting account is Charles R. Cross's bestselling biography, *Heavier Than Heaven*), and the artist was understandably gun-shy when dealing with the press before the release of *In Utero* in 1993. He agreed to grant only three newspaper interviews, and he singled me out for inclusion because he appreciated the reporting I'd done surrounding the controversy over the band's third album.

In an interview with my friendly competitor, Greg Kot of the *Chicago Tribune*, "recordist" Steve Albini (see Chapter Five) had claimed that Geffen was reluctant to release *In Utero* because it was too harsh and abrasive, and that Cobain was bowing to pressure to remix it, as he'd done with Andy Wallace on *Nevermind*. In fact, though he didn't want to admit it publicly lest he blow whatever "indie cred" came from hiring Albini in the first place, Cobain himself had decided to hire Scott Litt (the pop-oriented producer of R.E.M. and the dB's) to remix parts of the record, because he felt the vocals were too low in the mix and he wanted to emphasize the beauty of the more melodic tracks in order to make the impact of the noisier songs even more powerful.

Around the time that "Smells Like a Nirvana Feature" was published in *Request*, I reviewed two of the group's final American shows. The first concert at Chicago's Aragon Ballroom was the only time the band ever performed "You Know You're Right" onstage, and it was one of the best shows I've ever seen. The second was one of the worst. The contrast between the two was evidence that this was still very much a group that was living in

1

the moment, and that it was anything but the big, slick rock machine that the industry so desperately wanted. Nirvana was still a band where anything could happen, including imminent self-destruction.

Six months later, I was writing Cobain's obituary.

Life rolled on for the surviving members of the band, though bassist Krist Novoselic has yet to approach anything near the artistic and commercial accomplishments of Nirvana with either of his new groups, Sweet 75 and Eyes Adrift, and after the promise of their debut, Dave Grohl's Foo Fighters quickly devolved into hammering away at an increasingly tired and shallow formula. Meanwhile Cobain's widow, Courtney Love (see Chapter Two), instigated a bitter fight over who would control the group's posthumous legacy. For a time the contentious court case looked as if it might become the ugliest feud in rock since the conflicts over the estates of Bob Marley and Jimi Hendrix, but less than five months after "The Nirvana Wars" was published in *Spin*, the two factions reached a settlement. Generally underreported in news analyses was the fact that Love won, and the settlement closely mirrored the proposal that her husband's former bandmates had earlier rejected.

The Limited Liability Corporation that had been set up to administer Nirvana's business dealings was dissolved, and the band's future output will be overseen by a new entity controlled by a representative of each side—Jim Barber (a former Geffen Records executive and Love's significant other) and John Silva (Nirvana's former manager and the current manager of Grohl and Novoselic)—though Love, Grohl, and Novoselic can override their actions with a unanimous vote. Love has primary control over any film made about Cobain, but the former Nirvana musicians have a say over how they are portrayed. After their deaths, all control of Nirvana's future will go to Frances Bean, Cobain's daughter.

The settlement paved the way for *Nirvana*, the single-disc greatest-hits set that sits atop the charts as I write this and which finally includes the previously unreleased gem, "You Know You're Right." (The long-promised box set and a single-disc rarities collection are both expected by 2004.) At the same time, Cobain's journals top the bestseller list with their odd mix of voyeurism and insight. As with the posthumous cash-ins of so many rock legends, none of this product really does justice to the band's true legacy, which remains difficult to evaluate. I suspect that its real impact has yet to be felt and is being considered most significantly in some garage or basement studio as I write, via its inspiration on any number of smart, passionate, and emotional young artists prompted to pick up that guitar for the first time by "Smells Like Teen Spirit" or "Rape Me." I'm sure that's the gift that Cobain would be proudest of leaving us.

Smells Like a Nirvana Article
Request, November 1993

SEVERAL HUNDRED PEOPLE are waiting outside Club USA, a trendy New York disco in the heart of Times Square. It's the third night of the New Music Seminar, the music industry's largest annual gathering, and the crowd has come to hear the Boredoms, a jazz-noise group from Japan that's one of the seminar's biggest buzz bands. People are growing irritable in the heat of the muggy July evening because the beefy bouncers won't let anyone in, even though the place is as big as an aircraft hangar and only half full.

Nirvana bassist Krist Novoselic is standing with a small group that includes his wife, Shelli, and band biographer Michael Azerrad. Novoselic has gone unnoticed until now, even though he stands a foot taller than most of the people on line. Maybe it's because New Yorkers don't acknowledge celebrities in their midst, or maybe no one recognizes him since he cut the long hair and shaved the scraggly beard he wore in the video 'for "Smells Like Teen Spirit." In any event he hasn't asked for or received special treatment, which I find admirable, since it's in keeping with punk rock's central tenet that band members are no better than their fans.

I wince when Novoselic starts jumping up and down and shouting at the bouncers to let him in—until I hear what he's screaming. "Don't you know who I am?" he shouts. "I'm Andy Kaufman. I was in *Taxi!*"

The bassist bears more than a passing resemblance to the dead comic, but it doesn't matter to the bouncers, and soon he and his friends are shrugging their shoulders and heading off to another club.

SINCE ITS RELEASE in late 1991, Nirvana's second album has sold nine million copies worldwide. *Nevermind* was the first punk album to make it to No. 1, and its success resulted in a major-label feeding frenzy that injected obscene amounts of money into the once-marginal indie-rock world. "Alternative" suddenly became a viable marketing niche, and every move that Novoselic, guitarist-vocalist Kurt Cobain, and drummer Dave Grohl made came under the media's harsh glare.

That's a hell of a lot of baggage to carry to a recording session, and skeptics expected the group to self-destruct as the Sex Pistols did in a brilliant flash before it could even attempt an encore. But the members of the Seattle trio fought the pressures of addictions, fame, and money, hired Chicago producer and provocateur Steve Albini, and recorded the follow-up to *Nevermind* in two weeks for twenty-five thousand dollars, a fraction of the time and money spent on most major-label releases. And somehow they pulled it off.

In Utero—"in the womb"—is an uncompromising album full of harsh guitars and aggressive rhythms, but Nirvana's candy-coated riffs and sing-along choruses are present in force, and they're every bit as catchy as those on *Nevermind*. As always, Cobain's angry, passionate voice cuts through the chaos around it, demanding your attention. "Teenage angst has paid off well," he sings, acknowledging with the first line of the first song that the band has been changed by stardom. Then he proceeds to prove that it hasn't hurt the music a bit.

"Whether this record is released or the tapes are bulk-erased is less important than what the band has done up until now," Albini said in his usual acerbic manner when the album was finished last spring. "They got themselves in a position of influence and power by being a band that everybody liked, and at this point, everything that they do for the rest of their career is going to be secondary to what they've done up until now. Not secondary in quality, but secondary in impact."

Several months later, Cobain reflects on Albini's comments and grins. "We're certain that we won't sell a quarter as much, and we're totally comfortable with that because we like this record so much," he says in a measured, quiet voice. "I wasn't half as proud of *Nevermind* as I am of this record. We intentionally made an aggressive record. I'm really proud of the fact that we introduced a different recording style, a different sound, and we're in a position where we're almost guaranteed a chance of it being played on radio. They're at least going to try it for a while and see how it sticks. And just doing that is a satisfying accomplishment."

Cobain is sitting on a well-worn couch in the split-level living room of the house he shares with his wife, Courtney Love (leader of the band Hole), and their fifteen-month-old daughter, Frances Bean. The family outgrew the home it bought after Nirvana's initial success, and this place is a rental. Located on a steep hill in North Seattle, it's only yards from the shore of scenic Lake Washington. Frances Bean's playpen and wading pool sit in the living room near an enormous TV and a collection of plastic anatomy dolls, one of which graces the cover of *In Utero*. Beside the couch sit two new Fender guitars, prototypes that the company wants to manufacture as the "Kurt Cobain model." Cobain designed it himself: A cross between a Jaguar and a Mustang, he calls it a "Jagstang."

In six days Cobain's band will play its first high-pressure show in a year at the New Music Seminar; in eight weeks *In Utero* will arrive in record stores. Courtney and the baby are in England as Hole performs at the Phoenix Music Festival, and Cobain is alone except for Geffen Records publicist Luke Wood, who's coordinating his interviews. As our conversation begins, Wood puts his tape recorder on the coffee table next to mine—"Double-recording . . . for the band"—before going off to the kitchen.

GEFFEN IS PARANOID about the media, but the members of Nirvana seem just as concerned and annoyed. Shortly after *In Utero* was finished, several major publications ran stories quoting sources who said that Geffen considered the album "unreleasable." With comments like "I don't think that all the pussies and wimps who liked the last album will ever like this one," Albini didn't help matters any. Finally the band and the label bought a full-page ad in *Billboard* to set the record straight, lest anyone think that the group's satirical T-shirt slogan—FLOWER-SNIFFIN' KITTY-PETTIN' BABY-KISSIN' CORPORATE ROCK WHORES—had become a reality.

Albini's name in the credits was supposed to be insurance against such charges. With the exception of occasional high-profile projects like PJ Harvey's *Rid of Me*, he mostly works with hardcore punk bands, recording in his basement studio on Chicago's North Side. His underground credentials are flawless: As a musician he led Big Black, a grinding metallic trio that was enormously influential in the underground (including Seattle's nascent "grunge" scene). As a producer he takes a flat fee based on what bands can pay, rejects groups that don't live up to his punk ideals, and stresses immediacy in recording (one or two takes and a song is done, overdubs be damned).

"I've never really paid any attention to Steve Albini's personality or anything that he supposedly is a crusader for," Cobain says between bites of a cheap frozen pizza. "In fact, I've never really been much of a Big Black fan, to tell the truth. I think I had *Songs About Fucking*. It's good music; it's something a bit more innovative than a lot of stuff that was coming out at that time. I saw their last show here in Seattle at the Steam Room. But for the most part I wanted to work with him because he happened to produce two of my favorite records, which were *Surfer Rosa* [by the Pixies] and *Pod* [by the Breeders]. By listening to those records, I realized something that I had been trying to prove for like three years: Ever since we started recording, I've always thought that it would be really logical to record with a lot of microphones to get an ambience from the room. It just seems obvious to me that if you want it to sound like you're standing right next to the band, if you want that live feeling, then you have to use a lot of microphones.

"It just seems like an obvious thing to do," Cobain continues. "And every time we went in the studio, we would ask the person we were recording with to try this, and they just flat out refused every time: 'This isn't the way you record. It's not what I learned at engineering school.' During the recording, I felt totally comfortable, and I still have no regrets with the way the tracks were done, except I wish I would have added a few more vocal harmonies. For some reason, the vocals didn't turn out the way they should have. I'm not a big fan of multitracking, but I did that on *Nevermind* on quite a few tracks, and I didn't even realize it at the time. I didn't realize that that was what Butch [Vig] was doing; I thought he was just asking for a lot of takes so he could pick out which was the best. It should have worked [on *In Utero*], because we had these great microphones—we used three or four microphones. I stood in front of these amazing, expensive-looking mikes, and it sounded great in the playback. But the final mixes for some reason got squashed. We're a pretty vocal-oriented band, and that's one of the main things I regret."

Albini helped the band get the live sound it wanted, but when the trio returned to Seattle with cassettes of the finished album, problems in the mix became apparent. Most were solved in mastering (the process of preparing tapes to manufacture CDs and cassettes), but two songs were remixed by R.E.M. producer Scott Litt, and another ("I Hate Myself and Want to Die") was dropped because Cobain thought there were too many noise songs in a row. ("It was just such a typical, boring song," he says. "We could write that song in our sleep. There was no point to putting it on the record. . . . If you look back on the record, there are so many noise songs all in a row that it makes it seem like it's nothing but a noise record. It's really not; there are plenty of soft spots to it.") *In Utero* is now tilted in favor of pop songs, with seven catchy would-be anthems to five pure noise outbursts.

Cobain and Novoselic (who were interviewed separately) both laugh when it's suggested that the album begins with "Serve the Servants" and its "teenage angst" line for the benefit of rock critics. Nirvana is rarely so calculated. When I note that the song's jagged, angular guitar solo sounds like Robert Quine, neither musician recognizes the name. Alternative rockers from New York or Los Angeles would never admit that they didn't know the former guitarist with Richard Hell and the Voidoids, but Cobain and Novoselic grew up in small-town Aberdeen, Washington. Their punk discoveries were hard-earned, unpredictable, and incomplete, but they made a lasting impression.

"The guitar players I'm fond of are like from Scratch Acid and the first White Zombie EP," Cobain says, wiping tomato sauce on his T-shirt. (His fingernails are perfectly painted with bright red polish, but his toenails are chipped and fading, in need of a fresh coat.) "Fucked-up, bending strings, borderline in-tune—that type of chaos."

With a driving mechanical drumbeat and electronically treated screams, "Scentless Apprentice" is one of several discordant songs that recall Big Black. The tune is credited to the band, and it came together in rehearsal; the lyrics are a bizarre free-association nightmare about childbirth. "My lyrics are total cut-up, just because I take lines from different poems that I've written," Cobain says. "I build on a theme if I can, but sometimes I can't even come up with an idea of what the song is about."

There's little doubt about what the singer is addressing in the deceptively sweet "Heart-Shaped Box." As much as he's protested the idea that he's a spokesman for his generation, Cobain eloquently sets twentynothings' frustration against Baby Boomers' pious preaching. Following the formula of "Smells Like Teen Spirit," the verses percolate over a quiet riff until the song explodes in an angry, irresistible chorus: "Hate Haight! I've got a new complaint / Forever in debt to your priceless advice."

The opening chords of "Rape Me" also recall Nirvana's biggest hit. The song can be taken on several levels: as a statement against atrocities in the former Yugoslavia (Novoselic spent time there as a teenager and Nirvana played a benefit for Bosnian rape victims); as an angry comment against misogyny (in the liner notes of *Incesticide* Cobain attacks the "wastes of sperm and eggs" who raped a woman while singing "Polly"); or as a response to perceived media abuses ("My favorite inside source / I'll kiss your open sores"). When the song was written more than a year ago, Nirvana thought it would be a single. The group tried to play it on the 1992 MTV Video Music Awards, but it wasn't permitted, and Cobain was told that the network is squeamish about a "Rape Me" video. The track is the catchiest on the album, and it isn't hard to imagine it becoming a hit—and a Madonna-sized scandal.

Violence against women is a common topic on gangsta rap albums, but it's rarely addressed so directly in rock. Cobain says the band members may reconsider the song for a single and video in the future, but for now they're going with "Heart-Shaped Box" because it's "fresher and more of an epic first single." You can almost hear Geffen's collective sigh of relief.

"Frances Farmer Will Have Her Revenge on Seattle" is the album's most enigmatic song title, but the tune contains one of Cobain's most revealing choruses. "I miss the comfort in being sad," he sings, summing up the dilemma of someone who's found fame by complaining but who suddenly doesn't have much to complain about. "I guess I could consider that a personal thing," Cobain says thoughtfully. "But for the most part the song is about Frances Farmer, and I'm sure she felt that way, too."

The rebellious actress was a rising star in the late '30s, but she became an alcoholic and the center of Hollywood scandal, after which she was hounded by the press, institutionalized by her parents, and finally lobotomized. Cobain and Love named their daughter after Farmer, but the singer pauses when asked why he's drawn to her story. "The tragedy of bureaucracy and how people are treated," he says after a while. "Public humiliation is one of the most stressful things a person can go through."

In November 1992, after months of veiled references in numerous articles on the band, Cobain admitted to using heroin to Robert Hillburn in the *Los Angeles Times*. After dabbling with the drug for several years, he said, he developed a serious habit during the chaotic days following the success of *Nevermind*. After going through rehab, he started visiting a clinic to help deal with stomach pains from a serious ulcer. He maintains that the ulcer caused most of the sullen behavior journalists described as drug-related, but his position on drugs is clear: He's nonjudgmental, but says he learned the hard way that they're stupid.

"It was long overdue," Cobain says of his confession to Hillburn. "I tried to deny it for so long simply because I didn't want to influence anyone. There was just no point in bleeding my heart in front of the whole world; it's really no one's business. But I was pretty much cornered at that point. I couldn't deny it any more. Otherwise everyone would think I was a big liar."

"Dumb" seems to be a song about falling into addiction ("I'm not like them / But I can pretend") and discovering the pleasures ("I think I'm dumb / Or maybe just happy") and the pains ("Skin the sun / Fall asleep / Wish away / The soul is cheap"). But a sober and clear-eyed Cobain politely disagrees with my reading. "Actually, that was a song about a concussion. I wrote it two years ago, and the lyrics came to me in about ten minutes. It was just one of those four-track demo things late at night."

The second half of *In Utero* is more chaotic, hitting the listener with the album's hardest tracks in rapid succession: "Very Ape," "Milk It," the sarcastically titled "Radio Friendly Unit Shifter," and "Tourette's" (with mumbled lyrics transcribed in their entirety in the liner notes as, "Fuck, shit, piss"). The four noise tunes are divided into pairs by "Penny Royal Tea," a pleasant hook-filled number about a home-abortion method. The song mentions Leonard Cohen and contains another of Cobain's most memorable lines: "I'm anemic royalty." It was not, as reported by England's *New Musical Express*, cowritten with his wife, Cobain says.

"All Apologies" is a lulling, hypnotic track that features cellist Kera Schaley, a member of the Chicago group Doubt and a friend of Albini's. "All in all is all we all are," Cobain chants mantralike to end the song and the album, but the lyric that demands the most attention is shouted in the middle of the tune: "I'm married / Buried." "That was another line that was written before Courtney and I started going out," Cobain says dismissively, but it's sure to be cited by the legions of Love-bashers.

SINCE THEIR MARRIAGE in February 1992 at a quiet ceremony in Hawaii, Love has become the most hated rock wife since Yoko Ono. She's been the focus of several intensely negative stories, including Lynn Hirschberg's infamous *Vanity Fair* article charging that Love used heroin while pregnant, and a chapter in Britt Collins and Victoria Clarke's as-yet-unpublished *Nirvana: The Definitive Story*. (Cobain attempted to stop the Collins and Clarke book with nasty late-night phone calls, but he shouldn't have bothered: A reading of the advance manuscript reveals that the authors dig up no truly embarrassing dirt, rely extensively on previously published articles, and generally write some of the most flatulent prose ever committed in the name of rock journalism.)

To be sure, Love has courted her share of controversy and publicity, cultivating a sexually aggressive and sometimes obnoxious persona onstage, in interviews, and in her music. But it's doubtful that she could have foreseen the way things are amplified in the media, or the painful personal costs for her and Cobain. Azerrad's unauthorized biography, *Come as You Are: The Story of Nirvana*, reveals that the two were separated from their child for a month by Los Angeles County authorities because of the drug charges leveled in *Vanity Fair*. Cobain told Azerrad that he considered shooting himself after the article was published, and he vowed revenge on Hirschberg: "She'd better hope to God that someday I don't find myself destitute without a wife and baby. Because I'll get fucking revenge on her. Before I leave this earth, she's going out with me."

The media's treatment of Love is obviously a sensitive issue in the band. Novoselic dismisses everything that's been written about her supposedly bullying ways with two sentences—"It's just a story. People need something to write about"—but he is reluctant to discuss the subject further. Cobain meanwhile says journalists are trying to make the couple conform to stories that have already been written—the John and Yoko or Sid and Nancy models. "Why can't there be a Kurt and Courtney model? Why do they dwell on the past?" he asks. "I don't mean to put down Sid and Nancy or John and Yoko, but I just don't relate to them in any way."

In June Cobain was arrested and spent three hours in jail before being released on bail of nine hundred fifty dollars. He says he and Love were jamming together when neighbors called police because of the noise. The police report charges that the singer assaulted his wife, but Love denied this in *The Seattle Times* and said the couple only started arguing after police asked if there were guns in the house. Cobain said there weren't, but Love said there were, and she didn't appreciate having them around. The cops were obligated to arrest one of the partners for a cooling-off period, and they confiscated three guns and several clips of ammunition.

"Once the cops explained to me that they had to take one of us to jail because there was a domestic violence call from one of the neighbors, I understood that because they were so nice about it," Cobain says. "They explained it in full detail and made me realize that most domestic violence calls are real, and if one or the other people aren't arrested, then the cops will just be called back an hour or two later, and this time one of them may be dead."

The most surprising thing about the incident isn't the fight—"Kurt and I hardly fight," Love told the *NME*. "No one could ask for a better husband"—but the fact that Nirvana's leader feels the need to own guns. Guns come up several times in the lyrics on *Nevermind*, usually in a negative context. "No, I don't have a gun," Cobain chants in "Come As You Are," and in "In Bloom," he seems to attack as ignorant gun-toting fans of his music ("He's the one who likes all our pretty songs / And he likes to sing along / And he likes to shoot his gun / But he don't know what it means / He don't know what it means"). "Throughout my entire life, I had never shot a gun before," the singer says. "Growing up in Aberdeen, I had plenty of opportunities, but I was against . . . not really against the right to own a gun, I'm all for that, it's a right that we all have."

"But wouldn't America be a better place if we didn't all have guns?" I ask.

"It's true, but you'd never get rid of them," Cobain says. "I don't know, I just decided to buy a gun one day. Actually, a friend of mine gave us one for a wedding present, and I never used it. And finally I went to the range and started shooting one day and kind of realized that this is like a challenging thing—a nice pastime—to try and hit this target. And I came to the realization that you really have to be prepared to shoot a gun if you're going to defend yourself, because it's a really hard thing to hit a target.

"Have you shot guns before?" Cobain asks. I tell him that I haven't.

"It's amazing how precise you have to be. Like if there was a person right there in the corner, I'd probably still, because I've only had the experience of shooting like twenty times since I've owned guns since last year, I'd have to shoot off four or five rounds to actually hit the person. And that's a really dangerous situation. I want to be able to be precise and shoot their kneecaps or something. Shoot exactly where I want to, so I don't actually have to kill somebody."

"Do you worry that you need to protect yourself in a John Lennon way?" I ask. (Publicist Wood has caught the drift of our conversation and entered the living room, and he's listening intently with a look somewhere between consternation and horror.)

"Not in that way, no," Cobain says. "It's just kind of a vulnerable area. We've got big windows, and I have a baby and a wife to protect. Things like that happen. People come into your house, not to steal your stereo, but to rape your wife and sodomize your baby. I just could not survive something like that. There's no way I could ever live with myself without trying to get revenge on that person and putting him out of his misery. I wouldn't think twice about blowing somebody away if they came into this house."

I grew up in Jersey City, New Jersey, not Aberdeen, I tell Cobain, and where I come from, only idiots own guns, and they use them in stupid ways. I tell the singer that if somebody comes into his house, they're probably breaking in to steal his fucking stereo, and would he really want to kill someone based on such a slight offense? I was mugged once, when I was working my way through college. It was right before Christmas, and I had just cashed my two-week paycheck and Christmas bonus. Two kids tackled me from behind, held a knife to my back, grabbed my wallet, and ran off. I'd worked hard for that money, and I was furious. If I'd had a gun at that moment, I would have shot them both in the back—and I would have hated myself forever from that point on. A couple of hundred bucks meant a lot to me then, but it wasn't worth two lives.

For these reasons, I would never want to own a gun, I tell Cobain, much less consider using one in anger.

The singer stares at me with a vacant, detached look; it's clear that he doesn't really understand my point, and that the only way anyone will take his guns away is if they pry them from his cold, dead fingers. "There's a difference between owning a gun and having it safely put away in your house for an intruder," he finally says. "To carry a gun . . . I would never carry a gun."

I'm not convinced, and it's the only time during several hours of smart, friendly, and spirited conversation that I feel as if we have no connection.

THERE'S AN ELEMENT of danger in most great rock 'n' roll, a sense that anything can happen. This is a key to Nirvana's appeal: At any moment, the group might career out of control or come screeching to a violent halt.

"When we played in Buenos Aires, we brought this all-girl band from Portland called Calamity Jane," Cobain says. "During their entire set, the whole audience—it was a huge show with like sixty thousand people—was throwing money and everything out of their pockets, mud and rocks, just pelting them. Eventually the girls stormed off crying. It was terrible, one of the worst things I've ever seen, such a mass of sexism all at once.

"Krist, knowing my attitude about things like that, tried to talk me out of at least setting myself on fire or refusing to play. We ended up just having fun, laughing at them. Before every song, I'd play the intro to 'Teen Spirit' and then stop. They didn't realize that we were protesting against what they'd done. We played for about forty minutes, and most of the songs were off *Incesticide*, so they didn't recognize anything. We wound up playing the secret noise song ["Endless Nameless"] that's at the end of *Nevermind*, and because we were so in a rage, we were just so pissed off about this whole situation, that song and the whole set were one of the greatest experiences I've ever had."

The show sounds similar to dozens the Replacements played in their heyday. On any given night the Minneapolis quartet could deliver a passionate full-throttle blowout, a drunken self-indulgent mess, or a combination of both. But the night before interviewing Cobain, I saw former Replacements leader Paul Westerberg perform at the base of the Space Needle during the Bite of Seattle festival. Westerberg led his hired band through a tight, well-rehearsed, and boring set, stopping frequently to ask if everyone was in tune.

Anarchy doesn't age well, and it's impossible to sustain. In *Route 666: On the Road to Nirvana*, rock critic Gina Arnold makes a case that Nirvana's success was the result of a decade of underground activity. Punk rock failed to change the world in the late '70s, but it inspired a generation of musicians, writers, college-radio DJs, promoters, and indie-label entrepreneurs who built an alternative network. From that network came the Replacements, the Feelies, Hüsker Dü, Mission of Burma, Naked Raygun, Big Black, and many more bands that played uncompromising music powered by the emotion of the moment. For most of them, the moment came and went before conditions coincided to make a difference to the outside world. But for Nirvana everything clicked.

"There are different aspects of where we were culturally," says Novoselic, the band's resident philosopher. "In January 1990, George Bush had like an eighty-five percent approval rating, and in 1992 when *Nevermind* was happening, we elected this governor from Arkansas. Maybe it took until late 1992 for the '90s to happen.

"And now comes the exploitation part of it. There are some bands out there now that would easily fit into the repertoire of, say, Rick Springfield or Phil Collins. But they're young, they dress kind of hip and modern, and they're called alternative. It's just bullshit. It's just exploitation."

But there's got to be more to the story than that. Mudhoney's classic "If I Think" from 1988's *Superfuzz Bigmuff* EP is easily the anthemic equal of "Smells Like Teen Spirit." But Mudhoney didn't do what Nirvana did. Novoselic nods and stumbles for an answer.

"Yeah. No. Maybe it was the production," he says finally. "What 'If I Think' did was help to unite the Seattle scene. When that EP came out, it was a must-have, and those were magical times. *That* was the Seattle scene. When Mudhoney was playing and we were playing, and Tad and the Fluid. That was a little time in history that you can compare to the Liverpool scene, the Cavern Club. It was innocent. It wasn't exploited. Now look what it's come to. Everybody's older and wiser."

Says Cobain: "A lot of the bands who are finally getting their just rewards, like Soul Asylum—bands who have been around for a long time and have apparently been innovative—they seem to be in competition with each other now. It's mainly been quotes from most of these bands in articles; that's where I've noticed it. I don't understand how these people can come from an environment and a lifestyle after so many years of being in underground music and keeping that kind of music alive, and now it suddenly seems like a desperate attempt by some of these bands who've never been recognized at trying to say we deserve that. It's kind of sickening to see how these bands become careerists all of a sudden. That's what everyone was against when they started these bands. The reason I wanted to be in a band was to be in a band and write songs. You can be validated if you sell two thousand records, and you should be happy with that."

Maybe it was just a nostalgic window to the past, but the scene at the Crocodile Café the night before didn't seem too jaded. Novoselic is still holding his head from the festivities, and he's drinking coffee to clear the fog. Scream, Grohl's old hardcore band from Washington, D.C., played an energetic reunion gig at Seattle's hippest rock club, part of a tour to promote a new CD of previously unreleased material. (The drummer skipped Nirvana's week of interviews to travel with the group.) Novoselic danced awkwardly through the entire show, part of an enthusiastic crowd that included fellow Seattle legends Tad and Mark Arm of Mudhoney (but not Cobain). When the members of Scream took the stage, Nirvana's bassist welcomed them by shouting, "Stone Gossard Pirates!" simultaneously dissing the Pearl Jam guitarist and pathetic Pearl Jam wannabes Stone Temple Pilots.

Novoselic's life has clearly been changed by Nirvana's success, but it's just as plain that he hasn't lost much of his love for the music. He owns a beautiful two-story house in a pleasant, tree-lined neighborhood midway between downtown Seattle and the Cobains' place further out on the city's edge. But he seems proudest of his two jukeboxes, one in the living room for 45s, and one in the basement that plays albums.

Midway through our conversation, the Federal Express man rings the doorbell. Novoselic brings the package into the den and opens it to find a framed gold record signifying sales of five hundred thousand for *Incesticide*, the compilation of B-sides and rarities that Nirvana released after *Nevermind*. Today's *Seattle Times* carries a short item noting that *Nevermind* has finally dropped off *Billboard*'s Top 200 album chart after an impressive ninety-two weeks.

"If it wasn't for 'Teen Spirit,' I don't know how *Nevermind* would have done," Novoselic says. "There are no 'Teen Spirits' on *In Utero*. There are six or seven great songs, but no phenomenal big hit."

Regardless of how many copies the album sells, the band members believe they've already succeeded. They're working together better than they ever have, Cobain says, and he hopes they'll write more as a group in the future. The night before our interview, he and Novoselic sat up until dawn brainstorming over the storyboard for the "Heart-Shaped Box" video, which the duo envisions as a spoof of *The Wizard of Oz* filmed in a technique approximating Technicolor.

"I have my heart set on—everybody, the whole band has their heart set on—releasing 'Scentless Apprentice' after 'Heart-Shaped Box,'" Cobain says. "That's a really good example of the direction we're going in. We actually collaborated on that song. It came together in practice. It was just a totally satisfying thing to finally contribute equally to a song, instead of me coming up with the basics of the song. Obviously, we're pretty much on the same wavelength; there's never been a situation where I tell them what to do. But there are a lot of times where I've had to sit behind the drum set and show Dave what I've been thinking in my head, and he'll incorporate that idea. For the most part, it's always been like eighty percent my song that I've written at home and introduced to the band later on in practice. I'm just so pleased to be able to collaborate. I'm getting tired of being expected to be the sole songwriter. I would love to have a songwriting partner. And Krist and Dave for some reason have started to come out of their shell."

"There was a time when things broke down and got screwy after the success of *Nevermind*, but everything was pretty much resolved by communication," Novoselic says. "There were just so many factors; things were happening so fast. There was all this fame and all these people who might want something. You'd walk into Safeway, and people would be looking at you real strange, wanting autographs. We had different reactions to it. There was a time when the way I reacted to the band was, 'I don't care. Whatever.' And I think Kurt reacted to that: 'Well, Krist doesn't care anymore.' And it snowballed. But now I find myself getting more and more outspoken again, and I think that's healthy. I think Kurt respects that. He has somebody to bounce things off of and get some input from. He feels he has all this pressure on him as the center figure, the singer-songwriter, and he appreciates having some help."

The difficulties the members of Nirvana face now include accepting the responsibilities of platinum-selling rock stars ("We have to be a good role model to people," Novoselic says sincerely. "I try not to brag about being a drunkard or a pot smoker") while maintaining their punk credibility ("Do you think that we're still a pain in the ass for the music industry?" he asks. "Are we still uncooperative? Is there still that vibe in the air?"). They also have to focus their rage on the right targets and convince the massive *Nevermind* audience to grow with them. But there's every indication they're up to the challenge.

At Roseland during the New Music Seminar, the band takes the stage after an opening set by invited guest the Jesus Lizard, a Chicago quartet that's considered one of the harshest bands in the noise-rock underground. Augmented by a second guitarist, former Exploited player Big John

Duncan, Nirvana runs through a sloppy but intense twenty-song set that draws from each of its albums. This is the first time fans are hearing "Serve the Servants," "Heart-Shaped Box," and "All Apologies," but many are singing along by the final choruses.

There's an unusually heavy bonehead element at the show, violent jocks slamming with wild abandon in the middle of the floor, disregarding the etiquette of the mosh pit, and sending dozens of more peaceful fans scurrying to the sides of the room with bruises and bloodied noses. The group ends its set with four acoustic songs, sitting on stools at the edge of the stage like Led Zeppelin in its unplugged mode. "Fuck the folk shit," one of the boneheads shouts, but most people listen intently to the simple, eloquent versions of "Dumb," "Polly," and "Something in the Way." The show ends with Leadbelly's "Where Did You Sleep Last Night," which is treated as a sort of Appalachian folk song similar to the version done by Ricky Skaggs. Its sad, haunting strains provide the night's most moving moment.

Nirvana returns for a half-hearted, badly out-of-tune "Smells Like Teen Spirit" and a version of "Endless, Nameless." But the encore is anticlimactic. Tonight, the band members make their point by quietly strumming their instruments instead of smashing them.

THE NIGHT AFTER the Roseland show, I run into Novoselic as he's heading into Irving Plaza to see Pavement, one of the many indie comers pegged as "the next Nirvana." It's an opinion I don't share, and I'm leaving to catch the older but more reliable Buzzcocks at the Academy when the bassist stops me with a big, friendly hello.

"I know you," I say. "You're Andy Kaufman." And Novoselic smiles broadly.

THE DIFFICULT BIRTH OF IN UTERO

From the beginning, overseeing *In Utero* was an unenviable job. *Nevermind* established producer Butch Vig's career, but even he would have thought twice about working on its follow-up. "I love the band dearly, and I would love to work with them again at some point, but it would be a blessing-slash-curse to do this one because of the overwhelming scrutiny," he says.

In the studio, *In Utero* producer Steve Albini instituted a strict policy of ignoring everyone except the three members of Nirvana to prevent Geffen executives and the group's managers from interfering. "Everyone else connected with the band besides the band members were the biggest pieces of shit I ever met," he says with characteristic frankness.

Several weeks after the album was finished, the *Chicago Tribune* ran a story quoting a source close to the band who said that Geffen considered *In Utero* "unreleasable." The story was advanced by *Newsweek*, which inaccurately charged that the group was being forced to remix the album. Geffen and Nirvana fired back with a letter to the magazine (published as a full-page ad in *Billboard*), charging that *Newsweek*'s reporter "ridiculed our relationship with our label based on totally erroneous information. Geffen Records has supported our efforts all along in making this record."

But clearly, *someone* had problems with the album. The members of Nirvana say they were pleased when they left the studio, but they started noticing problems with the mix when they played their cassettes at home. Krist Novoselic thought that one of the guitar effects Albini used on "Heart-Shaped Box" sounded "like a fucking abortion hitting the floor." And Kurt Cobain began wishing they'd spent more time on the vocals or tried some of the subtle multitracking that Vig used on *Nevermind*.

"I've never been more confused about a session in my life. I just could not put my finger on it," the singer says. "I called up Steve, and I basically asked him for some advice. Like, 'Why don't I feel the same emotion I did on *Nevermind* or *Bleach*?' We achieved exactly what I wanted, and it sounded exactly how I expected it to turn out—at least the drums and the guitars did. It took me a long time to realize the vocals weren't loud enough and the bass guitar was almost impossible to hear. [Albini] assured me it could be fixed in the mastering if we really worked on it, and it turned out to be true. But by that time, our A&R man had expressed his opinion and pretty much said that he didn't like the record."

The A&R man was Gary Gersh, the executive who brought Nirvana to the label. At the same time the band was finishing *In Utero*, Gersh was negotiating with Capitol Records to become that company's new president. Now in place in his new job, he declined to comment for this story.

"When things like that are said to you, when Gary and I talk to one another, it's always on a personal level," Cobain says. "That was his personal opinion, and it never went beyond that. There was never any sense of a threat, like, 'We're not going to put this record out.' Because they can't."

But Geffen can and has: The label once sued Neil Young for making music that didn't sound enough like Neil Young, and it rejected the first version of Aerosmith's *Get a Grip*, forcing the band to return to the studio. If label executives did consider rejecting *In Utero*, they were prompted to change course when the story became public, or they risked damaging the "alternative" credibility of the band and the label. Asked whether the Nirvana camp spread the "unreleasable" story itself to force Geffen's hand, manager John Silva says, "That's a good theory, but there's no basis to it."

Searching for a compromise, Geffen suggested remixing with Andy Wallace, who had done the same thing for *Nevermind,* Silva says. Wallace had scheduling conflicts, so Nirvana called R.E.M. producer Scott Litt, who had been a candidate for producing *Nevermind*. Novoselic says the band never considered reworking the whole album, but it wanted to tweak "Heart-Shaped Box" and "All Apologies." Cobain added some harmonies to the two songs, and Litt brought the vocals up in the mix (he's credited with "additional mixing"). Otherwise the songs appear in the same versions completed by Albini.

"The record sounded so good, but it needed a couple more touches," Novoselic says. "My perspective was, we've got a single like 'Heart-Shaped Box' and 'All Apologies,' these really kind of nice songs, and most of the record's really aggressive. I wanted 'Heart-Shaped Box' to be a gateway for people to buy the record, and then they'd put it on and have this aggressive wild sound, a true alternative record."

Nirvana's Raw Power Shoves the Hype Aside
The *Chicago Sun-Times*, October 25, 1993

TWENTY-THREE SONGS into Nirvana's show at the Aragon on Saturday, the first of a sold-out two-night stand, singer Kurt Cobain stood atop a stack of amplifiers as the last wails of feedback from the group's improvised encore echoed through the cavernous Capone-era ballroom. From there he climbed to the top of a prop tree towering some fifteen feet above the stage. He appeared to consider diving headfirst into the drums like he used to in the old days, but instead he turned his attention to a giant replica of the winged anatomy doll on the cover of *In Utero*.

Both Cobain and the doll came crashing to the floor, the doll's head shattering in a thousand pieces, and Cobain landing in a heap. He picked himself up, casually strolled to the microphone, and said, "Thank you."

Those were the only words he spoke all night.

These days the only other platinum rock star who vents the emotion in his music in such immediate and physical terms is Pearl Jam's Eddie Vedder. But acrobatics aren't the only way that Cobain puts himself on the line. Through the course of an amazing two-hour performance, Nirvana built the crowd into a frenzy with full-throttle punk assaults ("Radio Friendly Unit Shifter," "Scentless Apprentice") and anthemic sing-alongs ("Penny Royal Tea," "In Bloom," "Smells Like Teen Spirit"), only to turn and slow the pace with breathtakingly beautiful acoustic numbers.

Augmented by former Germs guitarist Pat Smear and cellist Laurie Goldstein, Cobain, bassist Krist Novoselic, and drummer Dave Grohl challenged the audience they won with the nine-million-selling *Nevermind*. As they tamed the Aragon's notoriously muddy acoustics, they displayed a new musical maturity and proved that Nirvana is just as potent at any volume.

Cobain's soulful vocals on "Dumb" were even more heart-wrenching than they are on the album. "Polly" had a hushed solemnity, and Novoselic's accordion added a melancholy sweetness to a cover of the Vaselines' version of "Jesus Doesn't Want Me for a Sunbeam."

The band isn't immune to the trappings of stardom: The members are surrounded by industry hacks who shelter them and treat them like gods, and the garish stage set would have been more appropriate for the Black Crowes. But like its third album, *In Utero*, the first of Nirvana's two Chicago performances proved that the group is honest and unpretentious where it counts—in its music—and it's committed to the punk ideal that the band members are no better than their fans.

Nirvana handpicked a dozen bands to open its United States tour, with the groups trading places after a week. The modish punk trio Jawbreaker and Seattle grunge legends Mudhoney opened at the Aragon Saturday with enthusiastic sets. Hidden from view behind the monitor soundboard, Cobain sat cross-legged on the floor, rocking his head in time with every other punk in the crowd. He may be a star, but he remains first and foremost a fan.

He also remains a somewhat inconsistent performer—at least onstage.

Like the Replacements, one of the many punk groups of the indie-rock '80s who paved the way for Nirvana's success, the Seattle trio can be an almost completely different band on two consecutive nights. And while its first Chicago show was among the best I've ever seen, Sunday's concert was one of the worst.

Cobain apparently couldn't hear himself because of faulty stage monitors, and he griped about it several times. He also snapped at the audience because fans were throwing wet T-shirts onstage, shorting out the guitars' effects pedals. The band members took long pauses between every song—a sharp contrast to Saturday's fast and furious pacing—and they continually mocked the Aragon's notorious acoustics by mumbling nonsense syllables into the microphones. (How could the sound be pristine one night and crap the next?)

Nirvana walked off without playing "Smells Like Teen Spirit," and fans booed. Hearing the jeers, Cobain returned and flung himself into the crowd. When he emerged five minutes later, the fans had stolen the shoes off his feet, but he was grinning from ear to ear. It was the only time all night that he smiled.

Rocker Cobain Knew Pitfalls of Stardom
The *Chicago Sun-Times*, April 10, 1994

LIKE MOST TWENTYSOMETHINGS, Kurt Cobain knew that the rock star lying dead in a pool of his own vomit has become a pathetic cliché. He grew up well aware of the litany of fallen heroes: Jim Morrison. Janis Joplin. Jimi Hendrix. Brian Jones. John Bonham. Keith Moon. Sid Vicious.

But that knowledge didn't help him deal with the fame that came from fronting one of the most important bands of the '90s. It didn't stop him from abusing drugs, and it didn't help him cope with personal pressures that his fans will never fully understand.

Alone in his home in Seattle, Cobain apparently committed suicide Thursday by shooting himself in the head with a shotgun, police said. He was twenty-seven years old.

The shaggy blond rocker was quiet, intense, and possessed with a sly sense of humor. He didn't fight for anybody's right to party, and he didn't rock and roll all night long. Nevertheless, his name has been added to the list of musicians whose excesses ended their careers and their lives too soon.

Cobain had struggled with an addiction to heroin, and he spent twenty hours in a coma in early March after overdosing on champagne and tranquilizers. "Now he's gone and joined that stupid club," his mother, Wendy O'Connor, said on Friday. "I told him not to join that stupid club."

But if Cobain's death was in part about rock star indulgence, his life was about the opposite. His brilliantly simple music railed against complacency and alienation, exploding with the energy of the punk scene that inspired him. "We are stupid and contagious / Here we are now, entertain us," he sang with a sneer on Nirvana's biggest hit. In "Smells Like Teen Spirit" and songs like it, he spoke as well as anyone for a generation that shared his cynicism, skepticism, and ironic sense of humor.

Like many members of that generation, Cobain was the product of a broken home. He grew up an outcast in small-town Aberdeen, Washington. Nirvana bassist Krist Novoselic was one of his few friends, and the two never really felt like they fit in until they discovered the punk-rock underground.

Even after his band's multiplatinum success, Cobain stressed the punk ideal, maintaining that he was no different or better than his fans. In his shabby sweaters and torn-up jeans, he certainly looked like them. When Nirvana last performed in Chicago, he sat cross-legged onstage, hidden in the shadows, watching the opening bands and rocking his head in time, just like every other punk in the crowd. I can count on one hand the number of times I've seen a member of the headlining group so thoroughly enjoy the entire sets by the bands who opened for him.

When I last interviewed him in July, Cobain was optimistic: Nirvana was playing better than ever, he said, and he considered its third album, *In Utero*, to be its best. He explained that he had dropped a song called "I Hate Myself and Want to Die" from the disc because it had been too noisy. The title was a joke, and the passion in his vocals indicated he was feeling anything but suicidal. "I still haven't had my full," he screams in the song. "Fill in the someday."

People close to the band are wondering when he began to feel differently.

"The [overdose] in early March led me to believe that he was quite an unhappy person," says Michael Azerrad, author of the Nirvana biography, *Come As You Are*. "He was a teetotaler; he did not drink. Somewhere in my book he mentions that most of the people who died of overdoses drank, and that's exactly what he did. You can come to your own conclusions on that."

Come As You Are recounts how Cobain and his wife, Courtney Love, nearly lost custody of their daughter because of their drug use. Cobain told me that he had conquered his addiction to heroin, but a source close to the band said he had recently returned to the drug. The source said that Love, Cobain's managers, and bandmates Novoselic and Dave Grohl had decided to distance themselves from the singer in an attempt to scare him into quitting drugs once and for all.

22   *MILK IT!*

Love and daughter Frances Bean were in Los Angeles when Cobain died. Police said his body lay for a day until it was found by an electrician scheduled to work at the couple's lakeside home. It was a sad and lonely end, but before the end of the day Friday, the myth-making had already begun.

On MTV, *Rolling Stone* writer David Fricke compared Cobain's death to John Lennon's. But suicide isn't murder, and drug abuse is not an accident. Cobain would have scoffed at such romantic nonsense, just as he balked at the idea of worshipping the musician instead of the music. "I'm anemic royalty," he screamed on *In Utero*.

Remember him for that attitude. But above all, remember him for the music.

Foo Fighters, Foo Fighters
Request, September 1995

"I DON'T OWE you anything," Dave Grohl shouts in the early moments of his solo debut. True enough, but who was expecting anything from the former Nirvana drummer?

Timekeepers get as little respect on the alternative rock scene as they've gotten through the rest of rock history. (You know the joke: "What's a drummer?" "Someone who likes to hang out with musicians.") Consider the curse of the Minneapolis skinsmen: Grant Young, Ken Callahan, and Chris Mars were treated as disposable cogs in the rock machine by Soul Asylum, the Jayhawks, and the Replacements. Seattle has been no friendlier; witness Pearl Jam's treatment of Dave Abbruzzese. Gary Gersh, currently the president of Capitol Records but formerly the Geffen A&R executive who signed Nirvana, showed a lot of faith by not only championing Grohl, but giving him his own label, Roswell Records. It's damn near certain that nobody else was betting the farm on the Foo Fighters' self-titled debut. The fact that it's distinctive, accomplished, and just plain rockin' is an achievement for drummers everywhere, as well as a gift to fans of melodic punk.

Melodic punk—yeah, that's what Nirvana was, too, but Grohl has a different sense of hooks than the late Kurt Cobain. Cobain nodded to the Beatles with "About a Girl" on *Bleach*, then quickly progressed to darker, more twisted, and less conventional ditties. Grohl has a deep and abiding love for the early garage-rock Beatles (remember his participation in the

Backbeat band), as well as the optimistic psychedelic pop group of *Revolver*. Tunes such as "This Is a Call" and "I'll Stick Around" would fit right in on *Nuggets*, Lenny Kaye's classic compilation of one-hit wonders by post–British Invasion American garage bands, while "Floaty" and the nearly six-minute album-closer "Exhausted" are two of the most effective mergers of psychedelic jangle and punk-rock drive since Hüsker Dü's *Zen Arcade* and that band's version of the Byrds' "Eight Miles High."

If one of Courtney Love's gripes with Grohl in their simmering feud is that he's ripping off Cobain's style of songwriting, she's way off base. Of course there are touches of Nirvana; like Hole and countless others, Grohl employs the patented Cobain dynamic shift (quiet verse, loud chorus, quiet verse). He's picked up a few of Cobain's vocal mannerisms, but fewer than you'd expect given that he sang harmony vocals with the guy for three years. Overall, words are a lot less important to Grohl than they were to Cobain. The lyrics are buried in the mix under layers of fuzz guitar. Odd catchphrases emerge—"I don't doubt that anyway," "This is a call to all my past resignation," and "It's you I fell into"—but they're the sort that are hastily improvised at the microphone when a songwriter realizes the need for a chorus.

Recorded before Grohl formed the band of the same name, *Foo Fighters* was crafted during a week at Barrett Jones's studio in Seattle. Grohl played all the instruments himself (with the exception of a guitar cameo on "X-Static" by the Afghan Whigs' Greg Dulli), and he trips up on only two of the twelve songs. "Weenie Beenie" and "Watershed" are transparent tributes to Steve Albini's mid-'80s noise-rock band Big Black, complete with piledriver machine rhythms, distorted industrial vocals, and piercing guitar. (Grohl got along with Albini better than the other members of Nirvana. Love jokes that the only thing you have to know about the drummer to understand his personality is that he was the guy who liked to go out back with Albini and set his farts on fire during downtime in the studio.)

Now that he's a guitar-playing member of a tight and allegedly democratic unit—the touring Foo Fighters are completed by former Germs and Nirvana guitarist Pat Smear and the Sunny Day Real Estate rhythm section of Nate Mendel and William Goldsmith—hopefully Grohl can be dissuaded from further noisy flatulence. When they're concentrating on the catchier numbers, the Foo Fighters are simply too good to waste time on throwaway skronk. In fact, the only way they could possibly be better is if Grohl still played the drums.

Senator Krist

Rolling Stone, February 8, 1996

MOST ROCK FANS think of Krist Novoselic as the former bassist for
Nirvana, the impossibly tall and goofy guy who threw his bass up in the air
at MTV's Video Music Awards in 1992 only to have it come crashing back
down on his skull, knocking him senseless. But since then Novoselic has
awakened in more ways than one.

Drawing on the clout and cash that come from having been in one of the
most successful groups of the '90s, Novoselic entered the political fray in
his home state of Washington, fighting music censorship. He linked up with
the Washington Music Industry Coalition, a grassroots group dedicated to
fighting the so-called erotic music law, which would restrict minors from
purchasing records with "adult" or "objectionable" content. He went on to
co-found and fund the Joint Artists and Music Promotions Political Action
Committee, which hopes to persuade politicians to view musicians and
fans as tax-generating voters whose concerns deserve to be heard.

Novoselic remains reluctant to address the suicide of his friend Kurt
Cobain, but activism seems to have helped him through one of the most difficult periods of his thirty years. Now sworn off drugs and alcohol, he talks
about politics with the same infectious enthusiasm he displays when talking
about rock 'n' roll. And he has returned to making music: Sweet 75, his new
trio, is recording its debut album and preparing for a spring release.

Novoselic talked about JAMPAC during a long interview at a New York
hotel. "Senator Krist, my friends call me," he says, laughing. "Haven't I
emerged? I just hope I don't sound like a civics lecture."

Q. *Let's start with how you became politicized.*
A. I was politicized in high school. I had an open mind and didn't really
care for Reagan. I cut my teeth on radical punk rock—the Dead Kennedys,
MaximumrockNRoll, and MDC. Those were the anti-Reagan voices at the
time, especially if you were in Aberdeen [Washington] and were eighteen
years old. I didn't feel like reading dry political analyses. I needed something that spoke to me, that I could understand.

Q. *Still, MDC's sentiments weren't very sophisticated. How did "Fuck Reagan"*
lead to something more?
The state of mind I was in was just anti-establishment and feeling awkward. I realized that "It's not me, it's those people [who have a problem]."

They totally bought into the mainstream culture, and I disassociated myself from it. Republicans—even Democrats—it was like, "What do I care?" But I did vote when I was eighteen. I voted for Walter Mondale, and I've voted in every presidential election since.

Q. *Mondale went down in flames. What did that say to you?*

A. It didn't really break my heart. It wasn't like it was gonna change anything. Walter Mondale wasn't exactly radical. But I voted and I had my say.

Q. *What was the next step?*

A. Well, Nirvana was always political. We talked about things and how we felt. There was Operation Desert Storm in early '91, and it broke my heart that people bought into that. I was living in Tacoma, Washington, a real meat-and-potatoes town, and it was scary and surreal, the hypocrisy of the government and people buying it. Six months later, the mainstream culture that was duped by Desert Storm was all over us. We were repulsed. We were like, "Who are these people?" It took us a long time to deal with that.

Q. *How did you get involved with the Washington Music Industry Coalition?*

A. Back in 1992 there was this broad piece of legislation in Washington State that was really scary. Say that you have a song and you make reference to an ass, "ass" meaning buttocks. In the sponsors' definition, that was part of the human anatomy, and that could be considered adult material unsuitable for minors. Somebody could go to a county prosecutor and say, "I think this material is obscene." The prosecutor would decide whether to deem this material erotic or not. You could then challenge that in front of a jury. I was like, "Jesus Christ, this is totally un-American! This is unconstitutional." But the legislature passed it, the governor signed it, and it was law.

The WMIC, the American Civil Liberties Union, and the Recording Industry Association of America challenged it in the state Supreme Court, and it was declared unconstitutional, but [the bill's proponents] came back again the next year. Now if someone had a complaint against Nirvana, we could have afforded the hundred dollars an hour for attorneys. But if you're a struggling artist or a mom-and-pop record retailer, you couldn't afford to go to court, so you're more likely to just not carry it.

Q. *When did you jump into the fray?*

A. The first time I got involved, I went on this TV show, a sort of town-meeting forum, and I went up against this mother from Edmunds, Washington, who instigated all of this because her kids came home with a 2 Live Crew CD, and she thought it was terrible. I was really nervous. I wasn't well versed on the legislation or anything. I just dealt my cards from my perspective. She thought I was a nice young man, and she wouldn't go against Nirvana: "Nirvana's fine, but it's this crazy stuff, this 2 Live Crew . . ." They always go after the extremes, and I'm so sick of that.

Q. *Where did the legislation wind up?*

A. It keeps coming back, because you have these people who are zealots who are worried about children losing their innocence. What happened was, we had a wonderful governor elected in 1992, Mike Lowry, and he vetoed the legislation in '93 and again in '94. But last year was kind of funny, because in '94 the legislature changed. This thing sailed through the House, so we decided we had to lobby the Senate. I stood back and looked at the system and said, "Well, if you can't beat them, join them."

Q. *So you formed a political action committee so they would take you seriously?*

A. Exactly. I could have walked around with a petition or could have held rallies on the Capitol steps. But I said, "We've got to get in there, shake hands, develop relationships, make a few campaign contributions, and become part of the political culture." That's how it works if you want to be taken seriously. Over the last couple of years, Seattle bands have sold over one hundred sixty million records, and nobody's moved away. I thought, "God damn, look at us! We're the establishment now! We're making all this money." Microsoft has lobbyists. Weyerhauser, Boeing—they're all active on the political scene. You think state government is gonna move against those companies? No way.

Q. *OK, so I don't live in Washington State. You've defeated this legislation several times now. What are you all excited about?*

A. Censorship is popping up all over the country. You have Bob Dole out there; he's never seen *Pulp Fiction*, never listened to Nine Inch Nails. George Will's wife writes him a speech, and he comes out a total crusader. These guys all want to wave the pro-family flag. They go to bed dreaming of *Leave It to Beaver* and this '50s ideal. But if you look at the economy of the '50s, there was a lot of opportunity. I think they're pissing up a tree. They want to mandate morality, but if you give people opportunity, that's all anybody wants: to live and prosper. What I say about these social problems is, "It's the economy, stupid."

Q. *What did you think of the recent shareholders' attack on Time-Warner?*

A. The whole thing with Interscope Records . . . what percentage of music is overtly sexual or overtly misogynistic or overtly violent? It's a very small percentage, three percent or four percent. But they want to regulate the ninety-six percent that's fine. It just doesn't make any sense. It goes back to economics. If C. Delores Tucker was real, she wouldn't be banging down the door at Time-Warner shareholders' meetings and demanding responsibility, she'd be banging down the doors of these corporations that invest overseas instead of investing in the inner cities in our country.

Q. *Do you think that some people in the fight against censorship go too far in defending objectionable material? I'm thinking of rock critic and activist Dave Marsh comparing N.W.A to Henry Miller. "Yo bitch! Get in my pickup / And suck my dick up / 'Til you hiccup" is not exactly* Tropic of Cancer.

A. I'm not gonna defend that material, but if you want to look at it with an open mind, it's like, "Where are these guys coming from?" I think it's really immature, but I don't feel threatened by it. Maybe that's because I'm a white male, and I don't have to walk down the street alone and be afraid every time there's a guy standing in the shadows. As far as what Dave Marsh thinks, that's his interpretation, and that's fine. But I generally agree with him on the basic premise that rating records is censorship and creating an adult section of record stores is censorship.

Q. *So how does a legitimately concerned parent deal with monitoring music?*

A. If you're really concerned about your kids and you want to impress them, go out and get some rock magazines and see where it's coming from. Look at it as a parenting opportunity. If you were to play some really over-the-top thing for your child, and your child says, "This is really stupid," I think that would be great, because it shows that your values have really been instilled in your child.

Q. *You talk a lot about politics being fun, almost in the way that you talk about rock 'n' roll. What's so much fun about it?*

A. What's fun is the results you achieve and interacting with people. It used to be I would never sign autographs, and I was in a crisis and in denial [about my fame]. But now I meet people and I'm like, "How are you doing? What's your name?" I try to be real with them. It's also fun because it's a contest. You put your heart behind this person, you want them to win, you work for them, you've got an emotional stake. You want to be with the winner. You've got to utilize a democracy. Otherwise it's like if you're a member of a club and you pay fees, but you never go and you never enjoy the benefits.

Q. *Cynics could say it's easy for you to talk about getting involved—you don't have to work.*

A. Since I don't drink anymore, I get up in the morning and I drink my coffee-substitute barley drink and read the paper and evaluate what I read. I don't do anything unless I'm compelled. Otherwise it's a chore, it's a job—and you're right, I don't have to work. But if I didn't feel like doing the PAC or doing music, I could retire, live on my farm, grow potatoes, and have organic goat-shit soil. I could do watercolors or macramé or cake decorating or whatever I was compelled to do. But I'm compelled to do this.

I remember going to a Hoquiam [Washington] city council meeting when they were debating whether to have Lollapalooza come, and I got choked up. Everybody had the right to speak. You had the chief of police, who thought it was a bad idea because he didn't have the manpower. You had business people, who thought it was a good idea, because it would bring money into town. You had people who were concerned about the traffic, and you had kids testifying, like, "Hey, man, I just think you should give the kids a chance." And the council decided to do it. Just seeing those kids testifying before their city council was cool. That's democracy in action, man. If you feel disenfranchised, just give it a chance.

Q. *A lot of people who are feeling disenfranchised are turning toward the militia movement. Why do you think that's so appealing?*

A. I hate to talk about that. I think there have always been militia movements—it's just that they're getting a lot of publicity now. I'm an advocate for the First Amendment, but I'm also for the Second Amendment, so you can't really call me liberal. The NRA goes off on Janet Reno and accountability. But where was the NRA in the early '80s, when the MOVE house and a whole block of Philadelphia was burned down? Where were they in calling for Edwin Meese's responsibility? I own firearms, but I'm not an NRA member, no way.

Q. *You've seen guns do damage in your life. Why would you want to own one?*

A. [Deep breath] I wanna protect my family. There's a lot of stupid people with guns. The people who got caught without guns in the former Yugoslavia are more likely lying in a mass grave somewhere. But I don't want to make this interview revolve round guns.

Q. *OK, tell me how you met singer Yva Las Vegas and formed Sweet 75.*

A. Yva's from Venezuela, so the band has an international vibe. She sang at my birthday party in 1994. She was a busker at Pike Place Market [in Seattle], and a friend saw her and thought she'd be perfect to serenade me for my birthday. She started singing these South American folk songs, and she's a real powerhouse; she has a lot of raw talent. I had guitars hanging around and started pounding away on them and came up with a few ideas. I started collaborating with Yva, and these songs came together. It has a grunge element, but a different thing as well, especially having a woman in the band. This is only the second band I've ever been in.

Q. *Are you worried people will expect the band to be great because you were in Nirvana?*

A. We *are* good! I'm excited. If I wasn't, I wouldn't even be in the band. I don't have any problem about how to promote it, either. I don't have a celebrity identity crisis. I am who I am, and if people come to see the band because it's the ex-Nirvana guy, that's great. That's an advantage that I'll take, because I think people should really hear the band.

Q. *Neither you nor your former bandmate Dave Grohl has talked publicly about Kurt Cobain since his suicide. Why?*

A. There's nothing to say, really. It happens every day in America. Dysfunction, drugs—it was compounded by the fame, but it's nothing romantic. It's just tragic. It's real emotional pain, and it's nobody's business. Who cares?

Q. *A lot of people, because they were touched by the music the band made.*

A. It's not proper to say anything. The emotional stake that Dave and I have in it is a lot more invested than the person who got to know Kurt through his music. There are things that are private and nobody should know. You can't go through life tragedy-free. Your parents die, and one day you or your spouse is gonna die. Life is heavy, and it still hurts a lot.

The Nirvana Wars
Spin, May 2002

HE PULLED THE trigger, and the vultures descended. Kurt Cobain's 1994 suicide may have been one of the saddest days in rock history, but like many tragedies, it was also a field day for opportunists. Following his death, some fans gained access to his Lake Washington house, despite the guard Cobain's wife, Courtney Love, had placed at the door.

"I think stuff got taken; that happens," says Eric Erlandson, then the guitarist in Love's band, Hole. To prevent more thievery of his dead friend's possessions, Erlandson rounded up everything he could: Cobain's paintings and sculptures, twenty-three journals and notebooks, and his guitars, including the prototype "Jagstangs" that Fender made based on his design (a cross between a Jaguar and a Mustang). The most coveted discovery: a box of one hundred and nine cassettes.

Most of these tapes capture rehearsals or rough mixes, but others contain songs that Cobain recorded alone on acoustic guitar in his bedroom or taped during basement jams with visiting musicians like Erlandson, Hole drummer Patty Schemel, and Nirvana touring guitarist Pat Smear. The majority of this music has never been heard. "I was just the person who was together enough to go, 'I don't want anything to happen to this shit,'" Erlandson says. "And now all of this stuff is getting involved in books and lawsuits."

As the administrator of Cobain's estate, Love recently signed a four-million-dollar deal to publish her late husband's journals, and she'd like to do a coffee-table book of his artwork as well. The guitars sit in a secure storage space. As for the tapes, their fate remains uncertain. Last summer, Love sued Cobain's former bandmates, bassist Krist Novoselic and drummer Dave Grohl. She believes she should have the right to steer the group's posthumous career, just as her husband steered the band during his lifetime. Grohl and Novoselic would like to retain a corporate structure that gives the three parties equal votes, allowing them to veto Love if they deem it necessary.

The dispute has mushroomed into one of the ugliest legal battles in rock history, and the fans are the ones who are suffering. The fight derailed a retrospective Nirvana box set that had been planned for last fall, and it is blocking the release of any new music by the most important band of the '90s. Love knows that fans blame her, and she has a serious public relations problem—beyond even her usual headline-making peccadilloes or her boisterous crusade for contract reform within the recording industry. She'd like to turn public perception around, and the tapes are her strongest tool for doing that.

"COME LISTEN TO HIS SONGS and WRITE ABOUT what you hear," Love urged me via email. "These tapes are everything from collage noise of Kurt's to acoustic songs, which he seemed to frantically write one a day or more in the two months before he killed himself—almost like a roadmap for his immortality. There is a vast collection of Cobain solo acoustic songs—in the history of rock music NO ONE has left behind a catalogue of this scope and astonishing depth, the literal holy grail of rock—I'm sure he did it on purpose."

So it is that I find myself sitting in the living room of Love's Spanish-style mansion ("Leased, not owned," she notes. "They tell me I'm cash-poor"), two doors down from Angelina Jolie and Billy Bob Thornton's place on one of the toniest blocks in Beverly Hills. Cynics might say this is a motivating factor behind her lawsuit, but she insists that it's a matter of principle. "I'm gonna win because they don't have a case, end of story!" she says, sweeping into the room at the start of a promised thirty-minute interview that winds up lasting more than ten hours, fueled by a steady stream of Dunhill cigarettes, Diet Cokes, and half a corned beef sandwich. Novoselic has taken to referring to Love in emails as "COURTney," and several former allies suggest that she's become obsessed with litigation. As she rattles on about various labor laws, I tell her she's beginning to sound like standup comic Lenny Bruce at the end of his career, when he talked about nothing but his numerous trials for public indecency. This sends the part-time actress into a flight of high dudgeon.

"Data and statistics do not make me Lenny Bruce!" Love rails. "But when you find out what your money and your husband's money is being used for, it's enough to turn you into Lenny Bruce—and they didn't even like Kurt, that's the scary part! I can stop the worst of them from continuing to feed on the dead man. That's the Shakespearean part I want you to understand: There's a dead man! A kid without a dad! There's blood on the walls—my husband's! I'm supposed to just walk away from that and say it never happened?"

Love contends that the surviving members of Nirvana have bilked the band for personal expenses such as Novoselic's 1999 divorce and legal work for the Foo Fighters' record deal. "But Grohl isn't the problem—Krist is the problem," she says. (Grohl declined to comment for this story.) Novoselic befriended Cobain when they were both teens in their native Aberdeen, Washington, and the towering bassist stood by the singer's side from 1985 until the end of his life. He has been the major keeper of the Nirvana flame, overseeing posthumous releases such as 1996's live album, *From the Muddy Banks of the Wishkah*, which Love calls "a piece of shit." Each side contends that the other has failed to do right by Cobain's legacy; each blames the other for turning a private business dispute into a well-publicized pissing match. Both make some valid points, and both spread plenty of inflammatory rhetoric.

"Krist and Dave fucked me!" Love rants. Says Novoselic: "Everything Kurt ever had, she has, but she wants that deity thing. I told her, 'Be an artist. Be an activist. Be a matriarch. Don't sue me. Don't sue Dave. Don't sue Nirvana.' But she wouldn't listen. When this goes to trial, man, this is gonna be heavy-duty shit, and she started it, so it's all gonna be public record."

Judge Robert Alsdorf will decide the specific legal issues in September, but the case raises a larger philosophical question, about the very nature of a rock band, which will linger much longer. Should Novoselic, who helped nurture Cobain's genius, and Grohl, whose monster drumming helped

Cobain's songs explode onto the world stage, be considered equal partners in all decisions regarding Cobain's music? What exactly was "Nirvana": Cobain and his songs, or the unique collaboration of three talented individuals?

THE ROOTS OF the conflict can be traced to the spring of 1992, six months after the release of *Nevermind*, when the trio's second album had already sold a staggering three million copies. Until then, the group divided songwriting royalties equally. (This is the model famously adopted by R.E.M. or, more recently, the Strokes, even though singer Julian Casablancas writes most of that band's material.) With massive success Cobain had a sudden change of heart. He threatened to quit if his bandmates didn't change the split in his favor, seventy-five percent to twenty-five percent for the music, and a hundred percent for the lyrics, retroactive to the group's inception.

Angry and feeling betrayed, Cobain's bandmates nonetheless capitulated, lest Nirvana cease to exist. The change cost Grohl and Novoselic millions of dollars, and they blamed Love—whom Cobain married in February 1992—for their frontman's reversal. But Rosemary Carroll, the attorney who represented Cobain and Love individually as well as Nirvana as an entity, insists that the initiative was Cobain's. "He knew what he was worth, and he knew he deserved all the money," she says in Charles R. Cross's Cobain biography, *Heavier Than Heaven.*

From that point on, Cobain received ninety-one percent of the songwriting royalties. The second biggest chunk, almost five percent, went to Chad Channing, who co-wrote some of the songs on Nirvana's 1989 debut, *Bleach*, and who was one of five drummers before Grohl. Novoselic and Grohl got less than two percent each, though that included key co-songwriting contributions such as "Smells Like Teen Spirit."

Nirvana continued to divide profits from merchandise, touring, and recording royalties equally, and the band filed tax returns as a general partnership. But Cobain never signed a formal partnership agreement, and he died without leaving a signed will.

It's a sad cliché that death is often a great career move in rock, and Nirvana did not end with Cobain's suicide. Left in the band's wake was a considerable legacy of B-sides, compilation tracks, unreleased songs, demos, and live recordings such as those compiled on *Wishkah* and 1994's *MTV Unplugged in New York*. To oversee these albums and other projects, Grohl and Novoselic proposed the formation of a limited liability corporation—a partnership that gave the two musicians and Love equal votes on all band business. Love signed the L.L.C. agreement in 1997, nearly four years after Cobain's death, but she now cites several reasons why this was a major mistake.

For one, Love says, the deck was stacked against her. Los Angeles music business attorney Jill Berliner represented Grohl and Novoselic individually as well as Nirvana, L.L.C. Band manager John Silva—whom Cobain had come to "hate," according to the Cross book—managed the post-Nirvana careers of both Grohl and Novoselic, in addition to Nirvana, L.L.C. Love says the interests of Berliner and Silva were in benefiting Grohl and Novoselic at the expense of the Cobain estate. "Collusion! Collusion! Collusion!" she howls.

Love also contends that the L.L.C. should have reflected the fact that Cobain was the group's key decision-maker and major songwriter, and as his representative, her vote should have carried more weight than Grohl and Novoselic's. Why did a business-savvy woman like Love enter a deal that wasn't in her best interests? Love maintains that her judgment was impaired by her notorious heroin problem. Finally, she says that she got poor advice from her attorney, Carroll, who told her that Washington state law would allow the surviving band members to force the estate to sell its interest in Nirvana if the parties couldn't reach an agreement. (Attorneys familiar with the case say that this is true, but no one could have forced Love to sell the copyrights for Cobain's songs.)

To overturn the L.L.C., Love has hired O. Yale Lewis, Jr., a Washington state lawyer renowned for recovering the rights to Jimi Hendrix's music for the guitarist's family. "After Kurt's death, people wanted to force Courtney into the L.L.C. for all sorts of reasons—for convenience, and maybe to control her," Lewis says. He is optimistic that the L.L.C. will eventually be dissolved by the court. Not surprisingly, the attorney representing Grohl and Novoselic disagrees.

"What's really going on is [Love] has her stink with Universal over Hole, and she's using Nirvana as leverage," says Kelly Corr. (Universal is the mega-corporation that swallowed Geffen Records, which had been home to both Nirvana and Hole. In 2000 the company sued Hole for breach of contract for not delivering all of the albums it owed the label. Love filed a countersuit arguing that, under California law, companies cannot tie artists up in contracts that last longer than seven years.) Corr has filed motions to examine the details of the Cobain estate, including Cobain and Love's prenuptial agreement and their daughter Frances Bean's trust fund, and he has asked the court to conduct psychological testing of Love. "She is a fool if she doesn't settle with us, because we're going to go to court and we're gonna beat her," he says. "Come on out for the trial. It will be a hell of a lot of fun—a real circus!"

As the lawyers gear up to duke it out before Judge Alsdorf, their clients wrestle in the court of public opinion. "When Kurt was alive, Nirvana was an equal partnership of the three of us," Novoselic and Grohl wrote in a public letter to fans, defending the L.L.C. At Love's request, Cobain's mother, Wendy Frandenburg O'Connor, fired back with a missive of her own. "I know that Nirvana was never a partnership of any sort," she wrote. "I know that in the last year of his life, my son despised his bandmates and told me many times that he no longer wanted to play with them or have anything to do with them."

Love's lawsuit contends that Nirvana had split up at the time of her husband's death. When I interviewed him in the summer of 1993, shortly before the release of *In Utero* and nine months before his death, Cobain seemed happy with the state of the group. But he often used the singular "I" instead of the plural "we" when talking about key decisions such as choosing the second single.

"I have my heart set on—everybody, the whole band has their heart set on—releasing 'Scentless Apprentice' after 'Heart-Shaped Box,'" he said. "That's a really good example of the direction we're going in. We actually collaborated on that song. It came together in practice, and it was just a totally satisfying thing to finally contribute equally to a song, instead of me coming up with the basics of the song. . . . For the most part, it's always been like eighty percent my song that I've written at home and introduced to the band later on in practice."

Nine years later, I email that quote to Novoselic. "He says it was 'refreshing.' [I would have said to Kurt,] 'What planet did you come from, dude? We've been working together for years, we've been doing stuff like that forever, I've got publishing on "Teen Spirit" and quite a few other songs!' I don't know what kind of mood he was in then. He was a windmill—he was turning all the time."

Though all three partners in Nirvana, L.L.C., agreed to the plan, it was Novoselic who compiled the forty-five-track box set that was to have been issued in the fall of 2001, commemorating the tenth anniversary of *Nevermind*. When Love filed suit, Judge Alsdorf granted an injunction against issuing any new Nirvana material until the case is resolved. In less heated moments, Novoselic and Love both express a desire to settle and get on with the business of releasing Cobain's music. "It should have been done six months ago," Love says. Adds Novoselic: "We could work out a deal with Courtney. I'm always willing to work out anything—I'm easy."

In fact Love proposed a settlement in January under which she, Grohl, and Novoselic would continue to equally share profits from merchandise that bears the likeness of all three members and recording royalties from the songs they all played on. Unanimous agreement would be required on the content of new Nirvana releases, and Grohl and Novoselic would have veto power over merchandising or licensing songs to movies or commercials. However, the estate would have the right to release Cobain's bedroom demos under the name Nirvana, and the profits from those would be exclusive. Love would have sole power to approve a film about Cobain's life (she's discussed such a movie with respected producers Jersey Films), and Frances Bean would assume all control of the band's future after Grohl and Novoselic die. Their attorney never responded to this proposal, and he scoffs at the suggestion that it seemed reasonable.

"Why should we give away any of the powers that we have?" Corr asks. "Because she says she was on drugs at the time and not capable of signing the contract? Please!"

WHETHER A SETTLEMENT is reached or the case proceeds to trial, it's unlikely that the box set will be released in the form envisioned by Novoselic. As many fans know, the gem of the set was a song called "You Know You're Right." Love maintains that it's a potential hit that would have been "wasted" on a three-disc box selling for sixty-five dollars when it could spur platinum sales as the bonus track on a single-disc greatest hits set à la the Beatles' *1*. Even Novoselic now admits that she has a point.

I first heard "You Know You're Right" the only time the band ever played it live, in October 1993 at Chicago's Aragon Ballroom, when Cobain introduced it as "On a Mountain." It was classic Nirvana, hitting with the same impact as "Smells Like Teen Spirit" and boasting a similar structure—a slow, creepy verse suddenly exploding into a painfully cathartic but undeniably catchy chorus. The studio version that I hear in Love's living room is even stronger, but her initial offer of unfettered access to the hundred and nine cassettes has evaporated. She says her lawyers have advised against playing any of the solo Cobain songs that Grohl and Novoselic haven't heard. "There's some really melodic stuff, and there's some garbage," Love says. "Some stuff is box set-y, but other stuff, we don't want to pass it up. We don't want to get all 'Free As a Bird' about it, but there's stuff that's too good to bury."

When Love says "we," she's including her Harvard-educated boyfriend, Jim Barber. A former Geffen A&R executive, he is now her manager and the point person in the Hole and Nirvana lawsuits. Barber has yet to document the contents of all of the tapes. "How we pull it together and in exactly what form it gets released, it's too early to say," he says. "We feel like, 'Let's clean up the business situation before we go into that,' because it's going to be a lot of creative work to get this material in shape. I think there are amazing things, and there may be some things that are singles, if you salt them in a context where they work for people."

Novoselic is aghast. "Who is this guy, a chef? It's interesting that he uses 'salt' as a metaphor—there are so many wounds, big ones." For the bassist, who often acted as a shield between Cobain and the world, protecting his childhood friend so that he could pursue his craft, Barber's presumptuous role as a posthumous producer obviously carries a personal sting. And he is dubious about Love's claims of a treasure trove of "lost" Cobain songs. "Just from my experience, I don't think there's very much. And if there is, I doubt it's anything releasable."

The promised grail may or may not exist, but in Love's living room, I do catch an enticing glimpse of what's at stake. "Dough, Ray, and Me" is often discussed on the Web, but only a handful of people have ever heard the acoustic demo that Barber plays on his Discman. The sound quality is sketchy, to say the least, but when that gravelly voice wraps itself around a typically enchanting melody, the effect is compelling. The tune builds to a powerful climax as Cobain repeats the mantra, "Do / Re / Mi," making it seem as if those three syllables contain a universe of meanings. Deciphering the rest of his lyrics is no easy task in two listens, but I'm pretty sure I catch the lines, "If I may / If I might / Wake me up / See me . . . If I may / Cold as ice / I only have / Sue me."

As with so much else that he left behind, that last line is more poignant than Cobain could ever have imagined.

A LOOK AT THE "LOST" NIRVANA SONGS

"You Know You're Right"

In late January 1994, Cobain, Novoselic, and Grohl entered Bob Lang's studio in Seattle for their final recording session. Following a long jam, they captured this powerful tune in one take, including the gut-wrenching vocal, a spooky, ambient intro of echoed harmonics, and a fractured guitar solo.

"Skid Marks"

At the same session, the group recorded this oddly funereal, mostly instrumental lounge-music tribute to stained underwear (the chorus is simply the title, shouted repeatedly). Novoselic and Grohl also recorded several tunes of their own, but Cobain apparently didn't play on them.

"Opinion"

Cobain performed this angry, acoustic diatribe against a sensationalistic media live on KAOS-FM in Olympia, Washington, in 1990, supposedly on the night that he wrote it. The lyrics seem prescient: "Congratulations, you have won / It's a year's subscription of bad puns / And it makes your story our concern / And you set it up before it burns."

"Dough, Ray, and Me"

"That's a beautiful song," says Novoselic. In addition to the solo demo, Cobain recorded a four-track version in the basement of the house on Lake Washington in March 1994. Eric Erlandson played bass, Nirvana touring guitarist Pat Smear played guitar, and Cobain drummed and sang into a microphone duct-taped to a cymbal stand.

"Verse Chorus Verse"

Also known as "Sappy," this is another fabulously catchy pop tune. A version recorded by the band appeared unlisted on *No Alternative,* a 1993 benefit album for the Red Hot Organization. "I actually think that with a little mixing, it's a proper single," Jim Barber says. "No one's ever really heard that song."

"Old Age"

Recorded on a boom box before the *Nevermind* sessions, Cobain later gave this song to Love for Hole, which released it on the *Beautiful Son* EP. Cobain also appeared on a version of Hole's "Asking for It" singing backing vocals, but it has never been released. Barber says that he has yet to find any other songs that the couple recorded together.

2   THE GIRL WITH THE MOST CAKE

COURTNEY LOVE IS ONE OF THE GREAT self-invented characters in rock history, right up there with Johnny Rotten and Iggy Pop. You have to give her credit for that, as well as for her razor-sharp wit and lightning-quick intellect. During any fast, furious, and far-ranging conversation she is simultaneously insulting you, seducing you, doubling back to make a joke about something she said ten minutes ago, and steering you where she wants to go next.

Seeing as how Hole never topped its impressive second album, *Live Through This*, and Love's acting career has cooled after the accolades she won for essentially playing herself in *The People Vs. Larry Flynt*, Courtney's biggest talent is probably just being Courtney. But even as that most shallow of modern commodities, a celebrity, she remains uniquely rock 'n' roll: She's the only star of her stature that I can think of whose email address is well-known to just about everyone in the universe, and she will sit down and pound out a passionate ten-thousand word screed (with approximately nine thousand five hundred of those words misspelled) in response to a comment by a fourteen-year-old fan.

Some notes on these pieces: A year after her husband's suicide, Love gave a freewheeling two-hour interview on live radio to then–*Chicago Reader* rock critic Bill Wyman and me when we co-hosted the first version of *Sound Opinions* on Chicago alternative-rock powerhouse Q101–FM. After a while our engineer simply gave up trying to "dump" her curse words and let them all fly, the FCC be damned. "Courtney Unplugged" culls some of the highlights of that chat.

Love was still in rare form seven years later when I spent ten hours interviewing her in her Beverly Hills living room for "The Nirvana Wars." I wanted to focus on the court case, but there is no "steering" Courtney in an interview—you have to let her go where she wants, and eventually she'll come around to what you're supposed to be talking about. I ran out of tape at the six-hour mark (I had to borrow some cassettes from her boyfriend and manager, Jim Barber), but I was going to be damned if I gave up before Love did, and I hung in there until she finally slowed down enough to actually let me ask a question. Some of the more amusing and far-ranging snippets of that second conversation were compiled for the *Chicago Sun-Times* as "The Quotable Courtney."

One other outtake from that long day: I had last seen Love's daughter, Frances Bean Cobain, when she was a toddler playing in the dirt behind the second stage at Lollapalooza '95. Now a pretty, lanky nine-year-old with long, chestnut-brown hair and piercing eyes just like her father's, she bounded into the living room wearing a T-shirt that said AVOID THE BOURBON STREET HANGOVER: STAY DRUNK! "One of mom's funny fuckin' shirts," Love noted. Franny, as she's called at home, chided her mother for cursing and held out her palm. "She charges me five dollars every time I say the 'f—' word," Love explained. "And that's fine, I agreed to that, but she has to write it down in Mommy's little curse book—she can't just be random about it. She tried to do a dollar a smoke, but that's not fair!"

Mother and daughter hugged long and close for a moment before the pre-teen skittered off. When she was gone, Love told me that Franny can't listen to her father's music—"It makes her sad"—but while she professes to have no interest in rock, Mom has caught her secretly monitoring Los Angeles's alternative KROQ–FM.

Hole, *Live Through This*
Request, May 1994

IN A PERFECT world, it might be possible to review Hole's second album without mentioning what's happened to the band's leader since its indie debut, or the fact that she now signs legal documents as Courtney Love-Cobain. But since these developments are impossible to ignore, it's best to acknowledge the rants of those who believe that Love is a shrewd, manipulative, and sometimes unpleasant woman; the whispers that she owes her major-label deal to the success of her husband, Nirvana's Kurt Cobain; the charges that her best ideas have been stolen from former partners such as Kat Bjelland of Babes In Toyland; and the accusations that she endangered the health of her baby by using heroin while pregnant. It's amazing that *Live Through This* can be heard through all this noise at all, but the best testament to Love's talent is that her music cuts through loud and clear.

Live Through This isn't a masterpiece, but it is a damn strong album full of driving guitar riffs and catchy choruses. None of the twelve tracks disappoint melodically, and don't let anyone tell you that's it's not because of the songwriting, which is credited to the band. Paul Kolderie and Sean Slade (Buffalo Tom, Morphine) did a fine job producing, and Scott Litt (R.E.M., Nirvana) and J Mascis (Dinosaur Jr.) did an even better job remixing (five tracks and one track, respectively). But *Live Through This* ultimately succeeds on the strength of its songs. In the tradition of all powerful three-minutes-or-less punk-rock songs, "Jennifer's Body," "Violet," "Asking For It," "Softer, Softest," and "Doll Parts" are simply impossible to get out of your head after the first listen.

As a vocalist Love isn't distinctive—she often sounds like Joan Jett—but she has a way of grabbing your attention, varying her attack from a seductive purr to a window-rattling growl. Eric Erlandson (a holdover from the first album) is a tasteful guitarist who decorates the spaces between riffs with touches of feedback or short, melodic leads, and newcomers Kristen Pfaff (bass, piano, and backing vocals) and Patty Schemel (drums) are valuable additions. They get a lot of mileage out of the basic Hole song structure: quiet (sometimes acoustic) intro, noisy chorus, quiet verse, noisy chorus, big finish. This format wasn't invented by Nirvana—go back and listen to "Louie, Louie"—and its ubiquitousness is the sort of thing that would only bother an anal rock critic. As long as you can do something good with a formula, why not use it?

Love and her bandmates are obviously keen students of rock history, and they prove themselves to be skillful synthesists. Like L7, they mix the drive and anger of the riot grrrls with the garage-rock melodies of the womyn-in-rock circa '77, especially Patti Smith and Poly Styrene of X-Ray Spex. But Hole also creates some surprisingly gentle, introspective moments; even "I Think That I Would Die," written in a show of reconciliation with raging Babe Bjelland, has a tender acoustic side. The album's one cover, "Credit in the Straight World," comes from *Colossal Youth* by Young Marble Giants, an arty English postpunk trio (bass, guitar, and organ) led by the stunning vocalist Alison Statton.

To her credit, the album title and the Young Marble Giants cover ("I got some credit in the straight world / I lost a leg, I lost an eye") are the only places in which Love openly refers to the controversies she's weathered (it's one thing to listen to an established rock star whine, but it's another to hear it from someone who's still an up-and-comer). Instead the lyrics are cut-and-paste Beat poetry for beginners, with an emphasis on female imagery familiar to any high school sophomore. Three songs refer to flowers, three to milk, two to witches, three to dolls or babies, and three to anorexia or bingeing and purging. Occasional lines jump out as especially well-crafted, funny, or insightful ("Be a model or just look like one," "I want to be the girl with the most cake," "When they get what they want / They never want it again"), but mostly you just find yourself rocking along, happily oblivious to where a song came from and what it really means.

This is a good thing, because the one time that Hole's lyrics focus on a definite subject, in "Rock Star," the album closer, they're a petty and vindictive attack on the fey but harmless Beat Happening–K Records–love-rock scene in Olympia, Washington. And then you find yourself wondering if maybe, just maybe, some of the nasty things you've heard about Courtney Love are true.

With Love, Cobain Widow Delivers Heartfelt, Cathartic Set
The *Chicago Sun-Times*, September 6, 1994

"I GOT SOME credit in the straight world," Courtney Love sang on Saturday night at the U.I.C. Pavilion. "I lost a leg, I lost an eye."

Outside rock circles Love has grown in stature since the suicide of her husband, Nirvana leader Kurt Cobain, and the death of Kristen Pfaff, the bassist in her band, Hole. The singer recently appeared on the covers of two major magazines in flattering profiles that labeled her "a survivor." Not a bad turnaround for a woman previously portrayed as the most hated rock wife since Yoko Ono. But people who bothered to listen to Love before her husband's death already knew that the Oregon native was an intense performer with a captivating vocal growl. Cobain might have convinced her to emphasize songcraft on Hole's second album, *Live Through This*. But Love has always had the songs in her.

Sandwiched between forgettable openers Marilyn Manson and over-hyped headliners Nine Inch Nails, Hole performed its first major American show on Saturday since Cobain's death derailed the tour to support *Live*

Through This. The band—which included a new bassist named Melissa Auf Der Maur from Vancouver—needed several songs to shake off the cobwebs. The sound was initially a muddy mess, and Love was tormented by a guitar that kept cutting out.

But midway through the ten-song set, by the time Love covered the Young Marble Giants' "Credit in the Straight World," the sound had crystallized into a furious catharsis. Love's plaintive wails were spurred on by Eric Erlandson's monstrous guitar riffs and Patty Schemel's rock-steady drumming. Especially effective were "Doll Parts," "Violet," and a new song in which Love pleaded for "her beautiful son" to "come back, come back to me."

The tune was clearly inspired by Cobain, as was the set-closer, a version by Love and Erlandson of Leadbelly's haunting "In the Pines" (also known as "Where Did You Sleep Last Night," which Nirvana covered on MTV's *Unplugged*). At the end of the song Love smashed her guitar and amp in retaliation for the sound problems. Then she reflexively jumped into the crowd, emerging a minute later with her white party dress torn to shreds and a big smile on her face.

The scene recalled Nirvana's last Chicago performance at the Aragon Ballroom, but Love wasn't just aping her husband. Like Cobain at his best, she had seized the moment and made it her own.

There was nothing so spontaneous about Nine Inch Nails. Missing the mud and the moment that made them seem special at Woodstock '94, Trent Reznor and friends came off as horror-movie extras. They were the band playing at Disney's Haunted Mansion, or old Alice Cooper updated with synthesizers—scary, silly, and slight.

Courtney Unplugged
Request, August 1995

LIKE MOST ROCK stars, Courtney Love-Cobain has a high-priced publicist who earns her money by placing sympathetic pieces in celebrity-obsessed glossies such as *Entertainment Weekly* and *Vanity Fair.* But Hole's leader is a sharp, funny, sarcastic, and extremely opinionated woman who just can't keep her views to herself. In the great punk-rock tradition, she frequently ignores her publicist, managers, and record company and leaps into the verbal mosh pit, delivering outrageous diatribes in the music-industry-dirt folder of America Online.

On one memorable evening last May, Love-Cobain granted a freewheeling two-hour interview to Bill Wyman and me on *Sound Opinions*, our weekly rock 'n' roll talk show on WKQX–FM in Chicago. She made only one demand, insisting that we call her Courtney Love-Cobain. "I'm a feminist, but when you're married, you take you husband's name," she said. "That's how the credit in my new movie [*Feeling Minnesota*] reads." (This despite the fact that for the Hole album, Geffen's official publicity material refers to her as Courtney Love.)

Other than that, there were no rules and no limitations. Love-Cobain didn't answer every question—she failed to elaborate on the causes of her obvious animosity toward former Nirvana drummer and current Foo Fighters leader Dave Grohl—and she ignored questions about stories that she refused to appear on Lollapalooza if Dr. Dre and Snoop Doggy Dogg were on the bill. But she was frank and forthcoming on most of the subjects we brought up, as well as many that we didn't.

The conversation began with a question about her appearance, dressed as an angel, on the cover of the June issue of *Vanity Fair*. In September 1992 an article by writer Lynn Hirschberg in the same magazine cited unnamed "inside sources" who said the singer took heroin while she was pregnant. The article nearly cost the Cobains custody of their daughter, Frances Bean. The couple always maintained that the story was incorrect, a position that Love-Cobain partially amended on the air.

ON THE RECENT *VANITY FAIR* COVER STORY: "I think it's a little redemption. *V.F.* one ruined my life; *V.F.* two made it chic not to ruin my life any more. I have these dreams about running into [former *Vanity Fair* editor Tina Brown] in a really big car."

ON HOW *VANITY FAIR* WRITER KEVIN SESSUMS CAME TO INTERVIEW HER IN THE BATHTUB: "I was dirty. I was like, 'Come in the bathroom.' I kept my panties on."

ON THE FIRST *VANITY FAIR* STORY: "I did take heroin when I was pregnant in the very beginning of my pregnancy. I did. Otherwise I could have sued the hell out of them. [But Hirschberg was] completely wrong. She made it seem like I was taking drugs into my *second* trimester."

ON MEETING LYNN HIRSCHBERG EARLIER THIS YEAR: "So I'm at the Academy Awards, at this party at Mortons, right? I walk into this room with my friend Amanda De Cadenet, who's very Hollywood, and there's Quentin Tarantino and this really haggy lady. Amanda says to me, 'That woman hates you.' And I'm like, 'She's probably a manager.' I sit down and I'm picking up this Oscar, and they're really heavy, 'cause they're lead with gold in them. You can totally brain somebody. I'm like, 'Who do I hate in this room?' All of the sudden this little voice by [Tarantino] peeps up, and she's like, 'You don't like me,' and I see this homely face and these really big boobs and it's Lynn Hirschberg and I don't recognize her.

"So I'm waving this Oscar around. I only hate two people in the whole world, some insane singer-folk-songwriter person [Mary Lou Lord] who got an insane bidding war because I chased her down the street, and her. She said her name was Lynn Hirschberg, and she bolted and she hid under Madonna and Ellen Barkin and Jodie Foster's table, and they were kicking her under the table. Jody Foster was smoking cigars and she was putting them out on her and screaming, 'Face the music, you bitch!' And she ran out of Mortons without her coat and without her purse. Had I killed her, they'd just go, 'There goes Courtney again.' But I kept my poise."

ON HER HIGH-PRICED PUBLICIST PAT KINGSLEY: "I'm a charity case for her. She doesn't even charge me; she just wanted to see if she could do it. I called up crying and said, 'Can you take a challenge?' She gives everybody to everybody else, other than Tom Cruise, Roseanne, and Julia Roberts. Me and Roseanne are her cases."

ON LIZ PHAIR: "I sometimes want to say a minorly mean thing about her, but I don't."

ON RECORDING ENGINEER STEVE ALBINI: "I think Steve Albini organizing the *Newsweek* press conference in his house so he can get famous for not wanting to be famous is pretty gross. He wants to be mega for not wanting to be mega. I can't listen to the Polly Harvey record [*To Give You My Love*] because they're all songs about Steve. He told my [former] manager Janet [Billig] that he'll never talk really mean about me because he's afraid of me. He said, 'She's crazy, but she's smart crazy—like Hitler!' I love that."

ON DEPECHE MODE, SMASHING PUMPKINS, AND PJ HARVEY PRODUCER FLOOD: "He won't produce my band. I've got a real complaint with that. He just keeps going, 'No,' for the most sexist, gross reason in the world. Let me give you a metaphor: Five people are auditioning for Hamlet. One's a girl, three are guys—Billy Corgan, Eddie Vedder, Trent Reznor. They're gonna kick each other's butts, right? Add a little sex, a little hatred, a lot of rivalry. You kind of have the story of my present life. Flood's passing me over because of that."

ON WHY SHE WANTS FLOOD TO PRODUCE HOLE IN THE FIRST PLACE: "Flood understands the Alan Moulder [My Bloody Valentine's producer] part I want, the Neil Young *Harvest* part I want, the Mazzy Star good-stuff part I want. He understands the gnarly-ass 'Supernaut'-'Sweet Leaf' Black Sabbath part. I want to make *Led Zeppelin II*, full-metal Courtney!"

ON CHARGES THAT SHE HAD TO SING OVER GUIDING VO-CALS TO NAIL HER PARTS ON *LIVE THROUGH THIS*: "I'll make the next record, then tell me I didn't make that, either! If you heard the last song on *MTV Unplugged* ['Sugar Coma'], that's the best song I've ever written."

ON FORMER MANAGER JANET BILLIG, NOW AN EXECUTIVE AT ATLANTIC RECORDS: "She's very political, Janet, but she's smart as hell and she's twenty-four years old, so give her some slack. She signed Billy [Corgan] out of a demo pile. She managed me, she managed Evan [Dando], she found Billy, she basically managed Nirvana, she managed the Breeders. It's a huge load for such a small girl."

ON SMASHING PUMPKINS' BILLY CORGAN: "He's helped me a lot, so I owe him. He always wanted to be a metal god. He's calling [Smashing Pumpkins' forthcoming album *Mellon Collie and the Infinite Sadness*] 'The Wall for Generation X.' And I think he can pull it off. You do know what his road crew calls him behind his back, though, don't you? 'The pear-shaped boy.' Ha! I love that."

ON PERFORMING WITH METALLICA AND VERUCA SALT NEAR THE ARCTIC CIRCLE FOR A MOLSON BEER PROMOTION: "Four hundred grand, man; you wouldn't pass it up either! Money in the bank, my daughter goes to Yale, case closed."

ON VERUCA SALT, WHICH HAS OPENED FOR HOLE: "They're very business-oriented. Or one of them is. I think that Nina [Gordon] has a lot of bile in her and that bile might come out on her next record and it will really be great. I think Louise [Post] plays lead."

ON TRENT REZNOR AND NINE INCH NAILS: "When he told me that he liked Sade, I should have taken the hint and backed way off. He considers himself the biggest recording star since Elvis Presley. He's got the biggest ego, the biggest entourage, the most groupies. He's vile. He's the P.T. Barnum of alternative rock. He was like this really quick blip in my life that meant nothing, but it ruined so many things. If his fans only knew what a homophobe he is: 'Faggot this, faggot that.' I've never heard so much wretched homophobic bullshit in my life. And he's also a Republican. That's why he's friends with [MTV VJ] Kennedy."

ON ATTORNEYS: "I have twelve lawyers right now, like the twelve disciples. The thirteenth is an America Online case because there's this crazy girl who's obsessed with Trent Reznor and she's stalking me and stalking him. There's not a lot that our two camps agree on, except for New Orleans [which we both like] and this person, who we hate."

ON YOKO ONO: "I got worse press than her."

ON GREEN DAY'S BILLIE JOE: "When he calls me or I call Billie Joe, he's going through the same thing Kurt was going through. He's reading *MaximumrockNRoll* and *Flipside* and he's reading that one one-thousandth of one percent of the music population that's arguing whether vegan means you eat nuts or not."

ON ELVIS COSTELLO: "I lived in his house with him and his wife. It was 1986, I was eighteen, and I had just finished that horrendous movie of Alex Cox's [*Straight to Hell*]. I was the only person who knew who Sonic Youth was on the set, and I had all these tapes. I was kind of like his nanny because I couldn't get another job, so I stayed at his house for a while. There was an incident [with] his wife and him and there was this movie on the TV . . . aaarrrggghhh! I didn't do it! I ran out of the house."

ON FORMER BANDMATE KAT BJELLAND OF BABES IN TOY-LAND: "She's got this one-and-a-half-carat diamond ring of mine and she won't give it back. She should never have broken up with me. We had a really great chemistry. I'm a fan of [Babes In Toyland's] *Spanking Machine* because it's half my lyrics."

ON PEARL JAM'S EDDIE VEDDER: "He tried to make friends with me. As Kurt would say [sarcastically], *'He's a good guy.'* A little savvy, a little calculating, more than people know. I should be nice to him by all rights, but I can't because it's dishonorable because Kurt hated him."

ON THE BREEDERS' KIM DEAL: "She's very charming and sexy. She doesn't change her clothes a lot, but she's still sexy. She's the only girl that Kurt ever admitted having a crush on."

ON JULIANA HATFIELD: "I think he had this little thing for about five seconds for Juliana Hatfield. Juliana Hatfield had 'Juliana Hatfield-Cobain' written on her notebook during the *Bleach* era."

ON SONIC YOUTH: "I owe them my entire career. I owe them my marriage. I owe them my daughter."

ON HOLE DRUMMER PATTY SCHEMEL: "Lars Ulrich of Metallica is really obsessed with us because he can't conceive that someone with a uterus is a better drummer than he is. Mudhoney said in *Melody Maker* that Patty was their first choice, but Kurt had Patty until he found Dave. Dave had this [John] Bonham thing, and Kurt finally chose Dave over Patty."

ON FORMER NIRVANA DRUMMER DAVE GROHL: "There's not a lot of love lost between me and Dave. We don't hate each other because we can't hate each other. If we hate each other it will be a disaster. But what you have to know about Dave is he was the guy who'd enjoy going out back to set his farts on fire with Steve Albini. That's Dave."

ON FORMER NIRVANA BASSIST KRIST NOVOSELIC: "Kurt understood him musically, except for the Hawkwind aspect of it. And Kurt believed that Krist would never sell him to Nike."

ON JUMPING INTO THE CROWD: "I was wanting to get passed like a football hero. And I'm a feminist. It's like the whole 'Asking For It' concept. I'm singing 'Asking For It,' I stage dive, and I get raped. Don't you see the irony? For eight weeks, this thing would overcome me and I'd just jump where there were the most girls. Then I discovered at the Metro [in Chicago] that the girls were the ones taking off my bra, taking out my hair, going into the twenty-four-hour hip place with pieces of my barrettes."

ON BECOMING AN ACTRESS: "That's just because, A.) I don't want to be me, and B.) Because Madonna can't do it."

ON REMAINING ACCESSIBLE: "I come from punk rock, what am I gonna do? To anybody who's not an Xer, I'm the anti-Christ. Every four months some editor gets a boner and sticks me on the cover. Why? So sixty-seven million soap-opera-watching American women can hate my guts."

ON HAPPINESS: "I'm not gonna die. I like my career because it's like chess. It's like politics. It's like America Online—it's this video game about me. It's all fascinating. But you know what? The industry really is slimy."

ON KURT COBAIN: "I feel that people have a right to know about it so that it offers him some chance at dignity so people don't think things that aren't true. Our lifestyle, our parenting, our daily rituals, his honesty, his integrity, his beauty, everything. His drug addiction was nothing like people think. There are so many junkies who are so much worse than Kurt or me ever were."

The Quotable Courtney
The *Chicago Sun-Times*, March 10, 2002

COURTNEY LOVE IS by far the most challenging interview subject I've ever encountered, as well as one of the most wildly entertaining.

By necessity, journalists reduce Love's hyperactive stream-of-consciousness rants to manageable sound bites, but those don't really do justice to the experience of having a long conversation with her. It's like trying to ride a tornado, and she knows it.

"This thing about me being crazy actually works some times," Love says. "Let them think I'm crazy! In business, if they think I'm crazy, they'll fill out the fucking check! I've heard this story about Tom Petty: When he was dealing with people, he'd take this knife and stab the desk when he wanted to make a point!"

In lieu of a knife, Love uses a torrent of words and a razor-sharp intellect. But while her abrasiveness and her humor translate well on the printed page, the sheer agility, speed, and precision of her remarkable mind don't always come through. I spent more than ten hours in a rambling but fascinating conversation with Love before the fireplace in the *In Style*–perfect living room of her Spanish-style mansion in Beverly Hills. This setting was a stark contrast to the barren living room of the house on Seattle's Lake Washington where I interviewed Love's husband for the *Sun-Times* in June 1993.

Here are a few of the quotable highlights from my interview with Love.

ON HOW MARKETING RULES ROCK: "It's all about marketing money. Marketing money is the manna from heaven, and if they don't give you your marketing money—like they didn't do with Garbage or the Wallflowers or Sheryl Crowe—then you're dead. All you've got is your live act, and that's it. Now you can say that [Hole's last album] *Malibu* didn't have balls, but it should have sold three million. If it shouldn't have sold three million, I'll know, and I'll accept that. But why is *Cocky* [by Kid Rock] not doing well? That doesn't make any sense to me! Is it really that bad? Kid Rock can alienate an audience just by getting a little country on them? It's one of two things: It's either marketing money, or he's alienated the wiggers and they can only deal with black culture and they can't acclimate to redneck. Or maybe his chick [Pamela Lee Anderson] is a bad luck charm. Naked, she's gotta be amazing—I mean, I'd go there. But the real problem is Atlantic is not putting marketing money into his record!"

ON NIRVANA'S SUCCESS: "Krist says shit like, 'Nirvana didn't come to the public, the public came to Nirvana.' That's one of his favorites. But that neglects the fact that [Chicago independent record promoter] Jeff McCluskey sure as fuck got paid, and so did the rack jobbers, and so did the fucking handlers, and so did the guy in Thailand, and so did that guy, and so did that guy, and so did that guy! It was marketing money!"

ON WHAT SHE LEARNED FROM MADONNA: "I live in this house, I have this kid, I pay for my things, and if I am going to pay for that fucking stool, I want to see an invoice for it! When Madonna did that *Rolling Stone* cover with me and Tina Turner, she took me to her office and she said, 'You don't have photo approval?' 'No.' 'You don't sign your own checks?' 'No.' 'You're a fucking idiot! This is how you do it.' And she has this ledger, and once a week she sits and she signs her checks and she has a red pen and she writes, 'No!' or 'Fuck off!' And that's how you keep control."

ON DRUGS: "I did heroin once recently—I smoked it when I felt the entire world was going to hell [on September 11]. Me and a friend found somebody that knew somebody that knew somebody who could get heroin, and we were overcharged extremely for twenty dollars' worth, and we smoked it, because I thought the world was going to blow up. But the drug just doesn't like me anymore. Before that I hadn't done heroin since I was rehabbed, which was '95, before *[The People Vs.] Larry Flynt*. So heroin—no. Pills—I don't do pills. I have Ambien upstairs, but I've had that bottle for years. Ambien kind of makes you feel weird—it's trippy. It's pleasant, like Betty Boop is in the room and starts smiling at you, so I only take it if I can't go to sleep. A lot of people in Hollywood do blow, and I don't do blow. Nobody ever invites me to do blow, either! I walk into this room and they're doing blow and they hide it. When did I become a cop?"

ON LARRY FLYNT: "I'd been in a porno that you'll never find out about because Larry bought it. He tends to take care of me. He'll call [imitating Flynt], 'What were you doing running around San Francisco, naked, in a bean bag chair?' 'What are you talking about, Larry?' 'I just paid twenty grand for that!' You know, he's gonna keep the negative too, and if I ever go Republican or something, he'll fuck me! I'm raised on Gloria Steinem and it ends up being Larry Flynt who takes care of me!"

ON THE FUTURE OF THE MAJOR LABELS: "They're not going to fall, because they're distribution systems, and we need them. But we need them to do better accounting! They give a very, very unregulated accounting, and they're all crooked together. They hide money and they lie to their stockholders, and capitalism cannot work if the stockholders are being lied to. They don't know where the money comes from every quarter, so they cannot report accurately! Capitalism cannot function if the stockholders are being lied to!"

ON HER FUTURE IN POLITICS: "I don't want to do case law—the only thing that really interests me is the legislative intent of labor law. But I like going to [the California state capital in] Sacramento. It's funny! I like politics, you know what I mean? It might be something to do some day. There's power involved in it, and it's sexy. There was a poll in some women's magazine, and I was number two behind Tom Hanks for who would be president of this country. I was above Rosie and I was above Oprah. And I've never even had a big hit record! The problem with it is it's dirty. It's dirty and there's no way to clean it up. You go in, you do the best you can, but I don't think I could be in office because it's just too fucking dirty, and it would make me crazy."

ON EDUCATING YOUNGER MUSICIANS: "The fucking kids who've been in this business for three years—when I'm on the phone with Macy Gray, do you think she wants to talk about her fucking record deal? The best I can do for her is get her to *lease* the fucking Bentley, not *buy* the Bentley! [Imitates Macy Gray:] 'Macy don't want to talk about that!' Macy gets a fifteen-million-dollar push with marketing money, but just try to sit with these fucking kids to talk about their record contracts! I swear to God, it would have been easier in '95. They're not educated now. They weren't educated in '95, either. Hell, I'm not educated! But they're not interested in being educated! They wonder why I'm curious about things. 'You're so crazy! You're so weird!' And they're being taken to the cleaners!"

ON FORMER BEAU BILLY CORGAN: "I loved *Siamese Dream*. That was like cheating on Kurt—I couldn't listen to that in the house. When we were making *Live Through This*, I used to listen to it because Kurt wasn't around, and I knew those songs were all about me. But I never spent a week with Billy! When you're young and full of cum, you have these fake romances that are epic, so he writes all these epic songs about me, but they're not real.

"After Kurt died, Billy came out to the Canyon Ranch and he like took care of me for a couple of days, but it wasn't like sex. I kept trying to make him fuck me, but he wouldn't fuck me. Everybody thinks we had something, but I was so fucking high that I would have made the maid fuck me. I was crazy! But Billy came out, and we drove around the desert, and he took me to a cave and held me. His wife was nice enough to let him go, and he was like *my friend*! But [before that], I never had breakfast with him, I never woke up with him, I never saw him pee, I never had a burrito with him, I never went around the block holding hands with him. I fucked him, and I'd leave—that was it. That was our relationship, and then these songs came out of that."

ON FORMER BEAU EDWARD NORTON: "He was like, 'I'm the fucking actor of my generation. I don't give a fuck. I love this girl, she was married to that guy, I don't give a fuck, *I'm the man!*' He helped me with this drug problem, he was great to my kid, and we had a very symbiotic relationship. But he didn't want to deal with the vulgar business of all this [Nirvana] stuff, and that's why I'm only getting around to it now."

ON CURRENT BEAU JIM BARBER: "I'm shocked that I ever married a cute guy [Cobain]. The only reason I married a cute guy is that he was a bit of a gearhead. I don't go for cute guys. I had this thing with Gavin [Rossdale of Bush] for a while—I love him and he's a fucking loyal friend, but he's a cute guy. Not that Jim's not really cute, but he's kind of a gearhead. Jim went to Harvard. He took American history. He's like Holden Caulfield, plus he's a gearhead."

ON THE SURVIVING MEMBERS OF NIRVANA: "Dave going on Howard Stern and bitching about me was puerile. Grohl's benefited so much from Kurt's death! And I think he has a lot of resentment about Kurt being better than him [as a songwriter]. But Grohl's not really the problem. It's Krist who's the problem."

ON HAVING INTEGRITY VERSUS SELLING OUT: "Ask Fred Durst [of Limp Bizkit] what 'sell-out' means, and you know what he'll say? 'I sold every fucking ticket at the Forum, that's what sell-out means!' They don't have a problem with Pepsi commercials. When they call me for Mountain Dew commercials now, I sometimes wonder. I was sitting here the other day, and somebody's telling me I'm cash-poor. I've gotta raise some cash, and I'm like, '*Playboy* or Mountain Dew? Hmmm?' But I'd fuck a fucking Arab prince first, I swear to God! I've got my little fucking code, and I'm going to hang on to it. But I never said in my code that I couldn't go be a movie star!

"I've read Naomi Klein [author of the anti-globalization screed *No Logo*], and I think it should be required reading for everybody, but I already know all that shit! And the last thing we need is the word 'sell-out'! Look, you've got a girl with no father who left a suicide note that basically says, 'I'm gonna go now, I'm a sell-out, goodbye.' Beyond the genetics, beyond the Klonopin, beyond the fucking treatment, there's that awful word 'sell-out.' Fuck that!"

ON WINONA RYDER: "Apparently I taught Winona how to shoplift. That's what her lawyer told a friend of mine. I haven't shoplifted since I was in a certain state institution in Oregon! If we were really off the record,

I could tell you a lot more. But on the record—she's innocent, and she'd never do anything like that!"

ON MICHAEL DOUGLAS: "I tried to bag Michael Douglas for years; he was my older-man fantasy. I wanted to fuck him like you wouldn't believe, and he so didn't give a fuck. I tried every approach I could think of—aggressive, demure, painfully shy, dominatrix, pornographic, you name it. Then I saw him this year at this party that all the old Hollywood people go to—I got invited because of my political activism—and there's Michael Douglas, who has never in his life said my name out loud, and he looks at me like I'm his oldest friend in the world, and he goes [seductively], 'Hi, Courtney,' because now he's married to this young beautiful bride! Before that, I tried to hit on him every way to Sunday, and it was like, 'If I can't get Michael Douglas to fuck me, I'm worthless.' I mean, he's a fucking sex addict!"

ON GENERATION Y AND GEN X NOSTALGIA: "The weird thing when you're talking about Y is the Y kids have a nostalgia thing. I had a kid doing my hair—a young guy, twenty-one—who says, 'You were involved with all that. What was that like?' There's a group of kids that really think they're different and cool and weird because they follow the early '90s and they romanticize it, and it feels really strange. But the Chili Peppers are still around, and I'm still around. That's why I feel confident: I'm not in Stone Temple Pilots, I'm not in Pearl Jam, I was never grunge. I was always the idiosyncratic solo person that was out there being kind of a dick. I can take three or four years between albums, but I'm not going to worry about it as long as the quality is there."

ON CHRISTINA AGUILERA: "I got an email from Christina Aguilera. Know what she wrote? 'Na-na, wass up?' You know what I wrote back? 'I'm in bed watching an Eleanor of Aquitaine documentary. [Imitates a school teacher:] Do you know who Eleanor of Aquitaine was?' I am not gonna sit there and go, 'Wass up?' That fucking Disney tutor should be shot! And Christina doesn't understand why I don't want to sing back-up on her record!

"Aguilera was trying to get me to come over [to the studio]. The next day, her manager says to me, 'Don't you dare go ruin Christina's sessions!' My retort to that was, 'I'd like to see you put forth to any writer in America that I would ruin Christina Aguilera's session! I do believe that they would state that the opposite was true!' That girl was like, 'Please come over and sing back-up.' She was demanding it: 'I'll send over my limo!' I was like, 'Sorry, I have a new PBS documentary on Eleanor of Aquitaine.' Eleanor was one of the last truly powerful women who got to fuck. She didn't end so well, but she did get some in her life. She was beautiful, she was hot, she owned a lot of land, she produced a lot of progeny. I'm obsessed with her!"

ON ELVIS PRESLEY AND OZZY OSBOURNE: "Elvis manipulated doctors. He knew the game, and they knew what they were getting into. You're dealing with Elvis fucking Presley, he needs his fucking Demerol; I'm sorry, man, but he gets it! Ozzy Osbourne? He has a bodyguard! You leave him alone, he'll call the concierge and he will get Vicodan like that [snaps her fingers]. [Manager and wife] Sharon [Osbourne] has this guy who's been Ozzy's bodyguard for seventeen years, and all his job is is to make sure Ozzy can't call the concierge. The bodyguard went out for a fucking sandwich one day on the last Ozzfest, and the guy was coming with the prescription bag when he came back!"

ON WHAT MIGHT HAVE SAVED KURT: "[Cobain biographer] Charlie [Cross] has this theory that there was always suicidal ideation, and there was no way around it. I think that's bull; ideation can be replaced with other ideation. Now, I have a theory, and it sounds vulgar, and it sounds shallow, and it's capitalism coming from a capitalist. But if we were around folks who knew luxury, who were our generation, who had money, who were flying on Lear jets, who were drinking fine wines, who were feeling great fabrics, who knew what Ming was, and fine art, and thread count, things might have been different. We didn't experience what [R.E.M. guitarist Peter] Buck experienced when he was living next door. We didn't have *stuff*. We didn't know about food. We didn't have a cleaning lady! Wealth makes things nicer—it does, and that's just a goddamn fact! We were rich people, and we didn't get to *be* rich people. And I think that luxury might have replaced [Kurt's suicidal] ideation."

ON DAUGHTER FRANCES BEAN COBAIN: "Frances should never ever, ever, ever, ever have to worry [about money], and I mean that in the Lisa Marie Presley way. She should never have to have anything bad happen except having a tennis ball hit her once in a while. That's her life, OK? I am not raising a worker. But in her trust agreement she has to work three months a year after the age of eighteen, period. I don't care if it's volunteer work, but it's a pretty strict trust. And then I'm just gonna stand outside her door with a shotgun and make sure nobody comes near her!"

ON ROCK VERSUS POP: "Frances nailed the difference between rock and pop. She goes, 'Rock lasts a long time, pop doesn't last long.' I'm like, 'That's right!' She says, 'Pop sucks.' I say, 'That's not necessarily true: Pop can be good. A lot of pop lasts a long time because it doesn't know it's pop.' She thought of that herself. She's like, 'How can you be so old and be as famous as you are?' I said, 'Because I'm rock!'"

3 PUSH ME, PULL ME, YIELD

RACKING UP SALES OF SOME EIGHT million copies within months of its release in August 1991, Pearl Jam's *Ten* followed Nirvana's *Nevermind* as the second Seattle "grunge" album to broach the mainstream—though the two bands shared few similarities beyond their home base and the meaningless genre tag that they'd been saddled with. I initially found Pearl Jam's debut to be histrionic and melodramatic, and those traits grew from annoying to grating as the singles "Even Flow" and "Jeremy" became ubiquitous on modern-rock radio. But the group won me over when it performed as part of the second Lollapalooza tour (see Chapter Seven), as Eddie Vedder literally climbed the arenas' rafters in an effort to stir the crowd's passions.

The title of the group's second album was prophetic: When I asked, "Pearl Jam versus what?" the band's battle with Ticketmaster was not yet under way. I reported on that fight extensively as it unfolded, and it was disheartening to see so few musicians much less consumers support the quintet's noble but doomed crusade. While many readers called and emailed to complain about the giant ticket broker's monopolistic ways, more simply shrugged and asked, "What's the fuss?" And both camps kept supporting the machine instead of protesting with their wallets. When Ticketmaster adds eighteen dollars or more in "service fees" to your tickets today, don't blame Pearl Jam—look in the mirror.

One of the key points in the argument against Ticketmaster was that the company had set up a system that makes choice impossible. It has signed exclusivity agreements with most of the major concert venues across the country, and artists either have to use the service and hose their fans or find someplace else to play—and there are very few places indeed. For a while all of this made for a real "us against the world" vibe on the rare occasions when Pearl Jam *could* perform—as at a memorable 1995 show at Chicago's Soldier Field—and it added resonance to the musicians' sometimes generic sounds. You couldn't help but cheer them on.

Similarly burdened as a "spokesman for a generation," Eddie Vedder was even warier of the press than Kurt Cobain was. When I finally spoke to guitarist Stone Gossard, I found his backpedaling on Ticketmaster disappointing, though it confirmed what I had heard about a fundamental split in the group over the way the band was run. Insiders say the divide continues to this day, though Vedder seems to have wound up with the group he always wanted—one that benefited from the hype then shunned the machine, and which continues to make music more or less on its own terms today.

This section ends with a piece that was written during the same trip that produced "Smells Like a Nirvana Article." The fabled Seattle "scene" had long since dissipated by the fall of 1993, but Chicago was on the rise, and the comparison between the two says a lot about the alternative era and the way the major-label machine was able to market rebellion, turning even the most organic and distinctive sounds into mere commodities.

Pearl Jam, Vs.
Request, October 1993

THE QUESTION RAISED by the title of 1993's second most anticipated follow-up is, "Pearl Jam versus *what*?" The quintet's rather cryptic bio offers a list: "Transition, media, leeches, bullshit"—the same forces, in other words, that thwarted fellow Seattle legends Nirvana on *In Utero*. But a better answer is "itself." Over the course of these twelve tunes, the band members struggle to create a new definition of Pearl Jam that confounds both platinum rock-star expectations and the constrictive alternative rock world that the musicians have come to symbolize with an appearance on the cover of *Time* and their constant presence on modern-rock radio and MTV.

Like *In Utero*, *Vs.* is an angry, uncompromising album. Rather than duplicating the proven formula for "Alive" and "Even Flow," Pearl Jam explores aggressive new directions, but it isn't nearly as subversive as Nirvana. This band grew up listening to classic rock instead of punk and new wave, and truth be told it still prefers those sounds. Pearl Jam retools and revs up familiar riffs from the Doors and the Who with a glossy, FM–friendly production by Brendan O'Brien (the Black Crowes, the Red Hot Chili Peppers, and, ironically, Pearl Jam imitators Stone Temple Pilots). Yet Eddie Vedder's poetic lyrics and Jim Morrison–like vocal growl elevate the band above its wannabe alternative peers.

Like Kurt Cobain, Vedder is a reluctant spokesman for the twentynothing generation, even though his words perfectly embody that group's alienation, cynicism, and prevailing sense that things aren't what they seem. On the first few spins, "Alive," the key track on *Ten,* seemed to be a celebratory declaration. With time you realized it was a song about a guy contemplating incest with his mother after his father's death, which certainly gave new meaning to Vedder's trademark evil-eye scowl. Many of the songs on *Vs.* are just as complex and multilayered. The tender, acoustic "Daughter" revisits the neglected child of "Jeremy," this time a confused young girl. The lean lyrics of the snarling "W.M.A." ("He won the lottery / When he was born") gain new meaning when the liner notes state that it's a song about the white police officers who beat African-American Malice Green to death in Detroit. And the lilting "Elderly Woman Behind the Counter in a Small Town" is a sort of stylized Beat haiku.

Elsewhere Vedder is annoyingly coy (remember his "How can you judge art?" speech at the MTV Video Music Awards?) or overly preachy. "Animal" attacks wife-beating, while the ultra-hummable "Glorified G" calls for gun control. These are fine causes, but Vedder has nothing memorable to say about them. Of course, when the pretensions get a bit thick, you can concentrate on Stone Gossard and Mike McCready's fat guitar riffs, or groove with Jeff Ament and Dave Abbruzzese's new, Chili Peppers–flavored funk rhythms. Or you can just toss the CD booklet aside.

Vedder's vocals are distinctive in many ways, but good diction isn't one of them. The rousing chorus of "Go!"—"Don't go on me!"—sounds for all the world like, "Dunk the wombat!" And "Glorified version of a pellet gun" from "Glorified G" comes out, "Lost my version of a pelican."

Come to think of it, I like those lines a lot better.

The Courtship of Eddie Vedder
The *Chicago Sun-Times,* March 6, 1993

FANS BELIEVE THEY'RE the most important rock group of the '90s. Detractors say they're alternative poseurs. But everyone agrees on one thing: Pearl Jam doesn't operate like many other bands of its stature.

Industry insiders compare the current Pearl Jam tour to the Led Zeppelin outings of the mid-'70s. Then, rock critics and the industry establishment looked down on Zep as crass pretenders, mere kids' stuff compared to the great *artistes* of the '60s. But it didn't matter: The group ignored the press and took its music directly to the fans.

Both bands formed in similar ways. Zeppelin was founded by guitarist Jimmy Page, a session pro who played with the Yardbirds in their final days. Page saw the mistakes that group made and was determined to avoid them with a new outfit that would be the biggest rock band in the world. Similarly, guitarist Stone Gossard and bassist Jeff Ament learned from their time in the influential Seattle bands Green River and Mother Love Bone, and with Pearl Jam, they set out to knock the rock world on its ear.

Here the comparison falls apart. While Zep thundered across America like Viking marauders, Pearl Jam is to some extent influenced by the anti-hype ethic of punk—though not nearly to the degree that Nirvana is, and it may not be all of the band members who feel this way. Sources close to the group say that Gossard's vision for what the band should be is much different—and a lot more gilded—than Eddie Vedder's.

While Zeppelin's vocalist brazenly declared himself a "golden god," Pearl Jam's singer seems determined *not* to become a rock star. "If you think too much about that stuff, it can really change you from a normal person into what everybody thinks you are," Vedder told *Musician* magazine. "It makes you crazy, because you start to be what everybody thinks you are."

The story of how Vedder linked up with Pearl Jam is nonetheless the stuff of rock-star legend. By late 1990, Gossard, Ament, and Mother Love Bone bassist Mike McCready had already recorded the demo for the album that would become *Ten*, but they still needed a singer. Fate intervened when former Red Hot Chili Peppers guitarist Jack Irons handed a copy of the tape to his friend, Vedder, then twenty-six. Vedder lived in Evanston and Chicago until he was in his late teens. "He was Eddie Mueller then," journalist and filmmaker Cameron Crowe wrote in a *Rolling Stone* cover story. "After moving briefly to San Diego, both his parents returned to Chicago. Vedder, who subsequently took his mother's maiden name, stayed behind to pursue his career in music."

Vedder was struck by a tune on Pearl Jam's demo tape—a song he called "Dollar Short" which would eventually become "Alive"—and he wrote lyrics for it one morning while he was surfing. Within a week of his audition he had become a full-fledged member of the band. Powered by hard-hitting anthems such as "Alive," "Jeremy," and "Even Flow," Pearl Jam's hook-filled debut sold more than eight million copies. The group stole the show during Lollapalooza '92, and it proved its diversity and staying power with a captivating performance on *MTV Unplugged*. Vedder became a poster boy for alternative rock, and the media anointed him as a spokesman for disaffected twentysomethings everywhere. But the singer reacted to this sudden celebrity as if he'd thrust his hand into a vat of acid.

When the group was promoting *Ten* the band members spoke to any journalist who would listen, from national magazine writers to high school newspaper scribes. After *Vs.* the musicians stopped talking, "not because we think we're above the press, but [because] it separates you from what you're doing," Vedder says. Crowe, a friend who gave Vedder a cameo role in his film *Singles*, says the singer is first and foremost a *fan*. He's always willing to talk about music—as long as it isn't his own. "Here's a tip to Pearl Jam fans who see Eddie in public," Crowe says. "Be a rock fan—don't be an Eddie fanatic—and you'll spend all night with the guy."

Vedder has created a public persona based on articles he read as a teenager in *Creem* and other rock magazines. His hero is Pete Townshend of the Who, and he recently performed as part of Roger Daltrey's Townshend tribute show, singing "My Generation" and the rare Townshend solo track, "Sheraton Gibson." Like Townshend, much of what Vedder says to the press is for dramatic effect. But sometimes the group's actions have the opposite effect of what the band intended.

In an effort to thwart scalpers, the band has set a cap on ticket prices, fixing them at eighteen to twenty-four dollars. But tickets to the upcoming Chicago Stadium show sold out in fifteen minutes, and now scalpers are charging five hundred dollars a pair for seats in the first twenty rows. "This is the biggest band in the world right now, and that's the price," one ticket broker unapologetically told me.

Vedder's comments about the pitfalls of fame are often portrayed in the press as "rock-star whining." Members of the Chicago trio Urge Overkill say the singer is simply misunderstood. (Urge toured with Pearl Jam on the first leg of the *Vs.* tour, and it's opening for Pearl Jam in Chicago.)

"I don't know if he's whining so much, it's just that he tries to be so sincere all the time," says Urge bassist Eddie "King" Roeser. "He feels like if he hadn't gotten this tape, he would still be the guy working at the gas station, making his own tapes, and trying to do something that was honest. He really feels like he has this bond with people who aren't in his position, and he's saying, 'Hey, I'm still like you. I'm still fucked up!' We were skeptical at first, but after playing with that band, we saw that they're amazing players. We were blown away by how together and righteous and honest they are. This band *deserves* to be number one."

Pearl Jam, Vitalogy
Request, February 1995

LIKE DON QUIXOTE and the windmill, the key artists to emerge from Lollapalooza Nation have found their reason for living in battling superior forces. Exactly what forces is secondary to the fight itself; just being on the battlefield forges a connection with the audience. In Kurt Cobain's case, the enemy was Kurt Cobain, and in the end, his personal demons won. For Billy Corgan, the battle is with the cliquish indie-rock world and critics who "just don't get it." Judging by sales, the Smashing Pumpkins are on top. With Pearl Jam, it's been hard to say who the enemy was and who was winning. Until now.

The Seattle quintet's third album arrives at a point when its manager says the band is "fighting on all fronts." In an arena-rock analogue to Fugazi's five-dollar shows, Pearl Jam has taken on Ticketmaster, demanding more reasonable service charges. The band has refused to release singles or make videos; it has demanded that its albums be released on vinyl; and it wants to be more like its '60s heroes, the Who, releasing two or three albums a year. (Sources say *Vitalogy*, or at least a big chunk of it, was finished last spring. Depending on who you believe, the album's release was delayed by Epic, by the battle with Ticketmaster, or by some combination of the two.)

Since Pearl Jam makes the most conventional music of alternative rock's Holy Trinity, it's ironic that its enemy is the music business as usual. Then again, it was R.E.M. and U2 who ultimately made the biggest impact in the mainstream during the '80s, not Hüsker Dü, the Minutemen, or Minor Threat. Pearl Jam lacks Nirvana's eloquence and the Pumpkins' ambition, but its familiar classic-rock sound is exactly what makes it a potent force for change.

Vitalogy is Pearl Jam's first attempt to really show its range. The songs come in three basic styles: classic rockers, ballads, and studio wankery. The last category is the slightest. With wonderfully tuneless accordion and allegorical lyrics about insects deciding his fate, "Bugs" is Eddie Vedder's entertaining attack on the music biz, but "Stupid Mop" is the sort of sub–"Revolution 9" sound collage that should have been left to Ween; the instrumental "Aye Davanita" sounds too much like R.E.M.'s "New Orleans Instrumental No. 1"; and "Pry, To" is self-serving filler that features Vedder petulantly grousing about his lack of privacy.

In the ballad department, Pearl Jam gives us two strikingly similar offerings—"Nothingman" and "Better Man"—that effectively update "The Fool on the Hill" by the Beatles. Then there's the slow and anguished

"Immortality." Vedder denies that it's about Cobain, but with lines about an "auctioned forearm" and a "trapdoor in the sun," that's hard to believe. In any case the song sinks under its ponderous lyrics and tunelessness.

As in the past, Pearl Jam is best when it's moving quickly. Producer Brendan O'Brien cranks the guitars and drums, and Stone Gossard, Mike McCready, and the since-departed Dave Abbruzzese power through seven of the fourteen tunes. The soulful determination of their playing is what makes Vedder's preaching tolerable. On "Spin the Black Circle," he sings the praises of vinyl the way an addict talks about heroin; on "Satan's Bed," he screams about his genuineness ("I shit and I stink . . . I'm real!"); and on "Not for You," he stands up for "youth" by telling Baby Boomers his music isn't for them. Not only does Vedder bare his soul, the album's elaborate artwork includes his freaking dental records.

Thankfully the filler and the fuzzy lyrics don't overpower the riffs or Vedder's distinctive vocals. (He may not want to be a rock star, but he certainly sings like one.) And when the high points are as good as "Corduroy," "Last Exit," and "Better Man," you can put up with a few flaws—especially when a band is fighting the good fight.

Pearl Jam, No Code
L.A. New Times, August 24, 1996

ONE OF MY BEST FRIENDS, the head sports photographer for the *Chicago Sun-Times,* recently told a revealing story about Eddie Vedder. A longtime basketball fan who roots for his former home team the Bulls, Vedder had courtside seats for the championship series between Chicago and the Seattle Sonics. At one of these games, Kenny G. played an excruciatingly painful free-jazz version of the national anthem. It seems Kenny had to walk past Eddie on his way back to the sidelines, and Eddie stood there glaring at him the whole time and wielding him both middle fingers.

It was an obvious gesture—aside from a few grandmothers and grandfathers and maybe the team's owners, there probably wasn't anybody in Chicago's United Center who *didn't* want to give Kenny G. the finger—but it was touching nonetheless. Same with Vedder's addled "fuck you" to the folks who gave Pearl Jam a Grammy last year. A lot of cultural observers wondered why he turned out in the first place if he didn't believe in the notoriously conservative awards. But this betrays a fundamental misunderstanding of the two sides of the band's schizophrenic personality.

On the one hand, Pearl Jam has never wanted to reinvent the wheel. Its members are proud of their Everyman roots in classic rock—the Who, Neil Young, Led Zeppelin, etc.—and they have come to excel at the larger-than-life musical gestures that make arenas seem small. They *like* being rock stars. On the other hand, they love to thumb their noses at the establishment, not because they're revolutionaries (though their brave and solitary battle against Ticketmaster is not to be slighted), but simply because it's fun in a snotty teenage way. And this of course is why snotty teenagers love them.

Since the phenomenal success of its debut album *Ten*, Pearl Jam's recordings have been saddled with ridiculous commercial and artistic expectations. To its credit, the band has done its best to subvert these, refusing to make videos or play the usual promotional games and not being afraid to let its warts show. Quick and dirty, *Vs.* was its "angry" effort (Q: Pearl Jam versus whom? A: *Everybody*); diverse and dissonant, *Vitalogy* was its arty album. These weren't intended to be masterpieces, or even especially coherent. On the rare occasions when they talked to the press, the band members said they wished they could operate the way their heroes did in the mid-'60s, releasing two or three albums a year. Just throw it all against the wall and see what sticks.

A little bit angry, a little bit arty, Pearl Jam's fourth album is another effort in this mold, and like its predecessors, it's a source of small, obvious pleasures. Inspired either by Vedder's time spent hanging out with Nusrat Fateh Ali Khan or by the guitarists listening to "Kashmir" again, "Who You Are," the first single, glides along on a cool Eastern percussion track underscored by a magical, mystical sitar-like drone. The band goes back to ersatz Crazy Horse mode for "Smile"; does a fun Fugazi imitation on the one-minute-long hardcore-punk tune "Lukin"; throws a vocal bone to Stone Gossard on the catchy rocker "Mankind"; and kicks out the jams in top *Ten* style on "Habit" and "Red Mosquito."

Yes, the group occasionally founders under the weight of its pretensions. "Around the Bend" is a country-tinged ballad that sounds sort of like a grunge version of "Happy Trails." Even worse is "I'm Open," a swirly, atmospheric portrait of the artist as a young man, complete with an all-too-serious Vedder voice over: "When he was six he believed that the moon overhead followed him. By nine he had deciphered the illusion, trading magic for fact. No tradebacks. So this is what it's like to be an adult. If he only knew now what he knew then." Lord, get me the Maalox.

Eddie is at his best when he's just murmuring and emoting. One of the key lines on this album is in "Hail, Hail." "I don't wanna think/I wanna feel," Vedder sings. This is an admirable goal that places him squarely in the ranks of a lot of other soul singers who didn't make sense but didn't really have to (James Brown, Screamin' Jay Hawkins, Iggy Pop, etc.). The other line is in "Smile," when Vedder innocently asks, "Don't it make you smile/When the sun don't shine?" Well, *no*, Eddie, but I understand what you're getting at.

It's hip to make fun of Vedder and his bandmates these days and ask why they aren't enjoying themselves more, but the truth is they're having a blast being this miserable and self-important. One of the promo shots that Epic is handing out with the press materials for *No Code* shows the band in its practice studio/clubhouse, surrounded by its totems and candles and collections of guitars, feeling secure, isolated, and wonderfully insular by playing in a circle and reveling in its angst. It brings to mind any group of boys in a treehouse world of their own devising. It's a not unappealing place to visit, but I wouldn't want to live there.

Yield: A Sign of Surrender?
The *Chicago Sun-Times*, February 4, 1998

ALTHOUGH IT REMAINS one of the best-selling rock bands of the '90s, Pearl Jam is better known for the principled stand it took against business as usual in the concert industry. So what are we to make of the band titling its fifth album *Yield*?

"Soon the whole world will be different / Soon the whole world will be relieved," Eddie Vedder sings in the chorus to the rollicking "Brain of J," the opening track on the new disc. A few songs later, in "No Way," the Seattle superstar croons, "I'm not trying to make a difference / I'll stop trying to make a difference." In other words, Pearl Jam still wants to change the world. Or maybe it doesn't.

The *Sun-Times* has learned that the quintet will announce a compromise next week when it unveils plans for forty upcoming shows in the United States. Whenever possible, it will play non-Ticketmaster venues. But when it's faced with the choice of doing business with Ticketmaster or not playing in a city at all, it will deal with the monopolistic ticketing giant.

"We haven't lost anything, because we've learned from the experience," Pearl Jam singer and Evanston native Eddie Vedder says of the band's three-year battle in an interview to be published in next month's *Guitar World*. "There is no way that we, personally, could have lost. It wasn't a chess game. It was basically a case of our trying to be responsible to the people who come see the shows. . . . Basically, it's showing respect to the fans."

Vedder can call it whatever he wants, but Pearl Jam is throwing in the towel. There are plenty of critics who will call the Seattle superstars hypocrites for reversing their position, while others (like frequent Vedderbasher Howard Stern) will wonder why the band didn't stop "whining" sooner and start enjoying its position as rock stars earlier. Both of these are short-sighted views that ignore the fact that, for a time and however unwittingly, Pearl Jam held a unique position in the alternative era as a band that refused to let the bottom line dictate its every move. With that in mind, it's worth reviewing how the group got to this fork in the road in the first place.

Pearl Jam fell into the role of crusaders by accident. The group was touring in support of *Vs.*, struggling to keep ticket prices under twenty dollars, when it performed a powerful show at the Chicago Stadium on March 10, 1994. The next night it did a surprise gig for fan club members at the South Side's Regal Theatre. The musicians were outraged when they discovered that Ticketmaster had tacked a service fee of three dollars and fifty cents onto the eighteen-dollar tickets for both Chicago shows. It so happened that the government was investigating Ticketmaster's dominance of the concert field at the time, and the Justice Department asked the group to file a memorandum about its experiences with the company. It did, and Stone Gossard and Jeff Ament soon found themselves testifying before an investigative subcommittee on Capitol Hill.

It's important to remember that the government went to Pearl Jam, not the other way around. But the press covered the story as a personal crusade by Vedder, especially after the Justice Department dropped its investigation without prosecuting Ticketmaster. Generally overlooked in the media coverage was the fact that the company signs exclusive contracts with major venues in most cities. Artists can't perform at those halls without using the ticket broker and allowing it to charge service fees ranging from three dollars to seven dollars or more per ticket. In Chicago, for example, bands can't play the Rosemont Horizon, the United Center, the New World Music Theatre, and most other major venues unless they work with Ticketmaster. Fans have nowhere else to turn (none of these venues even have box offices), so they have to pay the price or miss the show. That sure spells "monopoly" to me.

Many who are close to the band say that Pearl Jam was surprised to find itself standing alone in the battle with Ticketmaster. Although Bertis Downs, R.E.M.'s attorney and co-manager, was among those who spoke out against the company at the congressional hearings, the group opted to use Ticketmaster for its recent tour. "We wanted to do our part to help improve the system and make suggestions in ways competitiveness could be reintroduced," Downs told *Billboard*. "But it's out of our hands. We're going to play buildings that are under exclusive contract with Ticketmaster. There's nothing we can do about that."

Some feel otherwise. "R.E.M. talked big, and then they just dropped the ball," says Chicago attorney Paul M. Weiss, who is representing consumers in a class-action suit against Ticketmaster. Pearl Jam manager Kelly Curtis says he has no hard feelings toward R.E.M. "I'm sure most bands will take the easy way," he says. "You can't ask everyone to go and do what we've done, to make the sacrifices we've made. We're taking a huge risk by doing this."

No kidding. Pearl Jam's decision not to work with the company had serious repercussions: With a handful of exceptions—including a galvanizing show at Soldier Field on July 11, 1995—the group has been unable to perform in the United States for the past three years. In part, it welcomed the break: The band members also stopped making videos, giving interviews, and releasing official singles. They retreated to Seattle, huddled together, and regrouped. "We were just moving too fast," Vedder tells *Guitar World*. "What were we doing? We were playing music. That's the one activity you do as a band—not all of these peripheral things."

But there's no question that the band suffered both artistically and commercially by withdrawing from the public arena. The three albums it has made since *Vs.*—*Vitalogy, No Code,* and the new *Yield*—all suffer from the sterility and self-indulgence of a group that hasn't ventured out of the recording studio nearly as often as it should have. And along the way, it lost a fine drummer in Dave Abbruzzese.

Industry observers have been quick to note the declining album sales. *Vitalogy* sold eight hundred seventy-five thousand copies in its first week. *No Code* sold three hundred sixty thousand. Predictions for *Yield* are for two hundred- to three hundred thousand, despite ads for the album that are airing regularly on MTV, and a Led Zeppelin–sounding single ("Given to Fly") that's getting a lot of radio play.

Cynics will say that Pearl Jam is yielding because it wants to reclaim past commercial peaks. But if that was what really mattered to the group, it could have compromised its principles long ago and embarked on lucrative tours charging fifty to seventy-five dollars a ticket or more, just like the Rolling Stones and the Eagles. Anyone who's tempted to call Pearl Jam poseurs ought to ask themselves if they'd throw away millions of dollars just to make a point.

And Pearl Jam did, indeed, make some points. It proved that a rock band which isn't comprised of greed heads can play stadiums and not milk the audience for every last dime. It showed that groups don't have to feed the relentless hype machine. And it indicated that idealism in rock 'n' roll is not the sole province of those '60s bands enshrined in the Rock and Roll Hall of Fame.

There are definite pluses to a more visible Pearl Jam. "If Pearl Jam is more active promotionally—whether it's a tour or video or both—it will make a difference," says Alex Luke, the program director at Chicago modern-rocker Q101. The group took over that station and a dozen other radio outlets for four hours Saturday night, broadcasting its live "Monkeywrench Radio" program from its Seattle hideout. The band performed live and hosted showcases by friends like Mudhoney. In between, Vedder interviewed feminist godmother Gloria Steinem about what can be done to prevent violence at abortion clinics, and he spoke to members of the band Sleater-Kinney about how young women can learn to defend themselves if they're attacked.

It was some of the best radio I've ever heard, and it was a suggestion that, even if they are yielding on the Ticketmaster issue, these quixotic rockers aren't about to stop charging at windmills any time soon. On the other hand, they're treading water musically on *Yield*. The rockers seem forced ("Do the Evolution," "Brain of J"), and languid, mid-tempo ballads dominate ("Low Light," "Faithful," and "In Hiding" boast some beautiful if hushed melodies, but they don't do much to get the blood flowing). As in the past, there are some slapdash in-jokes and studio toss-offs (witness the *stoopid* punk ditty "Pilate," or the self-consciously arty sixty-seven-second experiment, "untitled [red dot]"), but the band does deliver one bona fide classic by indulging its abiding fascination in classic rock, rewriting Led Zeppelin's "Going to California" as "Given to Fly."

We've been here and done this before, with more exciting results. In the end, no one is going to care if Pearl Jam wants to save the world if it doesn't deliver the rock 'n' roll goods.

Kicking Out the Jam
The *Chicago Sun-Times*, June 26, 1998

IN THE MIDST of their controversial battle with Ticketmaster, Seattle superstars Pearl Jam clammed up tighter than J. D. Salinger. I've been writing about this group for more than seven years, and I have a file three inches thick, full of faxes to its manager, publicist, and record company requesting an interview. But I've never talked to a member of the band until now.

Frankly, it wasn't worth the wait.

Guitarist and band founder Stone Gossard dodged my most interesting questions and spoke in the kind of rock-star sound bites that Eddie Van Halen delivers.

Is it possible that Pearl Jam isn't really the maverick group that some of us thought it was? Or are there two camps in the band: the iconoclasts (led by Evanston native Eddie Vedder) and the traditionalists, the artists and the rock stars? Has the band really yielded to the forces of the industry, as the title of its fifth album suggests? You're more likely to find answers to these questions at the group's upcoming shows than to get them from Gossard, but I tried.

Q. Stone, you're the one who testified on Capitol Hill against Ticketmaster, but in the media, it became Eddie's personal crusade. Generally unreported was the fact that it all started when the Justice Department came to the band and asked it to file a complaint.

A. I must have said that a million times. Ed loves to say this, but Ticketmaster was just one of the many things that we think about all the time. We think about having low ticket prices, low T-shirt prices, a great barricade, and well-informed security. Because we like lower ticket prices and we were selling out shows, that exposed what Ticketmaster was doing. It can tack on a ten-dollar fee, and there is nothing you can do about it.

Q. No other band joined you in the boycott, the Justice Department ultimately dropped the investigation, and nothing really changed. Do you feel at this point as if you guys were set up?

A. I'm sure we deserved it. I don't think anyone in the band has any regrets. There is definitely more independent ticketing now. There is definitely a bigger awareness of what Ticketmaster is all about. It's being policed a lot closer in terms of people questioning what it is all about.

Q. But the band paid a price: I hear that Eddie and bassist Jeff Ament wanted to continue the fight, but you and the other guys wanted to get back to being rock stars.

A. Does a band sometimes split over issues, or are there different personalities in the band that want different things at different times? Sure. There are definitely times when the band is split, but I think that's less true now than ever before. We do a pretty good job of communicating with each other, especially these days. When we joined the band, me and Jeff had a long history together, and probably some baggage. We didn't know Ed from Adam. I feel like I am just kind of getting to know him now in some ways.

Q. Pearl Jam has refused to make videos, and it's released eclectic records like Yield *and* No Code *without obvious hit singles. Has it been hard to do that in the music business as it exists?*

A. It's just natural. I think we are trying to write hits. We like having eclectic songs on records. That's a fun thing, whether it's three or four minutes of noise or a country ballad. Our favorite bands have always done that. I don't think there is any big-picture plan.

Q. Oh, come on: It's not that easy! Very few bands can do what you do on a major label!

A. The thing is, anyone can do it. I think that's the only way to make records. It might not be where the money is this week, but good record companies realize that bands and musical movements don't just happen overnight. Seattle is an interesting example of that. It started with bands whose sights were set on saving money for six months and going to play a show in New York with the Volcano Suns. Nobody's sights were set on, "We are going to be this huge national rock group."

Q. On those first tours, Eddie was literally climbing the rafters onstage, and the shows were explosive. The last time you played Chicago, the band was sort of huddled together, quiet and immobile. It was intense in a different way, but it wasn't as much fun.

A. In general, we don't drink as much now. What was fueling the band in the early era was a lot of pent-up anxieties, stress, and alcohol. Now it's probably not as frantic on stage, but it is a lot groovier. Both are cool. If anything, this tour will be a good blend.

Q. Is there a love-hate relationship with Chicago? You've had a well-publicized feud with Q101: The station bootlegged your concerts, appropriated your lyrics on billboards, and used Eddie's mom in a contest.

A. I think in general, just because of Ed's love for it . . . Chicago has a great energy.

Q. A lot of what you're saying is right down the middle of the road. Do people get this wrong: Is Pearl Jam not *the "us against the world" band?*

A. If you talk to any given guy in the band, you get a totally different answer. I tend to be the down-the-middle guy. I am going to give you the football coach clichés. We're just gonna put our heads down and go out there and give it all we can, and at the end of the day . . . whatever.

Is Chicago the Next Seattle?

The *Chicago Sun-Times*, September 5, 1993

SEATTLE—THE COMMERCIAL runs on MTV here every thirty minutes: A ferry crosses Puget Sound, then four long-haired guys in flannel shirts bang out some generic metallic punk. The spot advertises a local stereo shop, "Magnolia Hi-Fi—Part of the Seattle Sound," but to local fans, it's just more of the hype that killed much of the fun and innocence in this city's celebrated rock scene.

In a five-year span, Seattle gave birth to such acclaimed bands as Nirvana, Pearl Jam, Soundgarden, and Alice in Chains. Hailed as the center for a media-concocted sound called "grunge," the music became a tool to sell everything from wannabe groups like Stone Temple Pilots to designer ski caps.

Two weeks ago, *Billboard* magazine, the bible of the music industry, ran a front-page story that christened Chicago "the new capital of the cutting edge" because of recent releases by the Smashing Pumpkins, Urge Overkill, Liz Phair, and others. The package of stories came complete with a map of Wicker Park so that major-label talent scouts won't get lost as they descend on the city with their platinum credit cards and contracts in hand. But if Chicago is the new Seattle, what do we really have to look forward to?

"Chicago is going to explode this year," predicts Bruce Pavitt, co-founder of Seattle's influential Sub Pop Records. "It's been percolating for a long time, with Wax Trax and then Touch and Go, but things are really coming to a crescendo. It's obvious."

Reared in south suburban Forest Park, Pavitt left Illinois in 1978 to attend Evergreen State College in Olympia, Washington. From there he moved to Seattle and started Sub Pop with Jonathan Poneman in 1986. The label released the earliest recordings by Nirvana, Mudhoney, Soundgarden, and Green River, which mutated into Mother Love Bone and eventually Pearl Jam. Pavitt and Poneman realized the importance of creating a musical mystique, and their media-savvy attitude helped put Seattle on the map.

"What gets called 'the Seattle sound' really should be called 'the Sub Pop sound,'" says Soundgarden guitarist Kim Thayil, another transplanted Forest Park native. But while the media spotlight brought well-deserved attention to some bands, it also created some ridiculous impressions about the music scene outside the city limits, and the disinformation extended beyond the usual clichés about nonstop rain, lumberjack fashions, and Seattle's passion for coffee.

"The image you would get if you were reading about this scene and you weren't here was that five or six years ago, thirty people got together and said, 'Let's make a conspiracy to create this sound. Let's all sound alike and dress alike,'" says Charles R. Cross, editor of the Seattle music magazine, *The Rocket*. "It's insane to define all the musicians here with the words 'the Seattle scene,' as if the Beatles and Gerry and the Pacemakers had anything to do with each other in Liverpool. Nirvana and Pearl Jam and Alice in Chains are brought up in the same breath as if you have three bands that are interchangeable. These guys know each other, but nobody planned anything."

Every Seattle rocker has a favorite story about the clueless media. There's the time a reporter from the *New York Times* asked a Sub Pop intern about "grungespeak" and printed the words she made up as an official lexicon. Or the day a fashion reporter asked Cross to describe exactly what he was wearing—an orange hunting vest and hiking boots—then declared, "This will *definitely* be big next year!"

"One reporter called from a Toronto paper with something he read over the news wire about riots in Seattle," Cross says. "It was like nine at night, and I was working late. He said, 'Can you tell me what the police contingency plans are? A hundred thousand people are expected for a new Summer of Love.' Normally if you're talking to somebody, you're polite. But finally I said, 'You're nuts if you believe this!' And he just said, 'Look out your window. What do you see?' I told him there were a hundred thousand kids in flannel shirts coming to beat the shit out of me and I had to go."

In the wake of such frenzied sensationalism, many Seattle musicians have become amateur media critics. "It's just press stuff. They need something to write about," says Nirvana bassist Krist Novoselic. "There's a machine that needs information, and a lot of the time the information is compromised or the reality is fabricated. It's not real."

Seattle exploded into national consciousness in 1991 when Nirvana's second album, *Nevermind*, stormed to the top of the pop charts. A few months later director Cameron Crowe offered an idealized portrait of young Seattle in the film *Singles*, but by then many locals thought the scene had already peaked. "When Mudhoney's *Superfuzz Bigmuff* EP came out in 1988, it was a must-have, and those were like magical times," Novoselic says. "That was the Seattle scene. When Mudhoney was playing and we were playing, and Tad and the Fluid. That was a little time in history that you can compare to the Liverpool scene, the Cavern Club or something. It was innocent. It wasn't exploited."

"I go to these clubs now and there's all these twenty-one-year-olds, and I don't recognize any of them," adds Nirvana leader Kurt Cobain. "They all seem to be recovering from the embarrassment of being 'the Seattle scene.' And they're petrified that the media focus will come back."

Outside observers believe that, no matter how silly the "Chicago cutting-edge" hype gets, the Windy City's music scene will continue to thrive. Unlike many Seattle groups, Chicago bands don't share a similar sound or aesthetic, which means they can't be written off in one broad swipe. But the groups do have some similarities. For one thing there's the notion that Midwesterners have their feet on the ground. "I think the Chicago scene is immune to hype and hoodoo," says *Billboard* editor-in-chief Timothy White. "I think it would be ticking along and doing well whether we put it on the cover or not."

Then there's the fact that Chicago musicians are already as cynical as Seattle rockers have become. "Seattle was a totally different thing," Pavitt says. "It was a populist movement with flannel shirts and beer. Nobody wore glasses. In Chicago, everybody wears glasses and looks like Steve Albini. You need to have a few people in a community that give it focus. And Steve Albini, love him or hate him, sets a tone in the community."

The acerbic Albini has been influential on the Chicago rock scene since the mid-'80s, when he led the band Big Black and wrote for the fanzine *Matter*. As a producer he records dozens of local bands as well as occasional superstars like Nirvana. But he isn't exactly the head of one big, happy family. Albini's feuds with local bands are legendary: Once bosom buddies with the members of Urge Overkill, he now tells anyone who will listen that they're lowlife scum because of the way they left the Touch and Go label. That brings up a final unifying factor.

"Chicago has also been defined in a way by its divisiveness," Pavitt says. "But despite or maybe because of that friction, there's some energy. You get interesting people who complement each other in their own perverse way. And that's when things really become explosive."

"Chicago: The City That Works (On Hate)" is an idea that the leader of the city's most successful new band doesn't dispute. "If the Chicago musical community—the status quo, whoever they are—hadn't given us a hard time, I don't think we'd be the band we are now," says Smashing Pumpkins leader Billy Corgan. "For us, the negative pushed us that much harder. But if I was twenty years old in a band right now, I would definitely feel a lot better about Chicago because of bands like us and Urge Overkill. Because it says that you can actually get out of here."

4 MELANCHOLY AND THE PEAR-SHAPED BOY

OF ALL THE MEMORABLE ARTISTS and characters that the alternative era produced, Smashing Pumpkins bandleader Billy Corgan was the most traditional rock star, with all of the good and bad traits that that implies. His sometimes imperious attitude and my reluctance to abide by it led to a bit of a tiff, though the version of events presented in FAQ files on fan Web sites doesn't really get things right. ("A *Chicago Sun-Times* reviewer, Jim DeRogatis, gave Smashing Pumpkins a few bad reviews, saying of 'Hummer,' for example, 'the lyrics are sophomoric, and the song is stupid.' This got him barred from attending the Double Door shows. Some of Billy's statements on this can be heard on the *Drown* bootleg." Er, not quite.)

In the summer of 1993, shortly before the release of *Siamese Dream*, I spent several hours with the Great Pumpkin in his living room in the beautiful Victorian house that had been purchased with his share of the advance from Virgin Records. I liked the parts of *Gish* and *Siamese Dream* that evoked the English shoegazer movement (see Chapter Eight), but I had problems with the elements that were coming from the Cure's goth-pop and, even worse, classic-rock schlock like Journey. Corgan felt that I'd "betrayed" him with some of my criticisms in the piece entitled "Smashing Pumpkins Carve Out Their Niche"—notably with the dig in the sidebar about his lyrics (which, you'll note, I never called "stupid," though I did use the word "sopho-moric")—and a Virgin publicist subsequently told me that he'd never speak to me again, nor would I be welcome at future Pumpkins shows. At the Chicago gigs that followed, including one broadcast on live radio, Corgan endearingly referred to me from the stage as "that fat fuck from the *Chicago Sun-Times*," but I attended and reviewed the concerts nonetheless.

Some time later I faxed Virgin requesting a "bury the hatchet" interview. Corgan faxed me back himself (one of several letters I wanted to include in this book in its entirety, but Da Capo's lawyers nixed that idea). "must you continue to prove your nothing but a sniveling, jealous person," Corgan wrote, seemingly averse to capital letters and the rules of grammar. "i'm very sorry for you that you are fat and that your career choice (wire cover band) didn't work out. . . . please try to find a life for yourself, and attempt to reconcile the fact that some people actually like what we do. see you in hell. best wishes / go fuck yourself, billy c."

In February 1995, the band booked several nights at Chicago's intimate Double Door nightclub to road-test its new material before recording *Mellon Collie and the Infinite Sadness*. I was indeed banned from these shows (along with all other Chicago journalists, unless they agreed not to review), but the Double Door's stage is backed up against a large plate-glass window that borders Milwaukee Avenue, and I took a lawn chair, sat outside in the sub-zero chill, and heard better than if I'd been inside the hot, smoky club. I phoned in a report for the newspaper on deadline, and the notion that he could not control *everything* really got Herr Corgan mad.

Mind you, I was aware that this was becoming a sort of low-rent Lou Reed–Lester Bangs routine, and so was Corgan, I think, but he was always up for feeling aggrieved, misunderstood, and set upon; for a while he seemed to think that it made for better art (shades of the high school outcast who took to his bedroom and found solace in his guitar). None of this was personal on my part—I just disliked some of the melodrama and lyrical angst of the first three albums, which I will readily admit are the band's best-selling and the fans' favorites.

Adore and *MACHINA / The Machines of God* were a different story. Corgan made a huge leap forward as a lyricist after the death of his mother, a reconciliation with his father, the end of his first marriage, and the beginning of a meaningful new relationship. The whining and the self-pity disappeared, and the music, which had always been impressively crafted, became even more expansive as he extended his palette away from FM–radio clichés in favor of more electronic and experimental sounds. There weren't many critics who felt as I did, and I guess Corgan appreciated that. We started talking again—in addition to the interview included here, he spent three hours with Greg Kot and me dissecting the band's career on *Sound Opinions* shortly before the group broke up—and I had no problem gaining entry to review the Pumpkins' final show at Metro.

A few months later, Corgan sent me another fax to thank me for sending him a copy of *Let It Blurt*, and this was a very different Billy (though he still didn't have much use for capital letters). "it made me think a lot about the tangled relationship—even love / hate relationship—between critic and artist (note even in the distinction between critic and ARTIST there is a hint of condescension)," Corgan wrote of my biography of Lester Bangs. "as you are well aware this is something that has pained me unnecessarily over the years and reading the book brought a certain clarity to the way i feel and made me understand a bit more where you come from as a writer. in my older years i am becoming a bit more punk rock and am starting to agree with the basic manifestos that lester had written. i think if one can bring to bear the idea of a needed incandescence to recorded work without the negativity and cynicism that has become the nom de plume of most, i guess i am all for it."

This approach (and Corgan's new optimistic attitude) can be heard in his latest project, Zwan—he did indeed return as predicted in the final piece in this section, launching his new band with a strong album called *Mary Star of the Sea* in early 2003.

Smashing Pumpkins Carve Out Their Niche
The *Chicago Sun-Times*, July 18, 1993

AT TWENTY-SIX, Billy Corgan seems to have it all. As the leader of Chicago's Smashing Pumpkins, he's poised to reach a massive audience with *Siamese Dream*, the band's major-label debut. The group sold three hundred fifty thousand copies of its first independent album, *Gish*, and scored a million-selling hit with a song on the *Singles* soundtrack. But the introspective guitarist and vocalist dreads the trappings of the rock world. He describes recording *Siamese Dream* as a hellish ordeal, complains about the way he's portrayed in the media, and often thinks out loud about breaking up his "dysfunctional" band.

For somebody who's so successful, he sure is miserable.

"After *Gish*, the last thing I wanted to do was go back into the recording studio," Corgan says. "Because it was like saying, 'Let's start this process all over again.' Let journalists beat me over the head, let people throw things at me in concert. And part of you doesn't want any part of it. I like the part about making records, and I like the part about playing. But all of the periphery is in your face."

Nevertheless Corgan and the band entered Triclops Studio near Atlanta last fall. More than three months and two hundred fifty thousand dollars later, the result was the sophomore album which will be released on July 27 by Virgin Records. Produced by Butch Vig, whose credits include *Gish* and Nirvana's *Nevermind*, *Siamese Dream* is a solid collection of swirling but tuneful guitar-rock epics. Like the English "shoegazer" bands Ride and My Bloody Valentine, the Pumpkins use guitars to create disorienting walls of noise. But like the super-successful Seattle grunge bands Nirvana and Pearl Jam, they add catchy, radio-friendly riffs and stomping, heavy-metal rhythms.

"The minute you say 'psychedelic,' it conjures up hippies rolling in a muddy field," Corgan says. "I stopped using the word because people can't get beyond their own preconceptions. But the essence of 'psychedelic' in the true sense is exploring and trying to look for something different. I always had a problem with a lot of the punk ethic, because there's more of an art to the presentation. Maybe I'm just an art fag or something, but I like the idea of creating your own alternative universe: 'Welcome to Pumpkin Land, this is what it sounds like on Planet Pumpkin.'"

Tall, baby-faced, and ghostly pale, Corgan is wearing an MC5 T-shirt and sitting in the stately Victorian home that he and his wife recently bought in Chicago's Lakeview neighborhood, a few blocks from his beloved Wrigley Field. Most of the house is *Home and Garden* perfect. Sunlight filters through lacy curtains to fall on a grand piano in the living room, but Corgan seems most comfortable in the dining room, which has been converted into a sort of cluttered rock 'n' roll clubhouse. The room is lined with CDs, stereo equipment, and guitars, and the platinum disc for *Singles* is framed and mounted on the wall. "It makes a great conversation piece at parties," Corgan says, smiling.

The musician's father, William Corgan Sr., was a jazz-rock guitarist who played with members of Rufus and Chicago back in the day. Born in west suburban Elk Grove Village, William Jr. grew up in Glendale Heights listening to Led Zeppelin and Black Sabbath. He discovered alternative music via the Smiths, Bauhaus, and the Cure, and he started playing in bands when he attended Glenbard North High School. He moved to the city shortly after graduation and began gigging with the Pumpkins in 1988. Metro owner Joe Shanahan was an early fan.

"First and foremost it was the songs," Shanahan says. "There was a songwriting ability and a depth. And Billy was a guitar virtuoso; he could really play."

Shanahan booked the band into prime opening slots and gave its demo to record company talent scouts. Within two years the Pumpkins were selling out Metro (three thousand, three hundred tickets to its upcoming performances sold in twenty-three minutes), but Shanahan's patronage and the band's success earned the scorn of jealous scenesters. As a result, the Smashing Pumpkins are both the most loved and most hated band in Chicago.

The group's appeal to alternative-music fans is obvious: It's weird enough to alienate parents, but tuneful enough to attract kids weaned on Depeche Mode and the Cure. In concert, Corgan recalls Robert Smith's non-threatening, regular geek stage presence. But the band has scores of detractors who dismiss its members as poseurs and wannabes, and Corgan readily admits that he's partly to blame. "A lot of it, I think, has to do with me—the way that I carry myself or the way that I put myself across," he says.

Alternative rockers are rarely so self-analytical; Corgan often sounds like grizzled rock geezers James Taylor or David Crosby rehashing their latest therapy sessions. He believes fans relate to his honesty and appreciate the fact that he doesn't adhere to the rock 'n' roll myth. "When I was fifteen years old, I had my Jimmy Page poster on the wall, and all I could see was, 'Fun, sex, rock 'n' roll' and that whole bit," he says. "I saw all the myths and bought into the whole thing. So I went along and met chump after chump and got treated like shit and paid nothing, and I started to realize this is all a big fake. When I started to see the inside and how rotten and bitchy and backbiting the whole thing is, I said, 'Fuck it.' At some point, I personally had to get over my own connection to rock mythology, and as I've grown up somewhat in public, I made a decision that I'm not going to perpetuate the myth. There's this weird resistance to somebody actually being a real person. But that's not my life. My life is I get up every day with the express purpose of writing music. That's all I care about."

When he's talking about the Pumpkins' music, Corgan vacillates between the pronouns "mine" and "ours." He writes the majority of the band's songs alone (eleven of the thirteen tunes on *Siamese Dream*), oversees recording and mixing, dominates the stage show, and gives most of the interviews. To many people, Billy Corgan *is* the Smashing Pumpkins. Guitarist James Iha, bassist D'Arcy Wretzky, and drummer Jimmy Chamberlain are left in the shadows.

"There's what the press writes, and there's what actually happens in the band," Iha says in a separate interview. "A lot of articles don't mention that the drumming's awesome on the album, or the fact that [I'm] writing songs. I myself am comfortable with the way we work." Adds Corgan: "The best thing you can say about the band is there's an energy, and when it's on all cylinders and everybody believes in the idea and everybody's trying, it's transcendent. But the analogy I make is we're pushing a rock up a hill, and the moment you stop pushing, the rock rolls back. If it's not going one way, it's coming back the other way. I'd rather have the band explode at the seams than become fat, dull, and lazy, which is what we became last summer."

Corgan almost broke up the band before recording *Siamese Dream*. Chamberlain was sidetracked by drug and alcohol problems (he has since been through treatment), and Corgan thought the others weren't contributing their share. But relations have improved since he issued an ultimatum. "When I finally decided that being unhappy and being totally displeased all the time were no longer worth the band, then suddenly the band got better," he says. "It was like drawing a line: 'This is where we stand, and you're either in or you're out.'"

"It's frustrating sometimes," Iha admits. "Billy says a lot of dramatic things, and some of it might be self-defeating. But he has a pretty high set of standards, and we're used to the ups and downs."

Corgan and Vig have both been described as incurable perfectionists, so it isn't surprising that making *Siamese Dream* was an ordeal. Speaking from his studio in Madison, Wisconsin, Vig describes the Smashing Pumpkins' sessions as "arduous." Recording lasted for more than three months, and the band and the producer often put in fifteen-hour days. By the time the project was finished, Vig and Corgan were too emotionally spent to mix it. Corgan is a fan of My Bloody Valentine, and he suggested hiring Alan Moulder, staff engineer at England's Creation Records. Moulder made sense of tapes that sometimes included fifty or more guitar tracks, and he gave the album his trademark shimmering sound.

"We deliberately tried to push ourselves in terms of some of the things we were doing arrangement-wise," Vig says. "About half the songs were fairly finished when we came in; the band had been playing them and there were really good arrangements. But a lot of it was worked out in the studio, especially some of the detailed things like guitar parts."

The producer seems to agree with Corgan's description of the Pumpkins as "dysfunctional." "They were not necessarily a happy bunch of campers," Vig says diplomatically. "There was the typical stuff with bands, where there were a lot of things going on personality-wise. One day they'd love each other, and the next day they'd all hate each other. But they have it particularly bad. I think Billy sometimes puts the weight of the world on his shoulders. He is very sensitive about everything and can be real meticulous and also very passionate about what's going on. He would often push the band further or I would push the band further than what they were ready for at that time."

Both Vig and Corgan think the results were worth the angst and trouble. "There are some tracks on the record that make the hair on the back of my neck stand up because I remember when Billy was singing those songs how it affected me," Vig says. For his part, Corgan describes making *Siamese Dream* as a learning process. "The person who made *Gish* couldn't have made this record. That person wasn't capable of this kind of honesty and depth." Yet he still talks with some regularity about the possibility of disbanding the group, and he concedes that this topic makes his managers and Virgin executives extremely uneasy. "They don't like to hear it, but we've become a band that from here on out will be a band of the moment."

Whatever the future holds, it's hard to imagine Corgan quitting music. He's the archetypal rock nerd—someone who's most comfortable facing the world from behind his record collection, his guitar, and a multitrack recorder. "I've reached a point where I have confidence in what I do," he says. "I was watching this thing on TV last night about baseball players, about how when you're a rookie, you're not quite sure if you belong. And at some point you decide, 'Not only do I belong, I *deserve* to be here.' That's the way I feel. I feel I've earned it and I'm capable of continuing as long as I want to. If the Pumpkins can't do that, then that's the end of the Pumpkins and I'll do something else. But I feel I can make viable music as long as I want to. I'm past the point of no return."

••

The Smashing Pumpkins have had a short but successful recording career. Here is a discography. (Star ratings are based on the *Chicago Sun-Times's* four-star scale.)

Gish (Caroline, 1991) ☆☆☆

After a debut single on Limited Potential, the Pumpkins released the "Tritessa" / "La Dolly Vita" seven-inch on Seattle's hip independent Sub Pop Records. That disc was enough to attract offers from several major labels, but the band signed to the Virgin-distributed indie Caroline with the understanding that it would graduate to Virgin proper for its second album. *Gish* is a slickly produced introduction to the band's sound, which mixes swirling psychedelic guitars with Led Zeppelin and Black Sabbath–inspired rhythms (drummer Jimmy Chamberlain does a mean John Bonham stomp). But Billy Corgan's lyrics are often indulgent, trippy nonsense, his guitar solos can meander, and the album pales in comparison to truly innovative discs by new psychedelic groups like the Flaming Lips, Mercury Rev, Ride, and My Bloody Valentine.

Siamese Dream (Virgin, 1993) ☆☆☆

Several songs on the Pumpkins' second album are as indulgent as anything on *Gish* (notably "Mayonaise" and "Soma"), but the disc is generally more focused and direct. Corgan still can't be accused of undue originality: "Space Boy" is "Space Oddity"–inspired glam-rock fluff; "Today" recalls the California psychedelic pop band Game Theory, and several tunes ape My Bloody Valentine's distinctive guitar sound. But "Cherub Rock" is a strong single, and it's driven by a powerful riff that's hard to resist. In interviews, Corgan emphasizes the honesty of his lyrics, many of which seem to address his childhood, but too often they sound like sophomoric poetry ("Faith lies in the ways of sin / I chased the charmed but I don't want them anymore").

Up Against the Wall: Mellon Collie and the Infinite Sadness
Rolling Stone, November 30, 1995

WHEN SMASHING PUMPKINS leader Billy Corgan boasted that he would follow the triple-platinum *Siamese Dream* with a sprawling double album that would be *The Wall* for Generation X, the assumption was that he would make a concept album like Roger Waters's rock opera about the lack of communication and love in modern society. But the twenty-eight songs on *Mellon Collie and the Infinite Sadness* aren't linked by a libretto; they're only connected conceptually through the broad theme of being part of a day in the life of a typical, alienated teen. (The two discs are designated as "Dawn to Dusk" and "Twilight to Starlight," and the time frames in the songs roughly correspond to the passing of the day.) Maybe Corgan meant that he wanted *Mellon Collie* to be a lush, diverse soundscape that would be as state of the art for 1995 as Pink Floyd's album was for 1979. Or maybe he wanted to make an album that teenage fans could obsess over, getting comfortably numb while listening on headphones in their bedrooms. If so, he succeeded on both counts.

Although *Mellon Collie* clocks in at more than two hours, it's one of the rare epic rock releases whose bulk is justified in the grooves (it certainly beats the comparable length of, say, the *Use Your Illusion* records by Guns N' Roses, which were marketed as two separate CDs). The accomplishment is even more impressive when you consider that Corgan single-handedly wrote twenty-six of the songs, and he co-produced the album with Flood (U2, Depeche Mode) and Alan Moulder (My Bloody Valentine, Ride, and Nine Inch Nails). Corgan's role as the Great Pumpkin is undeniable, but *Mellon Collie* at least *feels* more like a band effort than its predecessor. Even as it incorporates such baroque textures as harp, strings, and grand piano, the album retains the rough edge and intimate vibe of old friends (and sometimes enemies) playing together in their rehearsal space.

Corgan and James Iha stretch out on several fiery guitar workouts, covering the gamut from Tom Scholz–style studio perfection to Sonic Youth noise-rock skronk. The Pumpkins deftly swing from unapologetic art rock (the nine-minutes-plus "Porcelina of the Vast Oceans") to pop metal in the Boston or Journey vein ("Tonight, Tonight"), and from techno-industrial lullabies ("Beautiful") to twisted cow punk ("We Only Come Out at Night"). Brimming with hooks, the songs quickly work their way into your subconscious, making the album seem a lot shorter than it is. The problem, at least for rock fans who want substantive content with their seductive form, is Corgan's lyrics.

Corgan is a romantic who believes in the redemptive power of love, but he's also a cynic, having been constantly disappointed by those he loves. "Believe, believe in me, believe / That life can change, that you're not stuck in vain," he sings in "Tonight, Tonight," the swelling ballad that follows the album's opening instrumental. But for much of the rest of the album, he's stuck in a lyrical rut, wallowing in his own misery and grousing about everyone and everything not meeting his expectations. "Intoxicated with the madness, I'm in love with my sadness," he sings in "Zero," just after the song breaks down into a chant of, "Emptiness is loneliness, and loneliness is cleanliness / And cleanliness is godliness, and God is empty just like me."

One could argue that Corgan's lyrics aren't intended to be analyzed under the microscope, that—like those of Depeche Mode or My Bloody Valentine—they're simply intended to conjure a mood along with the music. But the vocals are much too prominent in the mix to accept that. Musically, *Mellon Collie* solidifies Corgan's position as one of his generation's most ambitious songwriters—no one else in alternative rock's superstar stratum has attempted an album of such length, let alone scope, and it may even match *The Wall* in its sonic accomplishments. But his lyrics don't fare nearly as well in comparison. It may be too much to ask that Corgan be as poetic as Kurt Cobain or as earnest as Eddie Vedder, though his therapeutic self-examinations could at least probe as deeply as Trent Reznor's. But while Waters's tale of the rock star Pink only reached the literary level of a comic book, "We don't need no education / We don't need no thought control" seems deeper, more universal, more entertaining—and heck, a lot more inspiring—than, "Living makes me sick / So sick I wish I'd die."

(*The album was rated three stars on* Rolling Stone's *five-star scale.*)

No, Really: The Smashing Pumpkins, Adore
New Times Los Angeles, May 28, 1998

WATCHING THE SMASHING Pumpkins open for Cheap Trick with a strong set of new material a few weeks back, it seemed like we were seeing a new Billy Corgan: kinder and gentler, certainly, and maybe even (dare I say it?) "happy." Then bassist D'Arcy Wretzky paused to introduce hired drummer Kenny Aronoff, formerly with John Mellencamp. Aronoff wasn't paying attention, and he prematurely started the next groove. "Hey, nobody plays when somebody in this band is talking!" Corgan barked. He was kidding, but only partly. There was also a flash of the infamous dictator and egotist—you know, the Billy everyone knows and loves.

You're going to read a lot elsewhere about the revolutionary "new" sound on the band's fourth album, *Adore*. That's mostly a load of hooey. These are the same old Pumpkins, only more mature and self-confident. At long last the band members are curbing some of their most bombastic tendencies—at least on disc—while daring to expand (though by no means reinvent) their sound. And they're doing it in two distinctly different modes.

Our boy Bill has always been a notorious perfectionist; there are certain drummers who might also add "son of a bitch." (Joey Waronker reportedly quit Beck's band to join the Pumpkins at double his salary, then bailed after two weeks. Aronoff got the gig next, but you can't help but wonder: *For how long?*) Sure, you had to give the Great Pumpkin props for crafting amazingly ornate walls of sound in the studio, but anyone with half a brain also had to be disappointed with what he did with 'em. On *Gish*, *Siamese Dream*, and *Mellon Collie and the Infinite Sadness*, those mighty musical constructions—better than Journey! Styx! Queen, even!—were employed by the man to vent his raging angst and revel in his terminal miserableness. You know, that whole sorry "despite-all-my-rage-I-am-still-just-a-rat-in-a-cage" trip.

Either the music on *Adore* is strong enough to outweigh the lyrics (sample: "You remind me of that leak in my soul") and typically whiny singing, or those lyrics and that singing have gotten better. Probably a little of both, plus the fact that for all his talk about the ambition of previous efforts, Billy's never really put it on the line like he does here.

How so? For starters, he succeeds where David Bowie, U2, and Madonna have failed, successfully merging rock and techno for the pop-rock mainstream the way Blondie blended rock and disco on "Heart of Glass." Songs such as "Ava Adore," "Daphne Descends," and "Tear" incorporate electronic dance grooves and washes of ambient synthesizer without sacrificing rock's essential visceral kick, and they do it without a hint of grunge. Corgan and James Iha have dramatically expanded their six-string arsenals, delivering some of the coolest tubular-buzz E-bow leads since "Heroes" (the Bowie-Eno-Fripp version, not the damn Wallflowers cover).

That's half the album. In typically schizophrenic style, Corgan devotes the other half to tender acoustic ballads that expand on his earlier cover of "Landslide." There are some genuinely beautiful moments in "To Sheila," "The Tale of Dusty and Pistol Pete," and "Annie-Dog." The latter is particularly effective because the lilting, piano-driven melody contrasts with lyrics that seem to portray Corgan's pal and former lover, that whirling dervish Courtney Love. ("Amphetamine Annie-Dog has a leash and a face . . . She is Venus, she is Mars / She's electric.") Then there's "Behold! The Nightmare," which somehow combines both of the album's divergent approaches *and* a better imitation *Pet Sounds* vocal break than any of those indie-rockers like the High Llamas can muster.

Best of all is "For Martha," a moving tribute to Corgan's recently deceased mom. Naturally he pulls out the stops on this one, crafting an elaborate mini-symphony the likes of which hasn't been heard since Genesis's *Selling England by the Pound*. "I will follow you and see you on the other side," he croons, then builds to a thunderous climax with an elegiac, *way-over-the-top* guitar solo. Oh, mama! Even if you're a cynical, pierced, and multiply-tattooed alterna-teen, you won't have a dry eye after this one.

"My mother's death helped me to refocus my priorities," the singer-songwriter recently told *Guitar World*. "It showed me the true value of my life." Notice he didn't say it made him *love* life—that's still a problem. But at least he has grown up enough to be able to ask the key question, "Who am I?" at the end of "Crestfallen," and to observe in "Shane" that, "Love is good and love is bad / Love is drunk and love is blind / Love is good and love is mine / Love is drunk all the time." I'll take that over "Life's a bummer / When you're a hummer" any day.

Two other losses are key here. With original drummer Jimmy Chamberlain out of the picture, Corgan is free to play with samplers, sequencers, and synths. He made the most of the opportunity, but Chamberlain is still missed onstage. Corgan is also mourning the death of the genre that he helped usher in. "We blew it," he tells *Guitar World*. "There was a real purity in the early '90s scene that cut through everything like the white-hot blast of a laser gun. But we screwed up, because everybody got so caught up in it in the wrong way. Instead of taking over the world, we just gave it away. Kurt takes himself out. Pearl Jam doesn't tour. Soundgarden breaks up. Courtney decides she's not even going to start. I freak out on the world and have a nervous breakdown."

As usual Billy's romanticizing here: Nervous and broken down or not, he was always the most focused and productive member of the alternative nation. The difference between him and almost everybody else on that list is that they all rejected the notion of stardom. Corgan and Love embraced it from the start, though Love has opted for Hollywood these days, while Billy continues to make music. Are any of these sounds revolutionary, oh-boy!, brand-spanking-new? Hell no, but this is certainly the best music these goobers have produced. And now that alternative rock is officially dead and buried—one could trace this to the ascendance of Bush, but the history books will no doubt mark it by the dismantling of Lollapalooza—it leaves Corgan as the last American Rock Star of his generation. And that oughta count for something, no?

Billy Speaks
The *Chicago Sun-Times*, April 11, 2000

ALTHOUGH THEY HAVE released one of the strongest albums of their career, the Smashing Pumpkins have watched *MACHINA / The Machines of God* slide steadily down the *Billboard* albums chart after five weeks in the stores, falling from a debut peak at No. 3 to No. 54 with some three hundred forty thousand copies sold. As much as the phenomenal first-week sales of two-

and-a-half million by 'N Sync, this seems like concrete proof that a new wave of young pop fans has turned a deaf ear toward alternative rock. But the songwriter for the most successful rock band Chicago has ever produced maintains that he is not disappointed by his new album's performance.

"I'm very happy with it; I'm just glad we still have a pulse," Billy Corgan says. "I don't mean the record—I mean the band in general. We're just happy to be alive. We've been through so much that the ability to go out, make a good record, play good shows, and be ourselves without making any compromises is enough. It's probably one of the happiest periods in the band."

There is reason to believe that Corgan is sincere. The artist who brings his band to the Aragon Ballroom for two sold-out shows on Saturday and Sunday is a different man than the Great Pumpkin that I last interviewed one-on-one seven years ago, during the heady days before the release of *Siamese Dream*. This Corgan is more philosophical, less arrogant, slower to take offense—and he's producing his best work ever. I spoke with him last week upon his return to Chicago after a series of European shows, in the midst of rehearsals with guitarist James Iha, back-in-the-fold drummer Jimmy Chamberlain, and new bassist Melissa Auf Der Maur.

Q. *There's been speculation on the Internet based on something you said in* Rolling Stone: *that bands have a natural life span of about three albums. A lot of people read that as you saying, "This is it; we're breaking up after this."*

A. No, there's still more life in us. What form that takes and how we do it, I don't really know. Sometimes I say this for dramatic effect, and sometimes I really mean it, but it really is a powder keg, the intensity in this band. It's this sort of self-generated intensity to always be great, to always perform at a very high level, to never take the easy road out. We're rehearsing again today, we're going to rehearse all week, and we're trying to learn another ten songs to rotate in the set. Everybody wants time off. We could have just taken some time and basically done the same show we've been playing on tour, but instead we're rehearsing and changing songs around. That's the sort of intensity I'm talking about, and that can blow up at any second.

Q. *Would that change if you were recording alone, or is that just the way you operate?*

A. I've really wondered if that would be the case, if I was with a different set of personalities. I'd like to think it's somewhat unique to this unit.

Q. *You don't think that little voice in the back of your head would still be there?*

A. I guess so. [Laughs] But to their credit, my bandmates never balk at the notion of moving forward.

Q. *You're involved in a lawsuit with your old manager, Sharon Osbourne. How did things go so bad so fast? You were only with her for eight or ten weeks.*

A. Maybe twelve. That's a story for the ages, man. She's a total phony. When somebody tells you, "The way that you are is fine. The way that you are with business, I support that," and then suddenly out of nowhere it's a problem . . . It was a lie. It was a total deception. I've been had by the best, that's the best way I can describe it. I've been faked out by the best: Sharon Osbourne, Courtney Love . . .

Q. *Are the Aragon shows and the rest of this tour the end-all and be-all of what you're doing to support* MACHINA, *or will you be coming back for a shed or arena tour?*

A. There doesn't seem to be enough energy in the country to be looking at a big tour right now. A lot of people that are going out are gonna die. Nine Inch Nails is doing this big arena tour, and I don't see how they're going to do it. Right now we're viewing this as our only American tour. We're booked through December—we'll be touring the world—and we're sort of hoping that by that point these kids will wake up and say, "I'm so uncool, I've been listening to 'N Sync!"

Q. *What do you make of 'N Sync's success and the rest of what's been happening on the pop charts?*

A. I don't think it says as much about 'N Sync as it says about the future of our business, the entertainment business. All of the mergers, the Internet stuff—we're going to see more and more of this disparity of mega-acts selling huge amounts of records and other people being completely unable to compete. It's gonna be like Michael Jackson all over again, where if you're a good band with good songs, you don't have a shot. You might as well accept that you're going to sell twenty thousand records and that's it, because all of the money and all the energy is going to be going into blockbuster events. Where it gets really scary from an artistic point of view is, what if you don't agree with all of the corporate synergy? SFX and all that—what if you don't agree with it? Where are you going to go? Especially when you're competing with people who are willing to do whatever they are asked to do and say whatever they are asked to say.

Q. *Generation Y seems to view music differently from Generation X. They don't define themselves by what they're listening to, the way that you and I did as teens.*

A. It's an accessory. It's a commodity that can be traded like movie stars or wrestling heroes. It's trading cards. But to their credit they've been programmed this way. As a generation, they've been programmed to accept that it's OK that—I'm looking at a magazine here—here's Sarah Michelle Gellar promoting Maybelline. There's nothing negative to them, they probably think it's great. Whereas I look at it and think, "Shouldn't she be above doing a Maybelline ad? Why does she need the money? Why doesn't she just be a TV and movie star?" There's been an erosion of standards and standard-bearing. You and I know that as good as I think my band is, you know that I know that the Beatles are way better. My band still sits around and talks about the Beatles, like, "How the fuck did they do it?" We wish we could achieve that level of perfection or integrity. But if you look at Generation X and its mainstays, they've been ripped to shreds. Who in Generation Y would want to be like Generation X? If I was Generation Y, I wouldn't want to be like me!

A thing I hear from kids is that, "It's not easy being a fan of your band." What they mean by that is that they hear a sort of criticism. It's not a musical criticism, it's a criticism like, "Billy Corgan is a pain in the ass." How do they know I'm a pain in the ass? Because they've read it a thousand times. And if my band doesn't get the musical credit it deserves—and at this point we're more cartoon characters than a musical entity—then why would you want to be me? That's what I'm saying: The heroes of Generation X—there aren't any. They either self-destroyed or were destroyed by others.

Q. *You're saying people need illusions in order to have an ideal to strive towards?*

A. You know as well as I do that nobody's perfect. Everybody's got skeletons in their closet. But part of what made rock 'n' roll exciting to me as a kid was the idea that it was perfect. That's what made it so much fun.

Q. *Outside of music, you generally seem a lot happier today than you were seven years ago. Is that true?*

A. [Laughs] Yeah, I am.

Q. *Where does that come from?*

A. That's just sort of getting my personal life together. My girlfriend [photographer Yelena Yemchuk] has had a huge impact on my life—putting this sort of manic energy into my life. I feel I have a little more foundation. Five years ago music was all I had, because that was all I believed in and that was all I loved. In some ways having other things takes the edge off what you do musically. But at some point you do have to live. It's still an unhealthy balance. I love what I do, and I believe there's a reason I have talent for it, and I believe that there's a lot of good that can come out of it, besides just self-serving patting on the head. I guess it only gets complicated when the reviews start and when people start making assumptions about why I do things.

Q. *I would have thought that after* Gish *and that first experience of being reviewed, you'd have realized that it's all just people's opinions. Why did bad reviews register the way they did?*

A. You want a serious answer? It triggers the same button as child abuse for me. I know that may not really translate in a public forum, but it sort of seems to open up the same wounds. I don't know why, and I suppose I could spend a year in a therapist's office trying to figure it out. But it seems to stick a knife in the exact same wound that exists from those years in my life, and I don't think I've ever found the right balance. Though I will say that it rolls off my back a lot quicker these days. It used to be that if I read something I didn't like, it would be like weeks—the one line that I didn't like would repeat in my head like a mantra. Now it's like I read it and I just go, "That's not right; they've got it all wrong." My biggest complaint is that we're not reviewed these days as a musical entity. We're reviewed as a sort of a personality.

Q. *Let's talk about your lyrics. It's my contention that with* Adore *and* MACHINA, *you took a big leap forward as a lyricist. Do you feel that way?*

A. I do feel that, and I feel it's sort of an unspoken thing. In some ways I think I've let the words do more of the talking and the music do less of the talking.

Q. *What was the breakthrough?*

A. That's a really good question. There's a song on *Adore* called "Annie-Dog." If you read the lyrics, it's sort of like how it comes out on the page. It's hard to explain . . . I can't even remember how I used to write lyrics. It's sort of like I used to sit down and say, "Now I've got to write lyrics." Then there was a point where I would just write this free-flowing stuff and somehow let the context make it into the song. I let the lyric kind of take over the song instead of trying to force the song onto the lyric. "Annie-Dog" was one of the first songs where I just sort of wrote a bunch of stuff about this archetype of a woman who fucks for power. The ramble of it came out and made it into the song, and that was what made the song. That's where it started to change.

For me it's always like whatever part I feel weak about, that's where I go next. With lyrics it seemed like on the first couple of albums there would be the one great lyric song, and then the one song where after a couple of months I'd hate singing the lyrics. And it seems like if you let lyrics just sort of come out of your body, you never seem to have a problem with them later. Where if you sort of cerebrally say, "What am I trying to say? What am I trying to get across?" that's where you start cringing at lines later.

Q. *I hear "Everlasting Gaze" as posing an existential question: How does a sentient individual survive in a cold, corporate society of the sort you described earlier?*

A. It has a lot to do with spirituality and trying to find my place in the universe and sort of humbly accepting limitations and the things I've been graced with. It's more of a humanistic worldview. I'm not writing anymore for the tortured teen—both me and whoever was listening. I'm writing with the idea that everybody's experiencing these things all the time, and even if they're not experiencing them personally, they're affected by them. You can live in the street and write about the garbage, or you can try to get up a little higher and look down and try to see the bigger picture.

Q. *Do you feel that you've matured?*

A. Oh, I don't know. Just when I would think I wouldn't write about personal stuff anymore, I would turn around and a write a whole album about it. As I've always said, if I could have chosen what I wanted to do, I wouldn't have chosen these things.

Q. *There's that perverse streak. Do you enjoy confounding expectations?*

A. I enjoy the energy in that. I don't find comfort energizing. Inside, there must be some sort of thing in me that needs to be contentious.

Q. *Well, I can relate to that!*

A. [Laughs] Yeah, I know.

Perfect Timing:
The Smashing Pumpkins Say Goodbye
The *Chicago Sun-Times*, December 4, 2000

AND SO IT ended pretty much where it had begun: onstage at Metro. With a marathon four-and-a-half-hour set on Saturday night, one of the most successful rock bands Chicago has ever produced put an end to a career that spanned thirteen years and six studio albums with twenty-two million copies sold.

The Smashing Pumpkins will stand as a cornerstone band of the alternative-rock era, but the zeitgeist has changed since their mid-'90s heyday. Alternative has given way to sickly-sweet teen-pop and testosterone-crazed rap-rock, and the cynical, angst-ridden Generation X has yielded to the cheerfully consumerist Generation Y. Always an astute student of rock history, thirty-three-year-old bandleader Billy Corgan well knows that it's better to burn out than to fade away. Thankfully he did not define that well-worn rock cliché like his peer Kurt Cobain of Nirvana. Instead the Great Pumpkin decided to pull the plug on the band that was his life before it could live on past its prime. In so doing, the Pumpkins made history again, becoming one of the rare rock groups with the fortitude to retire while it was still at its artistic prime.

"Sorting through the ashes of the Smashing Pumpkins, there's a lot of beautiful stuff there, and that's the most important thing," the guitarist-vocalist said toward the end of a night designed to make that case. Divided into three "acts" and including a mid-evening acoustic set, the thirty-eight-song performance spanned the group's career, touching on every aspect of its complicated legacy: the laser-focused, ultra-melodic hard rock and the self-indulgent, artsy noodling; the petulant, self-obsessed whining and the poetic outpourings of heartfelt emotion; the great, the awful, and pretty much everything in between. It was as if the Pumpkins decided to play the entirety of their inevitable box set. But the friends, family members, industry insiders, and lucky fans in attendance didn't mind, nor did the approximately five hundred faithful without tickets who sat in the cold outside Metro. (They were accommodated with speakers that broadcast a portion of the show, which was also recorded for a potential live album.)

The highlights were numerous. Chief among them: a duet by Billy Corgan and his father on the breathtakingly beautiful "For Martha," an elegy that Billy Jr. wrote after the death of his mother from cancer. Corgan and James Iha's guitars never sounded better than on the roaring versions of "Siva" (from their debut album *Gish*) and "Starla" (a rarity included on the *Pisces Iscariot* collection). Drummer Jimmy Chamberlain was as always an astounding force of nature; the crowd sing-alongs on "The Everlasting Gaze," "Today," and "1979" were inspiring; and the moving hometown homage in "Tonight, Tonight" ("And your embers never fade in the city by the lake") was never more poignant.

On the flip side, however, were numerous stretches of merciless bombast of the sort that gave '70s rock a bad name and prompted punk to rise up in opposition. The nadir was the last song of the night, an endless twenty-minutes-plus version of "Silverfuck," Corgan's epic meditation on love and pain. It found the artist erasing the new levels of musical and lyrical maturity that he reached with the *Adore* and *MACHINA* albums and reverting to the insufferable mode of the tortured soul who loves to be miserable. *Ugh.*

Before the rosy glow of nostalgia sets in, it needs to be said that minus the emotion and history of the occasion, there have been many more memorable Pumpkins shows. Among those that I witnessed: the *Siamese Dream* record release gigs at Metro, the Lollapalooza tour, the pre–*Mellon Collie* show at the Double Door (even if I never actually made it *in* to that one), and the *Adore* show at the New World Music Theatre.

Despite the rampant pre-show speculation, there were no real surprises Saturday. Cheap Trick guitarist Rick Nielsen and former touring drummer Matt Walker came out for cameo appearances, but founding bassist D'Arcy Wretzky did not. Corgan did offer her a heartfelt thanks, as well thanking just about everybody else who'd helped in his career, including his ene-mies—"for pushing us to try harder and be better."

When the music stopped, the band members filed off one by one, tossing guitar picks to the fans as they left. (Concertgoers also got a commemora-tive CD of the Pumpkins' first show at Metro in October 1988.) When the mighty Chamberlain tried to toss a drum stick up to the balcony, it actually lodged in the ceiling above the dance floor, where it will no doubt stay for-ever as a testament to the evening.

At the very end, Corgan stood onstage alone, looking awkward in his sil-ver and black outer space priest outfit. He basked in the adulation of his Chicago fans, took their hands, made the "I love you" sign from his heart, and finally broke down in tears.

And so it ended pretty much where it had begun—the climax of a week that witnessed more farewell hoopla than when Michael Jordan retired for the first time. Remember, though, that Jordan came back. And so, too, will Billy Corgan.

5 POSITIVE BLEEDING

THROUGHOUT THE '90S, CELEBRATED "recordist" Steve Albini cast a long shadow over the Chicago music scene and alternative rock in general. I first met him when he was touring in the mid-'80s with his band, Big Black, and we were both writing for the influential Chicago fanzine, *Matter*. The group played a searing show to about two dozen people at Maxwell's in Hoboken, New Jersey, and I approached him afterward to say how much I enjoyed his music and his writing. I had heard that the trio did a killer cover of "Raised Eyebrows" by the Feelies, and I asked why they didn't play it that night. He sheepishly replied that he could never play a Feelies song in the club that served as their home base. I remember thinking, "*This* is the infamous Steve Albini?"

Shortly after arriving in Chicago, I spent a few hours watching Albini shoot pool while engaging in a typically opinionated conversation for the profile that became "Chicago's Leading Alternative," a piece timed to Touch and Go's reissue of the Big Black catalog. He remains one of a handful of truly incisive thinkers on the subject of rock 'n' roll—even if he's often wrong—and wrestling with him verbally is a treat. That is, as long as he thinks you're worthy of his time.

Albini and the members of Urge Overkill were originally the best of friends (he released their debut recording on his own label, Ruthless Records), but they fell out when Albini decided that Urge had been unethical in splitting from Touch and Go to sign with Geffen Records (though it seemed like a fairly typical business decision at the time). I loved *Saturation* and maintain that it's one of the best albums of the '90s, and I spent a long day hanging out with the band at its James Bond–style headquarters for the Sunday feature "Escape from Guyville." The Tuesday after that article ran, Albini called me at home to tell me I'd been duped by a bunch of weasels, sell-outs, and scumbags. I told him the Urge boys may well be all of those things, but I really didn't care because I liked their music. Ted Nugent is a fairly despicable human being, but I like his music, too.

I took the conversation in the spirit of good-natured but contentious debate between two rock 'n' roll obsessives, and I mentioned his comments in my review of Urge's record-release show to illuminate the rough and tumble scene with its many internecine feuds that had spawned all of these artists. Albini considered that some sort of unforgivable sin, prompting a letter addressed to "Jim DeRogatis, Music Pimp." He accused me of "cooking" him as a source and vowed never to speak to me again.

"I don't offend easily, and I don't give a fuck what you or either member of your readership thinks of me," Albini wrote. "I can however make up my mind about who is or isn't a useless fuck I should ignore, and you are one. . . . What's next, 'Smashing Pumpkins Uncork a Masterpiece'? 'Material Issue—Not *Really* a Complete Washout'? 'E'Nuff Z'Nuff—This is Their Year'? . . . I can see why it is in your best interest to ignore the obvious phoniness of Urge and other manufactured phenomena, but don't pretend you're trying to be 'fair.' You could elevate your job a notch if you stopped delivering predictably fatuous ink for the industry, and actually looked for something new and / or good to write about, but then you wouldn't be every flack's best lunch date anymore. I can imagine how important lunch must be to you."

Urge never did achieve the stardom it deserved—it broke up not long after the release of its second Geffen album, a dark night of the soul gem called *Exit the Dragon*—but Albini did. His credits include Nirvana, the Breeders, Bush, Jimmy Page and Robert Plant, PJ Harvey, the Jon Spencer Blues Explosion, the Pixies, and Shellac (the band he was obtusely alluding to starting during our interview). True to his word, he has refused to speak to me since sending that letter, even when I was the first reporter to call him with the news of Kurt Cobain's suicide. He simply hung up without saying a word.

Chicago's Leading Alternative
The *Chicago Sun-Times*, September 13, 1992

HIS ALBUMS HAVEN'T sold millions, and his work is probably unfamiliar to most mainstream rock fans. But in terms of his influence on other musicians, Steve Albini is the most important alternative rocker that Chicago ever produced.

The unnaturally skinny Montana native moved here twelve years ago to study journalism at Northwestern University, but he soon abandoned his notebook for a more active career in rock. Throughout the '80s, Albini played furious, hard-hitting postpunk art-rock with two trios, Big Black and Rapeman. In the '90s, he's become a much in-demand record producer (though he hates that term), thanks to the in-your-face sound on albums by the Pixies, the Breeders, and many other alternative rockers.

Big Black's relentless noise guitars, jackhammer rhythms, and lyrical tales of America's underbelly continue to inspire cutting-edge bands such as Helmet, Tar, and the Jesus Lizard, as well as industrial dance groups such as Nine Inch Nails and Ministry. Meanwhile Albini's uncompromising attitude and abrasive, immediate recording style are mimicked throughout the underground rock world, and his influence is sure to keep growing: The local independent label Touch and Go recently reissued the entire Big Black catalog, Albini has landed a coveted gig producing PJ Harvey, and his writing is included alongside Lester Bangs, Greil Marcus, and Tom Wolfe in the new *Penguin Book of Rock & Roll Writing*.

Although he just turned thirty, Albini is one punk who hasn't mellowed with age. Shooting three-cushion billiards at a Northside pool room, he talks nonstop for two hours, offering typically feisty opinions on a range of topics. The major record labels are "thieves," he says. Most alternative rockers "would sell their souls to get on a major label"; his former record company, Homestead, is "absolutely criminal"; and the only bad thing about living in Chicago "is the lunkheadedness and belligerence of the police department and the revolting corruption of city government."

Although he frequently apologizes during our interview "for being so testy," it's obvious that he doesn't mean it. Being testy is what Albini does best.

Quiet, spacious, and clean, the Chicago Billiard Cafe on Irving Park Road is the underground hero's favorite place to meet interviewers. He arrives shortly after it opens at ten A.M., carrying his own pool cues and wearing his familiar black leather jacket, close-cropped haircut, and John Lennon specs. "It's the closest thing to therapy I have," he says as he settles in at his favorite pool table. He doesn't ask me to join in the game, and I don't volunteer to play with him.

Outspoken on almost any topic Albini is uncharacteristically modest when it comes to talking about Big Black's influence. "I'm pretty embarrassed that Ministry keeps putting out our records," he says. "But other than that, when people talk about bands being influenced by Big Black, I think it's more that bands are voicing the influence of that era of music. The records in their reissue form are selling far more than they did in their original incarnation. At the time the Big Black records came out, they were ahead of their time in quality, theme, and style. And they're not ahead of their time now. Using my own criteria, I don't think they're as important now."

From the beginning, Big Black served as Albini's alter ego, a window to the darker side of his soul. The name itself was the opposite of his surname, whose Latin roots translate to "little white." Eloquent, soft-spoken, and extremely intelligent, he became a raving lunatic onstage. He would wrap his guitar strap around his tiny waist like a belt and flail away, controlling the drum machine by stomping on a foot pedal, and screaming until the veins popped out of his neck.

The soul of Big Black was always the two-guitar attack by Albini and Santiago Durango, described in liner notes as *"guitar skinng"* and *"guitar grrr."* But it was Albini's lyrics that garnered the most attention. Although he has dabbled in rock criticism for the Chicago fanzine *Matter* and the Boston magazine *Forced Exposure*, early efforts at journalism convinced him that he would have more freedom playing music than being a writer. Yet a flair for sensationalist reporting surfaced in songs lifted from bizarre headlines. "Jordan, Minnesota" was about a townwide ring of pedophiliacs, "Pigeon Kill" chronicled another rural burg's annual pigeon-poisoning celebration, and "Kerosene" depicted a bored arsonist. Other favorite topics included redneck truckers, gangland slayings, and dictator Benito Mussolini.

"I don't mean to be constantly negative in saying that people have the wrong idea about things," Albini says as the pool balls collide with a sharp crack. "But Big Black's lyrics have gotten entirely too much attention. I get the impression that people think about our songs in the same way they think about a pop song: That there's a subject and a literal set of lyrics. And that's not at all the way we did things. The lyrics to us were really just an extension of the mood we were trying to establish with the music."

This approach puts Albini in a tradition of rock songwriting that starts in the '60s with the Velvet Underground's voyeuristic descriptions of heroin use and sadomasochistic sex. But many critics attacked Big Black for advocating the behavior it portrayed, and Rapeman was picketed in the United Kingdom for having a sexist moniker (the name came from the hero of a Japanese comic book). "I've run afoul of that several times when the subject matter of a song is distasteful to some people," Albini says with a shrug.

"They make the argument that if you have something like that as part of the subject matter of your song, or Rapeman as the name of your band, then you are an evil person glorifying violence or the domination of women. If I wrote a song about a macho idiot, that doesn't mean *I'm* a macho idiot. That fact that I'm not a macho idiot makes it possible for me to make these observations. Our stuff was observations from the somewhat detached point of view of crazy people, people who weren't us. The kick for me was trying to figure out how close those people were to me."

Pronouncements such as these are delivered with a razor-sharp wit that can be easy to miss. Critics rarely mention that, in addition to being frightening, Big Black could be very, very funny, and all of this tough talk came from a guy who is about as threatening as Martin Short. Detractors also fail to recognize that Albini's anger is rooted in idealism. He is the first to admit he's disappointed that punk rock never took over the world. But he seems disingenuous when he says he isn't playing in a band because punk has gotten too commercial.

Big Black disbanded in 1987 when Durango enrolled in law school. Albini returned with Rapeman, featuring drummer Rey Washam and bassist David Sims, now a member of the Jesus Lizard. That group broke up in 1989 because of the usual squabbling, and its auteur hasn't made music since. "The current mode of behavior of rock bands I find absolutely repulsive," Albini says. "The majority behave in a way that I'm disgusted by. I don't associate myself with those people, and I don't particularly want to be thought of as part of that continuum." He takes a sip of coffee and stares at the pool table. "If I ever do anything again, I'll do it for my own entertainment. And if I do, probably the last thing I would do is admit it to someone who was going to print it in the newspaper. It would draw attention to itself, and it would be impossible to do it with a clear conscience."

More likely the guitarist realizes that it would be difficult to make new music as extreme or as trend-setting as his earlier work. Besides, working behind the scenes has been very, very good to Steve Albini. He claims that he now makes two hundred records a year, mostly in his basement studio in Chicago or at Pachyderm Studios south of Minneapolis. His earnings have helped purchase a house on the Northwest Side, a four-thousand-dollar car that he outfitted with a two-thousand-dollar stereo system, and his own twenty-four-track recording studio. He pulls out a black log book and runs down a list of recent projects including the Didjits, Dolemite, Union Carbide Productions, the Jesus Lizard, Scrawl, Boss Hog, Thinking Fellers Union Local 282, Fugazi, and Shadowy Men on a Shadowy Planet.

This week he's in Minnesota engineering the sophomore effort by the English trio PJ Harvey.

Albini prefers the terms "engineer" or "recordist" to "producer." He often insists that he not be credited on albums he's recorded, and he maintains that working with a band doesn't mean that he supports its music. In fact his contribution to *The Penguin Book of Rock & Roll Writing*, reprinted without his knowledge from *Forced Exposure*, is a collection of "eyewitness record reviews" that tear into bands he's worked with. "In the same respect that an auto mechanic can do a good job working on someone's car without delving into that person's morals or ethics, I can do a good job on somebody's record without endorsing the music," he says.

Albini refuses to take royalties on albums. Instead, he works on an hourly rate like a plumber. He says that his fee depends on the band's ability to pay and whether or not a major label is involved. "A conventional rock producer is paid a percentage of the retail price of every record that's sold, so it's to their benefit to make a record that's as commercial as possible. I work a certain period of time, I get paid for the time that I work, and it doesn't matter one whit to me whether the record sells one copy or ten million copies."

Most of the bands Albini has worked with praise his business skills and his professionalism in the studio. The ones that don't usually broke his no-credit rule and were severely chastised in person or in print. "He's really great, and he's really, really nice. He's like a big teddy bear," says Rose Marshack, the bassist with the Poster Children. Albini recorded half of the Champaign-based group's first album, *Flower Plower*, and all of its critically praised follow-up, *Daisy Chain Reaction*. "He documents bands' sounds really well. The way you sound when you practice and play live, that's exactly what you'll sound like."

Albini usually has some affinity for the bands that approach him—they tend to be loud, fast rockers—but he quickly rejects the ones he doesn't like. "When, for example, Pantera faxes me and wants me to do a series of in-your-face remixes for them, it's no effort for me to say I couldn't stand it," he says. It's rare for anyone in the music business to be able to turn down such lucrative big-name work. Albini is lucky, and his success doesn't quite jibe with his harsh attitude about the music business. He often sounds like someone who's been jilted by his true love. But if punk rock really broke his heart, why is it still his career?

"Everybody likes to do something he's good at. I'm a good recording engineer, and I enjoy doing that far more than photo-retouching, which is what I was doing before," he says. He claims he'd chuck it all and go back to a day job if there weren't any bands he was comfortable working with, but he seems to love the business of making records, and it's hard to imagine him stopping. "People who are genuinely doing whatever they're doing from a pure motivation, a real legitimate creative impulse, will be remembered and will be influential," he says. "People who are doing things for other motives will be forgotten or ridiculed."

He packs up his pool cues and dons the leather jacket. "That's the way it's been all through history. Great records eventually sell a lot."

....

Here are reviews of Steve Albini's recordings, plus his comments on his own work from our interview and the albums' liner notes.

Big Black, Lungs EP (1982) ☆☆
Albini is a one-man band on Big Black's debut. The key ingredients are all here, including harrowing portraits of redneck America, relentless drum-machine rhythms, and chaotic guitars, but the mix hasn't quite jelled yet. Says Albini: "Recorded in a living room on a four-track with one microphone. Has a couple of 'all right, I guess' songs, but is mainly of historical value."

Big Black, Bulldozer EP (1983) ☆☆☆ 1/2
The songs are stronger, but the best lineup still hasn't come together. Santiago Durango is on guitar, but the rhythm section of Naked Raygun's Jeff Pezzati and Urge Overkill's Pat Byrne is just visiting. (Albini went back to the drum machine on *Racer X*, and bassist David Riley finally joined on *Atomizer*.) The highlights are the furious "Cables," about Montana school kids who like to help out at the slaughterhouse, and "Seth," a cheerful tune about a guy who trained his dog to attack African-Americans. Albini says: "Probably my favorite record. It's the first record that we made as a full-fledged band, and it was probably more different from everything around than our other records were."

Big Black, Racer X EP (1985) ☆☆☆
Named for Speed Racer's brother, the third EP is a bit of a let-down. The highlight is a loosely interpreted, amped-up version of James Brown's

"The Big Payback," which is as close to hip-hop as Big Black ever got. Available with *Lungs* and *Bulldozer* on a compilation disc called *The Hammer Party*. Albini: "High production values on the band's first 'rock' record. . . . The next one's gonna make you shit yourself."

Big Black, Atomizer (1985) ☆☆☆☆
He wasn't kidding. The band's first full-length album is Albini's best record. Songs such as "Jordan, Minnesota," "Kerosene," and "Bad Houses" are as lyrically twisted and musically uncompromising as earlier efforts, but now they boast genuine killer hooks. Available on CD with the four-song *Headache* EP, which is memorable only for its gruesome head-wound cover and an excellent version of Wire's "Heartbeat." That compilation's title, *The Rich Man's Eight-Track Tape*, is Albini's comment on the digital format. Albini: "*Atomizer* had a lot of the crowd-pleasers on it. It's alright. I have trouble evaluating any of our stuff."

Big Black, Songs About Fucking (1987) ☆☆☆
As its title suggests, the group's final album is heavy on misogynist role-playing, but its biggest problem is the lack of the melodies that made *Atomizer* so effective. The best moment is an inspired cover of "The Model" by the German synth group Kraftwerk. Albini: "Hey, breaking up is an idea that has occurred to far too few groups. Sometimes to the wrong ones."

Urge Overkill, *Saturation*
Request, July 1993

THERE ARE SEVERAL things you have to understand about the Urge Overkill aesthetic before you can appreciate the Chicago trio's sixth and best album.

First and foremost, it's a retro thing. Urge Overkill rummages through the '70s trash heap with more devotion than any band besides Redd Kross. The nostalgia goes beyond the group's Matt Helm stage persona of velvet jumpsuits, gold medallions, and ubiquitous martinis to *Saturation*'s thundering drums, killer guitar riffs, melodramatic "Behind Blue Eyes" acoustic interludes, and cheesy "C'mon girl / People get ready now!" lyrics. Hip rockers and rappers proudly own up to loving Led Zeppelin; Urge Overkill wants to make it cool to admit adolescent obsessions with Ted Nugent, Boston, and Grand Funk Railroad.

Next, it's a guy thing. Only a dude who spent his sophomore year partying with good friends, a bottle of wine, and Nugent's *Weekend Warriors* could think the experience is worth reliving. (It isn't much of a leap from "Cat Scratch Fever" to Urge Overkill's "Bottle of Fur.") Most women I know are either insulted by this swaggering machismo or find it utterly ridiculous. Liz Phair offers her own sarcastic take on her Matador debut, *Exile in Guyville*, which takes its title from the Stones and a tune on Urge's *Supersonic Storybook*.

Finally, it's a Midwestern thing. Chicago is the classic-rock capital of the universe, the place where a "disco sucks" stunt at Comiskey Park turned into a full-blown riot. Urge Overkill has its roots in the groundbreaking early '80s punk scene that produced Big Black, Naked Raygun, and the Effigies, but the band members' hearts belong to the big FM–rock sound. (Rumor has it that Steve Albini left cassette dubs of the Enuff Z'Nuff album marked "new Urge demo" in rock-club bathrooms around town. Ha ha.) The merger of punk sarcasm and aggression and big rock sounds was present in earlier efforts, but *Saturation* is the first time the group had the cash and technical expertise (producers Joe and Phil Nicolo struck platinum with Kris Kross) to realize its vision. A between-songs snippet near the end of the album features the band talking about recording for the first time "in the big leagues" and includes a sample of Mary Tyler Moore's theme, "Love Is All Around," which pays tribute to both the '70s and the '80s (Hüsker Dü famously covered the song).

You might think these three factors limit Urge Overkill's appeal, but I find myself coming back to *Saturation* again and again, cranking the volume on the rollicking "Sister Havana," simultaneously being touched by and snickering at the pathos of "Positive Bleeding" ("People like me go it alone / Baby, I'm a rolling stone"), and getting creeped out by "Stalker" and the freaky "Dropout." I'm loathe to explain it, but *Saturation* pushes all the right slacker buttons. Besides that, it's fun and it rocks. Party on, dudes.

Escape from Guyville
The *Chicago Sun-Times*, June 6, 1993

THE MEMBERS OF Urge Overkill are lounging around their Humboldt Park headquarters, an old bank that's been converted into a grunge-rock version of the Playboy Mansion. A bar decorated with tiki lamps occupies a corner by the marble dance floor, and a large bong sits on the coffee table under a coat of arms. Stacks of vinyl albums and singles crowd the mantelpiece, and old wooden bookshelves are lined with the trashy best-sellers of summers past.

For the next two hours the band members crank album sides by Hot Chocolate, the MC5, and John Lennon. They also pour several bottles of fine champagne purchased at their insistence by the publicist from their new label, Geffen Records. The company is happy to indulge the trio. Executives believe that its sixth record, *Saturation*, is poised for the sort of alternative-rock breakthrough Nirvana achieved in 1991. With its encyclopedic knowledge of the '70s riffs that twentysomethings grew up on, Urge Overkill pushes all the right slacker buttons. "But the thing that makes these guys special," says Geffen's punk-rock publicist, Luke Wood, "is that they *live* it."

A chance encounter with one of the band members at a favorite hangout such as the Crash Palace or the Rainbo Club proves that's not just hype. The boys in Urge Overkill dress, act, and *sound* like the rock stars they soon hope to be. And what rock fan hasn't fantasized about having a hideaway just like the Bank?

Formed by bassist Eddie "King" Roeser and guitarist Nate "National" Kato, the trio has been kicking around the Chicago music scene since 1985, but anyone who wrote the group off early on should be forgiven. Urge began as just another in the pack of noisy, unimaginative bands imitating Big Black, Naked Raygun, and the Effigies. The group didn't really start to develop its own sound until the *Americruiser* EP in 1990. Drummer Blackie Onasis joined shortly thereafter.

Onasis had served as a temporary replacement on a tour several years earlier, but "they hated me and I hated them," he says. Both sides have since reconsidered. Onasis, twenty-six, is a native of the South Side Beverly neighborhood. Kato, twenty-seven, and Roeser, twenty-six, were both born in suburbs of Minneapolis–St. Paul, but they didn't meet until they attended Northwestern University in Evanston. The three were drawn together by Chicago's mid-'80s punk scene, but their influences were never limited to the faster-louder punk-rock underground.

Onasis says he "grew up listening to stuff like the Steve Miller Band," and Kato claims he was raised on funk. Since *Americruiser*, the band has incorporated more of these influences and slowly turned its back on the raw garage aesthetic personified by its former buddy, Chicago producer (er, "recordist") Steve Albini. On *Saturation*, the group turned to producers Joe and Phil Nicolo. "It sounds really airy, like someone just threw the windows open on every track," Kato says. "It's a perfect summer soundtrack."

This time the band knew what it wanted to avoid. "Between [Steve] Albini, [Butch] Vig, and Kramer, we ran the gamut on indie-rock producers, and we didn't want to do that again," Onasis says. The musicians had all enjoyed the debut album by the hip-hop group Cypress Hill, and a Geffen executive suggested the rappers' producers, the Nicolos. The Philadelphia-based "Butcher Brothers"—who earned their nickname through their tape-splicing skills—had also scored a major hit with teeny-boppers Kris Kross.

"They let us try everything," Onasis says. "We knew instantly that we had finally teamed up with someone more insane than we are." Adds Kato: "If we came into the studio and said, 'I want to track this vocal swinging by a bungee around my ankles,' in five minutes, they would have the crane rented." Concludes Roeser: "We wanted to get away from the idea of somebody deciding what the best song was or what was going to get on the radio. These Butchers were far removed from that; they didn't know who we were or what an alternative record sounded like. But soon into the recording process, it was clear that we were friends for life."

Joe Nicolo indicates that the admiration is mutual. "I had heard of Urge Overkill, but I wasn't a fan," he says. "I listened to the older records and thought, 'OK, there's a quirky, charming innocence about this stuff that's appealing.' But for me, the new record is by leaps and bounds their best effort."

True enough. Yet the clean but powerful sound of *Saturation* has more in common with old Van Halen than early Urge. It remains to be seen whether mainstream rock fans will connect with odd, brainy tunes such as "Sister Havana" and "Heaven 90210." Nevertheless, the band members are excited about what they clearly consider the looming prospect of stardom.

"It's so wrong to ever be considered a careerist," says the motor-mouthed Onasis, the group's most verbose spokesman. "But if all you do is your band, and that's how you make your money and that's who you are, then it *is* in fact your career, and what the hell is wrong with it? Urge is our baby and we are its parents, and we want our baby to grow up to be as healthy and happy as it can be."

The band is unusually honest about its ambitions, a trait that's generally well-masked in the alternative rock world. As a result, as with the Smashing Pumpkins, Urge has frequently been subject to charges of being all too eager to "sell out" to the corporate rock machine. The band members write this off as typical small-town backbiting. "Rose, the bass player from the Poster Children, told me that when they signed to Sire, they met Seymour Stein, the legendary head of that label," Onasis says. "Few people know that he was from Chicago, and he was in the Buckinghams or one of those Chicago bands. The first thing he said to them was, 'How's the Chicago scene?' Even before they could answer he said, 'It sucks, right? Nobody likes each other, all the bands hate each other and talk behind each other's backs, right?' He said that's the way it's always been in Chicago."

Urge is particularly sensitive to scene politics thanks to a celebrated feud with former producer Albini and former label Touch and Go. *Chicago Reader* critic Bill Wyman outlined the dispute several weeks ago in his Hitsville column: Touch and Go founder Corey Rusk accused the band of being unethical when it left the label, and Albini said it ruined his relationship with the Chicago Recording Company by monopolizing studio time there. Urge Overkill is already tired of talking about the squabbles. The band and Touch and Go "don't associate and haven't talked in a year," Roeser says. As for Albini, "We'd rather his name not be in the article; he has nothing to do with the band." Adds Onasis: "Only we know what's best for our band. Touch and Go doesn't know what's best for us, and Steve Albini doesn't know what's best for us."

If the feud has somehow become larger than life, that's in keeping with most things about Urge: *Everything* about this band is exaggerated, usually to comic proportions. While chart-topping grunge rockers wear de facto uniforms of long hair and flannel shirts, Urge sports flamboyant Vegas-style stage costumes and big gold "U/O" medallions. The group boasts of a "world domination" plan that includes its own magazine, *Bofonics*, and a KISS Army–style fan club to market medallions to the faithful. The band members are extremely image-conscious, and photographers who've worked with them say they preen like supermodels. But the group is even more obsessive about its stage presentation.

Urge Overkill turned down a coveted slot on Lollapalooza '93 because it didn't want to get lost in the mix, and it has added a bass player so Kato and Roeser can both play guitar for a live sound that's closer to the album. Christmas guitarist Michael Cudahy filled in on the group's last tour, but he was subsequently deemed "too busy" as a player. The band is keeping the identity of its new member secret until its record release party at Metro on Thursday, a blowout that also will feature an opening set by a Neil Diamond impersonator. Urge covered Diamond's "Girl, You'll Be a Woman

Soon" on the *Stull* EP, and the band members frequently praise the glitzy lounge singer in interviews. As with the uniforms, it's hard to tell if they're serious.

"We've met Diamond, OK? I don't know, but he seems to *believe*," says Roeser, the smaller of the two frontmen. "That's why he's Neil, because he always believed," adds Kato, his towering partner. "To us, punk rock always meant 'wrong,'" Onasis concludes. "*Stull* is so wonderfully *wrong*. I mean, *a Neil Diamond cover*?"

If there is any impediment to Urge's success, it's this kitschy sense of humor, which makes it difficult to distinguish satire from genuine homage. It permeates everything the band does, from Diamond covers to comically clichéd lyrics such as "People like me go it alone / Baby I'm a rolling stone."

"Everyone quotes that line at us," Kato says. "It's rockspeak. People might not take it seriously, but we're extremely sincere."

The question is whether this shtick will translate to a wider audience. "What it's for is really to just keep us entertained," Roeser says. "A lot of great rock 'n' roll has been way over the top." Adds Kato: "We're escapists, and we like escapist things. The great movies are escapist, and cool music is that way, too. We like getting lost in a fantasy world of our own design."

Kato leans against the rail of the Bank's back porch and flashes a wide Cheshire Cat grin. Onasis has just returned from stacking a new pile of platters on the turntable. He's carrying a fresh bottle of bubbly and flipping through the pages of *Sassy* magazine. Urge Overkill's fantasy world is a quirky but enticing place, and Geffen may be right about its appeal to the new rock audience.

"We're the lost generation," Kato says. "We're not catering to our generation, it's just what we are. We don't think about it, we just do it."

· ·

Saturation is Urge Overkill's best chance for national notoriety, but the group has already released six recordings in its eight-year history. Here is a discography.

Strange, I . . . EP (Ruthless, 1986) ☆

When these five Steve Albini–produced tunes were released, I wrote a fanzine review describing them as a "more garagey version of Big Black" and gave them a "B +." My tolerance for sub–Big Black noise may have decreased, but more likely, I was being too kind, because *Strange, I . . .* is almost unlistenable. The best thing about it is the cover, which lists goofy take-offs on the band's name, including Huge Overcoat, Large Coffeespill, Hedge Undergrowth, and Urchin Ovaries.

Jesus Urge Superstar (Touch and Go, 1989) ☆ 1/2

Only a slight improvement. Whatever melodies the band wrote are buried under the pointlessly noisy guitars and muddy production, although "Your Friend Is Insane" points to the direction the group is heading.

Americruiser (Touch and Go, 1990) ☆☆☆

Butch Vig (who went on to produce Nirvana's *Nevermind*) finally solved some of the production problems, and Urge Overkill started to hone its approach: lyrics full of "rockspeak," junk culture references, and fat guitar riffs reminiscent of the best '70s rock meet a solid funk backbeat and driving punk aggression. The highlights are the opening track, "Ticket to L.A.," and the appropriately titled "Faroutski." Reissued by Touch and Go on one CD with *Jesus Urge Superstar.*

The Supersonic Storybook
(Touch and Go, 1991) ☆☆☆ 1/2

By this point, the band was really cooking. The tuneful anthem "What Is Artane?" became a college radio hit; a cover of "Emmaline" turns the Hot Chocolate tune into a wonderfully creepy ballad, and "Bionic Revolution" is an effective '90s take on T-Rex and Mott the Hoople. On the other hand, "Henhough: The Greatest Story Ever Told" sounds dangerously close to Jethro Tull, or at least Trip Shakespeare.

Stull EP (Touch and Go, 1992) ☆☆☆

Recorded in New York with Shimmy Disc founder Kramer (Bongwater, Galaxie 500), *Stull* was the band's best-sounding record before *Saturation,* though the group was obviously saving its best material for Geffen (it already had been signed to the label when these six songs were recorded). "Stull (Part 1)" is stretched into an Allman Brothers–style jam, and the reflective "Goodbye to Guyville" signals the band's desire to move forward. But the Neil Diamond cover is a flop; regardless of Urge's praise, Neil Diamond will *never* be cool.

Urge Overkill, *Exit the Dragon*
Request, September 1995

IT'S NOT EASY being Urge. Despite strong support from radio and MTV, the Chicago trio only sold some two hundred fifty thousand copies of its Geffen debut, *Saturation*, a number that rates as barely respectable in these days of alternative-rock success stories. Former friend, producer, and indie-rock ethicist Steve Albini tells anyone who'll listen that he thinks the band members are sell-outs and weasels. The musicians are followed around their hometown by two female fans who've made dissing them into a sort of performance art, and this duo publishes painfully detailed accounts of their foibles and *faux pas* in an anti-fanzine called *The Stalker*. So it should come as no surprise that *Exit the Dragon* is a somber, brooding effort fueled by more than a touch of "woe is me."

There is no larger-than-life FM–rock anthem on this album; no Paul Shaffer favorite like "Sister Havana" or "Positive Bleeding." Produced once again by Philadelphia's Butcher Brothers, Joe and Phil Nicolo, the fifteen songs are almost all mid-tempo groovers. In place of the last album's shimmering guitars and thunderous drums are groaning synthesizers, heavy Hammond organs, distant horns, and clattering congas. Over this late-night juke-joint backdrop (perfect for crying in your beer), singers Nash Kato and Ed Roeser ruminate about how they hate walking in sunshine, can't get a break, never learned anything in school, made more than their share of mistakes, and don't pray anymore "because too many of God's children die."

Such whining sentimentality would be unbearable coming from, say, sanctimonious folkies Soul Asylum or generic grungemeisters Bush. But the members of Urge Overkill are post-modern pranksters who are well versed in every aspect of rock history and '70s pop culture. They're having the time of their lives being this miserable, and the dark night of their souls is illuminated by signposts pointing out the connections to legendary end-of-the-line classics such as Big Star's *3rd*, the Rolling Stones' *Exile on Main St.*, and Sly and the Family Stone's last great album. ("You have a right to be right and a right to be wrong / It's like a song Sly sang, there's a riot goin on," Kato warbles in "Need Some Air.")

"Jaywalking" visits a Nancy Sinatra groove by way of the Jesus and Mary Chain's "Sidewalking"; "Somebody Else's Body" is a jaunty detour that recaptures the old Urge sexual swagger; "Monopoly" uses the board game as a metaphor for a relationship (and Urge has all the hotels); and an odd studio toss-off called "The Mistake" hits closer to home than the group may have intended. "Traveling 'cross the U.S.A. / It's hard sometimes to keep it together," the Urge boys sing. "Nothing but the songs that you play / And a couple kids believing your sound."

Urge Overkill is still way too smart for its own good, and it's way too enamored of its own cleverness to allow listeners to connect on any genuine emotional level. But *Exit the Dragon* is a wonderful facsimile of a cathartic masterpiece in the same way that MTV's *The Real World* is an entertaining simulacrum of real twentysomething life. Savvy of the medium, nothing too real is ever betrayed, but the crises are engrossing nonetheless, and the fact that they're two steps removed spares the audience from feeling guilty for loving every minute of it.

6 IT WAS A RIOT, GIRLS

WITH ALL DUE RESPECT TO THE SISTERHOOD, there were entirely too many declarations of "The Year of the Woman" in the '90s and far too many "Women in Rock" features on the covers of the major music magazines. I say this as a feminist (none of this "post-" stuff for me), not as an (I hope) all-too-typically sexist male rock critic. Y'see, I've always agreed with the members of L7: Real progress toward gender equality won't be made in the music world until we talk about vulva-bearing rock bands as great rock bands, period, instead of segregating them and singling them out as great *female* rock bands.

The artists in this section are here because they rocked, riotously or righteously, and because they provoked thought and controversy. They also happened to pee sitting down. Yes, that does mean *something*. As my friend, Paula Kamen, author of the excellent book *Her Way: Young Women Remake the Sexual Revolution*, writes, "To me 'Third Wave' feminism and these women profiled seem to be about life and sex on one's own terms, embracing complexity and contradiction and ambivalence. They dare to have sexual desire *and* intelligence and a critical social view at the same time. And, as you say, here's the challenge: They're trying to do this while under intense commercial pressures and temptations to look and sound like Barbie dolls, to be yet another sexy product canned and consumed (like Liz Phair, Veruca Salt, etc.). In trying to fight sexist stereotypes, older feminists were generally more rigid, defining women as being this way, this way, and that way—and young women are now saying that they don't want any one set of rules of how to be, from the Patriarchy or from feminists."

I'm a rock critic, though, and in the end it was the music these artists made that mattered to me most. It's for this reason that I never cared for many of the celebrated "riot grrrl" bands—laudable though their politics may have been, their brand of punk rock simply sucked moose cock.

This chapter opens and closes with musicians from my adopted hometown, and while their music was extraordinary, their fates are illuminating of many in the alternative-rock era, regardless of their gender. Liz Phair's *Exile in Guyville* opened the door for a wave of imitators, from Alanis Morissette to Meredith Brooks to Fiona Apple, all of whom outsold her without ever approaching the hem of her bell bottoms in terms of artistic accomplishments. Devoid of the conceptual conceit but boasting nearly as many memorable songs, I preferred 1994's *Whip-Smart* and 1998's *whitechocolatespaceegg* to Phair's much-lauded debut at the time of their releases, but *Exile in Guyville* remains the album that fans revere and that I find myself listening to most often now, and it has only grown richer and more powerful with the passing of time and the waning of the hype that greeted its issuance.

Phair disappeared for several years after her awkwardly named third album (the title had something to do with a dream she had while she was pregnant, and the birth of her son, the end of her marriage, and a move to Los Angeles had something to do with her hibernation). She finally resurfaced in late 2002, singing backing vocals on "Soak Up the Sun," a hit by Sheryl Crow, whose pleasant pop is to Phair's best rock what Devil Dogs are to fine French éclairs. Crow seems to have been a bad influence: Crafted with a list of big-name, small-substance collaborators such as Michael Penn, Pete Yorn, Natalie Imbruglia, Vitamin C, and the Matrix (the three-person songwriting and production team behind teen-pop sensation Avril Lavigne), Phair's California-lite fourth album, *Liz Phair*, is a thorough disappointment, justifying the complaints by some longtime fans that she has "gone Hollywood."

The story of Veruca Salt's subsequent career is even less pretty, and if "The Making of a Buzz Band" is illuminating for the way it charts the rapid rise of a typical alternative phenom, a piece just as revealing could be written about how this modest but lovable garage-pop band was ruined by the music machine and its own inflated ambitions. After the modest success of its debut, the group proved all too willing to be molded into a slick, insubstantial, but well-marketed cartoon. Produced by Bob Rock of Motley Crüe and Metallica fame, the band's second album, 1997's *Eight Arms to Hold You*, is overblown, monolithic, and lacking the intellectual edge and emotional wallop of the debut. After its release, initially inseparable singers and songwriters Nina Gordon and Louise Post split amid considerable acrimony. Both resurfaced in 2000: Gordon tried to morph into Jewel crossed with Stevie Nicks on a wretched solo album, *Tonight and the Rest of My Life*, while Post put together a new version of Veruca Salt and made the brilliant if sadly under-heralded *Resolver*, a powerful effort that found her seeking catharsis from her professional split with Gordon and her romantic breakup with Dave Grohl of the Foo Fighters. As of this writing in early 2003 both women are missing in action, though you can occasionally hear a radio commercial that Post's reincarnated Veruca cut for the Illinois State Lottery.

As for the women sandwiched in between, L7, the Muffs, and Elastica never won the mainstream attention they deserved, at least compared to pop fluff masquerading as alternative rock such as No Doubt or the Cranberries. But PJ Harvey, Björk, Tori Amos, and Sinéad O'Connor continue to stand as some of the most vibrant voices and inspiring creative forces of their generation, mining their own triumphs and difficulties to produce art that is universal in its appeal, regardless of the sex of the listener. You go, girls.

Sex in Rock 101: Selling the Maiden Phair
BAM, March 24, 1995

SAYING THAT "SEX sells music" is a bit like saying, "Rock is often loud." Well, no shit. From Elvis shakin' his pelvis to Jim Morrison unfurling his trouser snake, from Trent Reznor's "fuck you like an animal" shtick to Boyz II Men's buppie lust, sex has always been part of the picture, and it probably always will be.

Some critics hold that only now, in the Year 1995 PM (Post-Madonna), are female musicians finally approaching sex with the sort of frankness that men have always shown (i.e., "Squeeze my lemon 'til the juice runs down my leg"). That, of course, is bullshit. From those raunchy, risqué, groundbreaking blues godmothers, whose lewdness would have prompted grandma to have a stroke, to the aforementioned Ms. Ciccone, whose sexual escapades have gotten so tired that they probably even put *her* to sleep by now, women have been on top in terms of making sexually charged music just as often as men.

Nancy Sinatra shocked the hell out of dear ol' dad with her go-go boot fetish, to say nothing of her dalliance with a vaguely sinister older man and mentor, Lee Hazelwood. Patti Smith reclaimed Van Morrison's "Gloria" as a horny bisexual fantasy and proudly confessed that she had her first or-gasm while watching the Rolling Stones play for Ed Sullivan (a *rilly big shew*, indeed!). Poly Styrene turned the tables on the male BDSM fantasy with X-Ray Spex's "Oh Bondage, Up Yours!," Debora lyall of Romeo Void baldly declared that she "might like you better if we slept together," and Cyndi Lauper she-bopped onto the scene with a delightful little tune about the joys of masturbation.

The only thing really new in the current wave of female rockers is that sex is a given, not a gimmick. PJ Harvey, the Breeders, Belly, Elastica, Veruca Salt, Hole, L7, and the Muffs all admit that women are as obsessed with sex as men are. It's a major part of their lives, therefore it's present in their music. "That should be the end of the story," their attitude says. "And if you ask me one more time about being a 'woman in rock,' I'm gonna beat the crap out of you!"

I'm not sure, but I think this is what egghead critics mean by "post-femi-nism," and I buy it because I know that Donita Sparks *could* kick my ass. In any event, I like L7 because it's a great rock band, not because it's a great *fe-male* rock band. But then there's the problem of Liz Phair.

Whether you love her, hate her, or vacillate between both positions as I do myself, Phair prompts extreme and schizophrenic reactions because she is an extremely schizophrenic artist. She has used sex to sell her music more blatantly than any other woman so far in the '90s. That's not to belittle her songwriting talent, her limited but expressive voice, or her and Brad Wood's ambitious studio visions. It is simply a factual observation, and one that Phair would probably agree with—depending on which Phair we were talking to. "I wanna be mesmerizing, too," she sings midway through her celebrated and oh-so-sexual debut, *Exile in Guyville*. And she certainly suc-ceeds in casting her spell.

Phair is quickly becoming the alternative-rock Madonna—a savvy, witty, and expert manipulator of the media. Both women revel in the use of titil-lating lyrics and photos while simultaneously mocking the fact that "sex sells." Both are happy to play the pretty pop pin-up, then turn around and use that pose to critique sexual stereotypes. But Phair is also alt-rock's Forrest Gump (she says simple things that are perceived as brilliant) and its Zelig (she has an uncanny ability to become what people desire her to be in any given situation). You can see this in action with different camps of her fans, but it's even more obvious in her dealings with the press. In *Out* mag-azine, she discusses her college flirtation with bisexuality. In the women's magazines, she talks about her views on feminism. And in *Rolling Stone,* she gets high with the writer, then confesses her sexual fantasies for Captain Kangaroo's pal, Mr. Green Jeans.

Phair is a cipher—the Maiden Phair, everyone's Midwestern dream girl—or at least the college-rock version of that ideal. The adopted daughter of Dr. John Phair (chief of Infectious Diseases at Northwestern Memorial Hospital) and his wife, Nancy (a volunteer historian at the Art Institute of Chicago), she grew up in Winnetka, a posh suburb northwest of Chicago. She famously attended summer camp with Julia Roberts, studied art history at Oberlin College, then became a Wicker Park beatnik, artist, and, in her words, "*Sassy*-style quasi-good-girl slutty type." Her first loves were painting and charcoal etchings, and she only started making music in her bedroom as a lark, joining the underground network of do-it-yourself four-track cassette artists with a release called *Girlysound*.

That tape caught the attention of Matador Records, and the praise it garnered in fanzines gave Phair the courage to attempt her ambitious debut: a double album following the blueprint (but not the exact sounds or lyrical topics) of the Rolling Stones' decadent 1972 classic, *Exile on Main St.* (Phair's title comes from the phrase she and her friends borrowed from Urge Overkill to describe the testosterone-heavy Wicker Park rock scene.) It was an audacious move, and Phair knew it. "Whether anybody likes the album or not, it was totally necessary for me to do," she told me shortly after the disc's release. "It was a complete vision that I achieved for myself, and that was really awesome. I was totally in the fever of it. I wanted to have a novel instead of a short story, and I learned a hell of a lot from trying to do that. That's what mattered to me, and then this other stuff started happening all around it. In my mind, it's just completely independent from what I was doing."

Well, sort of. Like many alternative rockers, Phair has always been ambivalent about her ambitions. When she was nominated for the best female rock vocal Grammy in 1994 (a startling honor for someone who can barely sing in conventional terms), a reporter from the *Chicago Tribune* asked her if that meant she was now a part of the establishment. "If you go backwards in my life, you would assume that I was *always* establishment," she replied. "I was only masquerading as something radical and liberal."

She was certainly masquerading all over the place. Chicago's *Pop Stock* fanzine nicknamed her "Savoir Phair" because, like the cartoon mouse that tormented Klondike Kate, she was *everywhere.* But while her bandmates and cheerleaders complained that people were focusing on the hype instead of the music, Phair was having a field day with all of the, um, exposure. Let's not forget that she *chose* to appear on the cover of *Rolling Stone* in her slip, to slip into a slinky bathing suit and climb in the pool with a toy guitar for the *Chicago Tribune* magazine, to regale Tabitha Soren on *MTV News* with the tale of how she lost her virginity, to sit in her Calvin Kleins while lasciviously licking a milkshake for *Newsweek,* and to strike a particularly acrobatic pose for a double-truck spread in *Option* that allowed the photographer to look straight down her cleavage to a strategically placed hole in the crotch of her shorts.

It was, of course, Phair's inalienable right to present herself as a sexy and self-assured woman of the '90s. But don't say it wasn't calculated, because then you're the one who's not giving credit where it's due. "I'm totally just trying to be mature about this and be responsible," Phair said when I asked her about all of the sexy hype in 1994. "I'm twenty-six and I've had many nine-to-five jobs, and I don't really like them. I always said I want to be my own boss. And this is sort of like, 'Well, here's your chance, see if you can stay on top of this and still make music that matters to you.'"

In other words, these lewd little slices o' Liz were as pre-determined as her efforts to grab men by the gonads with lines like the infamous "I want to be your blow job queen," "I'll fuck you 'til your dick is blue," "I ask because I'm a cunt in spring," and "You fuck like a volcano," all of which spiced up *Exile in Guyville* and hooked in the rock critics (men especially), because not only was Phair appealing to their perpetually horny selves, but she was doing it with an album that claimed to "respond" to the Stones' *Exile on Main St.* (thereby eliminating the guilt of indulging in sexist fantasizing by couching it as a feminist response to the best album by rock's most famous sexists—talk about a rock-writer hard-on!). But as Madonna has discovered, playing the sluttish coquette can backfire, because it can be hard to turn the Mae West routine off when you want to be taken seriously.

Phair *does* have serious things to say on *Exile in Guyville.* As a whole the album is a statement about what it's like to be a sharp, talented young woman who simultaneously loves and hates the men in her life. She can't live with them and she can't live without them, but she'll be damned if she stops trying to find her ideal soulmate—or to concede that the difficulty in doing so may be partly her own fault. "It's cold and rough," she sings on the rollicking opener, "6'1." "And I kept standing six-foot-one instead of five-feet-two / And I loved my life / And I hated you." In "Help Me Mary" she rails about sloppy male roommates who make lewd remarks behind her back and leave suspicious stains in the sink, but vows that she'll have her revenge, promising to "Weave my disgust into fame / And watch how fast they run to the flame." But like strong female rockers from Marianne Faithfull to Chrissie Hynde before her, Phair makes it clear that these are her own desires that she's expressing, and she isn't doing so simply to appeal to some male fantasy.

"The fire you like so much in me / Is the mark of someone adamantly free," the artist sings on the closing track, "Strange Loop." That credo and Phair's obvious talent for crafting humble but memorable melodies is the source of the album's enduring appeal. As for the conceptual link to the Stones' classic, well, I for one have never bought it; if there is any conceivable connection between, say, "Mesmerizing" and "Loving Cup," or "Girls! Girls! Girls!" and "Turd on the Run," I just don't hear it. Producer Wood hints as much. "Liz was into analyzing what each song [on the Stones' *Exile*] means, but I didn't care at all," he told me shortly after recording the album. "I was more concerned about trying to make a record that twenty years from now, you won't be able to know when it was made."

But we're talking sex here, not music, and to tell you the truth, neither *Exile* nor Phair's less conceptual but just as catchy follow-up, *Whip-smart*, ever gave me wet dreams. "I have no problem being sexy," Phair told *Details*. "I have a problem being generically sexy." And that's my gripe. Sure, she's a smart and sexy woman. But where's the unique style? The personal edge? The reality? *The rock 'n' roll?* Frankly, I think Patti Smith with her bushy armpits, Poly Styrene with her awkward braces and pudgy cheeks, Courtney Love with her many battle scars—hell, even Carnie Wilson with her bountiful bounciness!—are a hell of a lot sexier than La Liz. But beauty is in the eye of the beholder, as they say, and to each his or her own.

Now, uh, can I have that photo from *Option* back?

L7 Makes Anger Fun
The *Chicago Sun-Times*, October 2, 1994

HORROR NOVELIST ANNE Rice has said that she doesn't mind love stories so long as they're of the homicidal variety. The same can be said of L7. The Los Angeles quartet is midway through a fiery eighteen-song set during a sold-out show at the Vic Theatre Friday night. So far there hasn't been a love song in the bunch, and there won't be by the time the band is done, but they certainly haven't been missed.

One of the big hits at Lollapalooza '94, L7 is using its expanded headlining slot to direct the anger and energy of its rambunctious fans. "Think of an ex-friend, ex-lover, politician, neighbor, or your boss," guitarist-vocalist Donita Sparks tells the crowd. The band then launches into a furious rocker called . . . actually, I can't tell you what it's called in a family newspaper, but you probably get the idea.

The group also indulges in politics of a less personal variety, though drummer Dee Plakas insists, "We're *not* a political band. We don't want to lecture people. We want people to come to our shows and have a good time. But if we can make them think at the same time . . . "

L7's political activities started because Sparks was fed up with the Supreme Court's abortion-related decisions and increased activities by anti-abortion groups, and she decided to do something about it. Last year the guitarist and her bandmate, bassist Jennifer Finch, founded Rock for Choice, which has become one of the most energetic activist groups in the music world. "It started because we were frustrated about our disappearing civil rights," Sparks says. "This is such a hot issue, and nobody in the music community was really doing anything."

Sparks had organized benefits in the past, and she'd promised herself that she wouldn't do it again. "But this was so in need that we just decided to do it. We went to the Feminist Majority because we knew they had done some public service announcements with rock stars. Initially, they wanted to do a very big show with satellite hookups and all this pizzazz, and they were throwing out names like Bonnie Raitt and Jackson Browne. We were like, 'Look, why don't you guys work on that, and Jennifer and I will work on Nirvana,' who hadn't broken yet, but were big in the underground. We did it ourselves, and it was very successful."

Since then Rock for Choice chapters have been formed in Minneapolis and Boston. A benefit album featuring Gretchen Seager of Mary's Danish, TV actress and Bongwater vocalist Ann Magnuson, Rosie Flores, and other artists is planned, and its release will be celebrated with a concert at the Los Angeles Palladium. "It just kind of snowballed," Sparks says. Meanwhile, L7's career has also been gaining momentum—its new album, *Bricks Are Heavy*, is perched at No. 192 with a bullet on *Billboard*'s pop albums chart.

Formed in California in the late 1980s, L7 actually features two Chicago-area natives: Sparks grew up in Oak Lawn and Plakas was raised in the Roseland neighborhood on the South Side. The two only met after they moved west, Plakas because she was attracted by the music scene, and

Sparks because she wanted to surf. The group released an independent album on Epitaph in 1987 and an EP on Sub Pop in 1990 before signing to Slash Records for *Bricks Are Heavy*.

Part of the credit for the new album's success is due to ace producer Butch Vig. L7 selected him before his last project, Nirvana's *Nevermind*, became a runaway smash, but the band had been laying the groundwork for their success for years with almost constant touring. "It's not an overnight thing," Plakas says. "We've been together for a while and steadily working, and it's just all the sudden, we're getting known in parts that you wouldn't think we'd be known in."

The comparison with Nirvana goes deeper than the two bands sharing a producer. Like the Seattle trio, L7 (which takes its name from Beat lingo for "square") effectively merges aggressive punk energy and noisy guitar growl with deliciously catchy riffs and melodies. "Musically, we know what we like and we know what works for L7," Sparks says. "I like catchy songs. We weren't out to make a really ugly-sounding record. We weren't looking for anarchy in this recording or in our songwriting. We don't care about impressing people with time changes. We just wrote songs that we liked and that caught our ear."

One of the band's strengths is its lyrics, which are written by Sparks and guitarist Suzi Gardner. Songs such as "Wargasm," "Pretend We're Dead," and "Diet Pill" are hard-hitting and written from a strong feminist perspective. "In lyrics it's gonna come up that we're women," Sparks says. "What am I gonna sing about, being on a baseball team?" But L7 is as reluctant to be called "a female band" as it is to be pigeonholed as "a political band." "I think in the underground, there have always been a handful of bands who sing about things or organize benefits," Sparks says. "There are always a handful of bands that give a shit. And I'm not saying that people don't give a shit just because they're not singing about it. If it doesn't fit for you to sing about issues, people shouldn't feel that they have to. I mean, I love Nirvana. I don't know what he's singing about most of the time, but that doesn't matter to me. I just hope that what I see at our shows—all the people registering to vote—in our own little way, I think we're helping to destroy the apathy."

Back onstage at the Vic, the high points of the band's set come courtesy of the Ramones-style rhythms and sing-along choruses of "Freak Magnet" and the modern-rock radio hit, "Andres." Lollapalooza seems to have taught L7 something about arena rock: Sparks goofs around with her new toy, the guitar "voice box" gizmo immortalized by Joe Walsh and Peter

Frampton, while guitarist Gardner plays one chaotic wah-wahed solo after another. Sparks and Finch show off some fancy choreographed dance moves, Plakas pummels her drums like Linda Blair (a woman possessed), and the band unveils some bonafide special effects.

"How do you like our new smoke machine and flashing lights?" Sparks asks.

The fans eat it all up, just as they embraced everything about L7, including the anger. And, really, what's not to love?

Louder Than Words
The Chicago Sun-Times, June 9, 1995

POLLY JEAN HARVEY wants to be a star, but not for the reasons most musicians cite. The English singer-songwriter is hoping for fame and fortune so she can stop doing interviews.

"I'm not in the luxurious position of being able to do that at this point," she tells this interviewer, chuckling slyly. "I don't find interviews cathartic, and I hate doing them." Nevertheless Harvey is a warm and charming person whose very reluctance to talk offers insight into the way she makes music. "I see music in a very spiritual way. It's not to be thought about too much or rationalized or intellectualized. Everything I do is on a very instinctive level, and I don't like to dwell on how or why it comes about."

Since debuting on England's independent Too Pure Records in 1991, PJ Harvey (a name that can be used interchangeably for the band and the bandleader) has released four albums, including the newest, *To Bring You My Love*. Her gutsy, sexually charged merger of blues and alternative rock has won critical accolades and attracted a small but growing cult following, and few knowledgeable rock fans are without an opinion about her. In a recent interview, Courtney Love professed admiration but claimed she can't listen to *To Bring You My Love* because the songs are all about Chicagoan Steve Albini. (Albini produced Nirvana's *In Utero* and Harvey's second album, *Rid of Me*.)

Harvey laughs. Courtney's claim isn't true, she says, "but it is very, very funny. I have a lot of respect for Courtney Love, although I've never met her. I think she's great. The first contact I had with her, she sent me a fax saying, 'Look, just because I hate Steve Albini doesn't mean I hate you.' I was very grateful to receive that."

Harvey followed *Rid of Me* with an album of four-track demos featuring many of the same songs. Many critics contended that it was because she disliked Albini's production on the first version of the album, but she discounts this theory as well. "Steve and I find this all very amusing because people like to read so much into things," she says. "They like to think that I was dissatisfied with his work, and the rumors go on all the way down to I just had his love child. We're really very good friends, and I keep in very close contact with him. I turn to him for help and advice because I think he's very intelligent, and I trust him implicitly."

Besides, Harvey believes that she and Albini share a common problem. "People read things in and make him what they want him to be. He's the only other person I know that that happens to besides myself. People have a very specific idea of what I am—some kind of ax-wielding, man-eating Vampira—and I'm not that at all. I'm almost the complete opposite."

Harvey may well be the quiet "country bumpkin" that she likes to portray herself as, but it's easy to understand where the other image originates when you listen to her music and watch her perform. *To Bring You My Love* is another intense album by a very intense artist, and on this tour, she's leaving the guitar playing to band members Joe Gore and John Parish in order to step out as a galvanizing frontwoman. Wearing a summery dress and outlandish fake gold eyelashes, she vamps, vogues, and prowls the stage, at one point doing a sensual go-go dance while perched on a light box. She has always been frank when writing about sex in her songs, but she has never seemed so comfortable being a woman in the spotlight.

Harvey believes in music as catharsis the way that blues greats like Howlin' Wolf and spiritual rockers like Patti Smith believed. Instead of the self-loathing that so many alternative rockers waste their energies on, she purges herself by attacking her fans. One of her most powerful tunes ends with the pronouncement, "I might as well be dead, but I could kill you instead." In live performance she takes no prisoners and leaves few listeners unconvinced. And she is poised to reach her biggest audience yet, heading out on a major summer shed tour that pairs her with Live and Chicagoans Veruca Salt.

"It's something that I would not have usually done, but I do listen to my management," the singer says. "I've never done anything like it before, and before I rule it out as an option, I thought I'd try it."

Harvey is a bit concerned about the ramifications of wading in the mainstream. "I hope people won't look down on me for doing it," she says. Of course, if she's a hit, she'll be one step closer to not having to return inter-viewers' phone calls.

Harvey's Happy to Be an Outsider
The *Chicago Sun-Times*, May 10, 2001

IN 1995 ICONOCLASTIC rocker PJ Harvey toured the arenas opening for Live. Afterward, she vowed she'd never do anything like that again. "But I ended up here," she says with a sigh.

"Here" is the much-coveted support slot on U2's Elevation Tour, which comes to the United Center for four sold-out shows starting Saturday. It's a gig that any musician in search of fame and fortune would kill for. But Harvey has never been just any musician, and she isn't circumspect in voic-ing her complaints.

"It's a challenge for me to be playing in front of a U2 audience, and some nights it goes better than others," Harvey says. "In some places, people have really been quite ambivalent about it, and they're just waiting for U2 to come on. In other places, people seem to really love it, and there are actu-ally a lot of people that have come out to see me.

"A band in U2's position . . . they're in such a great position. They could go out onstage now and they could be playing shows that are really push-ing things forward, and I don't think they are, and I think that's a shame. Things have got to change. Music is in a dire position at the moment. The quality of the music that we're getting to hear is just so mind-numbingly boring. It's all the same thing regurgitated over and over again, but it sells millions.

"I get quite despairing about it when I think, 'Well, is this what people want to hear?'" Harvey continues. "And it must be, because it wouldn't sell otherwise. From my own point of view, I feel I can just go on following my heart and hope that it will touch something in people. I live in faith and hope that things will change, but I have to say, it's been looking pretty bleak for a long time now."

This attitude stands in sharp contrast to the more optimistic sentiments expressed on Harvey's sixth album, 2000's *Stories from the City, Stories from the Sea*. The disc may be the songwriter's most upbeat effort—a fact that's been widely attributed to a successful love affair. "This is love, this is love that I'm feeling!" she howls in the disc's most memorable line. As always, the enigmatic singer has no intention of discussing her personal life when we talk. But she's happy to talk about the musical progression from the stark, minimalist blues of earlier discs to the current lush and cinematic sound.

"Whenever I've finished any record and I'm starting another one, I always try to move into some area that I haven't explored enough yet, and I don't think I'd really explored the richness and complexity of melody and what it can bring to a song. I was really diving into that on this record, and not only the richness in the melodies and the voice, but also in the production. I wanted to create a very rich record full of lush sounds and a lot going on on a lot of different levels."

The first step down this path was *Dance Hall at Louse Point*, the 1996 album that Harvey made in collaboration with guitarist John Parrish. "People don't even count that, yet that's the record I'm really proud of," she says. "It was an enormous turning point for me. Lyrically, it moved me into areas I'd never been to before. Faced with John's music, which is so different to my own, it just made me write lyrics in a very different way and structure songs in a different way. Using somebody else's structures forced me to really change the way I was writing."

As for where she's going next, the artist says she's been listening to a lot of old Stones records, the Queens of the Stone Age, and punk rock. "I'm really into loud guitars, grunge, and quite violent music at the moment," she says.

If that puts her out of step with current trends, she doesn't mind at all. "I'm totally happy being on the outside of things and just going my own way and trying different things," Harvey says. "I don't think I fit into a lot of molds, but I don't want to, anyway."

The Do-It-All Icelander
The *Chicago Sun-Times*, August 4, 1995

AT THE RIPE old age of thirty, Björk Gudmundsdóttir has composed electronic film scores, played clarinet in a jazz band, produced a heavy-metal band, played drums in a punk band, and performed baroque music on flute.

"I've tried everything, to be honest," she says. "I'm not saying I was brilliant at it all. I'm not bragging about it. I'm just saying I have to taste everything. I've got this in my character that I'm really easily bored, and I have to try it all before I die."

Björk became famous as the singer for Iceland's first (and, so far, only) internationally successful rock band, the Sugarcubes. But that was never her only interest, and now that she's working as a solo artist, her wild eclecticism shines through. "When we're talking now, we haven't got a clue of what we're going to feel like at eight tonight," she says. "That's a reason why all the songs are so diverse, because we are all in different moods all of the time. The album is sort of a challenge, like, 'OK, life, you can throw whatever you want at me—an earthquake, a devaluation of all currencies, or maybe I'll fall in love—and I don't *have* to know what happens next. I'm just going to enjoy it to the max and go with the flow.'"

On her second solo album, *Post*, Björk follows the flow from twisted alternative rock ("Army of Me") to relatively straightforward techno ("The Modern Things") to a World War II–era big-band number originally recorded by film star Betty Hutton ("Blow a Fuse (It's Oh So Quiet)"). "Five or six years ago I was part of a group called the Jazz Legends of Iceland," she says. "We toured and played little villages that two hundred people lived in, from two years old to eighty years old, and that was probably the most critical period in my life. My own songs tend to be quiet and introverted, and sometimes when I pick songs that other people write, I tend to go for the opposite. 'Blow a Fuse' is brilliant. I can scream and shout, and it suited me perfectly because it balanced everything."

Another standout on the album is "Possibly Maybe," a No. 2 hit in England which made headlines as part of a sampling controversy. The song includes a snippet of telephone noise sampled from a record by Scanner, an English group that specializes in lifting cellular telephone calls (many of them risqué) from the airwaves. Björk says she contacted the group and it was happy to let her sample its own work. She intended the song as a tribute, and she paid the outfit one thousand pounds. Then Scanner signed with a publishing company, held a news conference, and announced plans to sue the singer for two hundred thousand pounds. The case has since been settled.

"Their philosophy was that all the noises in the world are for everyone, and I really admired that," Björk says. "Then they basically lied and said that I had never contacted anyone and I was this big star who was trying to step on the little guy."

Björk doesn't seem bitter about the controversy—that's clearly not her style—and she doesn't foresee changing the way she works because of it.

Her scattershot approach to music and life is ingrained. "I was in music school from the ages of five to fifteen, and I studied everybody from Beethoven to Stockhausen," she says. "My grandparents listened to jazz, and my parents listened to Janis Joplin, Jimi Hendrix, and all that. There is no such thing as Icelandic music; there are no roots.

"We're back to Scanner territory here," she concludes, laughing. "But I really do believe that everything belongs to everyone."

Tori! Tori! Tori!
The *Chicago Sun-Times*, February 6, 1994

TORI AMOS IS a study in contradictions. She's a singer-songwriter with the attitude of an alternative rocker, a classically trained pianist who stresses emotion over technique, and a sometimes spacey new-age chanteuse with a flair for cynical satire. The fiery redhead is an odd combination of gonzo punk and flighty faerie princess. Wind her up and she's off like a runaway train.

Amos proudly flaunts the conflicting sides of her artistic persona, leaving journalists to sort out what it all means. The downside is that, more often than not, they get it all wrong. "Journalists really drive me nuts," she says at the start of our interview. "I really have to go around the barn to get in the door with them sometimes."

The singer has talked to her share of reporters since the success of her gold-selling 1992 debut, *Little Earthquakes*. Spare but tuneful piano-and-vocal anthems such as "Crucify" and "Silent All These Years" were hits on adult-contemporary radio, while her striking cover of "Smells Like Teen Spirit" won her the admiration of modern-rock programmers and Nirvana bandleader Kurt Cobain. Critics placed Amos and Sophie B. Hawkins at the head of a new class of feminist singer-songwriters. But as the Tori-in-a-box cover art for *Little Earthquakes* indicated, Amos isn't easily walled in.

"The generalization thing just isn't working anymore," she says. "It's about individuals. I think there are a lot of women speaking about it. There *is* a next wave, but it's exciting, because it's not about 'me against you.' It's about what I'm feeling. It's about women exploring themselves."

Amos grew up in Baltimore, the outspoken daughter of a Scottish Methodist preacher and a mother who was part Cherokee. She was a child prodigy at the piano, entered the Peabody Institute at age five, and was expelled at eleven. In the late '80s, she fronted a pop-metal band called Y Kant Tori Read. The group released one album that flopped, prompting Amos to move to England in 1990. There she reinvented herself as a solo artist and began recording her debut.

Now the twenty-nine-year-old singer is back with her second album, *Under the Pink*. Working with Eric Rosse (who produced several of the best tracks on *Little Earthquakes*), she spent a lengthy eleven months recording on a portable studio set up at a hacienda in New Mexico. "I just felt so disarmed," she says. "All the stuff that was happening with *Little Earthquakes* was stripped away when I stood in the desert. I felt that I could listen to my voice again, and it had a lot to say. When I'm trying to get performances, I'm trying to tap into an energy. The 'Baker Baker' girl didn't come out every day; she might only show up once every two weeks. And because we had the studio in the house, I could wake up at eight A.M. and say, 'I'm cutting "Baker Baker" right now.'"

Once again the spotlight is on Amos's fluid piano playing and soaring vocals, but there are a few surprises. "God" boasts an elaborate groove that recalls Peter Gabriel, and Trent Reznor of the industrial-metal band Nine Inch Nails sings hushed backing vocals on "Past the Mission." "His voice, when he's not doing his thing, has a quality to it that I felt could be really supportive to the girl in the song," Amos says. "I thought it was neat to have a guy helping a girl feel good about herself."

"God" is the album's most striking track and its first single. The lyrics accuse the Deity of turning His back on humanity, suggesting that He might be more interested in a game of golf and "the nine iron in the back seat." It's the most effective pop single about the Man Upstairs since XTC's "Dear God." That single created a controversy in the Bible Belt, where it was banned by many radio stations, but Amos says she isn't worried about "God" prompting a similar reaction. "If the people of the South need to look at this as a prayer, then that's fine," she says. "But the way I'm praying is, 'God, things aren't so great here.'

"'God' is really about the institution," she adds. "My concept of God—goddess, the creator, energy force—is not what the institution taught me. The God we've been taught about on this planet is definitely male, and he's got very big feet. Whether it's Christian, Judaic, Islamic—the God we've been taught about has been patriarchal. I think this song is hilarious. It's like, 'Let's get a sense of humor, but let's take some responsibility.' We're projecting a lot—mankind, womankind—on God."

Religion has figured in several of Amos's songs, but violence against women is an even more prevalent topic. On her debut she portrayed a harrowing rape scene in "Me and a Gun." On the new album she fantasizes about killing her co-worker in "The Waitress." "And 'Cornflake Girl' is based on Alice Walker's *Possessing the Secret of Joy*, where the mothers took their daughters to the butchers to have their genitalia removed. It's that sense of betrayal, that deepest feeling of 'when is a generation gonna stand up?' I really tried to look at my part in it. Am I supportive of my female friends? Are they supportive of me? I say I want a guy to be more sensitive, but you gotta know I wanna be dominated for an hour a day. Yes, it's confusing, but that's the point!

"This record was really about capturing moments of feelings," Amos says. "To work through that victim's point of view, to say, 'I have choice here, but I've got to kind of hold hands with violence and take it out shopping and then I won't feel so freaked about it.'"

Amos will tour behind *Under the Pink* this spring, once again performing with just her voice and a grand piano. During her 1992 appearance at Chicago's Park West, she delivered a two-hour set that never faltered in its intensity. Though her musical approach is much different, this is the quality she shares with galvanizing rockers such as Nirvana. "I think Kurt Cobain is a genius," she says. "When I hear 'Heart-Shaped Box,' I don't think intellectually. I hear it internally; I feel it in my being. On *Under the Pink*—with 'God' and 'The Waitress' and even some of the ballads—it's not about what she's saying, it's about what is she feeling. That is what music is about. We're not just poets here: There's a whole other subtext that can't be defined as a language. You either feel it or you don't."

Sinéad's Not Bad (She's Just Misunderstood)
The *Chicago Sun-Times*, September 18, 1994

LIKE PRINCE, AN artist she famously covered, Irish singer-songwriter Sinéad O'Connor has taken many confusing turns in her career, and her personal and professional lives have become increasingly hard to separate. Confusing musical detours, lost custody battles, suicide attempts, a return to her rock roots, hair, no hair, an alternating attraction to and repulsion from Christianity—the most dedicated fan has had a hard time holding on during this wild ride. But through it all O'Connor has continued to produce music of startling beauty, and her new album *Universal Mother* is no exception.

Released earlier this year, the Peter Gabriel–inspired single "You Made Me the Thief of Your Heart" was a promising sign that O'Connor had reconnected with her distinctive muse and was back on track after her disappointing third effort, 1992's *Am I Not Your Girl?*, a collection of unremarkable readings of standards ("The songs that made me want to be a singer") such as "Bewitched, Bothered and Bewildered," "I Want To Be Loved by You," and, inexplicably, an instrumental version of "Don't Cry for Me, Argentina."

Oh, yeah—there was also the matter of that hidden track. Generally overlooked in the fall of 1992 during the pillorying that O'Connor took from the press after her infamous Pope-bashing appearance on *Saturday Night Live* was the fact that the hot-tempered artist had telegraphed the move with an untitled spoken-word diatribe against the Roman Catholic Church. It closed *Am I Not Your Girl?* following seven seconds of silence after the last track, the aforementioned Tim Rice and Andrew Lloyd Webber "classic." Asked the singer: "Exactly why do you think [Jesus Christ] was assassinated? Who was it that did the dirty deed? Who didn't like the answers they'd received? Look at the one wearing the collar. Then or now, there's only ever been one liar, and it's the Holy Roman Empire."

O'Connor has always been outspoken on issues such as abortion rights and AIDS, but many Catholics were furious after the *SNL* broadcast, while others found themselves newly wondering: "Who the heck *is* this rude, bald woman, and why is she so angry?"

Born to a strict Roman-Catholic family in the Northern Irish town of Glenageary, O'Connor took refuge in music after a difficult childhood. As a student at the Dublin College of Music, she began singing with the punk band Ton Ton Macoute. She first shaved her head as a statement against sexism.

U2 guitarist the Edge was an early fan, and his support led to O'Connor's solo debut, 1987's *The Lion and the Cobra*. Its 1990 follow-up, *I Do Not Want What I Haven't Got*, spawned the Prince-penned No. 1 hit, "Nothing Compares 2 U," and her first big controversy came shortly thereafter, when she refused to allow the National Anthem to be played before a concert at the Garden State Arts Center in New Jersey. O'Connor called "The Star-Spangled Banner" aggressive imperialist propaganda, and the fact that she was right made little difference.

Unlike her response to that contretemps, when she tried to explain her beliefs to the press with little success, O'Connor refused to comment on the *Saturday Night Live* incident, but she didn't fare any better: Two weeks later she was famously booed off the stage at the Bob Dylan tribute concert at Madison Square Garden in New York. (Big bad Bob didn't do a thing to help her, which left him looking squarer than Kris Kristofferson, who at least offered a consoling shoulder. And who would have ever thought that such a bearded granola eater would wind up looking cooler than Dylan?)

Now after all of that drama comes *Universal Mother*, a collection of a dozen songs that reaffirm O'Connor's status as an eloquent and poetic writer with an almost unbelievably powerful, penetrating, and soulful voice. If overall it falls just short of the stunning accomplishment of *The Lion and the Cobra*, as a whole, it goes even further than the almost painfully cathartic "Nothing Compares 2 U" in showing the emotional depths that her voice is capable of plumbing (and her fearlessness in going into those black and foreboding holes in the first place).

Here O'Connor's vocals are set against spare arrangements of guitar, piano, drums, and the occasional string part. The twenty-seven-year-old singer controls the dramatic dynamics and injects most of the melodic hooks. As indicated by the title, motherhood is a recurring theme. "Fire on Babylon" captures the rage of a parent watching her child being mistreated, "My Darling Child" is a heartwarming lullaby, and "Red Football" is a rampaging warning that this woman isn't going to be kicked around. "My body's not a football for you! / My womb is not a football for you! / My heart is not a football for you!" she wails. "I'm not no animal in the zoo / This animal will jump up and eat you!"

In this context O'Connor's tender acoustic cover of Nirvana's "All Apologies" can be heard as the singer reacting to Kurt Cobain's suicide not only as a peer and fellow misunderstood member of Generation X, but as a mother who felt the urge to comfort someone who was hurting by striking out at their tormentor's jugular. Like Cobain, O'Connor is deeply divided about many things in life—romance, religion, motherhood, and violence—but she is willing to explore these topics with heart-wrenching honesty and that crystalline voice, and we all benefit from her stumbling journey.

Powerful stuff indeed, and *Universal Mother* provides ample evidence that despite the celebrated missteps of the last few years, O'Connor remains one of the most vibrant forces in rock today.

Warming Up to the Muffs
The *Chicago Sun-Times*, September 1, 1995

LIKE IT OR not, the Muffs have become a footnote to one of the biggest success stories of the '90s. The Los Angeles group's spirited 1993 debut came out a few months before Green Day's major-label bow, *Dookie*. Members of that trio said in nearly every interview that one of the reasons they signed to Warner Bros. was because the company's roster included the Muffs, and the two groups shared a producer, Rob Cavallo. But while *The Muffs* unjustly sank without a trace, *Dookie* became the biggest surprise hit since Nirvana's *Nevermind*.

"I think the record company got lucky," says Muffs guitarist-vocalist Kim Shattuck. "I know everybody associated with that Green Day record, and it was so disgusting. Everybody was patting each other on the back, and none of them deserved to. It was totally a fluke." Nevertheless Green Day's good fortune may be rubbing off on its pals. "The record company is starting to get it, to understand where we're coming from, like we're not just freaks of nature."

The Muffs are touring in support of their second album, *Blonder and Blonder*, which takes its title from a passing crack that Courtney Love made about Shattuck dyeing her hair: "Hmmm, blonder and blonder, I see." The Muffs basically do one thing, but they do it extremely well, warping infectious '60s-tinged pop melodies by delivering them at mid-'70s Ramones tempos with a heaping dose of '90s aggression on top. All of this decade-hopping makes them a band for the ages, and the melodies on songs such as "Oh Nina" (think Beach Boys on speed), "Red Eyed Troll" (the even more evil flip side of Nancy Sinatra's "These Boots Are Made for Walking"), and "Ethyl My Love" (a sinister tribute to Bill Frawley's character Fred Mertz on *I Love Lucy*) are simply irresistible. "All my friends know: Do not play Kim any music unless it has melody," Shattuck says. "I'm a sucker for super-melodic hooks."

In the mid-'80s Shattuck mined a similar vein with garage-rock revivalists and pioneering pre-postfeminist rockers the Pandoras. But where that group's leader, Paula Pierce, emulated obscure '60s *Nuggets* heroes like the Chocolate Watchband and the Seeds, Shattuck was drawn to more accessible groups like the Beatles, the Kinks, and the Who. She formed the Muffs with another Pandoras veteran, guitarist Melanie Vammen, and the group was completed by drummer Criss Crass and Shattuck's former boyfriend, bassist Ronnie Barnett.

"We came out of a scene in L.A. that we really hated, which was bands like Jane's Addiction and bad metal bands," Shattuck says. "We were trying to offer an alternative to that by trying to have some melody and energy in a scene that was really dismal."

The Muffs released three strong independent singles (including one on Seattle's Sub Pop Records) before signing to Warners in 1992. Two years later Vammen and Crass got their walking papers. "The other two members became completely disgusting to me and Ronnie," Shattuck says with typical frankness. "Melanie couldn't take any criticism of her guitar playing. She told her friends we wouldn't let her play on the new album."

The Muffs recruited former Red Kross drummer Roy McDonald and forged ahead as a trio. Although the new album isn't much of a revelation or refinement after the debut, the hooks are still as addictive and enticing as those bowls of sugary-salty peanuts at the bar, and the group's energy is infectious. Onstage the band is even better. The group is legendary for shows in hometown Hollywood that end in chaotic brawls, and there's a theory that part of what made the old lineup work was that everyone hated one another. How does the band get on now?

"It's like night and day; we all get along much better," Shattuck says. "But me and Ronnie still hate each other onstage, so don't worry: We still have a good thing going."

Elastica Connects
Rolling Stone, January 25, 1996

IN A YEAR that witnessed what was hyped as yet another British Invasion, the English band that connected best with American critics and fans was Elastica. The band's hook-filled two-minute anthems recalled the no-rules invention of the late-'70s punk explosion (and occasionally borrowed riffs from groups like Wire and the Stranglers). Nursing a hangover from too much alcohol, Ecstasy, and techno the night before, Elastica's primary singer and songwriter Justine Frischmann took time to reflect on the band's accomplishments in 1995 (the group was voted the best new band by the readers of *Rolling Stone*), and to look ahead to where she, guitarist-vocalist

Donna Matthews, drummer Justin Welch, and new bassist Abby Travis are going in 1996.

Q. *Elastica toured the United States four times last year. What was the highlight?*

A. Lollapalooza, actually, because it was such an extreme American rock experience. I really did enjoy watching a lot of the bands we played with from the side of the stage. I think when we came here the second time, it was really amazing, because our video ["Connection"] was on MTV, and people were coming up and saying, "Do that face!"

Q. *You've been playing to ever-increasing crowds. Are you concerned about a backlash from the underground that originally nurtured the band?*

A. I think people appreciate what we're doing. I was wary coming here, because of the experiences Blur had, but I had no idea what we'd encounter. It helps that there's less hype here than in England. The whole MTV thing is insane, but generally the music press tends to be more responsible.

Q. *Perhaps. But were there any interviews where you weren't asked about Wire?*

A. Yeah, a few! It was interesting, because there are a lot of Wire fans around, obsessive ones, and it's great. I'm a fan. I think they inspire a kind of loyalty that goes beyond anything else, beyond the usual band-fan relationship.

Q. *You're very fond of the punk and New Wave eras. Do you see any parallels to the current alternative-rock boom?*

A. People were making their own rules then, which is a good thing. The press was really positive, and I think that's happening again in England. There's the feeling bands are doing something different, changing the mainstream. Oasis, Blur, and Pulp have all had No. 1 singles, and the last time anything like that was happening was the early 1980s.

Q. *Are you amused by the lengths that male writers have gone to in order to find a politically correct way to say that you're a babe?*

A. "Handsome" is my favorite; my mother hates that word every time she sees it. [Laughs] I seriously think that in rock 'n' roll, if you're a woman and you've got two arms and two legs, you're bound to be considered a sex symbol. Generally, people don't frighten me. I enjoy speaking to them. I feel quite unshockable. I don't mind it when they're flirting with me; I'd rather that than them being shy.

I had an interesting case of that the other night in Springfield, Massachusetts. I went to get a hot dog at this all-night truck, and I ended up at four in the morning eating hot dogs outside with these drunk men.

There was this incredibly drunk man kissing my hands, and these guys behind me were arguing about whether I was or wasn't the girl in Elastica,
and they were going [sings the riff from "Connection"], "Dah dah-dah
dah, dah dah-dah dah." But I was really drunk myself, so none of this
bothered me.

Q. *I gather you don't have a problem with eating meat.*

A. Actually, I was a vegetarian until the last American tour, but I fell off
the wagon. I still can't eat steak, but I love hot dogs. You can't really get
them in England. The first thing I did when I got home was go straight to
the deli, but they're not the same there. They're the best thing to eat when
you've got a hangover, and they're the only choice in airports.

Q. *You live with Damon Albarn of Blur and two cats. Who's more trouble?*

A. I had to give one of my cats away. It just got totally stressed because I
kept leaving it to go on tour. It kept relieving its bladder all around our
apartment. I was probably more fond of that cat than anything else, and I
had to pack it up in a box and send it off to a new home. I definitely felt like
I was making a sacrifice for my career.

Damon is definitely not good at housekeeping. He makes an effort, but
the last time I got home from tour, none of the light bulbs worked. There
was one bulb that he had to change and take with him whenever he went
from the kitchen to the bathroom. There was no food in the fridge and dirty
laundry everywhere. But he functions like this. I'm not going to pick up after him.

Q. *Bassist Annie Holland quit during Lollapalooza. What happened?*

A. She left on good terms. It was really her saying, "I love you guys, but I
don't want to do this anymore." She was tired of the grind. Either you like
this lifestyle or you don't.

Q. *So what's coming up for Elastica in 1996?*

A. We just recorded a single ["I Want You"] with Flood and Alan
Moulder, and we're gearing up to work on a new album. It's exciting because it's a new band with Abby. The dynamic has changed. With Annie,
there was a particular sound that she favored, and anything outside of that
she didn't really want to try. She was into the more punk stuff. I think we'll
be getting beyond the guitar, bass, and drums stuff, using more keyboards
and doing more with the rhythms and longer song structures. "I Want You"
is five minutes long, but I don't think it's going to bore anyone to tears.
Ultimately, everything we do is always going to be defined by our [punk-
pop] aesthetic. We played to a lot of people last year, and I'm totally happy
to stay at the level we're on as long as people are interested in our music. In

many ways I don't want to get any bigger. We're not compromised by the mainstream, but I feel like we've reached an audience. We've connected.

The Building of a Buzz Band
Request, January 1995

PEOPLE IN THE music world obsess over that elusive quality known as "buzz," but it really isn't so mysterious: At the most basic level, buzz means that someone gets excited about a band, tells his or her friends, and they tell their friends, and so on, and so on, until so many people are talking about the group that the major labels come calling. Eventually, if the band is lucky enough, it may even land on MTV, mainstream radio, and the *Billboard* albums chart. Sometimes a buzz develops spontaneously, by word of mouth, and sometimes it's manufactured by record company publicists and marketers. But it usually involves a measure of luck nonetheless.

The recent alternative-rock boom has sped up the timetable for this process considerably, and there is no better example than the buzz that built around Veruca Salt, carrying the band from its tentative first gigs in small Chicago rock clubs to the pop charts in a mere fourteen months. This is a trip that's well worth examining in detail, as much for what it says about this promising young band as for what it tells us about the music machinery circa 1995.

NEW YEAR'S EVE, 1992–1993

Nina Gordon first hears Louise Post sing and play guitar over the phone when a mutual friend hooks them up, knowing that the two women are each looking to form a band. The daughter of a Chicago attorney, Gordon, twenty-five, studied art history and French literature at Tufts. Post, twenty-six, grew up in St. Louis and studied English at Barnard before moving to Chicago to work with the New Crimes Productions theater company. Early in the new year, the two meet in person and decide to join forces. They search in vain for a suitable female rhythm section before settling on two men: bassist Steve Lack, twenty-four, and drummer Jim Shapiro, twenty-nine.

A veteran of several garage bands, Lack answers Veruca's "bassist wanted" ad in the *Chicago Reader*. Shapiro happens to be Gordon's brother

(Nina takes their mother's surname). He played with a band while attending Yale and is pressed into service when his sister and her friend can't find a suitable drummer for their new group, which takes its name from the bratty rich girl in the film *Willy Wonka and the Chocolate Factory.* In the movie, Veruca Salt makes no secret of her desires. "I want the world," she sings. "I want the whole world! / I want to lock it all up in my pocket . . . Give it to me now!"

Veruca Salt the band is just as ambitious, and this attitude prompts derision from cynical Chicago scenesters. But the band members bristle at anyone who questions their commitment. "I decided five months prior to meeting Nina that I was going to do whatever I could to make sure that I could make records," Post says. "I didn't know if I'd have a band or if it would be a solo thing. But when we met, I knew it was something serious. We played together for nine months, three or four days a week, before meeting Steve, and then we kept on working as a band. It wasn't like falling into it for me. This is the dream of my life. I always wanted to make really good records."

SEPTEMBER 1993

Veruca Salt's story is inextricably linked with that of Jim Powers. The thirty-two-year-old music lover stumbled into the business while studying journalism and political science at Iowa State University in the mid-1980s. A part-time job at a club in Ames led to a gig booking the joint, which in turn resulted in jobs with the Country Music Association, Chicago concert promoters Jam Productions, RCA Records, and finally Zoo Entertainment. As an A&R executive or talent scout, Powers signed the Cowboy Junkies to RCA and the Pooh Sticks to Zoo, but he left the company in 1992 when he tired of the corporate bureaucracy.

In the fall of 1993, Powers is living off his savings and just starting his own independent label, Minty Fresh Records. The company's first three releases are modest but well-received singles by Chicagoans Stump the Host, the British band Hit Parade, and Louisville, Kentucky's Love Jones. The aspiring label head is also booking local bands for events such as Around the Coyote, a weekend art fair in Chicago's rapidly gentrifying Wicker Park neighborhood. When a group scheduled to play a prime Saturday night slot backs out, Leroy Bach, the bassist in Liz Phair's band, recommends Veruca Salt as the replacement. Powers calls Post, and Post brings him a four-song demo.

"My first impression was that these songs were really outstanding," Powers says. "They got the slot, and subsequently we talked about recording together. After I saw a few more gigs, I realized that eighty percent of their songs were of album quality. I thought, 'This would be perfect for our first full-length release.'"

DECEMBER 1993

Critic Bill Wyman pens the first major article about Veruca Salt in the *Chicago Reader*. "To some extent, the band sounds as young as it is," he writes. "But there's still something about Veruca that's arresting." Meanwhile, Geffen approaches Powers about working in A&R. "They were aware of my singles and my past work," he says, "and I was interested in the possibility, but I wanted to get my label off the ground." Undaunted, the company continues pursuing Powers into 1994.

JANUARY 1994

Island and Sony A&R reps approach Veruca Salt. Geffen executive Luke Wood sees the band perform with Phair on New Year's Eve, and he, too, is impressed. The band members think this major-label interest is premature; they want their first release to be independently distributed. They begin recording for Minty Fresh with Brad Wood, Phair's producer and drummer, and the co-owner of Wicker Park's Idful Studio. Recording drags on after the first ten-day period, resuming whenever Wood is available in between recording and touring commitments with Phair.

The winter months are a slow time for national touring acts and a good time to catch local bands. Partly because of this, and partly because they want to see if Wyman is full of crap, the rock critics for the *Chicago Tribune* (Greg Kot) and the *Chicago Sun-Times* (that would be me) go to see Veruca Salt at Lounge Ax. The gig results in two favorable reviews. "It was clear on Saturday that a world of possibilities is open to the young Chicago quartet. Concentrating on a dozen catchy, well-crafted guitar anthems, the band's set was galvanizing, succinct, and thoroughly undeniable," I write.

"In some ways, their inexperience shows: At one point, Post asked that the stage lights be turned up because she needed to see the guitar frets while she was playing. But the band attacked its songs with confidence and an impressive control of dynamics, and Gordon and Post have instinctual talents as songwriters. Tunes such as 'Spider Man,' 'Seether,' and 'All Hail

Me' boast killer hooks, and they're infused with a biting wit and a sharp, feminist perspective. The quartet has drawn easy comparisons to the Breeders, but you can hear Veruca working to develop a distinctive voice. The guitarists harmonize effortlessly, and their combined vocals are uniquely breathy and lilting. Not that Veruca's music is without an edge— Lack and Shapiro propel the rhythms with Ramones-like intensity, and Gordon and Post rip holes in the melodies with buzz saw guitar leads and bursts of concentrated noise. Adopting the persona of a bullying boyfriend in 'Seether,' they sing, 'I try to keep her on a short leash / I try to calm her down / I try to cram her into the ground.' Meanwhile, their ferocious guitars cut like Lorena Bobbitt's knife."

MARCH 1994

Minty Fresh releases Veruca Salt's debut single, "Seether" / "All Hail Me." The label presses two thousand copies; only a handful are sent to the music press, and none are sent to commercial radio. The band performs at the South by Southwest Music and Media Conference in Austin, Texas, landing a showcase in the early evening, a time when the competition is slim. Partly because of this, and partly because they want to see if the Chicago critics are full of crap, many music writers from around the country attend the gig. Most of them are impressed, and many write favorable reviews of their own.

APRIL–JUNE 1994

Veruca Salt plays short tours throughout the Midwest and continues honing its chops onstage. The press is almost universally favorable.

JULY 1994

Veruca travels to Europe for the first time and begins to build a following in England. The gigs result in positive coverage in the *New Music Express* and *Melody Maker*, and the trip includes a taping for the BBC. In a one-week period back in America, three FM rock stations—KROQ in Los Angeles, KNDD in Seattle, and WKQX in Chicago—add "Seether" to their play lists. "My understanding is that Q101 was first, but it's almost irrelevant because they were all within hours of each other, if not days," Powers says. You might think Powers is thrilled by the attention, but he's not: Veruca's album won't be released until September 27, and the single has been sold out since April.

"In terms of timing, it would have been better if they were on it four weeks later. From those three stations, it spread—because lots of other stations look at their play lists—and it was all premature, because there were no records in the stores!" Powers says. Why the interest from radio? He cites similar successes by Beck and the Offspring. "Commercial alternative radio—for whatever reason and independent of any artists—has decided that it's cool to occasionally play songs by bands on labels that people have never heard of and that they can't even buy."

AUGUST 1994

Geffen and Virgin mount a bidding war to sign Veruca Salt. The band members are overwhelmed. They talk with several management companies and sign with New York City–based Q Prime, whose head honchos, Cliff Bernstein and Peter Mensch, are best known for managing Metallica, Queensrÿche, and Def Leppard. They also hire a New York publicity firm, Nasty Little Man, to field the increasing number of requests for interviews. I call the aptly named "Nasty" and am given the royal runaround—"The band isn't doing much press right now," I'm told, despite the fact that it seems to be in every magazine I pick up—so I phone Gordon and Post at home. We somehow manage to get together for lunch without the help of a publicist, and they insist on picking up the tab.

At one point Gordon explains why the band has been turning down requests to appear on the late-night TV talk shows ("We don't think we're ready for network television yet") and to tape "liners" for radio stations (these are recorded introductions along the lines of, "Hi, we're Veruca Salt, and you're listening to *station name here*"). "Right now, we're little media-hype-y kids, so it makes sense to have us on the radio," she says. "Whereas four years from now, it might sound really uncool."

I ask Gordon and Post if, given their still somewhat indie attitudes, all of the high-powered management and publicity muscle is really necessary. "I was worried with them being strange toward us as women—not having managed many women and being famous for managing these metal bands," Post says of Q Prime. "But in fact they treated us on a more equal level than the other people we had come in contact with." Adds Gordon: "Basically, what it came down to was they just seemed smarter than everyone else we met." Q Prime has a close relationship with Virgin, and sources at Geffen predict that Veruca will sign with Virgin.

Success does not seem to have gone to the bandleaders' heads, but others in the Chicago rock scene disagree. Earlier in the year, Veruca Salt agreed to record a cover of the Knack's "My Sharona" for Pravda Records. The Chicago independent label was preparing the third volume in its series of goofy albums featuring local bands covering the hits of the '70s. Several weeks before our interview—while the group's debut album was being prepared for manufacturing—Post called Pravda honcho Ken Goodman to say that the band had decided not to release the song after all. "They thought it was so good that it would interfere with their second or third single," Goodman says. "I tried to reason with her. I've had Smashing Pumpkins on one of these records, and it didn't interfere with their success. But she didn't want to talk about it any further and said I'd have to deal with their manager." Goodman called Q Prime and got nothing but threats. "They have a lot more money for legal fees than I do," he sighs.

Veruca defends its actions by saying that if the album had come out as scheduled a few months back, there would have been no problem. But independent releases are *always* late, and it's usually no big deal. "The fact was, it wasn't smart for us to do it anymore," Post says unapologetically. "It was important that we protect ourselves." Adds Gordon: "I like 'My Sharona.' But if we put out a second single and [radio programmers] don't want to play it because they think 'My Sharona' is cooler, then I have to hear 'My Sharona' on Q–101." That doesn't make Goodman feel any better. "I don't need this bullshit from Veruca Salt, Inc.," he says. "I think the hype machine just went a little extreme on them."

SEPTEMBER 1994

Powers signs a contract to work in A&R for Geffen, although his deal allows him to continue to sign bands to Minty Fresh. "Bands that sign to Minty Fresh don't have to sign to Geffen," he says. "It's a way of continuing a relationship with the band if they outgrow Minty Fresh, but they don't have to move up to Geffen if they don't want to." Named after a line in AC/DC's "You Shook Me All Night Long," Veruca Salt's debut album, *American Thighs*, is released on Minty Fresh. With money borrowed from Geffen, Powers is able to meet the initial demand for the disc, manufacturing and selling a hundred thousand copies in the first few weeks. The band is still free to sign with any label, though there is a tiny Geffen emblem on the back of its CD.

OCTOBER 1994

Veruca Salt signs with Geffen for a deal that sources say is worth half a million dollars. *Entertainment Weekly* declares Geffen "the winner of the week" for signing "the next Green Day." Geffen recalls all remaining Minty Fresh copies of *American Thighs* and replaces them with official Geffen copies. MTV begins to air the video for "Seether," and Veruca Salt joins its new label mates Hole on a high-profile five-week tour.

Throughout the band's rise, nasty graffiti about Veruca Salt has been scrawled on the bathroom walls of many Chicago rock clubs. Now a second wave of graffiti appears, accusing the group's attackers of spiteful jealousy. This prompts Gordon to crack that the band's debut album is actually its comeback effort.

NOVEMBER 1994

American Thighs enters *Billboard*'s Top 200 albums chart at No. 171 with a bullet. Veruca Salt doesn't have the whole world locked up in its pocket quite yet, but it may well be on its way.

7 LOLLAPALOOZA NATION

THOUGH I HOLD THAT NOSTALGIA IS the enemy of all great rock 'n' roll, and I see plenty of skepticism in my reports from the front while Lollapalooza was still a going concern, I have to admit that I feel a faint tinge of—regret? No, more like longing—for the musical diversity, optimistic energy, and boundless enthusiasm that the traveling, day-long, alternative rock fest represented at its very best. (At its worst, like the year Alice In Chains headlined, or what it had become by the time it ended in 1997, it was just another big, long, corporate rock concert. It remains to be seen where the revitalized concert circa 2003 falls.)

Woodstock '94 clearly tried to capture the Lollapalooza vibe, and it failed miserably. While it did not end in trashed ATMs and burning tractor trailers like the 1999 concert (and isn't it amazing that promoter Michael Lang got to pull the same con a third time?), it did set a new low for the blatant disregard of live music fans as anything but willing sheep ready to be fleeced for every last dollar while being bombarded by the forces of marketing. It finalized the perverse blueprint for the giant corporate concert promoter Clear Channel Entertainment, which dominates the industry today, the Microsoft of the live music world. Looking back at it makes me miss Lollapalooza all the more.

About Sonic Youth and Lollapalooza '95: I first saw the band ten years earlier, in the days before 1985's *Bad Moon Rising,* and I was a dedicated fan. By the time it headlined Lollapalooza, I'd become convinced that it had succumbed to the mistake of believing its own press, which was almost universally laudatory (this being the band that "discovered" Nirvana and "invented" alternative rock), despite the fact that it had just released its worst album, *Washing Machine.* I had written many pieces about the group through the years (see Chapter Nine for an example), but the band's two guitarists took great exception to my observation that people fled the concert in droves when it took the stage at Lollapalooza. They fired back in their Web diaries for *SPIN* online, and their comments were reprinted in the book, *Online Diaries: The Lollapalooza '95 Tour Journals* (Soft Skull Press, 1996). Greatly at odds with their stance as maverick trailblazers of the avant underground, it's remarkable how much these Boho giants cared about one sentence in a daily newspaper review.

"The *Sun-Times* has as music editor this guy from Hoboken who I remember seeing hang around named Jim DeRogatis," Thurston Moore wrote. "He used to write for this persistently weak bland-zine called *Jersey Beat* and for some reason unbeknownst to me, HATES us. I'm pretty sure it's just becuz he thinks we suck musically but he KILLED us in the paper saying we were inept, etc. charlatans hiding behind a silly light show. It was very mean-spirited and made us feel like shit. All I know about this guy is he used to play in a joke band called Ex-Lion Tamers who did all Wire covers. . . . As a rock writer this guy is unremarkable at best so my only feelings are what I usually share for hapless journalists of this sort—no writer should be protected by a byline if his or her goal is to 'hurt.'"

Added Lee Ranaldo: "Rock-Crit Crap: The saga of Chicago 'Writer'/DJ Jim DeRogatis and his 'vendetta' against SY continues. After he wrote that crappy review of our show Thurston left a msg on his answering machine, which he proceeded to play on the air during his next radio show. He went on to declaim about how 'twenty thousand kids left during Sonic Youth's show' that night. Yeah, right. This line about crowds leaving has been picked up by every empty headed small town journalist in the country. I am amazed at the poor quality of most of the regional press. The same whitebread middle America article is being written all across the country in these small-time papers. These guys (and they mainly are guys) seem to read the major wire svce. articles and basically plagiarize their own for the regional press without thinking at all."

This section ends with a piece on Jane's Addiction, because no consideration of Lollapalooza would be complete without a nod to its visionary founder, Perry Farrell, just as no book about alternative rock would be worth much without a nod to Jane's, who were pioneering in every way, good and bad. Farrell never did realize his ambitious vision of a world tour called the Jubilee, which is sort of a shame. But giving us Lollapalooza—a model of how good an American rock festival can be if it manages to minimize industry interference—was enough of a gift, and for that we should thank him.

Lollapalooza: Alternative Celebration or Big Business as Usual?
Request, June 1993

LOLLAPALOOZA MAY BE marketed as a slacker version of Woodstock, but behind the scenes, there's nothing alternative about it. Instead of celebrating the independent spirit, the traveling music festival is big business as usual in the music industry.

The day-long concert was launched in 1991 as the brainchild of former Jane's Addiction leader Perry Farrell. Farrell still owns a third of Lollapalooza, Inc., along with his manager, Ted Gardner, and the Los Angeles–based William Morris Agency, which acquired its share when it merged with the younger, hipper Triad Booking Agency in late 1992.

William Morris is one of the country's biggest talent bookers, with a roster ranging from Air Supply to Whitney Houston. Not surprisingly, six of the nine bands on the main stage at Lollapalooza '93 are William Morris acts: Rage Against the Machine, Tool, Front 242, Arrested Development, Fishbone, and Primus. (Of the remaining bands, Babes In Toyland and Dinosaur Jr. are booked by Twin Towers Touring, and Alice In Chains is booked by the powerhouse International Creative Management.)

Lollapalooza '91 was undeniably Farrell's show, but the wiggy singer has distanced himself from the day-to-day running of the last two tours. His new group, Porno for Pyros, played a few low-key shows on the smaller second stage in '92, but the band is noticeably absent from the bill this year, even though it just released its Warner Bros. debut. In a 1992 interview, Joey Ramone said Farrell wanted the Ramones to be included in the lineup, but Triad vetoed the veteran punk band because it's booked by another agency. The Red Hot Chili Peppers, the 1992 headliners, complained in *Rolling Stone* that the bill was "way too male" and said they wanted L7 to perform, but promoters dismissed the female quartet, saying it "didn't mean anything" in terms of the draw. This year, the only predominantly female group, Babes In Toyland, is performing on just half the tour.

All of the main-stage bands record for major labels, and so do many of the acts on the second stage. That platform was conceived as a showcase for local up-and-comers, but it has partly become a forum for established acts in need of a promotional boost. This year the acts included Cell (which records for D.G.C.), Mercury Rev (Columbia), and Unrest (4AD, which is distributed by Warner Bros.).

Perhaps the most telling evidence of the festival's big-business attitude is the way promoters treated fans in Chicago. Concert organizers put tickets on sale in the Windy City before announcing the lineup. As a result many fans shelled out thirty-five dollars a ticket believing rumors that Nirvana would headline, and they were no doubt disappointed when the bill was finally announced. Concert spokesman Ted Mico says the Chicago sale was an experiment to find out how much the Lollapalooza name is worth, and he notes that even without the lineup being made public, some twenty thousand tickets sold in four hours. "People finally got the idea of what the whole thing is about. It really isn't a package tour, it's something you go to for the day, like a renaissance fair for delinquents."

Ironically, Chicago's World Music Theatre is one of the least hospitable places Lollapalooza visits. The second stage and celebrated "village" containing arts and crafts exhibits, political displays, and ethnic food booths can be a lot of fun when they're spread out at spacious green venues such as the Blossom Arts Center in Cleveland and Harriett Island in Minneapolis–St. Paul. In Chicago, these attractions are crammed onto two tiny asphalt lots, and many concertgoers complained in '92 that they couldn't even find them. The only tent that was impossible to miss was the Lollapalooza merchandise booth, which sold T-shirts as a nifty memento at the not-so-alternative price of twenty-three dollars apiece, or thirty dollars for the more elaborate tie-dye version.

Rock of Ageless
The *Chicago Sun-Times*, July 17, 1994

COMING AT THE end of a week that brought Pink Floyd, the Eagles, and a new Rolling Stones album, Lollapalooza has never seemed more vital.

The traveling, day-long, alternative music festival is no less of a big business than the corporations behind any of those cynical and graying rock giants; the five-dollar burritos and twenty-five-dollar T-shirts are testament to that. But the energy of the performers onstage and that of the fans who filled the World Music Theatre on Friday and Saturday could power the city of Chicago for a year.

In terms of booking and the other midway attractions, Lollapalooza '94 is a return to form. Friday's show had plenty of highlights, starting with the first main stage set by the Boredoms. The sextet from Osaka, Japan, mixed the energy of hardcore punk, the invention of free jazz, and the flamboyant stage tactics of street theater. Nearly unlistenable at times on record, the band was transcendent live.

The Los Angeles quartet L7 was just as powerful in a more straightforward punk-rock style. The group tore through its set in classic Ramones fashion ("1–2–3–4!"), climaxing with the anthemic "Andres" and "Pretend We're Dead." The only question was why L7 chose to decorate the stage with giant Styrofoam snowflakes and a huge snowman in ninety-five-degree heat.

Later in the afternoon, Oklahoma's psychedelic rockers the Flaming Lips drew a huge crowd to the smaller second stage. A roadie used several big fans to blow bubbles over the crowd as the group launched into swirling, trippy tunes such as "Moth in the Incubator." The bubbles gently falling on the frantic moshers and bodysurfers was one of the day's weirdest images.

Meanwhile, a psychedelic veteran from another era and style held forth on the main stage. Aided by no fewer than fifteen members of the P-Funk All Stars, George Clinton delivered an hour of his uplifting "rhythm and rhyme." "They say this is an alternative show," Clinton said. "Well, we're some alternative people!" The All Stars' groove held Lollapalosers in its sway, and the crowd seemed sorry to see Clinton go after only an hour. Dr. Funkenstein left fans chanting, "Ain't no party like the P-Funk party, and the P-Funk party don't stop." But every act wasn't quite so successful.

The most polished thing about the Breeders was its well-coordinated stage gear: Everything was either spray-painted gold or covered in gold tarps. The group tried to show its underground credibility by covering a song by the cult band Sebadoh and dedicating a tune to Chicago producer Steve Albini. But the Breeders only really rocked in a satisfying way during their left-field hit, "Cannonball."

Nick Cave's solemn goth-rock didn't jibe with the afternoon's sunny, upbeat vibe, and New York rappers A Tribe Called Quest failed to show the musical diversity that marks their albums. Of course the best thing about Lollapalooza is that you're free to roam whenever the sounds aren't holding your interest, and this year the midway was more spread out, thanks to promoters claiming a chunk of the parking lot. There were lots of attractions dedicated to grabbing adolescent dollars, but there was also plenty to do for free. The biggest hits were the "rain rooms," tents fixed with sprinklers that sprayed a cooling mist on concertgoers. Computer geeks demonstrated "morphing" (the special effect used in Michael Jackson's "Black and White" video), and a virtual reality ride called the Chameleon drew long lines.

Lollapalooza's headliners have to be good to get a rise out of fans after a long and action-packed day in the sun. The Beastie Boys suffered from following Clinton, and they weren't nearly as clever, punky, or funky as they thought they were. Still, the trio's loud grooves and obnoxious shtick were well-received, especially the current high-octane hit, "Sabotage."

Following the Beasties and ending the day, the Smashing Pumpkins were determined to give their hometown their all. Billy Corgan even got to the World early and made a guest appearance with Milwaukee weirdoes the Frogs on the second stage.

Art-rockers at heart, the Pumpkins opened their ninety-minute set slowly, lulling the crowd with gentle, spacey sounds as spiraling lights and fog set the mood. But things soon picked up as the band ran through the hits from the phenomenally successful *Siamese Dream*. Corgan relished his vocal on "Cherub Rock," a song about the alternative scene, and drummer Jimmy Chamberlain was as dynamic as ever on "Today" and the new single "Rocket."

"I'm happy to be home for a couple of days," Corgan said. "Hopefully you more than anybody else in the world understands these songs. A lot of them are about this part of the world."

Nearly every tune included a moment when the house lights were turned on to expose the sold-out crowd of thirty thousand. Corgan seemed to be fascinated that all those people—his peers and neighbors—were watching him play. But he also seemed to be saying, "Look, I'm not that much different from any of you."

That attitude was echoed in different ways by nearly every artist who performed. That's what makes Lollapalooza different from the Eagles, Pink Floyd, and the Stones in 1994. And that's what makes it great rock 'n' roll.

Taking Stock of the Muddy Mess
The *Chicago Sun-Times*, August 16, 1994

SAUGERTIES, NEW YORK—Wrapping up three days of music, mud, and mess, a question lingers over Woodstock '94: Who ever thought this was a good idea?

Over the course of the weekend-long music-and-hype fest, the crowd peaked at what officials estimated as three hundred to three hundred fifty thousand people. Combined with a day and a half of rain, this human onslaught turned the once-scenic eight-hundred-forty-acre Winston Farm into a garbage-strewn disaster area. Calcutta never looked quite so good.

None of this should have come as a surprise to organizers: It rains outside. There is a reason why God made indoor arenas and rock clubs. But the twenty-fifth anniversary concert was ill-conceived from the start.

This wasn't because Woodstock wasn't worth commemorating, and it wasn't necessarily because of the much-maligned and ubiquitous corporate sponsorship. No, the problem with this Woodstock (and arguably with the one in 1969 as well) was that there wasn't *enough* corporate sponsorship— or at least enough forethought and money spent on preparations by concert organizers. If AT&T, IBM, or Microsoft had been a little more involved, maybe the phones would have worked, the food supplies would have been adequate, and the portable potties wouldn't have overflowed, resulting in literal rivers of shit running through the campgrounds.

Instead everything went to hell. Garbage pickup and toilet service stopped within the first few hours of the concert. Clean water was scarce, and many of the food tents had nothing left to sell by Sunday morning.

Back home in Chicago, eight hundred forty acres may sound like a lot. But Winston Farm wasn't nearly big enough to hold all of the concertgoers and campers. Tents were pitched inches away from one another, and people had to sleep in ditches, on the sides of the roads, and under tractor-trailer trucks. It's possible that this site could have accommodated seventy thousand. But the number of two hundred fifty thousand was pushed by greedy promoters and approved by politicians in a county desperate for something (anything) to boost the economy. "This is like trying to get ten pounds of stuff in a five-pound bag," the exhausted Saugerties police chief, William Kimble, sighed during one press conference.

Site preparation was a joke, and lax security virtually invited the additional hundred thousand gate-crashers. Most of the farm wasn't lighted, and the ground hadn't been cleared of stumps and other obstacles. Thousands twisted their ankles or slipped in the red clay mud. At the height of the concert, medical workers were treating a new patient every twenty seconds. In '94 as in '69, promoters told the media to focus on people pulling together and making the best of things. "A reaffirmation of the human spirit," co-promoter John Scher called it. But what was the alternative? Were concertgoers supposed to revert to the primitive savages running around in *The Lord of the Flies*?

"This was a royal rip-off, and I'd like to get my hands on the promoters," said twenty-five-year-old John Lail of Vermont. But as he spoke, another concertgoer shouted him down. "This is Woodstock, man," the muddy long-hair shouted. "Stop whining!"

The new Woodstock Generation is certainly media-savvy: A reporter walking through the crowd with a notebook was bound to hear several choruses of "Interview me!" Many concertgoers greeted any and all TV cameras by baring a part of their anatomy—women's chests and men's buttocks—and shouting, "Go naked!" But the best comment I saw came from a banner on the side of a van that had traveled from San Francisco: WE'RE NOT HIPPIES. WE'RE NOT GEN X. WE'RE JUST HANGIN'.

Hanging—and spending. Hundreds of merchants paid three thousand dollars each for a tent, and they sold everything from African food to clothing made from hemp to tambourines and bongo drums. The farm became a giant shopping mall, and the twentysomething crowd seemed right at home. The only impediment to commerce was the dumb exchange system that organizers had set up, presumably to keep a handle on and take their cut of any cash that changed hands. In order to buy food or merchandise, concertgoers had to buy special Woodstock scrip. Made of what seemed to be tin, the phony money was issued as ten- or twenty-dollar coins adorned with an image of a construction crane and the main stage. Don't ask me why.

I'm more than seven hundred words into this story and I just realized that I have yet to mention the music. Most of the bands on day one were relatively sedate, with the exception of the lightweight pop-metal group Jackyl. The lead singer tried to outdo Jimi Hendrix by setting a wooden stool on fire, then slashing it with a chainsaw. No fan of subtlety, he also exposed his genitalia during a tune called "She Loves My Cock." Big whup. Del Amitri, James, Sheryl Crow, and the Violent Femmes played sets that were slightly more effective musically, but only slightly. The hip-hop troupe Arrested Development was the band that best updated the spirit of '69, reworking Sly Stone for a joyous version of "People Everyday." But the amped-up California punk trio Green Day best nailed the vibe of '94: Band members taunted the crowd and started a giant mud fight, simultaneously protesting the conditions and celebrating them.

Much of Sunday was a procession of geezers, with the Allman Brothers, Traffic, Santana, and Bob Dylan delivering tight but unextraordinary sets. More successful was a morning performance by the Sisters of Glory, gospel singers Thelma Houston, CeCe Peniston, Phoebe Snow, and the incomparable Mavis Staples. The preening of Spin Doctors singer Chris Barron was as annoying as always, and their funky ten-minute jam on Joni Mitchell's "Woodstock" was probably the weekend's musical low point.

For me the most memorable experience was listening to Porno for Pyros as I hiked through the back campground. The low lands had turned into a lake of mud, and tents, clothing, garbage, and sewage floated by in free-flowing streams. A smoky haze from the campfires hung at head level as I spied a girl sitting waist-deep in a puddle, bathing in the filthy, shit-tainted water as a line of hikers walked over a makeshift bridge and ogled her dirty breasts. I have never been much of a fan of Porno for Pyros' musical mix of sex, sadism, and surrealism, but it seemed like the perfect soundtrack for the moment.

In the end, the music wasn't really the story; in fact it was barely an afterthought. The members of the Chicago band They Came In Droves thought they were lucky when they were pegged as one of three regional semifinalists in line for an opening slot at the concert. Their tape was ultimately rejected by PolyGram, one of the promoters, but four band members and four guests got to go to the concert anyway. They set up camp about a hundred yards away from the main stage on Thursday and watched the chaos build. "There was no control at all," said band manager Brett Kloepfer, twenty-six. "I thought it was very dangerous the whole time. It was insane."

Kloepfer said people were rude, shoving and pushing and walking right over their sleeping bags and camping equipment. "There sure wasn't any peace and love going on." David Prince, editor of Chicago's techno fanzine *Reactor*, enjoyed the late-night raves at the south stage—his personal highlight was hearing the Orb perform at sunrise on Saturday—but he agreed with complaints about the promoters and found the spirit of the crowd lacking. "There was no vibe here at all," he said.

The comments of twenty-four-year-old Oak Park resident Laura Anthony also seemed typical of the prevailing sentiment. "It was a mess, a muddy mess," she said. "But I guess I'm glad I was here, 'cause now I can say I was at Woodstock. Like a bumper sticker: I SURVIVED WOODSTOCK."

But survival should never have seemed like such an accomplishment. In 1969 no one was expecting five hundred thousand people, and the spirit of Woodstock was born from the resulting adversity. This time promoters created the problems. This is not to say that plenty of people didn't have a meaningful experience despite it all. They met and bonded with each other through music and the offer of a helping hand. But that had nothing to do with the organizers, who were all too quick to take credit and discount the screw-ups. Even those who enjoyed Woodstock '94 would have been within their rights to storm the stage, hog-tie David Crosby, and drop his bloated carcass right on top of co-promoter Michael Lang. Because they were had.

People paid one hundred thirty-five dollars—one-hundred forty-five with Ticketmaster service charges—to sit in the mud and be extras in a movie. And when they wanted to go home, they waited five or six hours for shuttle buses to take them to the parking lots. Garth Brooks fans or the symphony orchestra crowd wouldn't have put up with this. But rock fans are used to getting ripped off.

The real story is that rock fans deserve better than this. They deserve better than Woodstock '94.

Women Power Lollapalooza '95
The *Chicago Sun-Times*, July 17, 1995

ACCUSED IN THE past of favoring testosterone-crazed rockers, Lollapalooza '95 was clearly fueled by estrogen.

When this year's edition of the day-long, traveling, alternative music festival came to a packed New World Music Theatre on Saturday, the main stage belonged to a trio of women: Irish soul singer Sinéad O'Connor, the always controversial Courtney Love, and Kim Gordon, long the strongest link in the over-rated New York noise band Sonic Youth. But estrogen power was in evidence elsewhere, too, including the smaller second stage, where Georgia Hubley powered a galvanizing set by Yo La Tengo and singer Carla Bruce of Chicago's Sabalon Glitz performed while flanked by two go-go dancers adorned in silver body paint.

For the second time this summer, horrible traffic delays on Interstate 57 on the way to Tinley Park cost me an opening set, so I missed starting act the Mighty Mighty Bosstones. (New rule of thumb: Take the earliest departure time for the World that sounds reasonable, then add an extra forty-five minutes.) I arrived just in time for Chicago's Jesus Lizard. Unbeatable in smaller settings, the band's noise-rock assault was lost on the massive stage at the World. Its powerful musical barrage dissipated by the time it reached the lawn, and singer David Yow was unusually sedate, keeping his charms in his pants and minimizing the body-surfing.

Beck indulged himself with a half-hour of noisy noodling, then gave the crowd what it wanted with a lackluster version of the hit "Loser." O'Connor was the day's first revelation. Fronting a tight five-piece band, she came back with a vengeance, reworking some of the songs from *Universal Mother* into atmospheric trip-hop grooves, and turning others into dynamic showcases that soared from quiet a cappella intros to hard-rocking assaults.

Two disappointing sets followed. Pavement's music lacked focus or drive, and Cypress Hill was tedious in its single-minded devotion to lauding marijuana. (The rappers do get points, however, for a creative stage set featuring a giant inflatable Buddha sporting a big pot leaf on his belly.) Hole was obviously the crowd's favorite, and Love didn't let the fans down as she led her band through a precise, no-nonsense thirteen-song set which climaxed in a solo version of "Penny Royal Tea," a song she co-wrote with her late husband, Nirvana leader Kurt Cobain. "Don't you ever fucking forget!" she screamed.

Fans may not forget Cobain, but they seem to have forgotten Sonic Youth's status as influential alternative gurus. Concertgoers left the World in droves throughout the headlining performance by the New York noise rockers. I can't say I blame them, as Sonic Youth hid behind psychedelic lighting to deliver monochromatic and uninspired versions of pretentious art-rock tunes such as "Pacific Coast Highway" and "Expressway to Yr Skull."

As always Lollapalooza was as much about attitude as it was about music, and I'll close my report from the festival's fifth visit to Chicago with some random observations along those lines.

- Number of times Sinéad O'Connor stopped her set to praise Courtney Love-Cobain: Three. Number of times Love-Cobain praised O'Connor: Zero. Whatever happened to *mutual* admiration?
- Best T-shirt slogans: SMASHING PUMPKINS: ALTITUDE, NOT ATTITUDE; JEFFREY DAHMER: FINE YOUNG CANNIBAL; and I ❤ ALTERNATIVE ROCK, hand-drawn and worn with a sarcastic sneer.
- Most frequently imitated star: Love. There were at least two dozen Courtney wannabes walking around in torn baby-doll dresses.
- No sense of history: "This is a song from our first album."—Kim Gordon introduces "Bull in the Heather," which is actually from Sonic Youth's twelfth release; "This song was written before most of you were born."—Yo La Tengo's Ira Kaplan introduces a cover of "Tired of Waiting for You" by the Kinks; "This is a song about a jerk from here. I have a relationship with this town that's pure S&M."—Love introduces "Violet" with a reference to former beau Billy Corgan.
- Coolest sight backstage: toddler Frances Bean Cobain dancing to the sounds of Chicago space rockers Sabalon Glitz. She looks just like her father; it's all in those eyes.

··

LOLLAPALOOZA LINEUPS

1991
Jane's Addiction
Siouxsie and the Banshees (some dates)
Living Color
Nine Inch Nails (some dates)
Fishbone
The Violent Femmes
Ice-T and Body Count
The Butthole Surfers
The Rollins Band

1992
Red Hot Chili Peppers
Ministry
Ice Cube
Soundgarden
The Jesus and Mary Chain
Pearl Jam
Lush
Temple of the Dog (some dates)

1993
Primus
Alice In Chains
Dinosaur Jr.
Fishbone
Arrested Development
Front 242
Babes In Toyland (some dates)
Tool (some dates)
Rage Against the Machine

1994
The Smashing Pumpkins
The Beastie Boys

George Clinton and the P-Funk All Stars
The Breeders
A Tribe Called Quest
Nick Cave and the Bad Seeds (some dates)
L7
The Boredoms (some dates)
Green Day (some dates)

1995
Sonic Youth
Hole
Cypress Hill
Pavement
Sinéad O'Connor (some dates)
Elastica (some dates)
Moby (some dates)
Superchunk (some dates)
Beck
The Jesus Lizard
The Mighty Mighty Bosstones

1996
Metallica
Soundgarden
The Cocteau Twins (some dates)
Waylon Jennings (some dates)
Cheap Trick (some dates)
The Violent Femmes (some dates)
The Tea Party (some dates)
The Wu-Tang Clan (some dates)
Rage Against the Machine (some dates)
Steve Earle (some dates)
Devo (some dates)
The Ramones
Rancid
The Screaming Trees
Psychotica

1997
Orbital
The Prodigy
The Orb
Tricky
Tool
Snoop Dogg

....

Been Caught Squealing
New Times Los Angeles, November 27, 1997

PERRY FARRELL IS looking more than a little unsteady on his feet. Part of the problem is that he's wearing eight-inch-high platform shoes, a sartorial choice bound to give pause to even the most sure-footed of men. The other part is no doubt due to the bottle of wine that he's clutching, waving around, and spilling on fans who are seated in the balcony of the Aragon, the Capone-era Chicago ballroom that's the third stop on Jane's Addiction's Relapse Tour (or the fifth, if you count the two surprise Los Angeles shows that kicked things off last month). Before his own band takes the stage, Farrell has come up to the VIP section—filled on this night with assorted press, radio, and industry insiders—in order to witness a short, unannounced set by Windy City natives the Smashing Pumpkins, a gig performed to repay an old debt: Back in 1990, only four shows into the Pumpkins' career, the quartet pulled some serious strings and got the break of a lifetime, landing the opening slot for a Jane's gig at Cabaret Metro—a show that helped launch the Pumpkins on the road to alternative-rock superstardom (and also won them the lasting enmity of every other band in Chicago).

Decked out in a tight black-and-red dress and a garish red wig, Pumpkins leader Billy Corgan gives a short speech about his heroes' enduring influence. Meanwhile the lead singer of Jane's is sitting alone in the balcony, trying to appear incognito by hiding under his towering Cat-in-the-Hat chapeau. He's the only person in a ten-seat VIP section within the VIP section, and now he's spilling wine on his bell bottoms and patched-up jeans jacket. "It's a real honor and a pleasure to open for them again," Corgan says onstage. The Great Pumpkin proceeds to lead his band through five of its standards, including "Zero," "Tonight, Tonight," and "Thru the Eyes of Ruby"—

the same tight, professional rock-machine set that the band delivered only nights before when it opened for the Rolling Stones. Farrell yawns, gets up midway through the Pumpkins' performance, and wobbles off, occasionally reaching out for a chair or a wall to steady himself.

Farrell reappears about an hour later, taking the stage after first leaving his Jane's Addiction bandmates standing up there alone, noodling with their instruments for fifteen minutes. He's wearing the same outfit minus the hat and without the trademark braided hairdo that he's worn every other night of this tour. "Chicago was probably the worst show we've done," he says two weeks later, on the phone from Houston as Jane's Addiction forges a path across the country, making its way back to Los Angeles for two celebratory shows at the Universal Amphitheatre. "I was in not that great of a shape. I had, um, overindulged. That one night, I was overindulgent, and I lost my focus."

"Focus" is a word that Farrell uses a lot these days, and with good reason. The notoriously flighty frontman will need his feet (not to mention his financial planner) planted firmly on the ground if he's to pull off his most recent head-in-the-clouds Master Plan. It may be his craziest and most ambitious idea yet—and that's saying something for the guy who started Lollapalooza and conceived the ill-fated ENIT festival to welcome the arriving UFOs. Like most of his plots, it's partially about artistic expression, partially about communal experience, and partially about some loopy shit that only Farrell will ever fully understand. His description makes it sound like some new-millennial combination of Lollapalooza, WOMAD, and Woodstock—a gigantic traveling musical circus, conceived and executed in accordance with Biblical prophecy. As usual he's short on details, but he talks of a world tour with bands from across the globe, playing all styles of music, and artists, poets, and dancers doing their things, and "peace" and rampant sexuality on display for all to see and revel in. And the return of Jane's is all a part of The Plan.

IT'S BEEN TEN years since Jane's Addiction debuted with its self-titled album, recorded live at the Roxy. *Jane's Addiction* introduced the band's signature mix of glam-rock gender-bending, Led Zeppelin riff-pilfering, funky psychedelic wanking, and heroin-chic posing, all delivered by a singer who brought to mind Jon Anderson of Yes with stranger New Age ideas and less of a vocal range. It was a rough, intoxicating sound, and the band honed it on two subsequent (and much better) albums. The most faithful fans in the band's hometown speak of the group as the long-awaited Los Angeles answer to the Velvet Underground, or at least the most important band the city has produced since the Byrds. In fact Jane's always paled in comparison to such truly subversive '80s indie-rockers as Hüsker Dü, the Minutemen, Big Black, and Mission of Burma. Maybe the fact that the group was never really as daring and edgy as it pretended to be is the reason why it was so hugely successful.

That said, anyone who's tuned to modern-rock radio or MTV in the last seven years and grooved along to the anthemic singles from 1988's *Nothing's Shocking* and 1990's *Ritual de lo Habitual* can tell you that platinum-selling pop doesn't get much better or more inventive than this. Perhaps the truest testament to these discs' staying power is how they've turned up at any number of recording studios, and how they're always hauled out by over-eager engineers as evidence of exactly how rock 'n' roll *ought* to sound in these (post)modern times. Ten years on, we can argue about whether or not Jane's was the missing link between that vaunted indie era and the alternative rock revolution that began in earnest with Nirvana's *Nevermind* (released in 1991, just as Jane's was disbanding). But you still can't argue with those barking dogs at the beginning of "Been Caught Stealing."

Now Jane's is back. The official version of how this happened is that Farrell, drummer Stephen Perkins (who's been playing with Farrell in Porno for Pyros), and guitarist Dave Navarro (now in the Red Hot Chili Peppers) reconvened last December to record "Hard Charger" for the soundtrack to *Howard Stern's Private Parts*. Moonlighting Chili Pepper Flea took the place of original Jane's bassist Eric Avery, who declined Farrell's invitation to rejoin and continues to pursue his own course with Polar Bear. "Eric didn't want to do it, and he didn't give me any straight answers," Farrell says. "I wish I knew why." For his part Avery characterizes Farrell's version of their conversation as "absurdly incorrect."

"But so it goes in rock 'n' roll myth-making," Avery adds. "These are waters I want to navigate carefully. I have a lot of reasons why I didn't do it. Fundamentally, though, I believe that the past is the past for a reason. I haven't seen a reunion that's worked for me. I see them as being worse versions of past days. That's how I feel about them all, whether it's Fleetwood Mac or the Buzzcocks or Jane's Addiction. There's a certain time-specific aspect to great music, and when you try to force it, it doesn't quite come off."

Even without Avery, the press release says, things worked out so well that the new Jane's decided to tour and record two more new songs for *Kettle Whistle*, the underwhelming new Warner Bros. collection of old Jane's rarities and live tunes. (No mention of The Plan here.) Mindful of the kind of mercenary mediocrity that Avery alludes to, the remaining band members and everyone connected with them carefully avoid using one "r" word in favor of another. "We're not calling it a 'reunion' show, because we don't have all of the original members," Perkins says. "We're calling it a 'relapse.'"

Call it what you will, onstage in Chicago, all of the old Jane's Addiction contradictions are back, bigger and more troubling than ever before. For the night, the group has transformed the Aragon into Perry's Playhouse, with a main stage done up in a tiki-hut-turned-opium-den motif, strings of lights hung everywhere, two freestanding towers for gyrating female dancers, and a smaller second stage at the rear of the room. The last bit is a trick that everyone from U2 to the Rolling Stones has employed of late, but Jane's actually walks through the crowd to mount this auxiliary platform and deliver an intimate, touching version of "Jane Says." If only all of the music was as ambitious as the visuals.

Whenever the group starts to pick up some momentum, delivering fiery versions of "Ocean Size" and "Mountain Song," the show is derailed by another tune that's given to long and self-indulgent jamming, recalling the worst excesses of San Francisco '68. (I'm talking bad Quicksilver Messenger Service or Jefferson Airplane here, forget about the Grateful Dead.) Flea does his best to check his funkier impulses and play it straight, but Avery's looping bass sound is sorely missed. Perkins remains the secret weapon, mixing John Bonham's power with Mickey Hart's hippie fluidity and polyrhythmic world beats. But the band plays like it's only been together for a few weeks—which, for all intents and purposes, it has.

Farrell's long and addled monologues also have a dampening effect. He talks on and on about feeling the spirits brushing past him and wanting to "pray for E.T. to come and give us a magic mountain ride to Mars." A full three days after the holiday has passed, he tells us, "So, last night was Halloween." Another of his soliloquies is about the power of femininity—how we should all respect the feminine rhythms of our Mother Earth—but this touching sentiment clashes with the six scantily-clad go-go dancers who adorn the stage, feign fellatio and intercourse with the singer during the epic "Three Days," and climb the towers to thrust their vulvas at the crowds in the balconies. Farrell is defensive when asked about the apparent incongruity of his words and his stage show.

"I asked specifically not to have, like, strippers, but to have dancers, so that it wouldn't come off that way," he says. "But putting that aside, I must tell you, women are pound for pound more sexual than guys are, I believe. If you let a woman go unharnessed, if she wasn't going to be called a whore, she would be having sex I'd venture to say ten-to-one the amount of hours that a man would. So they're very sexual beings, and this is the way they operate. I'm not sitting there telling them to put their crotch up at anybody. It's too easy, and I would feel more tied with Motley Crüe than the Velvet Underground if that was the case."

Perhaps, but the fact remains that the smarmy, soft-core porn video that Motley Crüe has been screening on its own current reunion tour is actually less gratuitous than what the Jane's dancers are doing. Mulling this over as Jane's performs in Chicago, one could easily conclude that there isn't fundamentally much difference between Perry and Friends and Vince Neil and Company. It's all just rock 'n' roll; it's all just entertainment. But then Farrell disappears from the stage as the new Jane's launches into "Summertime Rolls."

The singer re-emerges a few minutes later: He's climbing the dancers' tower directly in front of the balcony where I'm sitting. The mass of metal scaffolding stands about thirty feet tall, and it would be scary enough watching him trying to get to the top under normal circumstances, risking life and limb while wearing those platform shoes. But the climb takes on added drama with the knowledge that he's impaired in other ways—"overindulged," as he says—as evidenced by his earlier wine-swishing escapade.

Miraculously, Farrell makes it to the top in one piece, but he isn't content to just perch up there. He takes the wireless mike and leans way, way over the edge of the platform, looking as if he's going to fall off at any second, just because he wants to make contact. He's turning the song into a matter of life and death, and he sings the familiar words about "me and my girlfriend" while straining to look directly into my eyes. I get chills, and I'm sure that everyone in the seats on either side and in front and in back of me feels the exact same thing. Farrell has got a rare hypnotic power as a performer, and despite all the contradictions in his art, it earns him a permanent spot on the list of all-time great, galvanizing rock frontmen, right there beside Iggy Pop, Johnny Rotten, and Kurt Cobain. On his best day, Vince Neil couldn't reach up to touch the hem of his bell bottoms.

EVEN WHEN ITS FRONTMAN attains such highs, the question of what Corgan called Jane's "enduring influence" remains. It was never easy to measure a band's artistic legacy against its commercial accomplishments in the alternative era, and Jane's has made it even tougher by coming back for an encore. Farrell would like to be remembered for constantly challenging his audience and pushing the boundaries of what can be accomplished in the commercial rock arena. Still, it seems too damn early for '90s alt-rock nostalgia, and the whole "cashing in on past glories" rock-reunion routine seems below him as a man who—love him or hate him—has always lived in the present.

When he's confronted with such questions about the reunion—er, relapse—Farrell begins rhapsodizing about his true intentions. This is where

The Plan comes in. "First of all, the answer to what is in a name has got no bounds," he begins. "It's eternally deep. I can tell you my name is Perry, or I can tell you my name is Porno, or I can tell you my name is Jane. What is in a name? But at the same time, it also declares that I'm not Jack or Jerry. What is in a name? The answer is boundless, and as I say, profoundly deep."

He's starting to roll now, and the spacey, surfer-dude-on-helium monotone is picking up speed.

"I will tell you why I went back to the name, and it has to do with the question you previously asked me, and that is A, at this time of life, I wanted to show that people can come to an understanding that had previously not understood each other, and make up, basically. It's about making up and letting go of one's debts to each other. This is a very, very important aspect of my life right now. That's A. B is back to what is in a name. If I say 'Jane's Addiction,' it does cause certain reactions. What I want to do here is I want to go out and be on a mission of peace. So I am going to break out my biggest peace gun, if you want to look at it from a soldier's point of view. To do that, I am starting now with this tour, and I want to increase the heat and increase the peace and increase the love. I want to go around and put together an important, important event that has been prophesied for over two thousand years: the Jubilee. The Jubilee occurs around this time next year, next Purim."

The singer is losing me here, so I ask him to back up a bit: What the hell is the Jubilee?

Farrell: "I'm talking about something that's been prophesied in the Bible for two thousand five hundred years."

Me: "I didn't know the Bible was talking about rock concerts. Cool."

Farrell: "The Bible was talking about Jubilee, when God will descend amongst men and live amongst men."

Me: "Isn't that what Christians call the Rapture? Or is that when everybody gets sucked up into heaven? I can't keep all that stuff straight."

Farrell: "I don't know what they call it. We look at it differently. We look at it that peace will preside on the earth for the next thousand years."

Me: "Ah, so it's a millennial thing."

Farrell: "It's millennial, but we—and when I say 'we,' I mean the race of Jews, the Hebrews, the Israelites—it's on a slightly different time, which is on the next Purim, so it's before the millennium that the Christian calendar is based on."

Me: "So what you're talking about is putting Jane's back together so that you can have the clout to pull off a really ambitious world tour. You know, that's actually a very pragmatic, capitalist tactic, Perry."

Farrell: "When you're going after the girl that you really see, and it's love at first sight, you buy her flowers and you scrub yourself behind your ears, you know what I mean? What I want out of life, I'm going to really go after this whole next year. I'm going to be ready at that door, you know what I mean? Whatever it takes to get peace to come down and for the Jubilee to go over. The Jubilee should be the ultimate event. So I have to show people we're capable of making money for them, and we can make money for ourselves, too; that's fine. But for me, this is an idea that I would sacrifice anything to do. I've got to rev it up, so when you're asking me why Jane's Addiction, why go back, you called it a capitalist attitude, but I have to show people that when shows get larger, at any size, we can still have an incredible event going on and this is what it looks like. With Porno, unfortunately, I don't know exactly why, maybe the music is more eclectic, but I was limited."

With sold-out Jane's shows across the United States, Farrell is no longer limited: He can do whatever the hell he wants. Maybe he'll pull off the Jubilee, taking some version of this traveling concert–arts show–orgy to the Middle East and Europe, as well as to Kansas and Los Angeles. Maybe he'll fall flat on his face, as he did with ENIT. One thing's for sure, though: He stands a better chance of making it happen come next Purim as the leader of Jane's Addiction than as the singer for Porno for Pyros or as plain ol' Perry Bernstein. He may be crazy, this wandering Jew. But he's crazy like a fox.

8

MEANWHILE, BACK IN THE MOTHERLAND

REVIEWING THE PLAY LISTS OF MODERN-ROCK radio and MTV through the alternative era, the distinct lack of British bands is striking: There was plenty of great music being made by groups from the United Kingdom, it just wasn't having much of an impact on the American mainstream, at least until Oasis and Radiohead came along.

In contrast to the days of the British Invasion, glam-rock, or mid-'70s punk, the major-label music industry in the United States was almost nationalistic through the '90s, keeping its focus local as it swooped in, signed up, and hyped to the high heavens any band that seemed as if it might appeal to the Lollapalooza Nation. The few exceptions like SBK mostly failed miserably. As is often the case, it was a different story among more curious fans in the rock underground, and as always, American musicians were certainly listening to the more innovative sounds from across the pond—witness Billy Corgan's internalizing and reworking of the Creation Records sound.

This chapter opens with a mini-profile of that label and its colorful founder, Alan McGee (a vastly entertaining and far more thorough account of the label's story can be found in David Cavanagh's 2000 book, *The Creation Records Story: My Magpie Eyes are Hungry for the Prize*). It moves on to reviews of the two best albums produced by Creation bands (My Bloody Valentine's *Loveless* and Ride's *Carnival of Light*), and pieces on Blur and Oasis, whom the English press pitted against each other in a much-ballyhooed feud. Oasis far outsold Blur on these shores, which prompted most observers to call them "the winner," but Blur's albums stand as much stronger art (including the discs that followed *Parklife*, *The Great Escape* and *Thirteen*).

While Blur did eventually make some dent on the American charts ("Girls & Boys" was only a modest hit, but "Song 2" wound up getting massive exposure as the soundtrack for Mercedes-Benz and Pentium computer chip TV commercials), bandleader Damon Albarn had the last laugh when the self-titled album by Gorillaz, his cartoon simian hip-hop side project, became a platinum smash. When I last spoke to him, before he toured the States in the spring of 2002, standing behind a giant video screen through the entire show, I congratulated him on pulling off one of the most brilliant scams in rock history: "Blur makes one great album after another, but you can't get arrested here. Then you invent these cartoon characters and sell a million albums! You have to be laughing your ass off!" He did indeed laugh heartily. "Well, it's not a Satanic kind of laughter," he finally said. "I do put a lot of work into it! When you use the word 'scam,' I know exactly what you mean, but it doesn't negate the fact that it requires probably even more work to pull off a good scam."

Oasis's scam has meanwhile grown rather tired: It continues to make the same album over and over again—and the Beatles did it much better in 1966 with *Revolver.*

Of the other bands included here, the Stone Roses seem even slighter now than they were when the English music press was ejaculating all over them. But Teenage Fanclub, Stereolab, and Spiritualized remain much-revered fixtures in the rock underground.

The Evolution of Creation
Request, September 1991

THE CYNICAL ENGLISH music press refers to it as "the scene that contemplates its shoes" or "the scene that celebrates itself." Enthusiastic American record executives call it "the next British Invasion." Whatever your perspective, it's hard to deny that the new wave of young English guitar bands is making some of the most exciting rock 'n' roll in years, and central to it all is a carrot-topped, wisecracking Scottish music fan, Alan McGee, president of Creation Records, the independent record company that he started "as a bit of a lark."

The best of the new groups—My Bloody Valentine, Ride, Teenage Fanclub, Slowdive, and Primal Scream—were all discovered by McGee, released successful records on Creation in the United Kingdom, and subsequently signed to major labels in the United States. Although the groups have some similarities—they all feature twenty-year-olds with guitars who tend to care less about lyrics and song structure than they do about sonic textures—there's no specific "Creation sound." "It's a totally selfish label," McGee says in his thick and sometimes impenetrable Scottish brogue. "The whole thing is just my taste."

Raised in the Glasgow suburb of East Kilbride, McGee hung around with the members of what became the Jesus and Mary Chain before relocating to London in 1981 "because of the drugs." He booked an alternative music club, the Living Room, and started Creation Records as a hobby, releasing 45s in batches of a thousand by his friends' bands and groups he met through the club. The label was named after a legendary band from the psychedelic '60s, the cult-favorite English psychedelic pop group that first inspired Jimmy Page to try bowing his guitar. (As a further homage, McGee called his own band Biff Bang Pow after the name of a Creation song.)

Creation Records' first release was by a long-forgotten oddball outfit called the Legend! "The first ten or twelve records we put out, nothing really happened to any of them," McGee says. "Then we did the Mary Chain record and sold like fifty thousand of them, and it all started developing from that."

Although the Jesus and Mary Chain jumped ship after its brilliant first single, "Upside Down" / "Vegetable Man," Creation continued to dent the English pop charts with releases by the Weather Prophets, the Jesus and Mary Chain offshoot Primal Scream, and the House of Love. "There were a lot of highs and lows with the success of people like the Mary Chain and the Weather Prophets and stuff like that," McGee says. "Then in 1988 it got quite serious, and we decided we wanted to compete proper."

Today Creation employs seventeen staffers, has released more than a hundred records, and is second only to Daniel Miller's Mute Records as the largest-selling independent label in Britain. The label's growth in the last three years is linked directly to McGee's championing of the new wave of British bands, although he resents the media's labeling of the scene. "The only time [Primal Scream's] Bobby Gillespie looks at his shoes is when he puts mirrors on them to reflect up," McGee says. "And the only time [Teenage Fanclub's] Norman Blake looks at his shoes is when he's passed out flat on his face drunk."

This may be true, but another of McGee's most promising bands, the Oxford-educated quartet Ride, certainly seems to fit both of the sobriquets bestowed upon them by the witty English critics. The musicians are indeed dedicated shoegazers, evincing an odd mixture of a stunning absence of personality and an almost haughty pride as they churn out the alternately melodic and feedback-drenched washes of sound in their intensely moody psychedelic guitar rock. The same is true of My Bloody Valentine. But who the hell cares if these blokes have attitude or stand stone still when their music is so hypnotizing and evocative?

American record executives obviously believe there's an audience for these sounds. McGee helped negotiate American distribution deals for My Bloody Valentine, Primal Scream, and Ride with Sire; for Teenage Fanclub with DGC; for House of Love with Mercury; and for Swervedriver with A&M, but he soon realized that dealing with so many American labels was confusing. Late last year he signed an exclusive American deal with SBK, Charles Koppelman's upstart label and the home of Vanilla Ice and Wilson Phillips. It doesn't affect the earlier deals with Creation bands, but SBK will have first shot at releases by any new bands on the label.

"I've always been interested in what Alan McGee has done," says Michael Mena, SBK's director of new music marketing and promotion. "We have a lot of faith in Alan. Creation has only been around for five years, and every year he seems to come up with a great band. We feel that Slowdive is definitely going to be in that category. They're a young band—they're between eighteen and twenty years old—and they're just gonna get better. They sold thirty thousand copies of their first album in the U.K. That's a significant amount of records, and they've gotten a decent amount of airplay. They're in the Top 35 of the pop charts there. It's not really music that is mainstream, but I think that bands like this, instead of them sneaking closer to the mainstream, they move the mainstream closer to them."

Neil Halstead, Slowdive's songwriter and guitarist, is optimistic that SBK will help break the group's ethereal first album, *Just for a Day.* "They've only got about twenty bands, which is quite remarkable for a major company that's got the high profile that SBK has got," he says. "If we signed to someone like RCA, they've got loads of bands, and we'd be at the end of the list. We're probably still at the end of the list at SBK, but at least we're the most different band they've got."

Slowdive's story is typical of the bands on Creation. "We'd only been together nine months when we got signed," Halstead says. "We did a gig in Reading and a friend of Alan's was there. He gave a tape to Alan and Alan phoned up the next day and said, 'Do you want to put a record out?' It was a shock because we'd always admired bands like the Mary Chain. They were the bands that we grew up with, and we'd always read about McGee and Creation Records. When he phoned, I actually thought it was someone taking a pisser, someone who was just phoning up for a joke."

McGee's style is more inspirational than hands-on, Halstead says. "Alan's a vibe person. He's very enthusiastic and very charismatic. He's very good at firing people up to do things."

Because of the present economy, McGee believes it would be next to impossible to start a successful independent label like Creation today. On the other hand, he says, "I keep making the charts with a twentieth of the amount of money that the majors spend on bands. And Creation will continue trying to do what we originally started seven years ago: To keep putting out records I like. I've given up women, and I've given up drugs. There's only music left."

A Love Letter to Guitar-Based Rock
The *Chicago Sun-Times*, December 2, 2001

THERE WAS A school of thought among some rock critics during the rise of hip-hop and techno in the early '90s that held that after five decades of rock 'n' roll, everything that *could* be done with guitars, bass, and drums *had* been done. But two albums arrived in 1991 to discredit that notion.

The first was Nirvana's *Nevermind*, which used the oldest of three-chord formulas to remind listeners that there is no more powerful musical force than a simple, indelible rock tune. The other was My Bloody Valentine's *Loveless*, an album that invented a sound all its own. It remains one of the most complex and disorienting albums in rock history, though in its own way, it is every bit as catchy and energizing as *Nevermind*.

While the supporting players were valuable, the story of My Bloody Valentine is really the story of Kevin Shields, just as the tale of the Smashing Pumpkins is really that of Billy Corgan. The two auteurs shared similar influences and musical ambitions, though Corgan drew more heavily from classic-rock bombast while Shields was devoted to psychedelia and the idea of creating a world that existed only in the space between the headphones. Born in Queens, New York, he moved to Dublin with his family when he was eleven years old, and he never shook the feeling of being a stranger in a strange land. School took a back seat to music—he learned to play guitar by mimicking the down strokes on the Ramones' concert album, *It's Alive*—and his parents let his bands rehearse in the living room on Sunday afternoons.

My Bloody Valentine formed in 1983 as a gloomy, mascara-wearing goth band enamored of the Cramps, the Doors, and the Birthday Party. In 1985 it recorded the *This Is Your Bloody Valentine* EP in Berlin. "The first one was crap," Shields said frankly a decade later, and the first version of the band split up in 1986. Relocating to London, Shields regrouped with veteran drummer Colm O'Ciosig and new member Bilinda Butcher on vocals and guitar (Shields and Butcher shared a romantic relationship that lasted until around the time of *Loveless*); Debbie Googe joined later on bass. The group started over with a pair of 1987 EPs, *Strawberry Wine* and *Ecstasy*, which ushered in a sunnier, more optimistic vibe reminiscent of West Coast '60s psychedelia, especially the Los Angeles band Love.

In 1988 the group signed to Creation Records, home of the Jesus and Mary Chain and the nascent "shoegazer" or "dream-pop" movement of modern psychedelic guitar bands. With *You Made Me Realise*, Shields hit on the sound that would become his signature. "Glide guitar" involved strumming the strings of his Fender Jazz Master while holding the tremolo arm or "whammy bar," a relic of the surf era that provided a unique pitch bend. As a result, the instrument was constantly going slightly in and out of tune, an effect Shields amplified with the backwards reverb from a digital effects pedal.

"In '88 a lot of elements came together at the same time, and a lot of extreme things happened," the leader of My Bloody Valentine told me in a 1995 interview. "What I did then was virtually invent my own way of playing. It didn't come about in any conscious way; it just came about from messing around on borrowed equipment. It felt playful, but on a much stronger level. Everything was adding up, and I was twenty-five then. Everything starts to come in and you go, 'God, what was I messing around with before?'"

The road had been paved for the band's crowning achievement, but it did not come easily. My Bloody Valentine spent almost three years crafting *Loveless*, and it cost Creation half a million dollars. ("I don't cry, but it drove me to tears—just drove me insane," said the label's founder, Alan McGee. Only the subsequent success of Oasis bailed the company out.) Some sixteen different engineers contributed to the project, though Alan Moulder emerged as the dominant sonic architect besides Shields, and Corgan would later tap him to work with the Pumpkins based on that experience.

Because of the album's labored creation fans assumed Shields was a perfectionist. "That's one of the great misconceptions about this band, that everything is intellectual and there's an awful lot of time spent in the studio perfecting things," he said. "Everything you ever hear on our records, virtually all the overdubs are first-take stuff, and all the guitar parts are first or second take. It's more like capturing the moment. For me, everything hinges on one critical thing, and that's being in an inspired state of mind."

Shields said that the goal on *Loveless* was to capture the feeling of walking downtown on a Sunday morning when the streets are deserted and you feel strangely uncomfortable, despite the familiar surroundings. The eleven songs are an odd combination of beautiful, lulling melodies and disturbing, unsettling noises. With the ever-swirling mix they are like an aural evocation of bed spins—or the rush of a powerful drug. "It was influenced a little bit too much by Ecstasy culture," Shields told me. "A lot of the melodies and hook lines that come from the instruments are extremely dinky and toy-like. For me, that was the aftereffects of experiencing too much Ecstasy."

Like the Cocteau Twins, the Valentines rarely wrote songs that were "about" anything. Titles such as "To Here Knows When," "When You Sleep," and "Soon" evoke more than they actually say, especially because the words are often inaudible, with the vocals placed behind the wall of guitars. The stray phrases that do emerge complement the sounds to underscore the band's recurring themes: lustful yearning, the longing for blissful escape, and feelings of overwhelming alienation. "Sleep / Like a pillow / Downward and / Where / She won't care / Anyway," goes the opening of "Only Shallow."

Adding to the mystery is the dreamy, sensual way in which the songs are sung. "Often when we do vocals, it's seven-thirty in the morning; I've usually just fallen asleep and have to be woken up to sing," Butcher said. "I'm usually trying to remember what I've been dreaming about when I'm singing."

Hypnotizing tape loops and the shimmering sound of Shields's glide guitar add to the dreaminess; it's as if you're listening to the album through a wall, or while submerged underwater. Even the propulsive rhythms are sonically slippery: Most of the percussion sounds were treated or triggered electronically. Yet for all of the audio trickery, the band could reproduce *Loveless* perfectly onstage. Although they barely moved while they played (they were indeed shoegazers), to this day the Valentines were the loudest group I have ever seen in concert. You didn't hear the music so much as you felt it in the pit of your stomach when they toured to support the disc in 1992. There are tales of the shattering volume and dizzying mix literally making some fans sick to their stomachs.

"A lot of what we've done is perceived by people as coming from somebody who's not quite sane, or a bit woozy or dreamy," Shields said. "That's why when we play live, it's quite aggressive or confrontational. What I do is about consciousness, being conscious of a feeling in my whole body. The trouble with the attitude toward psychedelic music is that it's about your head only. And to me, all non-Western people when they get into altered states of mind, it's the whole body that's involved."

Three months after the release of *Loveless,* the band parted ways with Creation and signed to Island. Shields invested the advance in building a home studio in London, but time dragged on; he ran into equipment glitches, suffered what he called "mental problems," and shelved one completed album because it wasn't good enough. The only post-*Loveless* Valentines music that I've heard to date is a relatively straightforward cover of Wire's "Map Ref. 41° N 93° W" on the 1996 tribute album, *Whore.*

"Too often when people make good records, there's an aftershock effect, and they collapse psychologically and emotionally," Shields said when we spoke six years ago. "Brian Wilson is a classic case of that. I'm trying to prove that you can make genuinely interesting music and come out with new ideas without an emotional drain to the point where you break down. I could make another record that would top the others we've made—I've been ready to for a while now—but to me it's extremely important to make that record in such a way that I'll be able to make another one. For lots of small, petty, human reasons that I won't go into, I'd like to be around in five years' time, making better and better records."

In fact, while various Web sites track his doings (Shields has contributed to recent recordings by Primal Scream, Curve, and J. Mascis) the follow-up to *Loveless* is still nowhere to be found, but that doesn't diminish the towering accomplishment of one of the best albums of the alternative era. No less a tastemaker than Brian Eno called it one of the most creative rock albums ever made; Radiohead's career is unthinkable without it; and Trey Anastasio pushed hard for Phish to cover it during one of that band's special Halloween shows. "*Loveless* is the best album recorded in the '90s," Anastasio told me. "History will tell, and twenty years from now that album will be considered a complete classic, while a lot of the albums that are real popular today will have been forgotten."

Ride, *Carnival of Light*
Request, September 1994

ENGLISH CRITIC SIMON REYNOLDS once dismissed so-called shoegazer bands like Ride as a "living, breathing archive of rock gestures—a mere footnote." I don't know about you, but I love footnotes, nuggets that are simply too choice to leave out, even if they don't fit into an author's neat and tidy outline of something. Pop music is full of footnotes, left-field surprises, and guilty pleasures, but eggheads like Reynolds are too hung up on sociological importance to enjoy them. While Ride doesn't do anything new, what the band does is simply too good to miss.

News about Ride's third album didn't bode well. Following an amazing two-year period that produced four EPs and two albums (1990's *Nowhere* and 1991's *Going Blank Again*) of ethereal but propulsive and very often transcendent psychedelic guitar rock, the quartet went into hibernation. Once the band finally started recording again, producer George Drakoulias (Black Crowes, Jayhawks) was jettisoned after a few weeks, and Stone Roses knob-twirler John Leckie had to finish the job. There were reports that songwriters, guitarist, vocalists, and co-frontmen Andy Bell and Mark Gardener were no longer speaking to each other. Yet *Carnival of Light* is Ride's strongest album, a breathtaking example of modern psychedelia that references and updates the best of what has come before.

The first two songs, "Moonlight Medicine" and "1000 Miles," both borrow from Rolling Stones song titles but boast riffs lifted from Pink Floyd's "Welcome to the Machine" and "Brain Damage," respectively. The angelic choir on "I Don't Know Where It Comes From" is straight out of the Stones' "You Can't Always Get What You Want," while an instrumental with the Dylanesque title "Rolling Thunder" actually sounds like the Incredible String Band, complete with tabla and sitar. Two songs pay indirect homage to the British indie label that gave the group its start: "Crown of Creation" is an effective, jangly, Graham Parsons–style ballad, while "How Does It Feel to Feel" is a cover of a song by the Creation, the legendary psychedelic-mod band of the '60s that gave the label its name. (The 1967 original included a chaotic bowed guitar solo years before Jimmy Page stole the trick, and it's faithfully reproduced here by Ride.)

It isn't necessary to know any of this to appreciate *Carnival of Light*; despite their art-school backgrounds, the band members may not even know from whence they appropriate themselves. What's obvious is that Gardener and Bell have internalized twenty-five years of inventive guitar sounds and trippy production tricks, drawing on an unerring sense of melody while turning poetry-notebook scrawlings such as "God is on my side" and "Angels come from time to time" into memorable, emotionally charged choruses.

Ride invites you to lose yourself in the melodies and the gorgeous ambiance and let the meaning be damned. Sometimes transcendence is in the footnotes.

Blur Shows Talent to Survive Passing Trends
The *Chicago Sun-Times*, September 14, 1994

OF ALL THE English rockers vying for attention in America these days, Blur is the most determined to retain its national identity. *Parklife*, the group's third album, is full of distinctly British characters, musical swipes, and cultural references. It has spawned an alternative hit with "Girls & Boys," which follows randy English youth on holiday to Greece. And it includes "Magic America," the best song about American cultural imperialism since "I'm So Bored with the U.S.A." by the Clash.

"I get physically ill when I go there," singer Damon Albarn says of our fine nation, but it's nothing personal: It turns out that much of Blur's bashing of the colonies is based on a rotten relationship with its American record company. The quartet's 1991 debut, *Leisure*, spawned two big English hits, "She's So High" and "There's No Other Way." The follow-up, *Modern Life Is Rubbish*, was a dense pop tapestry that stands as one of the best albums of 1993. But despite the success of the recent single "Girls & Boys," the group's American label, SBK (the company that brought us Vanilla Ice), has *still* been unable to bring *Parklife* to an audience beyond Blur's core following.

"I know there are people out there who are interested in us, but there's a remarkable ability to screw things up in that company," Albarn says with typical candor. "It's too depressing for words. [SBK executives] just don't have a clue about us. I'm afraid we're a little too intelligent for them."

Albarn's cockiness can be forgiven because he happens to be right. With *Parklife* Blur takes thirty years of cool English rock, throws it into an art-punk Cuisinart, and ends up with a masterpiece of timeless hooks and cockney attitude. There is Kinksian satire, early Small Faces swagger, wiggy Syd Barrett–via–Julian Cope production, XTC circa "Respectable Street" vocal looks ("ooh-we-ooh"), and a cynical Buzzcocks detachment. The band members are mods, of course, borrowing fashion tips from the pre-glam

David Bowie, revved-up tempos from the early Jam, and actor Phil Daniels (the star of *Quadrophenia*) for a vocal cameo. Stereolab's Laetitia Sadier sings backing vocals on a track, the Pet Shop Boys remixed the single "Girls & Boys," and the members of Blur love Wire so much that they hired that band's old road manager.

All of these stolen styles are synthesized and served up with a sly sense of humor and ultra-high energy. During a recent concert at Chicago's Vic Theatre, Albarn scaled a twenty-foot-high speaker tower during an instrumental break in the wild "Pop Scene." Then he jumped back down to the stage, landing directly in front of the mike, on the exact beat where he needed to begin the next verse. A former actor, the singer knows how to keep the audience's attention: He never stopped moving, jumping up and down, playing with his mod Fred Perry shirt, and even skipping rope with his microphone cord (a stunt that simultaneously pays homage to and betters Roger Daltrey's famous mike-swinging routine).

Albarn has a ready response to those critics who say that Blur is simply a clever distillation of well-chosen lifts from great bands of the past. "The trick when you go into the studio is to have all that information and all of those reference points stored in your head and then allow your own creativity to modify them," he says. "It's a case of stealing as much as possible but not borrowing. At the tail end of the century, there's a wonderful opportunity because there's so much in grasp that's still in touch with what's happening now."

The musician's knowledge of English rock history is inherited: His father was the road manager of the legendary psychedelic band the Soft Machine. "I had a very relaxed childhood, sitting around finger-painting and playing the violin," Albarn says. "I was extremely lucky. Then again, I missed out on things that I've caught up with now, like football and going to the pub."

Blur's visions of the motherland aren't all rose-tinted. Songs such as "Tracy Jacks," "The Debt Collector," and "Pressure on Julian" paint rather sad portraits of the title characters, whom Albarn describes as "trapped and trying to escape."

"It's all very visual," the singer says of Blur's music. "Both my parents are visual artists. I was never really gifted like that, so music is my way of doing it. I'm also a failed actor, so I've always been interested in characters. I suppose the combination is what we do." The fact is, few bands today—English or otherwise—are doing it better.

An Oasis in U.K.'s Rock Desert?

The *Chicago Sun-Times*, March 17, 1995

YOU'VE GOT TO admire a band that opens its debut album with a song that declares, "Tonight, I'm a rock 'n' roll star," then proceeds to back that up. Oasis is a quintet from England that makes invigorating rock music that's partly about the process of making invigorating rock music. The band members are clearly full of themselves—their CD booklet includes no fewer than twenty-six photos of the musicians in various mod poses—but they admit it and sing about that, too.

"I don't think there's anything better to sing about than having sex with women, taking drugs, traveling the world, and being in a band," says lead guitarist and songwriter Noel Gallagher. "To a kid on the street, that's going to sound exciting. I don't think kids want to hear about how tough life is and the war in Bosnia and, 'Oh, I feel bad today 'cause I have a headache.' If you sing about things that are enjoyable and you record them while you're enjoying yourself, that can only be transferred onto the record and people will enjoy themselves while they're listening to it."

The band's American debut, *Definitely Maybe*, fulfills those goals. Like their rival countrymen in Blur, the members of Oasis are obsessed with their homeland's pop-music history. They draw from different sounds and eras—the Who's maximum R&B, T. Rex's glam-rock, and the old Stone Roses' dance sound—but they add enough passion and attitude to make it all sound fresh. "It's not a blatant thing; it just so happens that that's how it comes out," Gallagher says. "The guys from Blur probably say the same thing. We don't set out deliberately to rip somebody off."

Gallagher formed the band in late 1991, and it signed to England's Creation Records a year later. The group is completed by rhythm guitarist Paul Arthurs, bassist Paul McGuigan, drummer Tony McCarroll, and Noel's brother, Liam, on vocals. The sibling team makes comparisons between Oasis and the Kinks inevitable—especially considering the sonic similarities—and Liam and Noel get along about as well as Ray and Dave Davies.

"We argue a lot, but the arguments are never about the band," Noel says. "They're about meaningless incidental stuff, like, 'That's my shirt you've got on!' When you're on the road for six weeks, you need someone to go off on, and who better than your little brother?"

At least Gallagher doesn't deny his status as band tyrant. "Everybody says, 'Ray and Dave Davies,' and I say, 'What about them?' They were both songwriters and they probably argued about band stuff. We don't argue about the band. I'm in charge and that's the end of it. I give them the songs and say, 'Play that,' and if it doesn't work out, they're fired."

The last few years haven't been kind to bands from England. The alternative rock boom has opened the door for legions of American one-hit wonders, but only a handful of British acts have dented the charts. Oasis may be turning the tide. The single "Live Forever" has become a radio and MTV hit, *Definitely Maybe* is climbing *Billboard*'s pop albums chart, and the album has sold an impressive two hundred fifty thousand copies.

"We're not saying we're the great British hope or anything like that," Gallagher says. "If other people say it, let them say it. But we're not going around saying we're representing England because we're just representing ourselves."

And, of course, the time-honored trilogy.

"Sex, drugs, and rock 'n' roll," Gallagher says, laughing. "That's us in a nutshell."

Oasis, Be Here Now
Audio, September 1997

ON THE FIRST track ("Rock 'n' Roll Star") of their first album (1994's *Definitely Maybe*), the members of Oasis brazenly announced their career goals. With 1995's *(What's The Story) Morning Glory?*, they made good on their boast and proceeded to give us two years of entertaining headlines about internal fights, external feuds, and other assorted scandals. *Be Here Now* is where they have to prove their staying power, and they do, with another batch of Noel Gallagher's skillfully crafted songs and a heaping dose of brother Liam's cocky attitude. "I'll put on my shoes while I'm walking slowly down the Hall of Fame," Liam sings in "My Big Mouth," and you better believe he will—as long as Noel doesn't trip him up on the way.

Beatles, Beatles, Beatles. It's impossible to write about Oasis without using that word, and so I will, noting that Noel's Fab Four fixation is still very much in evidence in lifted lyrics, borrowed riffs, and a George Martin–style production. Authenticity? Noel don't need no stinking authenticity. He offers his comment on the most tired argument in rock criticism on the album's opening track: "Fuck me," a backwards voice intones at the start of "D'You Know What I Mean?" and then the band tears into an epic rocker that uses the exact same chords as George Harrison's "Wonderwall" and incorporates drum loops sampled from N.W.A's *Straight Outta Compton*. No one can ever say these thieving Brits lack a sense of humor.

Noel knows that the only thing that really matters in rock today is whether or not a song moves you emotionally, and he writes indelible tunes that carry a visceral kick. "My Big Mouth," "It's Getting Better (Man!!)," and the title track recall the quicker tempos and angrier vibes of the first album with some effective Led Zeppelin bombast thrown in. The Stone Roses tried the same trick on their second album, overdid it, and failed miserably. But Oasis has always learned from the mistakes of its Britpop peers, and the band does arena rock without getting sloppy or self-indulgent.

Nor does the group skimp on the big ballads. Lush orchestrations and headphone-friendly layers of sound decorate prettier numbers such as the eleven-minutes-plus "All Around the World," "Don't Go Away," and "Magic Pie." The latter is the only tune that Noel sings, and he's said it's one of the five best he's ever written. "You see me, I got my magic pie," goes the massive sing-along chorus. What does it mean? Not a damn thing, as far as I can tell, but I'm willing to waive that demand when the hooks are this good. Sometimes we ask too much of our rock 'n' roll stars, when it ought to be enough to be darn good entertainment.

The Stone Roses, Second Coming
Request, March 1995

FROM THE VANTAGE point of these shores, England often seems a strange and curious place. Why the obsession with that backbiting pack of adulterers known as the Royal Family? What the hell are those women in *Absolutely Fabulous* talking about? And why was anyone ever so excited about the Stone Roses?

Nearly five years ago, the Manchester quartet released a self-titled debut that broke ground by combining '60s psychedelia—jangly Byrds guitars, swirling echo, and a bit of baroque-period Simon and Garfunkel—with the revved-up, Ecstasy-fueled disco beats heard nightly at dance clubs like the Hacienda. *The Stone Roses* was a pleasant enough effort, and it sold relatively well in the United States (about two hundred and fifty thousand copies) considering the group never played here. But apparently we Yanks missed the band's true sociological importance.

"A collision of drug economics, gifted players, and fashion bedlam had transformed the whole typography of young life in the United Kingdom," the editors of the *New Musical Express* recently wrote in a six-page spread devoted to the band's long-awaited return. "The Stone Roses gave rock 'n' roll back its thrilling provenance. That ability to reach beyond the normal core of music fanatics and to charm a whole generation, to change utterly the way you walk, talk, and dress. They were a band blessed with splendor and mystery." The British press is renowned for its hyperbole, but since I wasn't there, I'm willing to grant that this might have been the case in the merry ol' England of 1989. The only mystery now is how any group could have spent four years crafting an album as stultifyingly mediocre as the cheekily titled *Second Coming*.

The Stone Roses spent much of their hiatus fighting a lawsuit with their former record company, Silvertone, and the rest of it listening to Led Zeppelin. The group makes several attempts to craft Zeppelinesque anthems that build from gentle pastorals to bombastic rockers. "Daybreak" reaches back beyond Zep to Jimmy Page's first group, building to a spirited Yardbirds raveup, and "Good Times" is an attempt at genuine blues. But the ubiquitous "Madchester" beat (dugga-dugga CHA!, dugga-dugga-dugga CHA!) gives everything an unintended sameness, which is especially amazing when you consider these tracks come from at least five sessions over a forty-six-month period.

Originality was never a major virtue of the Stone Roses or the many Madchester bands that followed in their wake, including Happy Mondays, Inspiral Carpets, and the Charlatans (though the latter eventually blossomed into the strongest of any of these bands). Other English "if-the-'90s-were-the-'60s" groups made a game of stealing sounds and riffs, but Ride and Blur succeeded where the Stone Roses and their disciples failed because they had better hooks, weren't wedded to a mechanical dance beat, and had stronger senses of humor.

Second Coming's opening track, "Breaking into Heaven," is a long, drawn-out jam with lots of Steve Howe–style guitar. The title seems to be taken from Jay Stevens's *Storming Heaven*, the definitive history of LSD. "How many times will I have to tell you / You don't have to wait to die / You can have it all any time you want it / Yeah, the kingdom's all inside," Ian Brown sings. It's precisely this sort of ponderous preaching that gave psychedelia a bad name in the first place.

Guitarist John Squire (who wrote most of the songs) and bassist Mani give the Roses what little spark they have, while man-machine drummer

Reni and the band's flat, monotonous vocalist remain its weak links. During the unimaginatively titled Southern boogie "Driving South," Brown actually makes you yearn for Black Crowes frontman Chris Robinson. And his attempts to sound like the Incredible String Band's Robin Williamson on the Eastern-tinged "Ten Storey Love Song" and "Tightrope" are laughable.

Saying that *Second Coming* is a major disappointment plays into the English assumption that the band was ever really important in the first place. The four-year span that produced this album is the only thing that distinguishes it from countless other bogus follow-ups by once-promising newcomers. At best that earns the Stone Roses their place in perpetuity as a rock 'n' roll footnote, and not a particularly interesting one, either.

Adventures in Stereo
The *Chicago Sun-Times*, October 14, 1993

LIKE FRITZ LANG'S groundbreaking film *Metropolis*, the English sextet Stereolab has a distinctive vision that's both antiquated and futuristic. The group performs hypnotic, driving art-rock based on the unique gurgling and wheezing of early '70s instruments such as the Moog synthesizer and the Farfisa organ. "Today's instruments have no sound of their own," guitarist-keyboardist Tim Gane says. "The whole point of the Moog was that it didn't sound like anything else. It sounded like what it was: a weird view of the future that never happened."

Stereolab is one of several remarkable bands to emerge on Too Pure, one of England's most influential independent labels. But while labelmates PJ Harvey, th' faith healers, and Moonshake have built enthusiastic cult followings in this country, Stereolab so far remains largely unknown. (Its first three albums are available only as imports or hard-to-find indie releases.) This may change with *Transient Random-Noise Bursts With Announcements*, the band's first release on Elektra Records. The evocative title—along with previous efforts such as the single "John Cage Bubblegum," *Switched on Stereolab*, and *The Groop Played Space Age Batchelor Pad Music*—offers insight into the band's approach: The focus is on the sound, not the songs.

"We've probably recorded eighty songs on record since we got going two years ago," Gane says. "We pump out a lot of tracks because they're all just ideas, and I don't want to get precious about the records. The majority of the tracks are done first-take shortly after the band hears them because we want that spontaneity. Sometimes the music takes over and you don't know the direction it's going. The control is less than in other groups, but then you get things in the music that you didn't actually think of, happy accidents and weird harmonic clashes."

Gane jokes that he formed Stereolab with French vocalist Laetitia Sadier "about five minutes" after his first band, the jangly pop group McCarthy, split in 1990. The pair recorded several singles and EPs with various friends who came and went, including visiting members of th' faith healers and Moonshake. The lineup is now solidified with Gane, Sadier, Mary Hansen on backing vocals and guitar, Duncan Brown on bass, Katharine Gifford on organ, and Andy Ramsay on drums. But regardless of the personnel at the time, Stereolab's music has always been a fluid mix of simple, melodic drones that rise and fall around an insistent drumbeat.

In addition to such obvious influences as Brian Eno, Phillip Glass, and New Jersey cult legends the Feelies, the group draws inspiration from the early '70s Krautrock band Neu!, an offshoot of synthesizer geniuses Kraftwerk. Neu! specialized in an almost mechanical beat called *motorik* that was meant to evoke the feeling of speeding down the autobahn. Stereolab augments Neu!'s instrumental style with catchy hooks and Sadier's sweet, mysterious vocals, which are often sung in French or nonsense syllables. This approach can result in some varied and diverse moments: Compare the epic "Sister Ray" drone of "Jenny Ondioline" with the lilting "Tone Burst." But it also marks Stereolab as one of today's most single-minded bands.

"Sometimes I feel it's like a big block of music," Gane says, "and we just chip bits off and record them."

Thievery? Sure, But Inspired Thievery
The *Chicago Sun-Times*, February 9, 2003

AUTHENTICITY HAS ALWAYS been a thorny concept in rock 'n' roll. Critics love to laud originality and innovation, but this has always been a bastardized art form, wantonly stealing from any number of other styles and genres. The second album by Teenage Fanclub is a classic of tasteful thievery—it's impossible to imagine it ever being made without the band's three songwriters (guitarists-vocalists Norman Blake and Raymond McGinley and bassist Gerard Love) hearing the three influential albums that pioneering power-popsters Big Star made in the early '70s (*Radio City*, *No. 1 Record*, and *Big Star 3rd*, a.k.a. *Sister Lovers*).

As teens growing up in Glasgow, Scotland, a world away from the American South, the members of Teenage Fanclub had almost nothing in common with Big Star's twin auteurs, Alex Chilton and Chris Bell. Like Led Zeppelin or Derek and the Dominos reinterpreting the blues greats a generation earlier, the members of Teenage Fanclub applied Big Star's uniquely chiming guitars, moody atmospherics, and oh-so-romantic lyrics to their own cultural touchstones, substituting pubs for juke joints and jaded post-punk lasses for heartbreaker Southern belles. Rather than copping Big Star riffs and melodies wholesale (try spotting flagrant note-for-note rips and you'll come up empty-handed), the twelve tunes on the group's best album strive to capture a similar vibe and the melancholy but ultra-melodic essence of what made Big Star great.

As I said, Teenage Fanclub couldn't have made *Bandwagonesque* without Big Star. But you don't need to have heard Big Star to appreciate *Bandwagonesque*.

Blake and McGinley first teamed with Love in 1987 in a short-lived Glasgow group called the Boy Hairdressers, which issued one indie single before disbanding. After a short stint with the BMX Bandits, Blake and his mates reunited to form Teenage Fanclub in 1989; drummer and fellow BMX Bandit Francis McDonald completed the original lineup, though he was replaced by fan Brendan O'Hare during sessions for the group's debut, 1990's *A Catholic Education*, which was released on the revered Creation Records label in the U.K. and the ultra-hip Matador Records in the U.S.

Arriving a year before Nirvana's *Nevermind* ushered in the alternative-rock explosion of the '90s, *A Catholic Education* did its best to hide its sparkling melodies under hypnotic, droning rhythms and expansive layers of the sort of raw guitars that would soon be ubiquitously described as "grunge." But there were hints of what was to come, and of the band's nascent obsession with Big Star.

To their credit, Teenage Fanclub never denied the influence, and the musicians constantly lauded Big Star in interviews at the time. The title of their second album acknowledges a debt to their forbears—the bandwagon they're referring to was driven by Chilton and Bell—though it's also a typically snarky and sarcastic comment on the music industry post-*Nevermind*. Prior to the album's release, Teenage Fanclub became the subject of an intense major-label bidding war in the States (the group eventually jumped from Matador to DGC), and while Nirvana commented on similar circumstances with its famous cover photo of fishing for a baby with a dollar bill, Teenage Fanclub went the Seattle rockers one better with a simple cartoon of a big fat moneybag.

Blake has said that the disc's opening track, "The Concept," served as a blueprint for the entire album, which was expertly produced in rough and ready fashion by Don Fleming (former leader of the Velvet Monkeys, another group that knew a lot about appropriation and balancing sweet pop melodies with grungy raunch). The song finds Blake pining after a girl he knows isn't right for him (her taste in music clearly isn't as cool as his own—she likes bad '70s metal), but he's determined to have her anyway. Still, he's a nice guy (even if he'd never let his mates at the pub see that), and he hates the idea of breaking her heart, though he knows he'll probably do it eventually.

"She wears denim wherever she goes," Blake sings. "Says she's gonna get some records by the Status Quo / Oh yeah, oh yeah." Sublimely stoopid, that's the entire first verse, but the tune just gets better: "Still she won't be forced against her will / Says she don't do drugs but she does the pill / Oh yeah, oh yeah / I didn't want to hurt you / Oh yeah / I didn't want to hurt you / Oh yeah."

Not exactly genius poetry, but the sadly sweet singing adds a universe of meaning in the same way that Marc Bolan's faintest hint of a leer added unplumbed depths to the lyrics of T. Rex. And the words really can't be separated from the music: After a burst of ugly feedback (echoes of *A Catholic Education*), those gloriously sunny and chiming guitars kick in, and they're as colorful and irresistible as a bowl of M&M's. They reign supreme through the rest of the album, joined on occasion by expertly crafted string parts, while the opening track builds to a beautiful, worldless, elegiac climax and coda that hints that maybe, just maybe, our slacker playboy hero wound up finding true love where he least expected it.

The moment is as good as power pop gets—pure bliss and unfettered emotion—and many more follow, from the rollicking spoof of "Metal Baby" to the achingly lovely "December," and from the catchy and brilliantly inarticulate "Alcoholiday" and "What You Do to Me" ("There are things I want to say but I don't know / If they will be to you"; "I know, I can't believe / There's something about you / Got me down on my knees") to the indeli-

ble closing instrumental "Is This Music?" (which finds the musicians following in the footsteps of New Wave–era countrymen Big Country, mimicking the sound of Scottish bagpipes with their guitars).

Though *Bandwagonesque* was named album of the year by *Spin* magazine
(overshadowing even *Nevermind*) and the band found itself playing on
Saturday Night Live and as an opening act on several major tours, Teenage
Fanclub never achieved mainstream success in the States, racking up only a
fraction of the sales of Nirvana or Pearl Jam. (These were xenophobic years
in America, and until Oasis, very little English music topped the modern-
rock radio charts.) Nevertheless the album has influenced countless power-
pop bands that followed, from Chicago rockers such as OK-GO and Frisbie
to English bands like Travis and Coldplay. And if Teenage Fanclub never
quite got the mix of thievery and distinction, sarcasm and heart-on-the-
sleeve honesty quite so right again (though there are certainly rewarding
moments on efforts such as *Thirteen* and the recent *Howdy!*), it did give us
one album that is every bit as great as those produced by the giants it
lauded.

Acid Reign
New Times Los Angeles, November 6, 1997

WHEN IT COMES to the complex machinery of the modern recording studio, it's hardly a stretch to say that Spiritualized auteur Jason Pierce is as
much a master of his domain as Phil Spector, George Martin, and Brian Eno
were of theirs. It's ironic, then, to find him stuck in the English countryside
grappling with something as simple as a cell phone that has lost its charge.

"Sometimes technology just conspires against you, you know?" he finally
says when he manages to call on a land line, four hours late for our scheduled chat. Actually, I know all too well: It turned out that the batteries in my
recorder were dying as I taped our interview, which I discovered when I
started to transcribe it. Over the course of an hour-long conversation, Pierce
starts to speak slower and slower, until he's finally talking like Winnie the
Pooh's pal Eeyore on downers. But it's strangely fitting to hear Pierce this
way, since he's the man who helped write a new chapter in the book on
Quaalude rock with the hugely influential Spacemen 3, and the man whose
current band is one of the most intoxicating and disorienting combos in popular music today, not to mention one of the most underappreciated.

"All the best things in life fuck you up the most, whether it's love sickness or drug sickness," Pierce once told the *New Musical Express.* Rarely has the concept of "love is the drug" been explored with such intensity as on the group's third album. The disc represents the culmination of everything Pierce has done to date, a trip that began some twelve years ago when Spacemen 3 first started peddling its hypnotic, hallucinogenic drones.

Spacemen 3 was formed by guitarists-vocalists Pierce (who was Jason Spaceman then) and Peter Kember (aka Sonic Boom) when they were both attending art school in their industrial hometown of Rugby back in the early '80s. To people who care about the line of musical invention that stretches from early Pink Floyd, the Velvet Underground, and the 13th Floor Elevators through the Stooges and the MC5, Spacemen 3 were more than just a godhead rock band. They were *the next step.*

"By far the most important band of the 1980s, maybe one of the five essential bands of all time—they were one of the great psychedelic bands, capturing the essence of altered states of many varieties," wrote *Bomp!* publisher, label head, and Los Angeles underground legend Greg Shaw, who's certainly consumed enough psychedelics (musical and pharmaceutical) to be in the position to know.

After four proper albums and an armful of EPs, live discs, and assorted collections of odds and ends, Spacemen 3 came to a somewhat acrimonious end following 1991's Kraftwerk-obsessed *Recurring.* A lot of folks put their money on Kember after the split. But while some of the ambient ear wash he's made with Spectrum and the more snooze-inducing Experimental Audio Research has been, um, *intriguing*, Kember's post-Spacemen work pales in comparison to Pierce's. And don't think Pierce is above gloating. "I've never had any interest in remaking Brian Eno's ambient stuff," he tells me without invoking his former partner by name. "I mean, it's been done, hasn't it?"

Pierce set out to do something different. Spiritualized was formed around the core of himself, second guitarist Mark Refoy (now fronting Slipstream), and Pierce's girlfriend, Kate Radley, the only member besides Mr. Spaceman to play on all three Spiritualized albums. (In fact, Radley's Vox Continental and Farfisa Compact organs are as big a part of the band's sound as Pierce's Fender Jaguar and Vox Starstreamer.) Pierce was determined to craft what he called "a modern soul music" that used a different musical language than the one in the Book of Otis Redding.

The band debuted in 1992 with *Lazer Guided Melodies*, a mesmerizing mix of vintage Pink Floyd psychedelia, John Coltrane–style free jazz, and the sort of fervent speaking-in-tongues gospel music that's played in revival tents. The group took its first live bow in America a short time later as part of the Roller Coaster tour with Curve and the Jesus and Mary Chain. The extra cash that came from being part of a big road show enabled it to present the full light show that had become a trademark of its performances at home in England. During that first stateside jaunt, songs such as "Run" and "Shine a Light" ebbed and flowed into one another without a break as the band members stood in clouds of thick white fog that were penetrated only by the intense white lights shooting up from the floor. These blinding beams surrounded the musicians with luminescent columns that evoked the spotlight constructions of Nazi architect Albert Speer, or an alien visitation à la *Close Encounters of the Third Kind*. A religious experience it was, but Spiritualized hasn't duplicated it on these shores since.

"For lots of technical reasons that I won't go into because they'll bore you, we really haven't been able to bring over the full light show since that tour," Pierce says with a sigh of disappointment. "I mean, we do alright in New York, L.A., and Chicago, but in lots of other places in America, we just can't afford that. We keep trying to get there, though."

For a time around the release of its second album, 1995's *Pure Phase*, Spiritualized added "Electric Mainline" to its name. Lyrically the emphasis was on drugs and the drug experience. As if that didn't make Pierce's ongoing chemical fixation perfectly clear, the record's first single was entitled "Medication." Given that his first band once titled an album *Taking Drugs to Make Music to Take Drugs To*, this seemed like old hat for Pierce, and while the music on *Pure Phase* went even further in exploring the free jazz elements of the first album, one suspected that he was running short on inspiration. The album's most notable sonic accomplishment was that it simultaneously offered two completely different mixes of each song done six months apart—one in the left channel, the other in the right.

As the months and then the years ticked by while fans waited for another offering, Pierce started to develop a reputation for being a studio perfectionist who was unable to stop tinkering with his creations. Visions of My Bloody Valentine's Kevin Shields danced in journalists' heads. But that's a rap that Pierce resents. "I don't think it's not letting it go," he says. "I think it's getting it right. You see so many bands that release their records and at the time say, 'Yeah, this is our new record and we're really proud of it.' But then with subsequent releases, you find out they're maybe *not* so proud of it. They say things like, 'We've got the right producer this time.' Or, 'We've reinvented ourselves.' I don't know, none of *my* friends reinvent themselves every couple of years.

"I want to get it right," Pierce continues. "I want to get it one hundred percent, so that this record can't be any better than it is. I can't find any fault with any of the records we've put out because of that reason: I allow myself the time to get it right."

The resulting album justifies his meticulousness. Recorded at seven different studios in Bath, London, Memphis, New York, and Los Angeles, with engineering help from the likes of John Leckie and Jim Dickinson, *Ladies and Gentleman, We Are Floating In Space* is a breathtaking musical and lyrical catharsis. And it came at a cost.

Always gossipy (and we love them for it), the English music weeklies have characterized the disc as an album chronicling the unraveling of Pierce's soulmate relationship with Radley, who remains in the band, if not in his bed. "All I want in life's a little bit of love to take the pain away," Pierce sings in the symphonic title track that opens the album. He finds his ideal romantic union in tunes such as the orgasmic, Detroit-flavored "Come Together" and the idyllic "I Think I'm in Love," which is augmented by a horn section and the lulling strings of the Balanescu Quartet.

But things get rockier—and the music noisier—as the album progresses. In "The Individual" and "Broken Heart," love is lost, and the pain is worse than any drug withdrawal. "I don't even miss you / But that's 'cause I'm fucked up / I'm sure when it wears off / Then I will be hurting," Pierce declares. Nevertheless he moves on: The album comes to a gut-wrenching close with the jarring, sixteen-minute "Cop Shoot Cop," an epic collaboration with legendary voodoo pianist Dr. John that stands as Spiritualized's answer to "Sister Ray." By the end of it all, nothing is resolved, because there are no easy answers for Pierce. But you're left with the impression that the music has seen him through, just as it always has in the past.

A veritable Harry Houdini, Pierce deftly wiggles out of questions about the English media's take on the autobiographical elements of the album. "I don't read it," he says. "I'm not interested in that kind of press," he says. He doesn't mind talking about the album's other controversy, though.

Advance cassettes that were sent to press and radio included a different version of the title track, one on which Spiritualized covered part of the verse and chorus of Elvis Presley's "Can't Help Falling in Love" and folded it into the middle of the group's own tune. That brief snippet set the tone for everything that followed: Only fools rush in, but like an addict, Pierce just can't help himself. The choice becomes even more appropriate if you're aware, as Pierce reminded me, that a tape of Elvis's version was packed on the Voyager Space Probe before it was launched into the cosmos. Unfortunately, the Presley estate threatened legal action and forced the band to remove the Elvis portion of the song only weeks before the album's release.

"If I had wanted to re-title the song 'Can't Help Falling in Love' and given him the songwriting credit, then I could have done that, but it wasn't that big a part of the song," Pierce says. "I actually prefer the new version of it. It sounds now like a pop song written by a madman, whereas before it had this kind of familiarity to it—a safety net—because it revolved around this Elvis track."

In truth, the version with the ghost of Elvis was a near-perfect pop moment. But in 1997, you have to admire any rock visionary who is so consistently willing to work without that safety net.

"That's what I've held out for; I've always tried *not* to compromise," Pierce says. "Too many people are compromising massively, whereas my idea of success is putting out records that capture what we want to capture. We wanted to make a record that would fit alongside Sly and the Family Stone's *There's a Riot Going On*, Captain Beefheart's *Clear Spot*, and Elvis's Sun Sessions, rather than something that fits alongside the glut of contemporary music." And damned if he hasn't succeeded.

9 PIONEERS AND TRAILBLAZERS

I AM STRUCK BY JUST HOW MANY ARTISTS were cited over the course of the '90s as the "godfather (or godmother) of alternative rock," though not without justification. As I've noted earlier, the music did not develop in a vacuum—like all rock genres (or marketing trends) it was part of a continuum—and significant elements of the "alternative" sound, attitude, and approach to music-making can be seen in all of the artists included here.

This chapter opens with two of the most influential, Lou Reed and John Cale, the founders of a band that has been hailed as an inspiration so many times that it should really be tacked on as part of the name: the Seminal Velvet Underground. I prefer Cale's solo work to Reed's through the '90s—it's far less pretentious, more genuinely challenging, and a lot more fun—and it's interesting to note how Reed's adamant stance in 1992 against reuniting his most famous group was abandoned a few years later (though the Velvets reunion was short-lived indeed).

The piece on Brian Eno was written as a preview of U2's Zoo TV tour and was intended to introduce him to that band's audience as the wizard behind the curtain (though he is that and so very much more). I have interviewed Eno many times over the last decade and a half, and he is one of the most fascinating artists and thinkers I've ever encountered. His influence is pervasive—he was certainly an inspiration to the next three artists, Pere Ubu, Wire, and Wake Ooloo (the '90s incarnation of the Feelies)—and they in turn prompted a legion of rewarding bands that followed.

Some of these artists continue to make incredible music today, and some are quite clearly resting on their laurels (Patti Smith, Lee Perry). To acknowledge that is not to slight their previous accomplishments, only to hold them up to the high standards they originally set for themselves. If rock 'n' roll is really about "truth," not hype, even our heroes should be viewed sans rose-colored glasses.

Love & Death
Request, February 1992

FROM HIS WILD glam-rock days in the mid-'70s until he bottomed out in the early '80s, Lou Reed defined the words "high risk." He tied up with a microphone cord and shot speed on stage, had a torrid affair with a transsexual named Rachel, and sank deep into alcoholism and drug addiction. Not many rock 'n' rollers could tackle a sixty-minute concept album about death without sounding hopelessly pretentious. Reed isn't completely successful either, but *Magic and Loss*, his twenty-first solo album, carries the credibility of a survivor.

In one of the album's most effective moments, Reed, standing at the deathbed of a friend, writes, "If I was in your shoes / So strange that I am not / I think that I would fold up in a minute." "There's an understatement," he says, puffing on a foul-smelling Cuban cigar (he says he doesn't inhale). "Put it this way: I think it's possible that a listener might take my descriptions of things seriously because I have a track record to prove that I know what I'm talking about, and I have a background as an artist of being faithful to the listener and truthful. All great writers, at a certain point in life, have to deal with certain really basic, classic themes that go all the way back to the Greeks and Romans: Birth, life, and death—that's it. I think at this point I'm mature enough to be able to write with some veracity about one of those subjects."

Magic and Loss arrives at a point where Reed, fifty, is looking back at his long career, even though he claims to hate nostalgia. He recently compiled a three-CD box set for RCA that sums up his solo career before he moved to Warner Bros. for 1989's *New York,* and Hyperion, Disney's book division, published *Between Thought and Expression*, which collects lyrics from Reed's solo career and his days as the lead singer and guitarist with the Velvet Underground. "It's as close to autobiographical as you'll get from me," he says. According to his song, "Some Kinda Love," "Between thought and expression / Lies a lifetime." "Yeah, mine," Reed says.

Reed is one of rock 'n' roll's greatest chameleons, second only to David Bowie, who stole the concept of periodically reinventing yourself from Reed in the first place. At various times in his solo career Reed has been a gender-bending glam star (*Transformer*), an art-rocker (*Berlin*), a metalhead (*Rock 'n' Roll Animal*), and a punk (*Street Hassle*). After producing two brilliant albums about the tortures of kicking drugs and alcohol—1982's *The Blue Mask* and 1983's *Legendary Hearts*—he foundered for several years before finding his muse again on *New York*, an overweening album about the continuing decline of his beloved hometown, and 1990's *Songs for Drella,* a touching tribute to the Velvets' mentor, Andy Warhol, recorded with former bandmate John Cale.

The persona Reed has adopted these days is that of the Serious Writer; all that's missing is the cardigan and pipe. He proudly notes that lyrics from *New York* have been printed on the op-ed page of the *New York Times,* and he talks at length about the joys of writing on a laptop computer. His recent efforts sound less like his best rock songs—"Sweet Jane," "Rock 'n' Roll," or even "Walk on the Wild Side"—than long-winded prose poems set to music. In his book, Reed cites "The Bells" as his favorite lyric because it came all at once as he stood at the microphone, but there seems to be little of the spontaneous, improvisational spirit of the Velvets or his best solo efforts on his recent albums.

"Don't be too sure," Reed replies in his familiar nasal monotone. "When I'm writing, I try to leave a lot of room for certain things to happen. I saw Garrison Keillor on TV, and Larry King asked him this question about writing. He said something really interesting, I thought, because it applies to me. He was lucky, he said, because God made him an insomniac, so he's up at odd hours and he sits down and he writes. There's no one else around, it's totally quiet, and at that hour of the morning you can figure out things that a really smart guy wouldn't be able to figure out a couple of hours later. And that's how I feel. You really have direct access to things. Almost everything on *Magic and Loss* was written at like five in the morning on a computer.

"Writing is hard. Any kind of writing is hard. On the other hand, it's also really great, great fun. And it can also be excruciating."

"Excruciating" is a word Reed uses a lot when talking about *Magic and Loss.* The album was inspired by two close friends who succumbed to cancer last year, a woman known as Rotten Rita back in the days of Warhol's Factory and legendary songwriter Doc Pomus. But considering the number of gay friends Reed has lost and the chill that's fallen over the New York art and music scenes, the specter of AIDS looms large over the album.

"I think it's unfair to categorize the album as being about death. I think of it as being a celebration about friendship and love and dealing with the loss of that," Reed says. "I think it's a very positive album, especially these days with AIDS, where younger people are being faced with loss way earlier than people would normally be facing it. Everybody is losing relatives and friends left and right, this is just a fact, and there's no cure for it. You're talking about something that's fatal. You see these people doing ads on TV, HIV-positive, they look OK, but the rest of the story is that they will eventually die. There is no cure for this thing. HIV-positive means 'leading into.' What will Magic Johnson look like in a year? Will everybody applaud him when he comes out then?

"It's a terrible situation. How do you deal with loss? We're not trained to deal with loss. Our media keeps it away from us. People don't want to hear about it. And yet it can be a very, very positive and inspiring experience in real life if you happen to be in the situation I was, watching people who were absolute giants. The guy on the record says, 'Not a day goes by that I don't try to be like you.' And I'm trying to give that to the listener, that experience, because getting that from these people, then the loss is transformed. It's not just loss, these people live on. And I try to demonstrate it to you rather than just tell you about it. The demonstration of it is the magic."

Although he's often accused of being a cynic, Reed has always believed in the redemptive power of music. With the Velvet Underground he wrote of a girl whose "life was saved by rock 'n' roll." *Between Thought and Expression* includes a 1990 interview with Czech president Vaclav Havel, who talks of drawing strength and inspiration to fight the Communist regime from Reed's lyrics. And Reed seems genuine when he says he hopes *Magic and Loss* will help some of his fans come to terms with losing a loved one.

"I am, in fact, already hearing that from journalists, of all people," he says. "It's something they don't normally talk about, because who would you talk about that with? It would have to be someone very, very close to you. And yet I'm talking to people who will suddenly say, 'My brother'... or 'Six years ago, I had to go in,' or 'Both my parents died.' It's around a lot more than we know or speak about, and I don't think that's such a great thing. Talking is one of the cures. The thing that works for alcoholics and drug addicts is sharing, sharing of experiences. 'Now listen to this one.' They become funny. You can tell the most horrifying experiences, and it's actually funny. When that happens, you're on the way."

The idea of devoting an album to one concept certainly isn't new, though the form is usually associated with such overblown and mock-operatic works as *Tommy* and *The Wall*. Reed believes he's breathing new life into the genre, although he'd never link his recent efforts with the Who or Pink Floyd, or even his own overblown but sporadically brilliant concept album, 1973's *Berlin*. "I don't think there's ever been a really great album about just one subject at all ever, not that I can think of," he says. "I think that I've assiduously discovered what I would call a brand new art form, which is a CD with fourteen or fifteen songs connected by a theme with a beginning, a middle, and an end and lyrics that can stand on their own as poetry.

"With the Warhol thing, *Songs for Drella*, I thought, 'Jesus Christ, we could call this a new category, bio-rock.' And here's a chance for black rappers to do their constituents a great service. Just like I tried to introduce you to Warhol, the rappers could introduce you to Malcolm X or Langston Hughes or James Baldwin. I think Hammer should think about it. Michael Jackson should think about it. All they have to do is look at *Songs for Drella*, my Warhol album, this is how it's done. It's easy. It's the writing that's hard. You're talking about sustained thought, which in America right now is not easy. It's all quick editing."

Some critics have pointed to Reed's chronicling of the seamy underside of New York City as a prelude to the gratuitous sex and violence that gangsta rappers pass off as "urban realism." On 1986's *Mistrial*, Reed himself claimed to be the original rapper. But the first rapper to score a hit from one of Reed's tunes is Marky Mark, New Kid Donnie Wahlberg's pumped-up younger brother, who updated "Walk on the Wild Side." "For what Marky Mark was trying to do, I thought it was an honest attempt at it, and on that basis I thought it was really OK, and so I approved that one. Now it's a big hit, so that's kind of nice," Reed says, missing the irony of a lightweight popster crooning about the wild side. Then again, Reed didn't think it was ironic when he sold "Walk on the Wild Side" to Honda for a scooter commercial, either.

Reed dismisses most of the rappers who approach him to sample his work as "terrible, simply awful." Despite his long-standing love of new technology—he's always experimenting with new recording techniques, and before this interview, he fiddled curiously with his publicist's new computer Rolodex—Reed isn't interested in sequencers or samplers. He's a conservative when it comes to sticking with the two guitars, bass, and drums format. "There's all kinds of ways to expand the format through the tone, choice of notes, taking those progressions and turning them inside out a little bit, mixing progressions or two styles that you normally wouldn't think of, using space as a note. It doesn't have to be the same old thing over and over. Plus, from a sound point of view, it's astonishing the things you can do with guitars now.

"I finally have the technology working for me instead of against me," Reed says. "I was generally losing to it. I put out a lot of records that are like demos, just completely dry, because I couldn't stand the engineers and I couldn't get what I wanted, so rather than them make it even worse, I just put it out dry. It's been very, very difficult. I had to really immerse myself in the technical end of things by seeking out people who are much better than I am and asking them lots of questions. That's kind of one of my techniques. I'm always looking to be around people who are way more advanced than I could ever hope to be. 'Oh, how did you do that? Do that again. Show me how you did that.'"

The urge to pick the brains of the people who are working for him may be the reason Reed hasn't kept a band together for more than a few albums. He claims he has no interest in reuniting with any of his old bands, whether it's the powerful Robert Quine–Fernando Saunders–Fred Maher group of *The Blue Mask* and *Legendary Hearts* period or the Velvet Underground. But Reed is nothing if not inconsistent, and the Velvets did in fact come together for one song in the fall of 1990 at a Warhol tribute in Paris. "It will never happen again. It was purely a moment in time," he says now. "You must remember, I wrote, what, ninety-seven percent of the material for the Velvet Underground. These are things I've gone through on my way to making *Magic and Loss*. So I don't want to—and I don't, not in real life—look back. There's nothing to be gained from it. You're trying to grow and go forward, and the people you were with then are not where you are now. So it's not a fair match up."

Reed's most memorable sparring matches over the years have been with members of the music press, with whom he's had a love-hate relationship. He needs journalists' accolades to feed his sizable ego, but he dismisses their criticism as unknowledgeable. (Before our interview, he was griping to his publicist about something Jon Pareles had written in the *New York Times*.) No critic has had as intense a relationship with Reed as Lester Bangs, however. Reed has outlived his old nemesis (Bangs died in 1982 after overdosing on Darvon, a muscle relaxant), but Bangs seemed to predict Reed's future in a 1975 article entitled "Let Us Now Praise Famous Death Dwarves."

"Lou Reed's enjoyed a solo career renaissance primarily by passing himself off as the most burnt-out reprobate around, and it wasn't all show by a long shot," Bangs wrote. "People kept expecting him to die, so perversely he came back not to haunt them, but to clean up."

"I think sometimes when people get obsessed with your work, it's really dangerous for both of you," Reed says of Bangs and, by extension, any fan who draws too close. "You can disappoint someone like that so easily when they find out just how human you are. They'd rather have this illusion of this, that, or the other thing. I'm not dealing on that level of illusion. That's not the kind of magic I'm dealing in. What I'm dealing in is what's on the record. That's me at my best, when I have time and the ability for sustained thought to make it as good as I possibly can. Me in person can't possibly be as good as that."

Slow Dazzle
Request, January 1993

"I'VE BEEN CHASING ghosts, and I don't like it," John Cale sings in his deep, rich baritone on a stark new version of "Dying on the Vine," a tune he admits is autobiographical. Both Cale and his former partner, Lou Reed, have spent most of their lives chasing the familiar ghost of their former band, the Velvet Underground. The group's influence is so pervasive that everything Cale and Reed have done since parting ways has been measured against it, so it's only natural to compare the approaches they took in summing up their solo careers.

Reed, awfully scholarly in his current guise, compiled a three-CD box set and a hardcover book that presented his lyrics as works of poetry. More direct, less pretentious, and more of a natural performer, Cale—who started playing classical piano for the BBC at the age of eight—took to the stage with an acoustic guitar and a grand piano and recorded new versions of twenty of his best songs to form *Fragments of a Rainy Season*, a concise history of his work since leaving the Velvets twenty-five years ago.

"I don't look at it as a greatest-hits revue," the towering Welshman says in a lilting accent untainted by decades of living in New York City. "It's more of a diary of records that I did than anything." He pauses then laughs heartily as he thinks of Reed's fans shelling out thirty dollars for *Between Thought and Expression: The Lou Reed Anthology* CD box set and being treated to an excerpt of the almost unlistenable *Metal Machine Music*. "I actually believe Lou when he says he hates looking back. That's not nostalgia; he put it out, gritting his teeth just like I do. I don't want to get categorized, and I don't want to feel like this is the last gasp either."

Far from a last gasp, *Fragments of a Rainy Season* is a long-overdue reminder that Cale has written some complex, beautiful, and frightening songs that are as timeless as anything his former partner has penned. A passionate, dramatic singer and songwriter, he's capable of crafting the perfect musical accompaniment for the Dylan Thomas poem "Do Not Go Gentle Into That Good Night"; painting a colorful landscape of the Old West in the touching minimalist ballad "Buffalo Ballet"; or playing the role of a raging, homicidal lunatic in the horrifying "Fear (Is a Man's Best Friend)." And he attacks the piano and guitar—as he has in the past with bass, viola, and organ—with a frantic intensity that belies his virtuosity.

Cale's music has always balanced his dual passions for the classical avant garde (before the Velvets he studied with composer Aaron Copland and performed with John Cage and La Monte Young) and raw, stripped-down rock 'n' roll. Recording for Island through much of the '70s, he released such powerful albums as 1973's *Paris 1919*, 1974's *Fear*, and 1975's *Slow Dazzle*, and he worked with an impressive list of inventive musicians including Terry Riley, Robert Wyatt, Brian Eno, Roxy Music's Phil Manzanera, and guitarist Chris Spedding.

The stark, immediate sound of Cale's own albums and those he produced for other artists (including the debuts of Patti Smith, the Modern Lovers, the Stooges, and Squeeze) were a strong influence on punk and much of what has followed. His popularity as a solo artist began to wane in the early '80s, however; distracted by personal demons and short on inspiration, he toured with assorted pickup bands and released such disappointing albums as 1981's *Honi Soit . . .* and 1984's *Caribbean Sunset*. But Cale entered the '90s reinvigorated by three of his most interesting projects.

In 1989 Cale released *Words for the Dying,* an album produced by Eno and featuring a Russian orchestra and a Welsh choir on the ambitious thirty-one-minute "Falklands Suite." The album also included "The Soul of Carmen Miranda," a lovely pop song written with Eno that led to an upbeat album-length collaboration, *Wrong Way Up,* in 1990. In between Cale worked with Reed again for the first time in twenty years on *Songs for Drella*, a tribute to the Velvet Underground's mentor, Andy Warhol.

Cale drew the best out of both partners, lending Eno the technical prowess he lacks and spurring Reed with a passion that's missing these days as he takes shelter onstage behind his spectacles, music stand, and lyric sheets. Eno and Reed both swore off collaborations after working with Cale, however, and that seems to say as much about those artists' desire for control as it does about the difficulties of working with the Welshman (though he can reportedly be obstinate in his own right). For his part, Cale leaves the door open for working with either man again, and he has even expressed enthusiasm for a Velvet Underground reunion.

On *Fragments of a Rainy Season*, Cale shows what he gained from the collaborations. His creepy new version of "Cordoba" from *Wrong Way Up* permanently marks the song as his own, and his sentimental vocal on "Style It Takes" lovingly recalls Warhol's pride in Cale's old band, compressing all of *Songs for Drella* into one verse: "This here's a rock group called the Velvet Underground / They play when we show movies, don't you like the sound? / 'Cause they've got the sound that grates / And I've got the art to make."

Cale and Reed started *Songs for Drella* by taping their conversations as they reminisced about Warhol. "But at the end of the project, Lou just shut the door and came back and said, 'Here's the lyrics,'" Cale says. His work with Eno on "Cordoba" was more typical of the way Cale writes, using found art and the inspiration of the moment to build a song in the recording studio.

"When we got to ['Cordoba'], we had an instrumental track, and Brian and I were discussing lyrics to put on it," Cale says. "He had a textbook there, a Spanish-to-English translation book for students in high school in Spain. At the end of each chapter, it had exercises for each individual chapter telling you to translate the following sentences, and they were totally unconnected sentences. After a while of trying to hammer some sense out of them, we just turned the tape on and started singing in the same sort of stream-of-consciousness style of putting a song together out of disparate sentences. What started off as 'Exercise 54' became 'Cordoba,' and it turned into this portrait of a terrorist."

Songs such as "Cordoba" often take on new meanings as Cale performs them live. "Dying on the Vine" from 1985's *Artificial Intelligence* "gradually became the story of my childhood," he says. Another song that has evolved through the years is his cover of Elvis Presley's "Heartbreak Hotel," which appears as a tortured heavy-metal tune on the live album, *June 1, 1974*, a haunting dirge on *Slow Dazzle*, and a spooky jazz number on *Fragments of a Rainy Season*. "That was always one of my strong suits—different arrangements of things. But that song would not have stood up unless the words had been that great; I think I've explored more sides of that than Elvis's version."

The idea of recording a retrospective of his own songs in a stripped-down acoustic setting was the result of what Eno would call "a happy accident." "When I did the tour that this album came from, I started off with a

humongous MIDI system, and after about three concerts, something happened," Cale says. "I think we went into Italy, and the promoter said, 'I'm
sorry I couldn't get the equipment, do you mind doing it on the Steinway?'
I was kind of pissed off, but I did it, and as soon as that concert was over, I
just canceled the rest of the MIDI for the tour. It was much less of a
headache and a pleasure to play the real instrument, and all the technique
that I'd lost from playing electronic instruments started coming back."

Fragments of a Rainy Season was recorded during performances last spring
in Paris, Stuttgart, and Brussels. Cale is pleased with the results, but he
plans to work with a string quartet for the second release of his two-album
deal with Hannibal-Rykodisc. "I stopped working with a band because I
was always making my drummer miserable," he says. "I'd take the cym-
bals away from him; I did everything but took his snare away. But there's
life after back-beat. With the string quartet, it was great the way the arrangements worked; it was a lot more subtle and closer to what the songs
were about. And I could do acoustic and amplified strings, so I could get
back to the noise with that, no problem at all."

Cale has also been working with composer Robert Neuwirth on a musical theater piece called *The Last Day on Earth,* and the two hope to tour with
the project in January. But aside from a few scattered projects in France, he
hasn't devoted much time in the last few years to producing other artists.
"I'm lazy by nature," he says by way of explanation, then starts to laugh. "I
have no right to say I'm lazy when I'm as busy as I am."

Unlike his former bandmate Reed, Cale doesn't aspire to take rock 'n' roll
in bold new directions, and he isn't worried about being accorded proper respect in the history books. "A good eighty percent of my audience is young
people, and I don't know why they're there, but it's very exciting," he says.
At fifty he's content simply to follow his muse, and he's glad when someone
comes along for the ride. "I used to write poetry first and then turn them into
songs. I'd show them to Lou, and he'd say, 'Right there, that's the chorus.'
And I sort of learned to spot where poetry ends and rock 'n' roll begins."

Taking Advice by Strategy
The *Chicago Sun-Times,* September 13, 1992

ONE OF THE most innovative thinkers in the history of popular music,
producer Brian Eno is the man who makes U2's albums interesting,

among many other accomplishments. He first collaborated with the platinum-selling rockers on *The Unforgettable Fire* (1984), was back at the helm for the hugely successful *The Joshua Tree* (1987), and served as executive producer and artistic instigator for *Achtung Baby*, as well as helping U2 realize its concept for the Zoo TV tour, which returns to the Chicago area this week.

Eno helps U2 make music that doesn't sound like U2. It's a role he's filled with similar success for David Bowie and the Talking Heads, in addition to recording his own albums, which have been credited with inspiring both the punk and New Age movements.

"*The Joshua Tree* sold more copies in the first morning than all of the records I've ever made put together have ever sold, but I don't mind that," Eno says. "I think you can see certain things as a kind of research, things that are made for other artists in a way. It's what other artists take and use, like a single strong spice that then forms part of their work."

An English art school graduate, Eno played synthesizer on the first two Roxy Music albums before recording four electrifying solo albums that influenced the punk explosion by celebrating mood and emotion over technical virtuosity. In the late '70s, he abandoned rock to concentrate on several albums of ambient music that were a precursor to New Age. These sparse, sometimes static compositions were designed as background music that, he said, enhanced the thousand tasks of everyday life, rewarding close attention, but never demanding it. Last year, the forty-four-year-old artist returned to his rock roots on *Wrong Way Up*, a catchy, upbeat pop album recorded with former Velvet Underground viola player and bassist John Cale. *Nerve Net*, his new Warner Bros. album, continues in that direction. Although Eno is singing less, the songs are more hard-hitting and immediate, with a special emphasis on intricate but motivating rhythms.

Unlike most musicians, Eno has never been concerned about making a hit record. He refuses to tour, perform live, or make traditional music videos. "I always think of myself in sales terms much more like a jazz artist than a typical rock act," he says in his crisp, aristocratic British accent. "I get a peak in the first few weeks of people who've waited for the record, but then what quite often happens is things level off, and the albums keep selling for years and years. I don't really know how much difference it would make if I had a hit, because if that did happen, it would be so uncalculated that I would certainly not know how to do it again. The problem I'd be faced with is telling people that future records wouldn't necessarily sound like that. This is always a difficult problem for popular artists: They feel constrained by the expectations that have been generated by the fact that they made some hit records. Even U2 feels this."

Which is why the quartet hires Eno. "The good aspect of the relationship we have is they employ me to encourage them and to articulate their new ideas," he says between sips of tea. "Because they have a lot of people obviously who will encourage them to do more of what they've already done. It's much easier to encourage something you recognize, so people from the company and all the people they work with will come along and say, 'That sounds great,' because it sounds like the U2 they know and love. Well, I'm part of the small contingent that redress that by coming along and hearing things that I don't recognize and saying, 'Wow, now that sounds really exciting. Let's follow that for awhile.'"

Eno also helps the band articulate what its new sounds mean. Like the three albums he made with Bowie, *Achtung Baby* was recorded in Berlin, at a studio called Hansa Ton near a famous train depot called Zoo Station. The air was charged with the chaos and excitement resulting from the reunification of Germany. "There was definitely a very European feeling as well, as opposed to an American feeling on their other records," he says. "What 'European' meant was quite a few different things. It meant 'un-glossy.' It meant 'not nicely packaged' in what I would call a Hollywood way, of being neatly finished and presented as [in an officious voice], 'A professional product by one of the world's big bands.' They were very conscious of presenting something that when you put it on you went, 'Hell, this sounds a bit weird.' Where your initial reaction was, 'Christ, my hi-fi must be broken!'"

The band spent months working on the album, but Eno only flew in to join the group for several days every few weeks. "I would deliberately not listen to the stuff in between visits, so I could go in cold, as it were, and just listen through the material," he says. "I would say, 'Well, this one sounds fine, I don't think there's any reason for me to pay attention to this. This one has become a complete mess, and I suggest we spend half a day on it and decide from that half a day whether to just chuck it out or do something radically different with it. This one sounds radically confused, and last time I heard it, it sounded much more direct and clear'—those kinds of comments. Every visit gave the band a chance to marshal their resources and see where they were, assess the situation, and then when I left they'd go back to their dithering ways."

Eno also worked with the group while it was preparing its touring show, which will return to Chicago in an expanded version this week. "As is my usual role, I sort of took the overview position of saying, 'What do you want? You don't want a stage show where everything fits neatly into place, and it's all nicely organized and people know exactly where the center of attention is at all moments,'" he says. "That isn't what the music is about now, and it certainly isn't what this concept of a new Europe is about, so how can we make a stage show that has some of the feeling of defensiveness and chaos and information overload that we're trying to get across in some of the other places?"

Together Eno and U2 came up with the idea of using numerous video monitors with a quickly changing array of images. Eno suggested that the band make its own video discs so that images could be quickly and easily accessed to mesh with U2's live performance, instead of locking the band into prearranged tapes and effects. "I knew that that would be absolute death for U2, because their show depends on some kind of response to what's happening at that moment in that place," he says. "So if it turns out they want to do a song for five minutes longer, they can actually loop through the material again so that you're not suddenly stuck with black screens halfway through the fifth verse."

The stadium leg of U2's tour expands the Zoo TV concept with even bigger video monitors and more visuals, although Eno says his favorite part of the show is the stark acoustic set the band performs in mid-concert.

Although he admires them as musicians, Eno hasn't recorded with U2 on his own albums. "There's no good reason for that not having happened," he says. "They're always pretty busy, and I feel that they wouldn't be able to say no if I asked them."

Nerve Net came together at a variety of studios as Eno crossed the United States on a lecture tour; it was completed at his home studio in Woodbridge, England. Musical contributors include longtime collaborator Robert Fripp on guitar, former Led Zeppelin bassist John Paul Jones, drummer Jonathan "Sugarfoot" Moffett from Michael Jackson's band, and Tom Petty keyboardist Benmont Tench.

Eno is planning to release two more recordings before Christmas: an instrumental album called *The Shutov Assembly* that he describes as "non-rhythmic, scarcely melodic, and very atmospheric," and an EP of songs recorded before *Nerve Net* that were to have been included on a now-shelved album called *My Squelchy Life*. He's also finishing some music that will be released only as part of a home video, and preparing the written version of an illustrated lecture called *Perfume Defense and David Bowie's Wedding* ("That was sort of the summation of certain lines of thought about postmodernism, I suppose you'd say").

One of the few artists embraced by both the serious art and pop worlds, Eno is probably the only rock musician to belong to a think tank. His current interests range from the possibilities of virtual reality to perfumery (he recently wrote an article for *Details* on mixing his own scents). But despite his expertise on many subjects, he always champions the right of the "non-musician" and the "non-artist" to create, and he never comes across as pompous or pretentious.

"There's nothing worse than feeling too self-important when you work," he says. "If you get landed with this burden that 'I've got to do something great,' that's an awful thing. It's a bit like that situation at a dinner party where there's a silence, and suddenly, the silence gets longer, and as it gets longer, nobody knows how to break it, because you can't say something trivial. You know what I mean? You have to wait to say something momentous."

With Brian Eno, even the trivial seems momentous.

....

Here is a guide to Brian Eno's best solo albums and some of the most notable bands that he's produced.

Roxy Music
Originally the band's sound man, Eno graduated to synthesizers and tape manipulation, warping the other musicians' output and competing with singer Bryan Ferry as a focal point for attention. His wildly inventive playing is the highlight of such songs as "Virginia Plain" and "Editions of You" from 1972's *Roxy Music* and *For Your Pleasure*. Personality clashes with Ferry forced Eno's departure after the second Roxy Music album.

The "Pop" Albums
From 1973 to 1977, Eno recorded four brilliant solo albums that moved from creatively twisted progressive rock on *Here Come the Warm Jets* and *Taking Tiger Mountain (By Strategy)* to sparse, beautiful soundscapes on *Another Green World* and *Before and After Science*. Eno drew the best from contributors like Phil Collins, Robert Fripp, Roxy Music's Phil Manzanera, Fred Frith, and Bill Laswell, and these albums directly inspired proto-alternative bands such as the Feelies, Pere Ubu, and Wire. The pop albums and many of Eno's ambient efforts were recently reissued on the Caroline label.

David Bowie

Eno was at the console during Bowie's experimental Berlin phase in the mid-'70s, which included the LPs *Low*, *"Heroes,"* and *Lodger*. The albums, recently reissued on Rykodisc, were long on weird instrumentals, but also included pop gems such as "Heroes," "D.J.," and "Boys Keep Swinging."

The "Ambient" Albums

Eno believes listeners should be able to use music in real terms in their lives, and albums such as *Music for Airports*, *Music for Films*, and *Thursday Afternoon* are designed to serve as pleasant background listening for a variety of situations. His personal favorite is *Discreet Music*, because its calming sounds are frequently played in maternity wards.

Talking Heads

From 1978 to 1980, Eno was virtually the fifth member of the band. He produced *More Songs About Buildings and Food*, *Fear of Music*, and *Remain in Light*, overseeing the Heads' most exciting period as they shifted from minimalist New Wave pop to intricate African-inspired dance music.

The '90s

Eno returned to pop music after a long absence with 1992's *Wrong Way Up*, a cheerful, infectious album recorded with John Cale. That disc and his new Warner Bros. album, *Nerve Net*, are similar in approach to his '70s pop albums, but the rhythms are more mechanical and insistent and the compositions are much less song-oriented.

··

The Original Alternative Rock Band?
The *Chicago Sun-Times*, May 30, 1993

THE STORY OF Pere Ubu's long and twisted career is essentially summed up in the opening bars of "Wasted," the first song on the latest album by the veteran Cleveland art-punks. The tune begins with singer David Thomas playing a lulling sea chantey on the melodeon. "We were throwing time away," he intones. "Recklessly throwing time away."

The track sounds as if it's a melancholy middle-aged tone poem about wasted youth—until Thomas breaks the spell. "Rock!" he croaks, and the band kicks in with a chaotic guitar assault that leaves the listener dizzy and disoriented. If there's more to life than rock 'n' roll, the members of Pere Ubu aren't ready to admit it quite yet.

Thomas has long been one of rock's best and most unlikely frontmen. During the '70s punk explosion, he was an inspiration to self-conscious geeks everywhere: If an awkward, rotund fellow with a high, squeaky voice could be a rock star, there was hope for anyone. These days he wears 1940s suits and a tiny mustache that emphasizes his resemblance to Oliver Hardy, but his early, brooding stage persona (a character he called Crocus Behemoth) was nearly as menacing as the raging Iggy Pop.

At thirty-nine, Thomas has mellowed considerably. He still paces the stage during solos, chatting with imaginary voices and flapping his arms. But with his manic moves and animated faces, he projects the image of a lovable cartoon character. He is Ren's pal Stimpy come to life.

"I have people who come up to me and say how much they love me and stuff like that," Thomas says in his singsong manner. "I don't know why; I don't know if [my girth] has anything to do with it. I don't ask much because I don't want to know."

After Michael Jackson, Thomas is pop music's most famous Jehovah's Witness: He was reared in the strict religion and returned to it later in life. He practices the faith in London, where he lives with his wife. Great Britain is "alright," he says, but he would rather live in Iceland or his old hometown of Cleveland. "It's like you're on Mars or something; it's really unbelievable," he says, presumably referring to Iceland, not Cleveland (though who knows?).

People who have worked with Pere Ubu describe Thomas as "strict," "old-fashioned," and "extremely high-strung." During a memorable solo performance at Maxwell's in Hoboken, New Jersey, a few years ago, he stormed off stage because people were talking during his set. Both art diva Diamanda Galas and grunge wannabes the Buck Pets brag that they've made Thomas cry. But he is far from humorless. His lyrics and between-song monologues are sharp, witty, and filled with self-deprecating laughter. "We get hit with this 'art-rock' stuff, and it's not really fair or realistic," he says. "It's just because I rattle on, explaining things in ways that I explain them, and people listen and read what you will write about what I said and they'll say, 'This sounds worthy, but it doesn't sound very interesting.' But frankly, this is the way I am, and either we do it my way or we don't do it. So you'll write an article that will make me sound pretentious and arty, and you know what? I'm pretentious and arty. And I'm proud of it."

There is very little that's pretentious about *Story of My Life*, the ninth studio album since Pere Ubu first came together on Cleveland's industrial flats in late 1975. From the beginning, the band has turned rock 'n' roll upside down in an effort to create strange new soundscapes for what Thomas calls "the cinema of the imagination." The group's grooves and drones influenced the punk explosion that followed, and Thomas created a model for the DIY scene by releasing his band's early singles on his own label. Today, the band continues to inspire a range of visionary alternative artists, from Peter Murphy to the Pixies to Living Colour.

"My musical ideas haven't changed an iota since 1974," Thomas claims. But Pere Ubu's recorded history is a diverse collection that includes raw but ambitious punk (*Terminal Tower: An Archival Collection*), jagged New Wave dance-pop (*The Modern Dance*), and minimalist art-rock (*Dub Housing*). The group disbanded in 1982, but it reunited six years later to record *The Tenement Year*, and it has been active ever since. Unfortunately, Pere Ubu Mach II was a low priority for Mercury Records. In 1990 the label refused to ante up the cash for the band to fly to New York to tape *Late Night with David Letterman*. The group responded in true punk fashion with a fax campaign asking its fans to donate to a "Ship Ubu to Letterman" fund.

Mercury executives were furious—one publicly threatened to tear the head off Ubu's manager—and the band and label soon parted ways. "I really don't like to talk about the Mercury thing anymore, because it was a terrible, stupid, and ugly episode that should never have been allowed to happen," Thomas says. The usually affable musician turns somber for a moment, but he recovers quickly. "We like record companies!" he says. "They give us money! I don't understand; I wouldn't sign us, but if they sign us, we're happy!"

Story of My Life is Pere Ubu's first album for the upstart Imago label, which Thomas calls "the only American company that's ever said, 'We really like you guys and we want to sign you.' It makes me deeply suspicious." When the band reunited in 1988, the lineup included six members: veterans Thomas, Allen Ravenstine on homemade synthesizers, Tony Maimone on bass, and Scott Krauss on drums, plus new guitarist Jim Jones and legendary art-rock percussionist Chris Cutler. Since that time, Ravenstine and Cutler have quit the band, and keyboardist Eric Drew Feldman (a veteran sideman for Captain Beefheart) joined but then left to play with Frank Black. Pere Ubu was a spare guitar, bass, and drums quartet when it recorded *Story of My Life*, but Thomas laughs when the band is described as "the Incredible Shrinking Ubu."

"I was happy to be able to work without a keyboard because I wanted to try some things that were a bit more guitar-oriented," he says. "It was really just a useful series of coincidences." When the group started recording, it made a conscious decision to avoid the studio perfectionism that made *Cloudland* (1989) and *Worlds in Collision* (1991) such long and arduous projects. "We had done records that were heavy studio experiences, and we don't really feel comfortable in that mode," Thomas says. "We were happy to try it for a while and see what can be done with it, because we never worked that way. But we were happy to get back and find a producer like Al Clay to work in the usual quick and dirty mode."

Reflecting the album's immediate, stripped-down sound, the original title was going to be *Johnny Rivers Live at the Whiskey A-Go-Go*. "That was the name of the album up to the very last minute," Thomas says, laughing. "It was already in production when cooler heads intervened and persuaded me that this was going to end in tears."

The title would have been the sort of sophisticated rock-insider joke that Pere Ubu fans love but which has always left casual listeners baffled. Unlike many alternative bands, the group has never consciously tried to alienate listeners. Underneath the noise and chaos are songs as catchy as the '60s AM radio hits the band members grew up listening to. It just takes some work to hear them.

"In the end, we're doomed people," Thomas says. "We were young and came to manhood musically in a time when music was still considered by most people to be important. I have a very specific definition of music, and it's totally impractical. It has to do with being the voice and language of the heart and the true ear of experience and real life. It sounds stupid, but frankly, that's what I think, so tough."

The Real Live Wire
The *Chicago Sun-Times*, May 5, 2000

BRIAN ENO ONCE said of the Velvet Underground that although the group didn't sell a lot of records in its time, everyone who bought one went out and started a band. Through the '80s and into the '90s, the same could be said of Wire.

The musicians have been cited as influences by Sonic Youth, the Feelies, Hüsker Dü, Ministry, the Minutemen, Minor Threat, and countless others.

They've been covered by R.E.M. ("Strange"), Big Black ("Heartbeat"), and My Bloody Valentine ("Map Ref. 41° N 93° W"), slotted into the soundtrack of *The Silence of the Lambs*, and ripped off wholesale by the likes of Elastica and Blur.

Originally uniting in the wake of the Sex Pistols during London's original punk explosion, guitarist-vocalist Colin Newman, bassist-lyricist Graham Lewis, guitarist Bruce Gilbert, and drummer Robert Gotobed released three extraordinarily diverse and groundbreaking albums. *Pink Flag* (1977) was a masterful suite that essentially condensed the history of rock into twenty-one short, brilliant vignettes; the artier and more ambitious *Chairs Missing* (1978) prompted some critics to call the band "the Punk Floyd"; and *154* (1979) incorporated synthesizers and ambient, Enoesque textures and inspired the next few albums by David Bowie. Then Wire broke up—for a time.

The quartet first reconvened in 1986. It toured America for the first time the following year, but it refused to play its most heralded material. The musicians preferred to move forward, performing new songs from the *Snakedrill* EP and *The Ideal Copy* album. But they didn't ignore their past—instead they hired a young cover band from New Jersey. The Ex-Lion Tamers opened every show on the month-long tour by performing *Pink Flag* in order in its entirety, part homage, part postmodern prank. (In interviews, the members of Wire said that the Ex-Lion Tamers were the only band that had ever influenced them.) I know this part of the story fairly well because I happen to have been the drummer and a vocalist for that group.

In addition to forging some lasting friendships, the experience of touring with Wire afforded me a front-row seat with unprecedented insight into how one of the most significant rock bands of the last two decades actually operates. It's for this reason that I don't feel compromised in writing about them now that they're back for round three and another tour of the States, performing together for the first time since 1990.

What's surprising is that this time they're playing material from every era of the band, returning to what they have derisively called "the beat combo" of guitars, bass, and drums after spending the past decade on various electronic, ambient, and DJ projects (all except for Gotobed, who became an organic farmer). This is a unique group of four extremely smart, opinionated, and strong-willed individuals, as you'll see from the answers below, and the members all have different explanations for the current reunion. I posed the same questions to each of them, and they all answered separately via email.

Q. *To quote the intro of "12XU": "Alright, here it is, again." Why, and why now?*

NEWMAN: This can be answered in two ways; one is particular to Wire, and the other more relevant to the prevailing artistic climate. In pure Wire terms, there are periods when the reasons for doing Wire outweigh the reasons for not doing it. Although there are practical concerns, fundamentally these reasons are artistic and relate to an interest in doing "that thing" with those people. There's no comeback agenda and no record company underwriting it. I do it because it could be fun and because it represents an "itch that can't be scratched in any other way."

In terms of the general artistic climate, there has been a move (at least in the U.K. anyway) in the last few years towards a more "played" aesthetic and actual live performance. In many ways, bands like Chicago's Tortoise have been very influential in this. This relates more to a crowd who have moved forward from the electronic scene, rather than something which relates to the past. This has created a more healthy climate for Wire to take the form they are currently taking. It would have been much more difficult to do this ten years ago.

LEWIS: First, we did in fact congregate for the purposes of marking the fiftieth birthday of the Gilbert in 1996—a secret performance to inaugurate the commencement of the building of a club on the Southbank site. The club subsequently was not built, but communications were reopened between the members of Wire. My second daughter timed her arrival perfectly, being born on Bruce's birthday. A year later, Gareth Jones, producer of two Wire albums, asked Colin, Bruce, and myself to play guitars with the object of realizing a re-mix for Erasure ("Figures in Crumbs"). None of us had played guitars for years, but the harmelodic chemistry and ease of execution was apparent after two days. We managed to realize the four-part "Vince Composition" into one shifting mesh. The ability to work together, producing a particular sound picture, I think explains the "why?" part of your question.

The "why now?" is in some way explained previously, but the triggers were added to by an invitation from [Mute Records founder] Daniel Miller to take part in his Mini-Meltdown Festival on the Southbank in '99, which Robert declined. However, it stimulated the debate as to "Could there be a Wire?" I'm sure me stating emphatically that there was no need for "it" at all, six months earlier in an interview, further increased the possibility! When the invitation was extended by the Southbank for Wire to play the Royal Festival Hall, and curate the entire evening, with a fee which would enable us to rehearse extensively and produce the event independently of any outside interference (no record companies, etc.), instinctively I said "Yes!" The subsequent meetings with Robert, Colin, and Bruce in London were extremely direct and clear; whatever was to be attempted should consider all of our previous compositions (including "12XU") plus that which could be realized from new text which I had written. Above all, the process would be fun . . . learn to play again from scratch in two weeks and present another version of Wire. A challenge.

GILBERT: Why? We were asked. I liked the idea of the context—given that we would have to approach it in a retrospective manner, which was practical, and of course playing the old things was always something we'd avoided and therefore something we should investigate. The now of it is a little hard to answer. I think it is a kind of instinct.

GOTOBED: There is still enthusiasm from inside the group and outside. I feel there is an indefinable bond between the four members, and a stage is the most likely place that bond can be. It is also the outlet for my drumming work.

Q. *What does each of you bring to the group? Can you briefly sketch for me the others' roles as you see them?*

NEWMAN: I try to bring organizational skills both in the making of the music and in other functions of the band. Bruce's role is more of a savant and philosopher. Graham's concerns are tied a lot to meaning. Robert is very practical.

LEWIS: Robert—drums; Colin—text memory and guitar; Bruce—tone guitar; Graham—bass and new text.

GILBERT: This time it is harder to answer a question like that—there has always been a kind of swapping of roles and defining those roles is not something we have spent time on. At present it is more about being collectively cohesive in order to achieve *realistic* goals rather than pushing the creative pace, etc.

GOTOBED: Bruce—ideas, planning, songs, interesting noises; Colin—official skills, tunes; Graham—ideas, words.

Q. *I hold that nostalgia is the most insidious corruptor of great rock 'n' roll (or art in general, if you gentlemen are still rejecting the "rock" tag). Wire has always taken a strong stance against wallowing in the past. How then does the retrospective nature of the current set list fit with that?*

NEWMAN: For me this is all tied up with the first question. In Wire terms it is of course a novelty to play older material. Our refusal to do so in the past had less to do with an obdurate refutation of our own accomplishments and more to do with the fact that we are unlikely to have brought enough conviction to the material to make it "new" again. Enough time has now elapsed for the pieces to be a challenge and it is for sure that we are not in the re-creation or nostalgia business. People should be aware that there is a finite period during which we will be able to present this material with enough conviction to satisfy our own exacting demands. It also has to be said that the older material is somehow suffused with the spirit of the age in which it is being performed. I'm not able to be objective about how subtle that effect is but it certainly doesn't feel like "old" material. In fact people have commented on how "fresh" and somewhat contemporary we sound.

LEWIS: This is the only Wire retrospective.

GILBERT: I felt no nostalgia for any of the items we are performing—for me this is a series of presentations of retrospective exhibits. In the process of executing these items, I hope that something unexpected will happen. It's still a sculpture, Jim.

GOTOBED: For Wire, this is radical.

Q. About rock 'n' roll—three of you were emphatic about the "beat combo" having run its course. I never understood that; it always seemed to me that if that was a given in how Wire was to be defined, why not do "an Eno" (à la the Oblique Strategies) and make it a creative challenge? You know: "If drums are to be part of the mix, how much can we warp everything around them?" In any event, have you resolved this matter of electronic versus organic rhythms?

NEWMAN: It is a point of fact that in terms of general artistic development the U.S.A. lags many years behind the U.K. This despite the fact that it is very often American artists who spark new trends and directions. It just happens that so often it's the Brits who sell your own music back to you. I don't really have an answer to your failure to understand why or why not to pursue a particular direction due to your cultural inadequacy. The drums versus electronic debate is so outmoded and irrelevant to anything that is going on now in art that we may as well be talking about rock 'n' roll versus jazz. For God's sake, grow up Jim!

LEWIS: Personally, I thought all of the recordings we made at Mute addressed the "beat combo" problem. Listen to "The Drill" again. As to the organic-electronic rhythm, I have no problem. Check out my [current solo] work . . . I believe in "different" rather than "versus." The discussion in the late '80s within Wire was of its time. I certainly believed we could have pushed the envelope further. As to the future, rhythmically, no possibilities exist for nostalgia, given the freedom the individuals have worked towards. However, organic drums sound like . . . ?

GILBERT: As long as Rob is keen to play acoustic drums, we have to work around that—the beat combo approach. I don't have to resolve anything; learning to play the guitar again has been fascinating and laborious, but it always was. I don't think any of us entertain doing THIS version of Wire for very long.

GOTOBED: Still thinking on that one.

Q. *Since you began your career by "cocking a snoot" at the history of rock 'n' roll on* Pink Flag, *and spent much of the rest of it trying to explode the bloated carcass of the same, where does Wire now fit in the grand scheme of things, popular-music-wise?*

NEWMAN: Up its arse.

LEWIS: The Beatles, the Velvet Underground . . .

GILBERT: Come on, Jim. You know how it works: All we are doing is revisiting the scene of the crime. Of course it is interesting to be called traitors-heroes by maggots still feeding on the carcass.

GOTOBED: No answer given.

On the Beat
The *Chicago Reader*, August 30, 1996

IF THERE WAS ever any doubt that the founding fathers of punk could become clumsy dinosaurs just like the Eagles and Pink Floyd, the Ramones and the Sex Pistols have done a damn fine job laying it to rest this summer. Nobody calls it quits anymore, not when there's a nickel to be made in the sheds. But with so many former heroes proving once again that there's no way to grow old gracefully in rock 'n' roll, it's rewarding to meet the exceptions. I count three of them, all alumni of the class of '77, and all at the artier end of the punk-rock spectrum.

David Thomas continues to lead Pere Ubu in his wonderfully iconoclastic way, carrying the weight of that band's considerable history while focusing on its future. Five CDs worth of vintage Ubu (1975–1982) has been collected on the forthcoming *Datapanik in the Year Zero* box set, but for my money, last year's *Ray Gun Suitcase* more than holds its own and sounds just as inspired. There's also the English band Wire, which reunited in 1986 after a six-year split but refused to yield to nostalgia and play any of its old material. After disbanding again, its key players are pursuing solo projects in the techno and ambient house arenas, mostly on their own labels. Finally we have Wake Ooloo, a different band in name, but for all intents and purposes the '90s incarnation of New Jersey's late, lamented Feelies.

The Feelies made their live debut at C.B.G.B. during punk's first heyday, and in 1980 they released a hyper-kinetic minimalist masterpiece called *Crazy Rhythms* on the British independent, Stiff Records. The title was appropriate: The group took the primal tom-tom groove of the Velvet Underground (which Maureen Tucker had in turn borrowed from Bo Diddley and the African drummer Babatunde Olatunji), sped it up, shifted the emphasis to one and three instead of two and four, and wound up with an irresistible rhythmic undertow. In the face of commercial indifference, the band faltered for a few years, regrouped, and came back strong with three albums between 1986 and 1990. *The Good Earth, Only Life*, and *Time for a Witness* had in common guitars that rang in your ears, joyous nods to the Velvets and the Stooges, and, of course, those crazy rhythms.

Broke and disillusioned with their last label, A&M, the Feelies split up in 1991. Guitarist Bill Million dropped out of rock for good, taking a gig as a locksmith at Disney World. Fellow founding Feelies Glenn Mercer and Dave Weckerman took day jobs, too, but they hadn't lost their desire to make a joyful noise, and at night they returned to the garage in Haledon, a blue-collar suburb of Paterson, New Jersey. There they formed a new group less concerned with pristine instrumental sounds and mannered dynamics and more obsessed with turning it up and letting it rip.

More aggressive than 1994's *Hear No Evil* but more focused than 1995's *What About It*, the new *Stop the Ride* is the best of Wake Ooloo's three albums, all of which have been released by Chicago's Pravda Records. In the Feelies, Mercer played sustained melodic leads over Million's frantic rhythms; in Wake Ooloo, he does an admirable job juggling both roles, letting keyboardist Russell Gambino fill any gaps with trashy *Nuggets*-style organ. Weckerman is a loose-limbed drummer from the Charlie Watts school—his backbeat packs a mighty wallop—and bassist John Dean provides the requisite rumble. They combine most impressively for a distorted epic jam on "Get Caught Up," out Crazy-Horsing recent Crazy Horse.

Mercer, the most prolific writer, doesn't spend a lot of time on his lyrics. The chorus of "In the Way"—"We're alright / It's OK / It's alright / Hey, hey, hey"—sounds as if it's lifted right out of the Iggy Stooge song book (cf.

"No fun / My babe / Uh, no fun"). Weckerman contributes three tunes, and his are a lot weirder: "Just when everything was going well / I was wondering how the bell ringers will tango in hell," he sings in a plaintive whine on "Final Warning." But songcraft isn't the point. This is a rollicking party album based on the assumption that all anyone needs to get off on a Saturday night is a dumb but fun singalong chorus, an overdriven but tuneful guitar solo, and—you knew it was coming—that highly caffeinated Feelies beat. I've been riding this groove with them since the beginning, and damned if it doesn't work as well for me as it did the first time I heard it.

Stop the Ride builds to a climax with a closing cover of the Byrds' "So You Want To Be a Rock 'n' Roll Star," which features Mercer wildly bashing away on the riff and Weckerman thrashing his drums and howling the backing vocals with tuneless glee. You might think it's a bit creepy for two guys on the far side of forty to be yearning for the girls to tear them apart, but there's more than a little irony here: The Feelies were never really stars, but they sure met plenty of agent men who let them down.

We could argue about whether or not Pere Ubu, Wire, and the Feelies would have sold out over the years if anyone had been interested in buying, or whether their DIY approach these days is the result of choice or the fact that no one else wants to do it for them. But the more important point is that these punk veterans are making music that doesn't suck, and they haven't lost the energy or individualistic spirit that drove them when they started out. We should be thankful that unlike so many of their peers, they *didn't* die before they got old.

Five Alive
The *Chicago Sun-Times*, March 24, 1995

WHEN THE PUNK rock time line is traced from the garage rock of the '60s to the current sounds of Green Day and the Offspring, it's impossible to overlook the contributions of the MC5. "I've done the same thing, connecting the dots from the Five and the Stooges, to the Dolls and the Ramones, to Black Flag and Bad Religion," says former MC5 guitarist Wayne Kramer. "I think it's those of us who are addicted to the sound of Marshall amplifiers, blistering drumbeats, and lyrics that have some sense of political consciousness. If not overtly, they tell the truth on some level. And the truth is always more interesting than anything you could make up."

That certainly holds for Kramer's life story. Starting with *Kick Out the Jams* in 1969, Kramer and Detroit's Motor City Five called for revolution over white-hot rock 'n' roll that combined garage-rock's drive with the experimental intensity of Ornette Coleman's free jazz. When the Five broke up after three albums in 1971, Kramer was twenty-four years old. He was disillusioned and directionless, and he fell into a life of drug dealing and drug abuse. "As an organized criminal, I was really lousy," he says. "I'm not a killer, and that's what it ultimately means. Prison saved me, because at the rate I was going, I would have ended up dead one way or another."

Kramer landed in the federal penitentiary in Lexington, Kentucky. Whether by chance or through the efforts of a well-meaning prison official, his cell mate was Red Rodney, the jazz trumpeter who played with Charlie Parker. "To have met Red Rodney in the pen was an unexpected music lesson and lesson in life of the highest order," Kramer says. "He was just brilliant, and he taught me as much as he could about bebop, a whole music course in writing and arranging."

The guitarist emerged from prison clean, sober, and a better musician. He went on to play with everyone from Johnny Thunders to Leslie West. Now he's experiencing a career resurgence, spurred on by members of the Los Angeles punk scene who were inspired by his work in the '70s. Epitaph, the Los Angeles label that launched Bad Religion and the Offspring, has just released *The Hard Stuff*, a hard-rocking Kramer solo album that features contributions from modern punk notables such as the Muffs, Suicidal Tendencies, Rancid, Clawhammer, and the Melvins.

"The MC5 not only talked about revolution, we believed it," Kramer says. "The part about destroying the government and taking over and shooting it out with the pigs and all that, that didn't work. But the other part about the concept of possibilities, the revolution of ideas, that has changed the world. The best part of what's happening in the punk world today is the idea that our creativity and our ability to think will get us through. For me to have a great history in the MC5 is not enough. What gets me through is the records I make today and the records I'll make tomorrow."

Kramer is touring with a tight three-piece band, and he considers himself lucky to be alive and rocking. Two of his MC5 bandmates, singer Rob Tyner and second guitarist Fred "Sonic" Smith, died of heart attacks in recent years.

"We all lost each other at the end of the MC5, and the loss of the band took a long time to grieve over," Kramer says. "But I had reclaimed my lost brothers and got them back in a spiritual sense. To then lose them in the physical sense really tells me that our time is the most valuable thing we have, and it's not for wasting. If you're gonna make a contribution, if you're gonna make a difference, if you've got something to say, you'd better start saying it."

Patti Smith, *Gone Again*
The *Chicago Reader*, June 14, 1996

DURING MY MERCIFULLY short tenure as an editor at *Rolling Stone*, one of my more tedious tasks was compiling the results of the 1995 critics poll. By a ridiculous margin of eight or nine to one, Patti Smith claimed "Comeback of the Year." Yet her last original recording had been released in 1988. It should come as no surprise that now that there's a new album— *Gone Again*—critics are falling all over themselves rushing to give enough accolades.

Part of the credit for the hoopla is due to the fem-crit movement, which rightly celebrates punk poetess Smith as the godmother of '90s artists including Kathleen Hanna, Polly Jean Harvey, Liz Phair, and Courtney Love. Another reason is the sympathy vote (the Yoko factor, if you prefer), which judges *Gone Again* in the light of Smith's personal losses—among them her husband, Fred "Sonic" Smith; her brother, Todd; her longtime friend, photographer Robert Mapplethorpe; and her keyboardist, Richard "DNV" Sohl. But finally, it comes down to the fact that critics and fans miss the Patti Smith of "Gloria" and "Free Money," of "Dancing Barefoot" and "Rock n Roll Nigger," and even of "Because the Night," the song Smith wrote with Bruce Springsteen and her only Top 40 hit. And this is where I have a problem, because rock 'n' roll's biggest enemy is nostalgia—whether it's for the halcyon '60s or the punk-rock '70s.

The truth is *Gone Again* isn't as good as any of Smith's '70s releases. Yes, her voice remains strong, distinctive, and rich with character if limited in range—the female Bob Dylan or Lou Reed. And if anything, her writing skills have gotten sharper: There are fewer cringe-worthy lines of awkward poetry, and the sentiments expressed in songs such as "Beneath the Southern Cross," "My Madrigal," and the title track are universal and open-ended, even though they're clearly inspired by the deaths of people close to her. (Thankfully, Smith edited the lyrics of "About a Boy," the long, plodding dirge about Kurt Cobain, taking out the embarrassing lines about

Cobain being "just a boy who will never grow old" that were heard during a short East Coast tour with Dylan in December.)

Where the album falls short is the music. Smith is accompanied by long-time cohorts Lenny Kaye on guitar and Jay Dee Daugherty on drums as well as by Television's Tom Verlaine on four tracks. But only the tribal, tom-heavy "Gone Again," the breezy, upbeat "Summer Cannibals," and the relatively straight cover of Dylan's "Wicked Messenger" rock out, and they do so with such weak grooves and laid-back attitudes that they would have elicited yawns from the amped-up crowd at C.B.G.B. in 1977. The rest of the eleven tunes are gentle, lulling, and mellow, full of ringing acoustic guitars, lilting rhythms, and folkie textures such as mandolin, dulcimer, fiddle, and accordion. The result is more like a mediocre Richard and Linda Thompson album than anything by the old Patti Smith Group.

Dream of Life had these same problems—remember the lullaby to Smith's son, "The Jackson Song"?—coupled with an earnest leftist spirit that simply sounded naive in the midst of the Reagan-Bush years ("People Have the Power"—not at the time, they didn't). Released in 1988, midway between her '79 retirement and her '96 comeback, *Dream of Life* was mostly ignored by critics, who didn't want to dis Smith even if they couldn't bring themselves to champion her. Now they're so overjoyed to have her back, they'll applaud anything she does.

This isn't to say that, after seventeen years in self-imposed exile as a suburban housewife and a period of tremendous grief and loss, Smith isn't allowed to come back as a different person, or to reinvent herself as an artist. (Or to completely mythologize said exile, which some close to her say was never the idyll she portrays.) But it's certainly fair to judge her new offerings by the standards she set with her own work. Smith has dealt with the issue of mortality before—for instance, on "Gloria," the first song on her first album—but in the past, her inclination was to celebrate life with all the energy she could muster, even on the quieter songs, rather than to withdraw and solemnly meditate. As a musing on death and dying, *Gone Again* is a better album than Lou Reed's *Magic and Loss*, but neither contains anything as eloquent and powerful as "Pale Blue Eyes" (which Reed wrote and Smith covered), let alone as life-affirming as "Gloria" or "Real Good Time Together."

"When I was younger, I felt it was my duty to wake people up," Smith recently told *Interview* magazine. "I thought poetry was asleep. I thought rock 'n' roll was asleep." Well, things aren't a hell of a lot livelier right now, and *Gone Again* ain't gonna stir things up. Me, I wish that Smith had raged against the dying of the light instead of serenading it.

Great Gobs of Guitar Grunge
The *Twin Cities Reader,* October 17, 1990

IF YOU'VE PICKED up a rock publication in the last three months, anything from a Xeroxed one-page fanzine to BMW-subsidized *Rolling Stone,* you're no doubt aware that Sonic Youth is The Most Important Band in the World.

Rock 'n' roll is a dying art form, so the critics say, forty-some years old and plum out of fresh ideas. That most time-honored tradition—the two guitars–bass–drums combo—is the hoariest of its tired institutions, an anachronism from which nothing innovative or challenging or particularly exciting can come. Or at least it was, until Sonic Youth came along to save the day with *those guitars.*

Oh, those guitars! First, there are the famous weird tunings: backwards, upside-down, and inside-out, anything so long as it ain't the same familiar keys and chords. Twenty guitars on stage at a time. Then there's the way Thurston Moore and Lee Ranaldo play: frantic flailing, with hammers, with fists, with screwdrivers stuck in the necks. Lead and rhythm are moot; those guitars twist around each other like copulating snakes, building layers of harmonics and feedback, a wash of sound, a glorious wall of noise (but noise you can hum along with).

Sonic Youth certainly isn't the first band from New York to reinvent rock guitar by deconstructing it—there's a long history of that, from the Velvet Underground to Television to the Voidoids' Robert Quine to No New York to Glenn Branca, who gave Moore and Ranaldo their start as members of his guitar orchestra. But Sonic Youth has survived the longest, and thrived to the point where it outgrew every independent label it recorded for, with a total of six albums for five different companies since 1982.

A few myopic denizens of the underground will accuse Moore, Ranaldo, bassist Kim Gordon, and drummer Steve Shelley of "selling out" by signing to David Geffen's DGC Records last year. In fact they were "buying in"—to better distribution, promotion, and (God forbid!) radio play. Hey, you can't fault a band for wanting thirteen-year-olds to be able to hear 'em on KJJO–FM and buy their album at Target. The two records that most influenced Sonic Youth—the Velvets' *White Light/White Heat* and the Stooges' *Funhouse*—were both released on major labels. And besides, *Goo* is hands-down Sonic Youth's best album yet.

Unlike almost every rock fan I knew before moving to Minneapolis from Nu Yawk, I never equated Sonic Youth with God. I was always bothered because the band members were too damn serious—the underground Beatles, fer chrissake. I preferred Pussy Galore's piss-take Stones. True, it was impossible to deny the brilliance of those guitars, but whenever Moore opened his little black book to recite poetry during shows in the early '80s, it was always a bit too much.

Up through 1988's *Daydream Nation,* most Sonic Youth songs were musically fascinating but lyrically vacant (with a few notable exceptions, such as "Death Valley '69," "Halloween," and "Catholic Block"). I could never help thinking that The Most Important Band in the World should have something more to say. With *Goo,* Sonic Youth has finally given up trying to say something important and opted for writing great, simple, stupid rock songs, and it's about time.

This places 'em firmly in the "Louie Louie," "Surfin' Bird" tradition ("We feel we're very traditional," Moore says in the label bio. "We bolster and progress rock tradition"). The words may still be vacant, but instead of being pretentious, now at least they're fun. Witness "Kool Thing," with its wonderfully catchy chorus of "I don't wanna / I don't think so" and guest babbling by Public Enemy's Chuck D.; "Goo," a third-grade nonsense singalong about a punk rock gal; "Dirty Boots," which Moore says is about "touring in a van . . . that ZZ Top rock thing"; and the loving tribute to Karen Carpenter, "Tunic (Song for Karen)."

It all adds up to a goddamn great rock 'n' roll record, hence the critics' mad rush to outdo each other with superlatives. In fact, I'll add my own: Sonic Youth is not only one of the most innovative bands to burst out of New York since the Velvets, now it's coming on as heir to the Ramones' crown as Kings of Great Dumb Party Rock. Gabba gabba hey!

Gordon, talking by phone from DGC's New York offices last week, says the band never made a conscious attempt to change the way it writes. "I think we're getting to be better, more conventional songwriters," she says. "But I don't think we've changed lyrically so much, subject-matter-wise." When I point out that it's a pretty far cry from the *sturm-und-drang* of 1985's *Bad Moon Rising* to "Goo," Gordon laughs. "The songs have always had humor in them, it just hasn't come across as much sometimes."

Call it maturing. Too many bands get older and "progress" by getting so serious and sober that they finally collapse under their own weight. Sonic Youth is doing it by getting simpler and more accessible, shedding all those ugly, unwanted pounds like a housewife on Slim-Fast. But whether or not the kids will buy it is anybody's guess.

"I don't think [DGC] thinks they can make money on us like Guns n' Roses," Gordon says, but I tell her she's being naïve. The company wouldn't be investing big bucks if it didn't think there was the possibility of a hit somewhere down the line. And it *is* possible; weirder things have happened in the world of pop music.

"Maybe," Gordon says. "I think they probably think that, maybe not with this record but the next record, they can gradually build up to selling a reasonable amount to justify having us on the label, after they've lost interest in the fact that we've given them some hip credibility or whatever."

However reluctant Gordon and Company may be to admit it, they *are* on the road to stardom. Sonic Youth just turned down an opportunity others at their level would kill for: opening the much-ballyhooed Go-Go's reunion tour, coming soon to an arena near you. "They were offering us an awful lot of money, but I'm sure they would have hated us," Gordon says. "Also, I just didn't want to do it for the morale end of it. It would have been after our U.S. tour, and we want to take at least a month off before we start Japan and Australia."

The band recently returned from its most successful European tour to date, sharing stages with Minneapolis's own Babes In Toyland. Sonic Youth has been one of Babes' biggest supporters; Moore even sports a Babes T-shirt in some of the *Goo* cover photos. Gordon says she's happy to be in a position to help bands she likes. "But we did more with Babes than we could really afford. This is the first time we actually took a band and they traveled in our bus. We rented a van, and they were in this plush bus with our crew. Usually when we've toured with a band like Mudhoney, they've had their own tour happening and we just played a few dates with them. But for some reason, Babes just didn't get it together, and we still wanted them to do it, so it was kind of weird. I don't think we'll ever do that again."

After exactly twenty minutes, Gordon abruptly interrupts our conversation, and I imagine the publicist gesturing from across the room. "I've got to terminate this," the bassist says. DGC publicists are obviously among those who believe that Sonic Youth is The Most Important Band in the World.

If Gordon has any thoughts about that title, she isn't talking. "It's too weird to think about," she says of the hype. "I'm really happy that somebody is so enthusiastic and likes it and it's really great, but I don't think about it. It just gets in the way of other things." Me, I vacillate, but if you ask me during the middle of Sonic Youth's set on Monday, I'll probably grin madly and answer in the affirmative, seduced once again by those guitars.

Mudhoney's Dirty-Sweet Mix
The *Chicago Sun-Times*, November 4, 1992

INDIE-ROCK FANS are a possessive lot obsessed by obscure arcana. Talk to true devotees about a rising underground band and they'll almost always tell you that the group was better when it was called (fill in the blank), or that it ripped off its entire sound from (insert band name here). But occasionally they're right: If you like Nirvana or Pearl Jam and someone tells you you've *got* to hear Mudhoney, you'd better believe 'em.

Formed in 1987 by veterans of the legendary Northwest bands Green River and the Melvins, Mudhoney wasn't the first Seattle group to merge '70s-inspired hard-rock riffs, punk attitude, and a sense of humor, but it wrote the best songs. The name described the quartet's sound: an irresistible combination of dirty fuzz guitars and sweet pop melodies. Four years before Nirvana followed this formula to the top of the charts, Mudhoney was recording such memorable anthems as "Touch Me I'm Sick," "In 'n' Out of Grace," and "When I Think (I Think of You)" for the independent Sub Pop label. But timing is everything in pop music, and the group was ahead of the curve.

Guitarist-vocalist Mark Arm, guitarist Steve Turner, bassist Matt Lukin, and drummer Dan Peters aren't bitter that many of the groups that followed in their wake struck gold first. "Nirvana's Nirvana, and we're us," Arm says. "'Touch Me I'm Sick' is a lot different from 'Smells Like Teen Spirit,' and I don't think at that time a major label would have really known what to do with us. I think it took a series of bands to open more and more doors, starting with Hüsker Dü and the Replacements through R.E.M. and Metallica and Sonic Youth and Nirvana. It was a series of little tiny breakthroughs."

Mudhoney is geared up for a breakthrough of its own with *Piece of Cake*, its first album for a major label, and "Overblown," a song on the soundtrack to the film *Singles* that pokes fun at the heavily hyped Seattle rock scene. *Piece of Cake* perfectly captures the band's onstage intensity and offstage irreverence by mixing its trademark aggressive pop ("Living Wreck," "Suck You Dry," "When in Rome") with tongue-in-cheek song fragments (including a tune featuring a rhythm track of fake flatulence) and chaotic raveups ("Youth Body Expression Explosion," a fitting title for a group that doesn't stand still for a second on stage).

Fans of indie-rock arcana may object, but Mudhoney deserves to be more than somebody's secret.

Overrated: Alex Chilton
Request, July 1994

FEW CULT ARTISTS have done as little as Alex Chilton to justify their semi-legendary status. After being drafted as a teenager to sing with the '60s pop group the Box Tops ("The Letter") and being manipulated by managers and producers throughout the experience, Chilton elbowed his way into a band started in Memphis by his childhood pal Chris Bell. The dark, sophisticated jangle of Big Star has influenced rockers like R.E.M., Teenage Fanclub, Matthew Sweet, the Bangles, and the Replacements, who paid tribute in a song called "Alex Chilton." But the accomplishment wasn't all Chilton's.

Big Star recorded three brilliant albums, but a large part of the credit for #1 Record (1972) and Radio City (1974) also belongs to Bell. Effectively Chilton's first solo album, Big Star 3rd (aka Sister Lovers), recorded in 1974 after Bell split, works only because Chilton was in the process of killing himself after a romantic fiasco involving twin sisters; he was overindulging in sex, drugs, and alcohol, then purging his soul in the studio. (While it may be effective, this isn't exactly healthy behavior to encourage in a musician.)

During a twenty-four-year solo career, Chilton hasn't even come close to matching Big Star's best. Recording hastily compiled collections such as Like Flies on Sherbet (1979) and High Priest (1987) for a long line of indie labels, he has paired sneering, jokey, hillbilly-punk originals such as "Bangkok," "No Sex," and "Lost My Job" with sneering, jokey, tossed-off covers such as "Tee Ni Nee Ni Noo," "B-a-b-y," and, worst of all, "Volare" (rich Corinthian leather anyone?). Alternating solo jaunts through the indie-rock club scene with Box Tops reunion gigs at state fairs and on package '60s nostalgia tours, Chilton has often taunted crowds with snippets of Big Star's "Back of a Car" or "September Gurls" before breaking into wanky twenty-minute jazz jams. His contempt for his audience was only slightly less obvious during the much-ballyhooed Big Star reunion, preserved on the thoroughly mediocre recent album Columbia: Live at Missouri University.

"If people offer good money to play those songs, well I'm not against it," Chilton said of the reunion. Onstage in Chicago with original drummer Jody Stephens and '90s acolytes Jonathan Auer and Ken Stringfellow of the Posies, Chilton sang Big Star's songs but couldn't help needling his fans, adding a line about "all you creeps" to "Thank You Friends" and refusing to do an encore. It was clear that whatever muse inspired those tunes escaped long ago, and these days, Chilton is only in it for the cold, hard cash.

Mercenary Visionary
The *Chicago Reader*, July 18, 1997

IN OUR ZEAL to make sense of new and ever-evolving musical genres, we're always quick to hold up a sound from the past as (Lord, I hate this word) "seminal." But in honor of *Arkology*, the new collection of reggae rarities produced by Lee "Scratch" Perry at his Black Ark Studios in the '70s, my fellow critics have set a new standard for this practice. Not since punk pried open the rock pantheon to make room for the Velvet Underground have so many superlatives been thrown at a misunderstood cult figure.

"*Arkology* is an essential dub document, but the real treat is hearing how Perry's vision infects so many different strains of '90s music," Rob Sheffield wrote in *Details*. "Work your way through everything you know about hiphop, electronica, punk rock, and postrock, and somehow, some way, you always end up at Black Ark," crowed David Fricke in *Rolling Stone*. Valiantly refraining from using the word "postmodern" (though you know he wanted to), Rob Michaels added in *Spin* that Perry had "no use for 'songs,' as pop fans know them, with authors, owners, beginnings, middles, and ends. His medium was one of total flux."

The young Prodigy fan or Wu-Tang devotee who is inspired by such hyperbole to invest upwards of fifty dollars in the three-CD box set may be shocked to discover that *Arkology* isn't nearly as radical as he or she was led to believe, and that it's basically a collection of—hold on to your hats—plain ol' *reggae* music. Michaels's claims to the contrary, it contains a lot of songs; fifty-two, to be exact. Some of them are memorable, some of them are duds, and some of them are extended or otherwise warped by Perry's production techniques. The latter are indeed impressive, but all the chatter about what came after makes it harder to hear his actual accomplishments.

Rainford Hugh Perry was born in 1936 in Kendal, a small town in northwest Jamaica. He became "Lee" when he gravitated to Kingston in the late '50s and started his musical career—as a gofer at Clement "Coxsone" Dodd's famous Studio One and a DJ with the Downbeat Sound System, a group of DJs that helped take the new hybrid music, ska, to the streets on Dodd's equipment. In the years that followed, Perry became a recording artist himself, and in 1965 scored a hit with "Chicken Scratch," which spawned his second nickname. He was one of several key musicians who instigated the shift from upbeat ska to slower and more sinister rock steady and finally to reggae. He ran his own label, Upsetter Records, from 1968 to 1974, and he recorded the early efforts of Bob Marley and the Wailers.

Through it all Perry constantly complained of being screwed—out of both money and recognition—by other producers. Two of his best-known early reggae recordings, "I Am the Upsetter" and "People Funny Boy," are thought to be diatribes aimed at Dodd and Joe Gibbs, another former employer. Yet Perry himself has been accused of shortchanging the members of his band, the Upsetters, when they became the first reggae group to tour England in 1969, and he allegedly never paid royalties to the Wailers, resulting in a legendary cold war with Marley and the Marley estate. These items are conveniently left out of Perry hagiographies.

Arkology only goes back as far as 1975, the year Perry signed a worldwide distribution deal with the man he called "a vampire sucking the blood of the sufferer," Island founder Chris Blackwell. In 1973, Perry had purchased a house in the Kingston suburb of Washington Gardens—not an inexpensive spread for the time and place—and built himself a concrete recording studio christened "Black Ark" in the backyard. There he recorded his own music with the Upsetters (whose lineup varied depending on which session players were sitting around at any given time), produced the likes of Max Romeo, Junior Murvin, and the pioneering female reggae singer Susan Cadogan, and built on the dub experiments of the groundbreaking King Tubby.

No, Perry didn't invent dub, but he did embrace it. The word is thought to refer to the practice of "dubbing out" various tracks on the master tape, putting sudden and unexpected emphasis on elements that are usually in the background, like the rhythmic interplay of the hi-hat and bass. The word "dub" closely resembles *dup*, patois for "ghost." Perry's dub productions are marked by a haze of reverb and sound effects like pistol shots, crying babies, and falling rain that do jump out like ghosts in the machine. "It was only four [tracks] written on the machine," Perry says in the box set's liner notes, "but I was picking up twenty from the extra-terrestrial squad."

Although *Arkology* is divided into three "reels" called "Dub Organizer," "Dub Shepherd," and "Dub Adventurer," and kicks off with Perry's declaration that, "This is dub revolution / Music to rock the nation" (on "Dub Revolution Part I"), it is by no means "an essential dub document." Listeners in search of one handy package compiling Perry's freakiest dub productions would be much better served by Trojan's two-disc collection, *Open the Gate.* Key tracks such as Perry's own "Bionic Rats" and the Heptones' "Babylon Falling" are missing from *Arkology,* and there's nothing included by Cadogan. The collection assumes a certain fluency with Perry's output that many young listeners (and apparently some reviewers) lack, offering such arcana as alternate takes, previously unreleased tracks, and multiple versions of the same basic song. The latter illustrate the way Perry could use a rhythm track to sculpt different tunes. But this was a habit born out of economic necessity—young artists couldn't always afford to start from scratch in the studio—rather than a prescient vision of a drum 'n' bass future.

Five versions of a tune is overkill by anyone's standards, even when the song is as galvanizing as Junior Murvin's "Police and Thieves." Studying the variations in the mixes—dramatic as some of them are—is an activity that is only going to appeal to obsessive collectors and academics, just as casual listeners have little use for the early demos on *Peel Slowly and See,* the Velvet Underground box set. The alternate mixes of lesser tracks are even more useless. Perry may have been a sonic prankster, but he wasn't much different from other producers such as Phil Spector and George Martin in that he was ultimately as good as the songwriters he was working with. Paired with talents such as his old friend Romeo or reggae veterans the Heptones, the result could be magical. But not even Perry's chirping crickets and bellowing elephants can elevate a cookie-cutter reggae jam such as Errol Walker's "John Public."

The secrets of Perry's success were good taste in choosing the right collaborators and the ability to create a vibe that encouraged artists to use their imaginations to transcend the ordinary. In order to summon the ghosts, he would blow ganja smoke on the master tape as it rolled. The feeling of druggy disorientation permeates Perry's work to such an extant that you can get a pot hangover just by listening to too much of it. This places him firmly in the continuum of psychedelic rock: Perry wasn't reinventing the use of the recording studio or abandoning conventional song structure as much as he was trying to capture the experience of being stoned, plain and simple.

Like psychedelic avatars such as Syd Barrett and Roky Erickson, Perry eventually flew too high for his own good. He overindulged in rum and ganja, split with his wife and children, angered his business partners, unwisely ignored the thugs who shook him down for protection money, and finally saw Black Ark destroyed in 1979 by a fire that many people believe he started himself. (He covered the ruins with cryptic graffiti such as, "Moses + Satan + dead spit" and "all robots all winds all seas all brains all minds all water all air.") He's been playing the role of the mad genius ever since, granting colorful interviews in which he rambles about outer space, aliens, sex, Rastafarianism, and being ripped off by the "bald head" white man, then returning with his second wife and manager in their BMW to the house they share overlooking Lake Zurich in Switzerland.

He's crazy like a fox, Scratch is, and he's more than happy to have the bald heads credit him with whatever damn fool thing they can come up with—as long as it contributes to the legend and helps move even mediocre collections such as *Arkology*.

Curiouser and Curiouser
The *Chicago Reader*, February 14, 1997

IN THEORY, AT least, rock 'n' roll is the music of freedom and individuality and antiauthoritarianism, so it follows that we make heroes (if not millionaires) of those who forge their own distinctive paths, from Screamin' Jay Hawkins to George Clinton to that guy who used to be called Prince, and from Roger McGuinn to Alex Chilton to Polly Jean Harvey. This phenomenon can be traced to the old romantic idea of the lunatic as speaker of truth. As often as not, rockers not born loony have tried to reach this state with what Rimbaud called "a systematic derangement of all the senses," or what the rest of us call "drugs." Unfortunately, some of the best have paid the steep price of losing their minds for good, as evidenced by premature dropouts Syd Barrett, Roky Erickson, and Brian Wilson.

Genuine rock eccentrics are so hard to come by these days that we settle for transparent poseurs in bad Halloween makeup. "Never has there been a rock star quite as complex as Marilyn Manson, frontman of the band of the same name," *New York Times* rock critic Neil Strauss recently told us in the pages of *Rolling Stone*. Obviously he's never met Julian Cope. Whether Cope's insanity is organic or the result of being "out of my mind on dope and speed," as he once sang, he has successfully eluded the straitjacket and prolifically delivered great rock records for more than two decades now. His twentieth album, *Interpreter*—available only as an independent import because Cope proved too strange for Mercury, Island, and even American Recordings, the label that embraced Wesley Willis—is one of the finest efforts of his long and twisted career.

That career can be divided into three phases: Cope's early days in the Liverpool "bubblegum trance" group The Teardrop Explodes, which produced the sort of moody but infectious new wave you hear in mid-'80s John Hughes movies; part one of his solo work, which veered erratically but effectively from acoustic "acid campfire songs" to brilliantly bombastic MTV hits ("World Shut Your Mouth"); and the third and current phase of sounds, which can only be described as "Julian Cope music"—which is, perhaps, the ultimate compliment for a true individualist.

Starting with 1991's *Peggy Suicide*, Cope began crafting elaborate, sprawling conceptual paeans to his various obsessions. The title character in *Peggy Suicide* was an earth-mother goddess being raped by pollution-spewing technology. *Jehovahkill* (1992) was about a conspiracy by the Christian church to destroy paganism and its sacred stone circles, which of course were built by aliens. *Autogedden* (1994) returned to a subtheme of *Peggy Suicide* about cars poisoning our atmosphere and killing their drivers, and *20 Mothers* (1995) was a heartfelt homage to incest in the sense that Cope believes we're all related and we all ought to *really* love one another (at least, I think that's what he was talking about).

There's a basic New Age subtext to all of this, but Cope is no Tori Amos. His vocal role model is Iggy Pop, and his attitude is vintage Johnny Rotten, which is to say sarcastic, self-deflating, and bitingly funny. His musical approach is equal parts punk and psychedelic. It's his ability to merge these contradictory impulses—to annihilate and to transcend—that saves the self-professed Saint Julian from the pitfalls of either.

Cope divides all of his albums in the style of old vinyl LP sides. On the first half of his latest he offers six of his strongest tunes since *Peggy Suicide*, embellishing the massive hooks in songs such as "I Come From Another Planet, Baby" and "The Battle for the Trees" with beautiful Mellotron and real string parts, driving acid guitars, burbling analog synths, and rollicking rhythms. On what would be side two, he offers a thumbnail history of psychedelia, showing his mastery of ornate Beatlesesque pop ("Arthur Drugstore"), Krautrock ("S.P.A.C.E.R.O.C.K. With Me"), Clinton-style freak-funk ("Re-Directed Male"), and progressive rock ("Maid of Constant Sorrow") before building to a spectacular finale with "The Loveboat" and "Dust," grand anthems built around the eccentrics' rallying cry, "Celebrate who you are."

All of Cope's favorite topics are represented—environmental panic, pagan mystery, goddess worship, technological fascism—but this time he explains how they fit together. See, aliens visited earth in ancient times and gave us the secrets to personal happiness and preserving the health of our planet. We've turned a deaf ear to them, but the clues remain if you know where to look (say, Stonehenge, or the local acid dealer's pad). Salvation is ours if we tolerate our differences and care for each other and Mother Earth. This theme echoes in the liner notes through quotes from Che Guevara, Martin Luther King, Jr., and MC5 manager John Sinclair, and in lyrics that can be taken as pure goof, strict gospel, or a little of both, as I believe Cope intends. (After all, he named his indie label Kak, which is English slang for "shit.")

"I was feeling that time was peeling from the twentieth century / And I was given to warmth and healing—the patterns of eternity / The beauty of life force is all over me," Cope sings. Then he delivers the chorus, the title of the song, and his all-purpose motto: "Since I lost my head, it's been alright."

Kraftwerk at the Riviera Theatre
The *Chicago Sun-Times*, June 12, 1998

THERE EXISTS A GENERATION of fans for whom the German band Kraftwerk is more important than the Beatles.

The upper-middle-class sons of a doctor and an architect, Ralf Hütter and Florian Schneider met at the Düsseldorf Conservatory and began experimenting with electronic sounds in 1968 as a band called Organisation. After adopting a new name from the German word for power plant, they pioneered the use of synthesizers, samplers, and sequencers, introducing techniques of electronic music-making that are now taken for granted in alternative rock, dance music, and hip-hop. More importantly, they created a perfect pop group—one in which presentation, subject matter, and sound combined to create a timeless archetype. Not for nothing has Kraftwerk been called the Beach Boys of Düsseldorf.

In typical fashion the duo has modestly downplayed its accomplishments. "We are playing the machines. The machines play us. It is really the
exchange and the friendship we have with the musical machines," Hütter
said in the late '70s. He and Schneider have rarely spoken since, and even
though the group came to Chicago Friday as part of its first American tour
in fifteen years, it steadfastly adhered to its policy of letting the music do
the talking. "There is no new album," a friendly but stern female voice told
me when I phoned Kling Klang, the band's famous Düsseldorf recording
studio. "There are no interviews, just the show. Thank you." *Click.*

No matter: Sometimes it's best to let your heroes remain shrouded in
mystery, and Kraftwerk's music does indeed tell the story. After one album
of Philip Glass–style minimalism as Organisation, the renamed Kraftwerk
made three discs of similarly proto–New Age electronic Muzak before morphing into the band that has come to be considered legendary. In 1974 the
duo turned away from the avant garde and made a calculated attempt to
"go pop." In their friend, visual artist Emil Schult, they found a guru with a
talent for conceptualizing their music and presenting a unified multimedia
image, and in the then-new Mini-Moog synthesizer, they found an electronic instrument that was perfectly suited for their vision of rock 'n' roll. It
was as if Chuck Berry had just discovered the electric guitar.

Autobahn was conceived as an aural evocation of driving on the German
highway. The title track is powered by an incredibly catchy synthesizer riff,
and it isn't clear whether Hütter is singing in German or English; the lyrics
could be "Fahr'n, fahr'n, fahr'n on der autobahn" ("Riding, riding, riding
on the autobahn"), or a very Beach Boys–like "Fun, fun, fun on the autobahn." The album became a huge hit in the States after Chicago record producer Robin McBride edited "Autobahn" into a three-and-a-half-minute
single that was equally popular on rock radio and at cutting-edge disco-
theques. Expanding to a quartet with the addition of percussionists
Wolfgang Flur and Karl Bartos, the group presented itself as a new kind of
all-electronic band. Ladies and gentlemen, meet the robotic Beatles.

More extraordinary albums followed: *Radio-Activity* (1975), *Trans-Europe
Express* (1977), *The Man-Machine* (1978), and *Computer World* (1981), all
recorded at Kling Klang, and all boasting rich, complex, multi-layered syn-
thesizers and electronic drum sounds that many have envied but few have
been able to imitate. The band was hailed by the likes of Brian Eno and
David Bowie (who dedicated a song to the group on *"Heroes"*) and nascent
New Wavers such as Devo and Gary Numan. Rap innovator Afrika
Bambaataa sampled Kraftwerk; Chicago's Big Black covered the group; and

the trailblazers of techno and house music here and in Detroit paid homage in interviews and on record.

As its popularity grew, Kraftwerk withdrew from the spotlight. One of the best songs on *The Man-Machine* is called "The Robots," and it plays with the musicians' image as stiff automatons. But it wasn't long before the band actually took to sending finely crafted robots out to appear at press conferences, pose for photos, and even perform some concerts while Hütter and Schneider stayed home at Kling Klang. In the early '80s the pair became more interested in pursuing their new passion for bicycling, which was reflected in a 1983 single called "Tour De France" boasting a rhythm track based on a bike racer's heavy breathing. Following in 1986, *Electric Cafe* was a disappointment. As critic and biographer Pascal Bussy noted in *Kraftwerk: Man, Machine and Music*, it brought the band full circle, "building up atmospheric pieces of music rather than writing conventional songs."

Kraftwerk hasn't released any new material since. The (un)dynamic duo spent five years doing digital remixes of classic songs such as "Computerlove," "Pocket Calculator," and "Trans-Europe Express" for an album called *The Mix*. Frustrated by the glacial pace of the band, Bartos, Flur, and Schult departed, and the music world has been waiting for Hütter and Schneider to re-emerge ever since.

They finally did last year, making a highly anticipated appearance at England's Tribal Gathering rave. The group was a quartet once again, completed by Fritz Hilpert and Henning Schmitz, and its mix of electronic music and computer visuals was reportedly as breathtaking there as it was at the Riviera Theatre on Friday. When the curtains parted at exactly eight P.M. (nothing like German punctuality), the renowned Kling Klang had literally been reconstructed onstage in Chicago. Dressed in matching black uniforms, the four musicians moved behind their sleek work stations. The Man-Machine was thus complete, and Kraftwerk proceeded to deliver more than two hours of "Music Non Stop," to borrow the title of the closing number.

With the exception of one new song, a hyper-rhythmic techno instrumental, it was a greatest hits set: "Autobahn," "The Model," "Computer World," "Trans-Europe Express," "Radioactivity," "The Robots." But the show was anything but nostalgic. All of the tunes were rebuilt with new digital computer sounds as opposed to the analog synthesizers of the old albums—by way of comparison in the impact, imagine Stravinsky coming back to re-orchestrate "The Rite of Spring" for a rock band—and the show put to the lie the notion that Kraftwerk hasn't done anything "new" since

1986. There was as much imagination and reinvention here as there is when Bob Dylan reinterprets his best songs live onstage.

Careful observation of the players also disproved the idea that they're letting the machines do all the work, or they're simply manipulating the incredibly impressive visual images rather than playing music. Hütter sang and played all of the keyboard "leads"; Schneider controlled sound effects, including the computerized vocals, and Hilpert and Schmitz manned electronic drums and ambient keyboards. There was actually a fair amount of live interaction, as evidenced by two or three minor mistakes that offered welcome reassurance of these fellows' humanity.

In terms of sheer sonic artistry as well as inventive stagecraft (the visuals ranged from nostalgic black-and-white movies to the band's renowned dancing robots), Kraftwerk left every other electronic musician of the '90s in the dust. Only the Orb and Aphex Twin have come close as live performers. But the real lessons were less obvious.

One was that Kraftwerk's songs are timeless because of the melodies and rhythms, not the technology. The other was clear when the musicians stepped out front to perform an encore of "Pocket Calculator" with tiny hand-held instruments. At age fifty-one, Hütter and Schneider danced like awkward teenagers, even breaking character to smile at their devoted fans' enthusiasm. After thirty years of making music together, these guys are still having fun. Long may the Man-Machine rock.

10 OUT OF TIME: R.E.M. AND U2

THROUGHOUT THE ALTERNATIVE ERA two bands loomed larger than any of the others that had come before, hovering over the scene as inspirations for their business models as much as their music, and being hailed as venerated elders who had helped open the doors at mainstream radio and MTV. R.E.M. and U2 have always shared many similarities, and not only because they both straddled the line between pop and art as bass, drums, and guitar quartets with charismatic frontmen. Both were also expert at manipulating the media to promote their own mythologies (which sometimes had little to do with the facts), and both seemed absolutely impervious to bad press. These were Teflon Rock Stars in the age of the Teflon President.

Myth-making is part of what rock 'n' roll is about, of course, and I never begrudged R.E.M. and U2 that indulgence. But that doesn't mean I was willing to give them a free pass on the inherent contradictions.

Through the '80s and into the early '90s, I preferred R.E.M.'s music to U2's. I still haven't tired of the layers of mystery on R.E.M.'s greatest album, *Murmur*, and the many shows I saw the band perform as it graduated from tiny clubs like Maxwell's in Hoboken, New Jersey, to mid-sized theaters remain some of the best rock concerts I've ever seen. (I remember making a five-and-a-half-hour road trip to Boston with the fellow staffers of *Jersey Beat* fanzine, editor Jim Testa and columnist Patti Kleinke, because the three shows we'd seen on the Reckoning tour in New York and Passaic, New Jersey, just weren't enough.) But while I never had any illusions about the musicians being heroes—those had been purged early on when I witnessed some very Aerosmith-like behavior at an after-show party in Hoboken— I was nevertheless disappointed to see how many of the principles and

artistic goals they compromised as they became a part of the music-indus-
try establishment, a progression that is well charted via the three cover stories that I wrote about the band for *Request*.

It's as a disappointed fan that I say that R.E.M. hasn't made much music
of worth since the poignant last gasp of *Automatic for the People*, but even
now I hold out the hope that it's still possible (and I would love to see the
small-theater tour that Peter Buck has been promising for years).

As for U2, while I was enamored of the majestic, reverb-drenched
sounds of the first three albums, the band's posturing and literal onstage
flag-waving always struck me as extremely silly, and that shifted to pure
annoyance once the group began lionizing Elvis Presley and Martin
Luther King, Jr., as it bulleted the blue skies. While I generally consider
irony a cheap tool for any artist to hide behind, with U2 circa *Achtung
Baby* and *Zooropa*, it was actually a refreshing change of pace, and the
newly acquired ability of the musicians to laugh at themselves as well as
their courage in challenging themselves artistically via the provocations
of the brilliant Brian Eno (see Chapter Nine) resulted in their very best
work. Unfortunately, U2 returned to its old, self-important form on the
aptly titled *All That You Can't Leave Behind*. Applaud Bono for trying to
cure AIDS and solve Third World debt if you will, but his band's new music is a snooze compared to *Achtung Baby*.

Today R.E.M. and U2 both show all the signs of carrying on in perpetuity,
the Rolling Stones or the Eagles of the post-Boomer era, alternative to nothing, and very much a part of the machine that they once set out to upend.

Musical Perversity
Request, May 1991

THERE AREN'T MANY landmarks in Athens, Georgia, but the handful that
are there are memorable. The Civil War's only double-barreled cannon
stands in front of City Hall, and even though it killed its inventor the one
time it was fired, it still points north "just in case." The Tree That Owns
Itself juts out from an island in the middle of Findley Street, protected
against the march of progress by a far-sighted, arbor-loving gent who
granted the oak its freedom and protected it in perpetuity in his will.
Finally there's the crumbling steeple on Oconee Street, all that's left of the
abandoned Episcopal church where R.E.M. played its first gig in April 1980.

Like the cannon and the tree, the church looms larger in its legend than in life. Bertis Downs and Jefferson Holt, R.E.M.'s managers, suggested that the group buy the place of worship, but guitarist Peter Buck laughed at the idea. "Man, I lived there. It leaked, it was cold, and it had fleas. Dogs lived in the back. There was a grave under the stage. But," Buck adds with a touch of pride, "everybody who comes to town to see us always goes there to take a look at it."

Buck and his bandmates haven't discouraged such pilgrimages; they encourage journalists to interview them at home in Athens, the better to absorb the R.E.M. mythology. The most successful guitar band to emerge from the American rock underground in the 1980s, R.E.M. climbed to the top of the charts over the course of eight imaginative records, slowly expanding its fan base without sacrificing much of its credibility. For rock stars, they remain amazingly accessible, good-natured, and down-to-earth people.

Nevertheless, they're as image-conscious as any heavy-metal band ("I never look good on the cover of *Spin*," Buck complains when a publicist shows him the March issue). They maintain they've never had any goals more specific than making good records and having fun, but they're well organized with firm control of their career ("They've always had as many strategy meetings as practice sessions," says one Athens scenester). They know mythmaking is part of rock 'n' roll, so they promote it, repeating oft-told tales of the band's origins at the church and early tours that criss-crossed the country in an old Dodge van fueled by speed and visions of Kerouac.

"It's a very small-level myth. We haven't set ourselves up as legendary characters," Buck says. "We're relatively faceless for someone who sells as many records as we do. People still walk up to me and say, 'God, Bill, you're the greatest drummer in the world.'"

This seems disingenuous coming from a member of a band whose last two albums sold almost two million copies each and spawned two Top 10 hits. *Green* and *Document* reached the largest audience of R.E.M.'s career, but with typical perversity, the band has veered away from the straightforward pop of the last two efforts to produce its strangest, most textured, and best album since 1983's brilliant *Murmur*.

Out of Time marks several departures from the typical R.E.M. sound: The band is augmented by such odd instruments as flugelhorn and harpsichord, and there are strings on almost every track; Buck plays as much mandolin as guitar, leaving many of the six-string chores to Peter Holsapple, the former dB's leader who joined R.E.M. for the Green World

Tour; and for the first time, singer Michael Stipe is joined by two guest vo-calists, Kate Pierson of fellow Athenians the B–52's and Kris Parker, aka KRS-One of Boogie Down Productions. Bassist Mike Mills also contributes two rare lead vocals.

The first single, "Losing My Religion," is slow and moody (the title is a Southern colloquialism for bottoming out); the follow-up, "Shiny Happy People," breaks into a waltz midsong. The naive optimism of the latter song and the varied instrumentation and layered harmonies throughout the al-bum recall the Beach Boys' masterwork, *Pet Sounds*. Buck, Mills, and drum-mer Bill Berry say that album was on their minds when they were in the studio, although Stipe says he's only heard it two or three times.

"The first two people that heard ['Shiny Happy People'] said, 'Boy, that's the most cynical song, you're really digging in that one,' and I'm not," Stipe says. "I wrote this to be the happiest song I've ever written, and I think I succeeded. I wanted this to be a really up, positive record. I feel like these are incredibly troubled times, and people need something—not to distract them or take their minds off of it—but something that says there is good-ness around. You can laugh at this. You can dance to it. You can't sing along without smiling."

Stipe is the most written-about and least understood member of R.E.M. His subtle sense of humor is easy to miss. "I've always thought that the most gullible people are the ones who can lie the best," he says, "and I'm a really gullible person, so I can really pull the wool over someone's eyes if I want to in a joke situation.

"The whole willful obscurity tag has gotten a little tired at this point. And the Southern mystic eccentric tag has gotten a little tired, too. It should be dead and buried," the singer says. "I'm a lot more normal than most people. I maintain that media figures, people who are seen in the public eye, are always seen as much bigger, and every gesture is seen as much broader than the average person, when in fact it's an average person mak-ing simple gestures that are then hyperbolized through media."

As if to illustrate his point, Stipe wipes his face on his shirttail after fin-ishing a slice of pizza, and he occasionally drops out of our conversation to grab at an imaginary dust speck floating in the air.

On *Out of Time*, Stipe moves away from political songs such as "Orange Crush" and "Green Grow the Rushes" to focus on the more personal themes of time, memory, and love. "It was an incredible challenge to try to write an album of love songs, because I've always despised love songs per se," he says. "At the same time, I didn't want to be pigeonholed or categorized as a political writer. I've spent fully a third of my adult life trying to duck categorization."

Stipe reached a new audience with *Document* and *Green,* and many of these young fans were politicized in part by the band's well-publicized examples (R.E.M. supported Dukakis in the '88 election and has touted groups such as Greenpeace and People for the Ethical Treatment of Animals). He's proud that fans share some of his views—he's made several visits to a peace camp set up by students at the University of Georgia to protest the war in Iraq—but he's suddenly grown uncomfortable with being a leader.

"Clearly, people need media figures or someone who speaks common sense," Stipe says. "Nothing is ever just sensibly thought out any more. It's all complicated and it's all run through these levels of propaganda so that by the time it reaches Joe-Grab-a-Sandwich or Jenny-at-College, there's nothing there. I think unfortunately people are going to be looking to us to try to get some idea of what's going on, and I would only hope that they'd try to figure it out for themselves. I don't really want to be the political spokesperson of my generation.

"Hopefully the things that have brought me to be politicized will prompt our fans to do a lot of investigating and try to figure out what's going on, and most important—'Shiny Happy People'—keep their sense of humor about it."

As much as some of its members enjoy reveling in the myth, R.E.M. is no longer the wild young band living a beat lifestyle. They're all in their thirties, Buck and Berry are married, and they've made more than enough money to be considered yuppies. A member of the Feelies, a band Buck produced in 1986, recalls that the R.E.M. guitarist was very upset one day when he arrived at the studio. When asked what was wrong, Buck said his accountant had just told him the members of R.E.M. had each earned a million dollars that year.

"I think there was something kind of similar, maybe not millionaires," Buck says evasively when asked about the story. "It's just kind of odd to have to think about that shit. It's all intangible, money. It's an idea. I really don't even think about it too much. I have an accountant who pays my bills. I don't think I've ever balanced a checkbook."

But not worrying about bills is a luxury, as is Buck's stately mansion and swimming pool. The band members all own comfortable homes and other properties in Athens. Since they share the concerns of any tax-paying resident, they've become politically active in the town. When the county commission wanted to tear down several historic warehouses to make way for a civic center, R.E.M. funded a five-thousand-dollar study to determine the feasibility of saving the buildings. Unfortunately, the study was ignored.

The group was more successful when it supported a liberal commission candidate, Gwen O'Looney. R.E.M. gave O'Looney several thousand dollars, and when her conservative opponent, E. H. Culpepper, spread scandalous literature about her, R.E.M. withdrew the band's account from Culpepper's bank. "It was a savings and loan, so it was probably a good move anyway," says Downs, who is also their attorney.

When Mills arrived in Athens as a college student a decade ago, he never imagined his band would one day give him some local political clout. "And I never would have wanted it at the time. But when you get older, certain things become more important to you. The peace and quiet of the area in which you live becomes one of the overriding concerns in your life." These days, the thirty-three-year-old bassist probably wouldn't want to live next door to a rock 'n' roll party house like the one he and Berry shared on Barber Street in the early '80s.

R.E.M. won't be abandoning the comforts of home any time soon. For the first time in its history, the band that made its name on the club circuit by constant touring plans to stay home after releasing a new album. "We're still trying to get our wind back from the Green World Tour," Stipe says. "Nine months is a long time to be completely without base and to be moving that much."

"I love to play live. We all do," Berry says. "Ten years ago, we were a band that played live, and we'd occasionally pull off the road just long enough to make a record. There's a lot of great things about success, but one of the downfalls is that now we're a band that makes records, and touring has gotten to be a pain in the ass. The only way for us to do it now is to play those big halls and feed that big machine, and you've got to get it started six months ahead of time, and there's huge salaries, and in order to pay for it all you've got to stay out for nine months. And we just didn't want to do it this time."

Although they said for years that they'd never play halls larger than twelve thousand seats, the Green World Tour included shows at the largest indoor arenas. The band members bristle when they're reminded of their earlier comments. They say it was necessary to play arenas or fans would have been shut out or forced to pay large sums to scalpers.

"It's easy to say you won't do it when you think you'll never see the backstage of Madison Square Garden," Mills says. "But playing Madison

Square Garden is not a big rock-star thing, it's just being successful and doing well at your job."

Nevertheless, some longtime fans resent the band for going back on its word—something that seems to be happening more often as the group becomes more popular. Stipe often said he'd never lip-sync on a video, but he reneged when filming the clips for "Losing My Religion" and "Shiny Happy People." "I fainted the first time I had to do it. I'm still trying to get over the cold," he says. "I feel like we pushed video as far as it could be pushed without lip-syncing. I'd taken such a strong stand against it, I think I finally had to prove to myself that I could do it.

"There's gonna be people who cry sellout no matter what we do in our career, and that's just something we've kind of come to terms with," he continues. "We could put out *Metal Machine Music*, and someone somewhere would find some reason to consider us having sold out to corporate America. I can't even answer to that any more, it's such a ludicrous suggestion. Anyone who listens to the record will see that it may be the strangest thing we ever recorded, and yes, within that, there are elements of pop songs that are surely to make it to the Top 10 on radio. But I think that says more about the way radio has changed in the last twelve years than the band."

R.E.M. can't be accused of softening its sound for radio or kissing up to the AOR powers-that-be. "Radio Song," the lead track on *Out of Time*, is a scathing indictment of the state of radio that charges programmers with avoiding adventurous music, whether it's by a rock band like R.E.M. or a hip-hop artist like KRS-One.

"We were lucky to have two Top 10 hits, really lucky," Berry says. "Radio is no friend of ours. They play us because kids request us, and we sell out eighteen-thousand-seat halls, so they have to. Our songs barely get into the Top 10. They're there for a week, and it's like, 'See how fast we can get you out of there,' and they do. Payola is still the thing. They think we should pay money. That's what they want. They want indie promoters. But we're just not going to play that game."

Berry, Buck, and Mills have all read *Hit Men*, the best-seller that detailed the record industry's controversial practice of hiring independent promoters who can assure a record Top 40 airplay or block it out altogether. "We considered [hiring indie promoters] one time," Berry says. "We were doing rehearsals in Knoxville, Tennessee, before the Work Tour started, and we had a meeting backstage, and Jefferson said, 'Here's the way it is guys. This is how you get hits.' We always pooh-poohed the idea. We didn't want to have anything to do with it. We weren't even sure if that was really the case, but people were telling us this is how you do it. So we actually sat there and thought about it for a few minutes, until Mike Mills shook us out of it."

R.E.M. refused to compromise, and the gamble paid off. "Things have gone well for us because we've done them the way we've done them," Berry insists. "We slowly built a fan base that got bigger and bigger and bigger. If we didn't get a Top 10 hit, we'd sell 1.1 million records instead of 1.9 like the last one did. That's still OK. We can go out and sell out a twelve-thousand-seat hall instead of an eighteen-thousand-seat hall because we don't have a hit, and that's OK, too. There's worse things, and one thing worse is doing things you don't feel good about."

Since the beginning, the members of R.E.M. have maintained an equal partnership that requires unanimous decisions and allows any member to veto a move he strongly disagrees with. It's the reason the group thrives while many of its contemporaries—from the Bangles to Hüsker Dü to X—ended in bitter feuds. "By everyone having veto power and knowing that they're never going to have to do anything that they're not happy with ar- tistically or physically or mentally, it also makes you feel more positive about the entire approach and more willing to give in here or there," Berry says.

"It's a very volatile situation to be involved with a creative, moving force with as much independence as a rock band and be able to maintain friendship and creative energy," Stipe says. "It's hard enough for two people to keep it together and keep it going and keep it fresh, much less four or six including Jefferson and Bert. It's pretty extraordinary that we've persevered."

....

FROM THE DB'S TO
R.E.M. AND BACK AGAIN

When R.E.M. needed someone to flesh out its sound for the Green World Tour, it was natural for the band to turn to Peter Holsapple. As a member of the now-defunct dB's, Holsapple was a major influence on the group in its formative years, and his easygoing personality—as well as his abilities on guitar, bass, and keyboards—made him a logical candidate.

In the late '70s and early '80s, the dB's (who grew up in Winston-Salem, North Carolina) and the B-52's (based in Athens) showed rock audiences there was more to the South than the Allman Brothers and Lynyrd Skynyrd. They helped pave the way for R.E.M. by constantly touring up and down the East Coast and drawing attention to the new wave of Southern pop. Holsapple also introduced R.E.M. to Mitch Easter, who produced *Chronic Town, Murmur,* and *Reckoning.* And R.E.M.'s decision to team up with Scott Litt was influenced by Litt's sparkling production on the dB's wonderful 1982 album, *Repercussion.*

You'd think it would be hard to become the fifth member of a group that's been a quartet for the last decade, but Holsapple "really fit in mentally with the chemistry of the band," Bill Berry says. He even joined R.E.M. in the studio, playing on six of the eleven basic tracks for *Out of Time.* "I just came in and played my parts. I don't want to make it sound like it was anything less than that or anything more than that," says the self-effacing Holsapple. "I just did as much as I could to make the overall sound sound more like they wanted to sound."

Holsapple will continue playing with the group—"They know my number, and they can always call me when they want me"—but now he's concentrating on *Mavericks,* an album that reunites him with high school chum Chris Stamey. The two shared the singing, guitar-playing, and songwriting duties on the first two influential dB's albums, *Stands for Decibels* and *Repercussion.* Stamey left the group in 1983 to pursue a solo career, and Holsapple continued fronting the band for two more albums before calling it quits in 1988. Although Holsapple is living in L.A. and Stamey resides in Hoboken, New Jersey, the pair linked up several times over the last two years for shows as an acoustic duo, and those casual performances inspired them to record together again. The project grew more ambitious as recording began, and now they plan to tour in a five-piece band.

Fans of the dB's should appreciate *Mavericks* for Holsapple and Stamey's beautiful harmonies, carefully sculpted hooks, and quirky, literate lyrics on gems such as "Angels," "I Want to Break Your Heart," and "Haven't Got the Right (To Treat Me Wrong)." The two have an obvious chemistry that, despite some fine moments in their later work, makes this album the most consistently rewarding from either musician since *Repercussion.* But Holsapple and Stamey want to avoid comparisons to their old band.

"This is a different thing from the dB's, and I think it's really important to make that clear," Holsapple says. "There's a reason why we're not going out under the name 'the dB's,' and part of that is that [drummer] Will

[Rigby] and [bassist] Gene [Holder] are not along. And the other thing is that we want to think this is a few years down the line, and maybe we can do something slightly different."

....

Grand Old Men of Modern Rock
Request, November 1994

IN THE WEEKS before he took his life, Kurt Cobain frequently asked those around him how Nirvana could have avoided the bad publicity, retained more control over its career, and continued to have fun as its performances shifted from rock clubs to sold-out arenas. In short, Cobain wondered how his band could have been more like R.E.M.

It's not surprising that the favorite sons of Athens, Georgia, were role models for Cobain, or that they continue to influence and inspire rockers ranging from Pearl Jam to PJ Harvey. As they move into their late thirties, Michael Stipe, Peter Buck, Mike Mills, and Bill Berry have become the grand old men of alternative rock. Like grandpa talking about how far he used to walk to school, Buck is fond of telling every interviewer how the band slowly and surely built its audience from the days of cross-country tours in a beat-up van to its current level of multiplatinum success.

"I don't know what would have happened to us if our first record had been *Nevermind*," Buck says. "If *Murmur* sold five million copies, I don't know where we'd be. I'd like to think it wouldn't have gotten as far as it did with Kurt, but I don't know if we'd be here now."

In fourteen years, the members of R.E.M. have made very few wrong turns. The group is one of the few bands that surfaced during the postpunk '80s to have infiltrated the ranks of rock superstars. U2 is the only band that compares, and the new *Monster* is R.E.M.'s *Zooropa* (although not quite as good). Like U2's last effort, R.E.M.'s ninth album of new material is an attempt to mess with the band's recognizable sound by adding a harsh, aggressive edge, radically altering the vocals, and playing with a lyrical approach that's the musical equivalent of channel surfing. And the results are mixed.

The sound does seem tailor-made for rock arenas, however, and the band is gearing up to hit the road for its first tour since 1989. When it does, it will have three albums to draw from. Since the end of the Green World Tour, R.E.M. has released *Out of Time* (1991), with its lush *Pet Sounds*–like orchestrations; *Automatic for the People* (1992), a quiet, introspective, and brilliant effort that the band considers "a small album" but which still sold eight and a half million copies worldwide; and now *Monster*.

The new album is partly a calculated effort to prove R.E.M. hasn't gone soft. "It's a loud and obnoxious rock record," Mills says proudly. Buck named it, and he says that the title comes from "the stupid big guitar sound, as well as the fact that a lot of the characters aren't so nice." None of the band members brings it up, but one suspects there's also a touch of mid-life crisis involved. *Automatic for the People* opened with "Drive," a song that could be heard as the members of R.E.M. wondering if they're still in touch with younger rock fans ("Hey kids, where are you / Nobody tells you what to do"). *Monster* begins with "What's the Frequency, Kenneth?," a tune that Buck describes as "an older guy's perspective looking at the younger generation and wondering what's going on."

There's nothing like a little fuzz guitar and some feedback to drown out questions about whether you're too old to rock—just ask Neil Young. Clearly, Buck, Berry, and Mills still love at least some aspects of the rock 'n' roll lifestyle. They enjoy being stars, and they're good at it, even if they do work hard to project regular-guy images. Stipe is quiet and intense, but his version of what R.E.M. is doing and why is more genuine and better articulated than his bandmates'. As a whole, R.E.M. has always manipulated its image, flying journalists to Athens so that the town's artsy, eccentric vibe would be intertwined with the R.E.M. mythology. The band usually insists that interviewers talk to the entire group, offering time with each member individually or splitting up into pairs. Stipe seems to prefer it this way: It presents the image of a united creative front instead of the lyricist-frontman on one side and three musical cohorts on the other. And it gives him a way to retreat if he tires of unwelcome queries or if the interviewer isn't in tune with his sly and playful sense of humor.

Through the years, fans have become well acquainted with the band members' public personas. Buck is the rock aesthete, group historian, and chief mythologist. Mills is the most talented and versatile musician, the band member that Buck fingers as "most likely to do a solo album." Berry is the affable, good-natured drummer who doesn't mind that his contributions as a songwriter, backing vocalist, and sometime bassist and guitarist are generally overlooked. They are all necessary components of the band, as are comanagers Bertis Downs and Jefferson Holt, who are listed as group members in *Monster*'s liner notes. But Stipe is R.E.M.'s heart and soul, and its major source of mystery and inspiration. Here are the highlights of my talk with the voice of *Monster*. (True to form, Stipe and Mills were interviewed together, though the bassist's comments were limited to occasionally amplifying or amending Stipe's replies.)

Q. Automatic for the People *was quiet and introspective, an album that listeners had to spend some time with. In contrast,* Monster *sounds like your* Zooropa: *It's in-your-face and experimental, R.E.M. turned upside down and inside out.*

A. Inside out, there you have it. We wanted to take a new tack with this record. With *Automatic,* we set out to make a punk-rock record. It turned out to be a very quiet and introspective record, and it had a very obvious and constant theme. But I maintain that it's truly a punk-rock record.

Q. *In what sense?*

A. Doing things on your own terms. What else was going on musically when *Automatic* was released, and what did we do? Completely the fucking opposite. I'm really proud of that. We took a big chance. I can't always articulate it, but it makes sense to me.

It's really a pity when people go in the studio and come out with something that sounds just like everything else. There are limitless possibilities to what you can put down, but at the same time there's this language and lexicon that everybody understands. The pop song is very limited, but you can take those boundaries and smash them out. I like that: No rules. We do some pretty wild shit, and hopefully by the time it gets to the record it hasn't been normalized. I sang through a Walkman on three songs on this record.

Q. *There are two extremes to your vocals: a heavily processed sound and a real soulful voice like on "Tongue."*

A. I discovered the soul voice a couple of records ago. These guys have been throwing these songs at me and kind of daring me ever since. Every good singer has gotten to sing a song like "Strange Currencies" or "Everybody Hurts." I've got the pipes, I may as well use them. Sinéad O'Connor gets to sing these wild blues things, why can't I?

Q. *The first three songs on* Monster—*"What's the Frequency, Kenneth?," "Crush With Eyeliner," and "King of Comedy"—seem to have a common theme about media obsession. [The first song takes its title from something an alleged mugger said to CBS news anchor Dan Rather, the second is about sexual obsession from a distance, and the third takes its title and theme from Martin Scorsese's movie about a kidnapped celebrity.]*

A. The other guys sequenced the songs. I don't really have much to do with that. "King of Comedy" took a real turn. I took the original lyric and trashed it. Originally, it was about someone who was media-obsessed with some completely nondeserving media figure, some ancillary person who's involved in some ridiculous thing and becomes a media figure. The subject of the song had volunteered for money to become part of a research study, but instead of being given drugs, he was given sugar pills and put into isolation with piles of magazines and a VCR. Through that he becomes obsessed with this media person. He wrote these letters saying, "I don't want your money. I'm not going to sue you. I'm not the King of Comedy." As the song went on, it became obvious that this person, who thought he was completely normal, because of the isolation that he was in, he was really wigging out. The only stimulus was the media. But I took that whole idea and trashed it and just wrote a simple song.

Q. *Has it become easier for you to deal with being a celebrity yourself?*

A. I think I stepped into it in a big way, and I did it in a very public way. There was a point where I said, "OK, no matter what I say or do or how I look, people are going to perceive me the way they want. I may as well take what I want to say and truncate it into sound bites that are at least understandable or that show a little bit of the original intention." I feel really fortunate that we have the jobs that we have. There are some bad parts to it, but so what?

Q. *Thurston Moore plays on "Crush With Eyeliner." How did he get involved?*

A. We called him up and asked him. I thought that I had stolen the song from the Sonic Youth record. In fact, I had stolen it from a Coca-Cola commercial. But at the time that I thought I'd stolen it from Sonic Youth, I thought, "Well, if we're going to rip them off, we should have them on the song." He and Mike played together in the *Backbeat* band.

Q. *The second half of* Monster *has a grouping of songs about jealousy and placing blame: "Strange Currencies," "Bang and Blame," and "I Took Your Name." Is there a blame thing going on?*

A. It's probably more of a rhyme thing! [Laughs] Blame, fame, name.

Q. *I like the Iggy Pop line in "I Took Your Name." ["I wanna be Iggy Pop if that's what it takes."]*

A. Thanks. Somebody thought it was "indie pop." [Laughs] I like that. I almost changed the lyric. I don't know. I'm still just writing love songs. I wanted the record to have a lot of sexy songs. I wanted it to be really foxy and kind of swaggery. I think I succeeded.

Q. *You're preparing to tour for the first time in five years. Are you doing anything different this time to avoid the burnout that you complained about after the Green World Tour?*

A. [Laughs] Yeah, I'm not going. I'll get a doppelganger.

Q. *The members of Kraftwerk famously sent robots out on tour while they stayed home, and Andy Warhol sent impostors out to do interviews for him in the '60s.*

A. Seriously, I have a friend who looks a lot like me, and I was considering sending him on the road once. This was when my hair was really long and you couldn't see my face anyway. Anybody could sing like I sang in 1983.

Q. *Your attorney and comanager, Bertis Downs, appeared at the congressional hearings about Ticketmaster. He made it clear that R.E.M. supports Pearl Jam's stand against what it calls Ticketmaster's monopoly of the sale of concert tickets. Are you in a position to do anything about that?*

A. We've been out of the loop on it for quite a while, since we haven't toured since '89. There are things we can do and we're going to do them, but I can't say more than that.

Q. *You knew Kurt Cobain and were talking with him shortly before his death about collaborating.*

A. I talked to Kurt a lot in the weeks before he disappeared and died. I knew that he was in trouble and presented the idea of us working together as a way to get him out of the head that he was in. I sent him the plane tickets and got a car to go pick him up, but at the last minute he backed out.

I felt a real alliance with Kurt in terms of what he was doing, musically and lyrically and public-image-wise. There's not that many people that I feel that alliance with, people who are really pushing in terms of what is media image and really fucking with it. The last time I talked to him, he was burning a pizza, and I had to call back because the oven was on fire.

I talked to Kurt's mom the other day, and she said she was glad when she heard that we had dedicated a song to him. "Let Me In" is about Kurt.

Q. *How has R.E.M. avoided that absurd level of celebrity? People don't camp out in trees outside your house, and I don't read about you in* The National Enquirer.

A. Quite simply, I think we're pretty boring.

Q. *But you've also had a strong support system with Bertis Downs and Jefferson Holt. It seems as if you prepared for stardom from the very beginning. There are stories about the early meetings when you determined that if one member of the group ever strongly objected to something, he could veto it even if the others disagreed.*

A. That came from Peter having read every rock magazine and rock book. He knew what broke up bands, and we said, "If we're going to do this, let's do it right."

Q. *One of the things Kurt Cobain was doing was challenging sexual mores and attitudes about homosexuality: writing about the issue in his lyrics, talking about being bisexual, and appearing on magazine covers in a dress. You've addressed similar themes, going back to the videos for "Pop Song 89" and "Losing My Religion." Why is that important to you?*

A. I like gender-fucking, fucking around with the roles that have been handed us. Sexually speaking, they're very binary, very black-and-white. I disagree with that. I think that sexuality and sex and what turns people on and what turns people off is a really slippery thing, and it's not right to categorize it with labels. I really like slipping back and forth.

Q. *Cobain was bothered that there was a segment of his audience that didn't get it. In the liner notes to* Incesticide, *he rails against people who are homophobic and asks them not to buy his music. Do you think about that?*

A. There's a degree of preaching to the choir. I imagine that those people in his audience didn't really belong in his audience. It's great that he put that in there, but it's almost better to have those people come to the show and really challenge them, to have them surrounded by other people who disagree with them.

Q. *The pop-music landscape has changed dramatically between the first time I saw R.E.M. playing with the Neats for two hundred fifty people at Maxwell's in Hoboken, New Jersey, and now, when Lollapalooza routinely draws crowds of thirty thousand or more. Do you think there's a new vibe in the rock scene, and do you feel responsible to any extent?*

A. I kinda do. I think there's a lot of the same old thing, but I do think there are a profound number of people who are finally getting it, or who are at least open to trying to figure things out a little bit. The thing that I wrestled with in the late '80s was idealism versus cynicism, and I don't think that's quite gone away yet. I really feel an incredible kinship with people who are fourteen years my junior. I seem to be motivated by the same things they're motivated by, I have the same cultural references, blah, blah, blah.

I was talking to Tori Amos a couple of nights ago. I saw her perform. We were talking about the whole Kurt thing, and she said that there was this performer—I don't want to name who it is—but X performer was trying really hard, but not really capturing his feminine side. Overtly, you would think that that was there, because there are all these trappings and he seemed to be fucking with it. But he wasn't really making himself, as a performer, vulnerable to his audience.

"Everybody Hurts" was a very fucking ballsy song. It could be and can still be heard as one of the most sappy, maudlin, sentimental, cry-in-your-coffee songs. But it succeeded. For some reason, the majority of people think that that song speaks to them in some way. That really worked, but we could have just as easily taken a step that didn't work. To leave yourself vulnerable and open to that is difficult. That's where I feel that Kurt Cobain and Tori Amos and Eddie Vedder are important, and when one of them drops out for whatever reason, it sucks.

Q. *When I first heard "Everybody Hurts," I heard it as a song that was reaching out to people who are HIV-positive and saying, "Hold on." Does the specter of AIDS influence you as an artist?*

A. I honestly don't think it does any more than anybody else who is our age. At the same time that *Automatic for the People* came out, we hadn't toured for a long time and there was a rumor that I was HIV-positive, that I had AIDS. We put out this record that was about mortality and death, and a lot of people—I'm not saying that it was misinterpreted—but I'm not HIV-positive. I don't have AIDS. Initially, I refused to publicly answer that.

Q. *Did anyone ask you directly?*

A. We would get calls to the office, and I would say, "No comment." I felt like it was a ludicrous claim. But I realize now that a lot of people were asking out of genuine concern. I thought they were just being "Kibbles 'N Bits" journalists or nosy tabloid reporters.

This is really naive, but I kind of thought that by not answering the claim, people who were fans or who knew me just as a celebrity might actually think twice about how they mind their own business and how they feel about people who are HIV-positive.

I think that a lot of people interpreted that record through that. That was a pretty popular rumor, especially in England and overseas. I'm skinny and I've got a funny haircut and we didn't tour. People put two and two together, but to me it kind of seemed like it came out of nowhere.

Q. *After* Out of Time, *you talked about moving away from politics in your lyrics. You said that people know where you stand and that the new generation of rock fans doesn't need to be lectured because it's turning to activism on its own. What do you think now that we're a couple of years down the road?*

A. People definitely know where I stand. I go somewhere, and my reputation precedes me. The activism we exhibited in the '80s was a very direct response to the leadership we had in this country, and it was out of sheer desperation. I was no more a Dukakis fan than anybody else. It was just the idea of bringing in another Republican administration.

"Ignoreland" was like the last nail in the coffin for me. Like, "OK, I will no longer go on and on about the Reagan-Bush years." Of course, it's not over. We have to live with the specter of it for the next 30 years, and we are the privileged ones. You and I are going to make money doing what we like to do, like write and make music, but there are a lot of people who are really getting the short straw.

Q. *Are we really any better off under President Clinton?*

A. I'm a huge Clinton fan. I think he's unbelievably radical, and he's in a position of incredible compromise. He can't even begin to do everything he wants to do, but he's working hard to get as much done as possible and to stay in office long enough to actually have a go at it. He's made some really fucked-up decisions and mistakes, but so did Jimmy Carter. His mistakes do not even begin to match Reagan's mistakes in the first year in office in terms of how they affect people.

Q. *I know you practice what you preach locally. When I came to Athens in 1991, you were working hard to get Democrat Gwen O'Looney elected as mayor. You gave her campaign a lot of money, and when her opponent started spreading rumors about her, you took R.E.M.'s account out of his family-owned bank.*

A. We're still working for her! She's up for re-election. Let's have a silent moment and hope for the best. [O'Looney won the Democratic primary on August 9. The mayoral election is November 8.] The guy she's up against is the worst. His father was mayor, and he's like a Dan Quayle character. He probably knows as much about running the town as I do.

Q. *So when are you going to run for office?*

A. I'd rather not put myself in that position, thank you.

··

THE MAKING OF A MONSTER

While R.E.M. has often created an aura of mystery and reveled in it, the band's three instrumentalists have never been reluctant to talk about their working methods. The most obvious change on *Monster* is that the group has returned to the basics of guitar, bass, and drums, with each of its members in their old positions after two albums of varied instrumentation and role-swapping.

"I hadn't played loud electric guitar in years," Peter Buck says. "When we said we were going to do this—Bill on the drums, Mike on bass, me on electric guitar—it was really refreshing, and it kept getting louder and louder. When we started rehearsing, the quiet ones got loud and the loud ones got really loud."

"We originally thought that *Automatic* would sound like this album," Mike Mills says. "But when we looked at the songs we had, that went out the window."

Monster represents a change in the way R.E.M. writes and records. Buck no longer lives in Athens, splitting his time between Seattle and New York City. Gone are the days when the three instrumentalists got together every day to jam, with Michael Stipe coming in later to add vocals.

"The only thing that's really changed is that we stay in the same room longer," Bill Berry says. "When we were all down in Athens, we were really lazy. We'd get together every day, but we'd wind up going for a beer after half an hour. This time, we spent six or seven hours together every day when we were together, and that was great."

The new method was productive enough to yield forty-five songs, including the tunes that wound up on *Monster* and what Buck calls "a whole album's worthy of pretty good acoustic stuff." During preproduction, the band set up as it would to perform onstage. Rough eight-track demos were recorded, and the version of "You" that closes the album comes from these tapes. (The performance was so powerful the band members decided not to rerecord it, even though the drums were recorded in mono.) Like every effort since 1987's *Document, Monster* was produced by Scott Litt.

"We've kind of broken him in," Buck jokes. "We're hard to work with. If we ever did work with anyone else, I don't know how it would work. We're at the point with Scott where we communicate without talking. I really feel that if any one of us was given complete control, he could produce the record, and it would sound great. But we don't work that way, and thankfully we have Scott to moderate."

Buck estimates that the set lists on R.E.M.'s upcoming tour will be "ninety-five percent songs from the last three albums," and also will include tunes that the group hasn't recorded yet. The band likely will perform an acoustic mini-set in the middle of its concerts, allowing members to trade places and instruments as they did on *Out of Time* and *Automatic for the People* and during the live taping for MTV's *Unplugged*. R.E.M. will be augmented by a small string section and a guest guitarist-keyboardist, but the stage will be relatively bare and unadorned.

"When all is said and done," Mills says, "it all comes down to the interaction between the four of us."

Automatic for the Press
Request, December 1996

MICHAEL STIPE IS doing something that he vowed he'd never do: He's lip-synching as R.E.M. films the clip for "Bittersweet Me," the second video from its tenth album of new material, *New Adventures In Hi-Fi*. It's late July in Los Angeles, and the favorite sons of Athens, Georgia, are gathered on a small platform in the middle of a cavernous soundstage on the lot of A&M Studios. The carefully orchestrated media campaign that greets each new R.E.M. album is about to begin, and the crowd that watches the video shoot from the sidelines includes Chris Heath of *Rolling Stone*; Bobbie Ann Mason, a Southern novelist hired to profile the band for the *New York Times*; a couple of foreign journalists; and myself.

We're all here to collect what we writers call a little bit of "color" before interviewing the band the following day. Guitarist Peter Buck and bassist Mike Mills are plugged into their amps, and Bill Berry is sitting at his drums. In between takes of fake performances, we're treated to instrumental versions of "Winchester Cathedral," "Kingdom of Love," an old Soft Boys song written by Buck's pal Robyn Hitchcock, and "Catapult," a tune from R.E.M.'s first album, *Murmur*, that the band never plays at regular concerts anymore.

If you go back and look at the avalanche of press clippings that herald the release of every new R.E.M. album, you'll notice that a theme runs through all of them. The band members clearly decide what the emphasis of each new round of interviews will be, and they stick to the program and stress the same sound bites. Seduced by their plentiful charms, journalists willingly comply by writing the same stories. (I've done it myself.) Hence *Green* was portrayed across the board as "the political record." *Out of Time* was "the experimental-orchestral record." *Automatic for the People* was supposed to be "the loud record," but it turned out to be "the quiet record." *Monster* was "the long-awaited loud record," as well as "the record where Michael Stipe talks about bisexuality but says he isn't HIV-positive."

Over the next two days, I get the impression that the group wants *New Adventures In Hi-Fi* to be portrayed as "the record where R.E.M. proves that it's still got it." It arrives at a critical point in the band's history: It's the last album owed to Warner Bros. under the group's first contract with the label, and the first to be released since the news that R.E.M. has signed a new eighty-million-dollar mega-deal with the company. It's also the first album without the group's longtime manager, Jefferson Holt, and the first after the assorted health problems suffered by Berry, Stipe, and Mills during the Monster tour showed that the musicians are no longer the indefatigable, indestructible indie-rockers who crisscrossed America in a van.

R.E.M. is one of the biggest businesses in popular music today. After months of speculation that the group might jump ship for DreamWorks SKG, the new label run by old friends Lenny Waronker and Mo Ostin, or Outpost, the MCA-distributed boutique label started by longtime producer Scott Litt, the band re-upped with Warners for a five-album deal that's the largest recording contract ever awarded. It tops the seventy million dollars that Janet Jackson received to sign with Virgin in 1995, and Jackson's attorney, Donald S. Passman, helped R.E.M. negotiate the pact. The result was announced in late August during Warner's annual corporate meeting at the Anaheim Convention Center, and thousands of employees jumped to their feet for a standing ovation.

In late July, the band members weren't tipping their hands about which label they'd wind up with, but in retrospect, their comments shed light on the strategy they'd use to drive up the price. "Even if you know you're gonna buy a car from Honest Joe, you would cross the street to see what kind of a deal you're gonna get over there just so you can tell Honest Joe what you want," Buck said. Added Mills: "We're in a great position now in terms of leverage, and we're just going to take advantage of it." (That leverage included the fact that Warners, besieged by two years of corporate infighting, couldn't afford the black eye it would get from losing its biggest act.)

Back on the video set, the band resumes its pantomime, and the sounds of "Bittersweet Me," a melancholy ballad in the mold of *Automatic for the People*, fill the air. "I don't know what I'm hoping for," Stipe sings on tape and mouths onstage. "I don't know what I want anymore." More than anything the musicians will say in the current round of interviews, these lines seem to sum up where the group is at right now, as well as answering the questions that many fans are posing: After eighteen years as a band, what is motivating the members of R.E.M. to continue? And, perhaps more important, has their incredible success boxed them into a corner where it's impossible for them to challenge themselves artistically?

THE DAY BEFORE the "Bittersweet Me" video shoot began, a few advance copies of the August issue of the English music magazine *Mojo* arrived in Los Angeles. It was the first sign that R.E.M.'s designated message circa *New Adventures in Hi-Fi* might not be delivered exactly as planned. The group was pictured on the cover in a typically enigmatic Anton Corbijn photo, but the cover line was "R.E.M.: The Final Act?" Inside, writer Barney Hoskyns painted an unflattering but fairly innocuous portrait of a band adrift after parting with Holt and limping through the Monster tour, but determined as ever to control its public image. The piece ended with speculation that the group's long career might be drawing to a close.

Hoskyns was clearly mistaken on the last point, but the members of R.E.M. have seen the article, and they're not happy. "It's just more journalists looking for an angle," Mills says peevishly. "Every bit of information they had in there was wrong. It's all anonymous sources and making things up. I've got one thing to say to all those people who commented there, and that's 'Mind your own fucking business.'"

Warner Bros. had something else to say: The company retaliated by pulling all of its advertising from *Mojo* and making it clear that R.E.M. will never speak to the publication again—this after the group refused to comment for Hoskyn's story in the first place. The magazine's primary sin seems to have been daring to run a story about R.E.M. that R.E.M. and Warners did not explicitly sanction or control. "We've had our knuckles rapped," says *Mojo* editor Mat Snow. "They see press merely as an aspect of promotion as opposed to what you might call journalism, which has an institutional position in reporting on events of what you might call public interest. And they're not interested in that."

The lack of bad publicity that the members of R.E.M. have received through the years is extraordinary considering the band's fame and stature. "They were randy young rock stars who did all the things—drugs, sex, drinking, you name it—that you would imagine that they'd do," says a music industry veteran who was a close associate of the band through the late '80s. "The only thing was, you never read about it."

This is what led Nirvana's Kurt Cobain—whose every stumble was well-documented—to ask with envy how they did it. The members of R.E.M. maintain that it's because there were never really any tales to tell out of school. But in fact, they worked very hard to become the Teflon Rockers, skillfully setting the tone of press coverage by controlling access and cultivating relationships with friendly writers and editors who, if aware of any shortcomings, were nonetheless united behind a group that they saw as a true, fresh alternative to corporate-rock behemoths like Aerosmith, Van Halen, Madonna, and Michael Jackson.

The members of the tight-knit core of R.E.M./Athens, Ltd., the band's corporate entity—the four musicians plus Holt and attorney Bertis Downs

IV—always banded together like the good ol' boys they were, and they never let any of the really sensitive stuff escape the smoke-filled rooms in which strategy was plotted. "We come from the South, where everybody gossips," Mills says. "But you're not supposed to inquire into other people's business, so we don't. It's just part of our ethic that whatever is a person's private business remains a person's private business, and that stays within our group. We're a little more boring than most rock bands are thought to be. We're a little smarter than most people who get caught doing some of those stupid things. And maybe we're a little lucky, too. But I think that we're all people with more or less genuine good will, and that gets reciprocated in the end."

One person whose store of good will seems to have eroded is former manager Holt. A record-store manager from North Carolina, Holt hopped in the van with the group in 1981 and never got out. He was immortalized as the driver in the song "Little America" from *Reckoning* ("Jefferson, I think we're lost!"), and album credits always listed the group as "Berry, Buck, Mills, Stipe, Downs & Holt." But Holt resigned abruptly in May just as the band was gearing up to negotiate the biggest contract in rock history. R.E.M. announced that Downs would oversee its business affairs on his own, and a subtle change appeared in the credits of the new album. R.E.M. is listed as "Berry, Buck, Mills, & Stipe," and Downs is credited separately as "advisor."

In a story attributed to sources close to the group, the *Los Angeles Times* reported in June that R.E.M. asked Holt to leave after investigating allegations that he sexually harassed a female employee at the band's offices on West Clayton Street in Athens. Holt denied the charges and told the newspaper that the decision to part was mutual. "I've agreed to keep the terms of my agreement with R.E.M. confidential," he said. "However, fifteen years is a long time, and as time passed, our friendships have changed. I think we found as time passed that we have less and less in common. I've become more interested in other things in life and wanted to spend more time pursuing those interests." (Holt could not be reached for this story.)

Buck denies that anyone connected with R.E.M. planted the sexual harassment story. "We had nothing to do with that. If we *were* to speak to the press and talk about things, we would look a lot better than that," he says. "I personally don't have anything to say about it—I'm legally not allowed to—but the four of us always make all decisions, and we always have. Because of some experiences we might have had in the last six months, nobody likes the word 'manager' anymore, Bertis the least of all. So he's 'advisor.' But the fact is the four of us manage ourselves. In every aspect of what we do in our lives, we try to work on our moral level. Every decision we've ever made has had elements of the moral and ethical standpoints that we all encompass, that are part of our lives, and we're all feeling really, really positive."

But some of the group's most loyal devotees are starting to question whether its moral compass has been damaged. Online discussion groups dedicated to R.E.M. were full of complaints about ticket prices on the Monster tour and the fact that the musicians often seemed stiff and bored onstage. It's often noted that the band now regularly breaks promises it made early in its career, such as Stipe's vow that he would never lip-sync on video, or Buck's pledge that the group would never play halls with more than five thousand seats.

An editorial in the Summer 1995 issue of *394 Oconee*, one of the best of the dozen or so fanzines devoted to the group, summed up the feelings of many of its readers. "R.E.M. have become millionaires who really don't identify with the working class anymore," editor Pattie Kleinke wrote. "They're not the band I fell in love with thirteen years ago. In a three-page article, Michael used the phrase 'media figure' at least ten times. I'm even beginning to question their political correctness. Is it just photo ops and chances to hang out with their 'peers'—other glitzy celebrities who clutch their drinks, snort their coke, and mainline their smack at trendy parties? How could Bertis stand beside Pearl Jam during the Ticketmaster hearing and then charge fifty dollars as base price [for R.E.M.'s concerts]? Maybe it was good P.R. at the time."

The Ticketmaster charge is the one that stings the most. Downs testified with Pearl Jam against Ticketmaster during congressional hearings into whether the company was a monopoly, but then R.E.M. allowed Ticketmaster to sell tickets and charge its usual service fees on the Monster tour. "All Bertis ever said was that we don't like monopolies," Mills says. "They're bad for business and they're morally untenable. That's all we said. I was 100 percent behind Pearl Jam in their efforts. However, touring is a very, very important part of my life, and I was not about to not tour just for the sake of saying 'Fuck you' to Ticketmaster. I'll say 'Fuck you' to Ticketmaster right now and mean it, but that doesn't mean I'll stay home and not tour if I have to use Ticketmaster."

"We were the only band in the world besides Pearl Jam that testified against Ticketmaster," Buck says. "Our lawyer testified right with Jeff [Ament] and all those guys. And the fact of the matter is it did hurt us.

They cut no slack for us. You've got to understand, Ticketmaster has legally enforceable contracts with all the halls. Let's not use the word 'kickback,' because they have libel lawyers, but they get a portion of the service fee. We were pretty sure at the time that because there was a Democratic congress, that it would be investigated and something would be done, because it is clearly a monopoly. We thought we could testify and by the time we went on tour, we wouldn't have to use Ticketmaster. But the Justice Department let everybody down [when it determined that Ticketmaster is not a monopoly]."

Still, R.E.M. did control its ticket prices. While top alternative bands such as Pearl Jam and Green Day were charging twenty dollars for their concerts, the cost for tickets on the Monster tour averaged between forty and fifty dollars, plus Ticketmaster service fees.

"Honestly, the ticket prices were probably too high," Buck says now. "We wanted to be in the middle of the market. We threw out the Rolling Stones and the Eagles' prices of one-hundred-fifteen dollars a ticket because we didn't want to do that, and we sat down in every market and determined a price so that we were exactly in the middle between the high end and the low end. In retrospect, maybe I would have come back and said, 'Let's be lower.'"

Mills responds with obvious annoyance. "Are you saying that fifty dollars is too much for a ticket?" he asks. "In New York City, that's not too much. And I think that our moral integrity is such that we do not ruin it by charging middle-of-the-road ticket prices. If all of our good work over the years means nothing because we were charging fifty dollars for a ticket in New York, than so be it. I work real hard for this, and going out on the road for a year is something that's really tough. I don't mind being paid for it."

The members of R.E.M. are being paid well indeed. By signing their eighty-million-dollar mega-deal, they have joined the ranks of the superstars they once opposed, including Barbra Streisand, Madonna, and Michael Jackson, all of whom signed sixty-million-dollar pacts. To date, none of the artists who have signed mega-deals have produced work that stands alongside their best, and none of them have taken significant artistic chances.

In fact, signing a contract of such magnitude may be like putting a gun to your head, since it brings with it an enormous pressure to perform up to the label's commercial expectations. Industry analysts say that mega-deals often wind up losing money, but label executives continue to pursue them because, in a business full of uncertainty and one-hit wonders, they are the closest thing to a sure bet. The problem is, nobody's happy when a sure bet doesn't pay off.

THE "BITTERSWEET ME" video features R.E.M. performing in an empty movie theater while a bogus Italian art film in the style of *La Dolce Vita* is projected behind them. The fake '60s film scenes are taped on the second day of shooting at the Chapman Park Building, an ornate art deco structure in downtown Los Angeles that's doubling for an Italian villa. The movie stars actor Richard Edson, now a regular in the films of Jim Jarmusch but once the drummer for Sonic Youth. Director Dominic De Joseph spends the day filming Edson and various beautiful models in period fashions cavorting on the set. The band members don't need to be present for any of this, but today is also the designated press day, so they're here to be ushered in and out of fancy air-conditioned trailers to meet the journalists for their allotted thirty-minute chats.

Three long trailers are parked by the curb on the street outside the Chapman building: one for the actors, one for Stipe to hang out in, and one for Buck and Mills to do their interviews. Each has two separate rooms nicely appointed with couches, chairs, and a mini-bar. There's plenty of space for the business at hand, but Mills is angry because he wanted to have two interview trailers, one for him and one for Buck. Assistants are scurrying to see if another can be brought to the set, and I'm thinking about statements the band made in the early '80s mocking former tour mates the Police for arriving at shows in three different limousines.

In the old days, up through *Out of Time*, R.E.M. invited writers to come to Athens for interviews. Journalists usually stayed for a few days. They soaked up the ambiance at sites like the old church at 394 Oconee Street where the group played its first gigs (and which gave the fanzine its name), and they casually interacted with band members at their homes, in restaurants, and at the famous 40-Watt Club. These days, Buck lives in Seattle, Mills is in L.A., Berry has a farm outside Athens, and Stipe bounces around a lot. Since *Automatic for the People*, R.E.M. has done press in Los Angeles in a much more regimented fashion, revealing much less of themselves and sticking to the schedule set by Warner Bros.

Stipe, by far the most interesting band member and the group's biggest celebrity, only meets with most of the press for every other album. He talked for *Out of Time* but not *Automatic for the People*, and for *Monster* but not *New Adventures in Hi-Fi*. However, he does chat with *Rolling Stone*'s Heath, and he gives a few short quotes about Nabokov to the *New York*

Times's Mason, acknowledging those publications' positions at the top of the journalistic pecking order.

Berry, usually an affable sort, isn't talking to anyone, probably because he doesn't want to hear the inevitable questions about the brain aneurysm he suffered onstage during the Monster tour. I am granted separate interviews with Mills and Buck. The bassist is cranky and terse as usual, but Buck is effusive as always and happy to talk a mile a minute. After Stipe, Buck is R.E.M.'s most media-savvy member. He's got a neat trick of making journalists feel as if he's confiding stuff that he's never told anyone before: I've talked to three of my peers who have all gotten variations of the line, "Wow, what a great question, no one's ever really asked me that before." I've gotten the line myself all three times I've interviewed him.

"I personally like this record at least as well as *Automatic*, and *Automatic* I think is our best record," Buck says as he begins the process of using me to promote another new R.E.M. album. He goes on and on in his rapid-fire manner about how the rough tracks were recorded in different cities along the Monster tour; how sound checks were the most creative time for the band and a source of a lot of the new material, and how the instrumental "Zither" was taped in the shower stalls of a basketball arena in Philadelphia. "I think the album's up there with our best work," he says several times, sounding as if he's trying to convince himself as much as me.

New Adventures in Hi-Fi is a good album, not a great one, and its initial charms fade fast the more you listen to it and realize that it's rather generic R.E.M.: one part *Monster*, one part *Automatic for the People*. It's evenly divided between lilting, atmospheric, mostly acoustic numbers and fuzz 'n' feedback–soaked glam-rock grooves. There isn't a single tune that hints at a new direction, let alone a noble failed experiment like "Radio Song," "Ignoreland," or "Let Me In."

Buck notes that R.E.M.'s only real peers in the world of rock are U2. But the members of U2 have bravely reinvented themselves on each of their recent albums. They have purposely hired producers like Daniel Lanois, Brian Eno, Flood, and trip-hop guru Howie B. to force them to make music that doesn't sound like U2. It's a tremendous gamble that could have blown up in their faces, but instead it has produced some of their best work. In contrast, the members of R.E.M. have been working with the same producer, Litt, for almost ten years. They aren't taking any chances.

I'm thinking about all of this as Buck is yammering on about how R.E.M. isn't going to tour behind *New Adventures in Hi-Fi* but will probably be back on the road after the next album in 1998. Tour, don't tour—it's the sort of classic non-story that will appear in every article written about R.E.M. in the next few months. We all know that sooner or later, the group will perform again onstage—bands that sign eighty-million-dollar contracts always do. I'm determined to try to force Buck to address a real and much more interesting dilemma.

The central crisis in rock right now involves nostalgia and the problem of how a band grows old gracefully in an art form that is about doing absolutely nothing gracefully. Groups like the Rolling Stones make new music as an excuse to tour and play the old hits for paying crowds; the albums are just souvenirs. The members of R.E.M. say that what they care about is making challenging new albums, and then they tour every few years almost as if it's a perfunctory chore. Is it possible to be a working, creative band and not care about both functions equally?

"When I was younger, touring was why you were in a band," Buck says. "But no matter how loose we keep it now, it's still not going to be very loose at our level. So no longer is it this really creative process. Most of those bands like the Stones really are nostalgic. They know they can get sixty thousand people if they play all the hits from the '60s, and they can get three thousand people if they play the new record. To a certain degree, I understand that, and there may be a time in my life when I'm more interested in celebrating the past than working on the present or the future. But whatever tour we do, I'm just going to want to do the new songs and songs from the last couple of records. I'm totally willing to see the audience decline in numbers if that's the case."

But signing the mega-deal suggests that R.E.M. really hasn't learned anything from the Stones. Surely Warner Bros. isn't quite so willing to see the band's audience decrease. Nostalgia is pervasive in rock today because it's safe and it's a sure-seller. The most successful tours this summer were by the re-costumed KISS, the reunited Sex Pistols, the reshuffled survivors of the Grateful Dead, and good ol' Neil Young and Crazy Horse. All of them cheerfully cranked out the sounds of yesteryear.

"Well, this is show business," Buck says. "It is lucrative, and if your option is to wash dishes somewhere or play the hits from twenty years ago, most of us will probably play the hits from twenty years ago. But nostalgia just gives me the creeps. It's not even a real emotion, it's just a pandering to past emotions. When I go see Neil Young, I want to see him do the new record. I've seen him do 'Cowgirl in the Sand' for twenty-five years, and it's a great song, but I just don't need to hear him do it again. It's a real tough thing, and we're in a place now where we're lucky that our early stuff wasn't big hits because we'd have this huge tail of a comet wagging behind us. As it is we have to think about it—we played one song from *Reckoning* every fifth night—and I like that song, but do I really want to play that stuff? Probably not."

Buck says that the thing that keeps R.E.M. going is that the group is still doing good work, and its members can't yet envision what will stop that. But I note that no artist ever recognizes or admits when he or she has started to suck.

"Believe me I hear it from everyone," the guitarist says, laughing. "I don't think people give us a lot of slack. They come up and say, 'I don't think you were very good live and I don't like *Monster*.' I think about it a lot. It's the one thing I think about more often than anything. I'm very cognizant of how old I am, that this is passing and that every year the opening bands get younger and younger and the bands that I go see, I realize, 'My god, I was having sex with my girlfriend in the back of a car right around the time you were born and your parents are maybe five years older than me.' I'm cognizant of that and I know that it's gonna happen and the creative thing—very few people maintain it."

It all comes down to the definition of what exactly good rock 'n' roll is. I define it as a spontaneous explosion of personality. Some people have two and a half minutes of personality: The Kingsmen recorded "Louie, Louie," and that's as good as rock gets, but that's all they had in them. Some people have a lot more. The Rolling Stones were good until *Some Girls* in 1978; that's a lot of great music and heck of a lot of personality. Most bands fall somewhere in between. R.E.M. may or may not be at the end of the line. The question is whether its members will be honest enough to admit it when they get there.

"We're trying to keep it as forward-looking as possible and not embarrass ourselves, and I think we're succeeding," Buck says. "I want to be the one. There's never been a rock band that's lasted and kept at it. I'm thirty-nine now. By the time every one of the major classic great bands, when the songwriters were my age, they had been a nostalgia band for ten years, or five years at the very best. I want to be the one. U2—they're our age—maybe the two of us can do that. I want to be fifty and turn in a record that's great. And I know that probably then we're not gonna sell ten million copies, and that's cool. It would be nice if we could go gold and have people go, 'You know, those old fuckers really keep at it. No matter what people say, it's a really good record.' It will all trail down—we won't be sitting in four trailers talking; I'll be on the phone with you—but I think that I can do this when I'm fifty.

"I've seen a lot of the pitfalls that bands have gone through, and I'm going to try to avoid most of those," Buck continues. "Everybody makes mistakes, and maybe mine won't be to become a nostalgia act. But if I find myself playing eight-hundred-seat clubs and all of us are on one bus, I could do that. Maybe not every night of the year, but we're not stupid people, I'm not going to have to work like that. We're talking about maybe doing a theater tour some time, and maybe having a vibes player and a cello player and a piano player and doing some of the quieter stuff. Which is something I could do when I'm fifty."

But the truth is that bands on the mega-deal level rarely have the privilege of playing small theaters with vibes and cello players. Buck and I both know this. Superstars aren't allowed to "trail down"; it's in the music industry's best interest to keep them pumped up and on the straight and narrow course that's likely to yield the greatest dividends. The only people who ever really challenge artists are the artist themselves. The fans and the press are all too willing to fall in line and buy whatever they're being sold.

A knock comes at the trailer door, and Buck and I exchange pleasant goodbyes. My time is up, and the next journalist is outside waiting to take my place.

U2 Pumps Up the Power with Zoo TV
The *Chicago Sun-Times*, September 17, 1992

THE JOKE GOES like this: Stevie Ray Vaughan dies and goes to heaven, where Saint Peter introduces him to Elvis Presley, Buddy Holly, John Lennon, and Bono. "Wait a minute," Vaughan says. "U2's singer ain't dead!"

"Oh, that's God," Saint Peter replies. "He just *thinks* He's Bono."

U2's performance at the World Music Theatre Tuesday proved that if Bono heard the joke, he'd not only get a laugh out of it, he'd probably broadcast it on the band's massive Zoo TV screens.

The group (which performs its third and final show at the World tomorrow) used Zoo TV to deflate the rock-star myth at the same time that it delivered a slick, captivating, stadium-rock spectacle. The band members turned a half dozen video cameras on themselves to provide warts-and-all close-ups that showed they're just regular guys, then they blew the picture up one hundred times larger than life.

Technologically, Zoo TV represents the future of arena rock, providing a sensory overload of videos, swirling lights, and electronic messages. Musically, the Irish quartet is at its peak, and if you took the high-tech gimmickry away, it'd still be an incredible show. But U2 knows the music is even more powerful when connected to strong images.

The same could be said of Public Enemy, the acclaimed New York hip-hop crew that followed Big Audio Dynamite II's torturous opening set. Public Enemy has never played to such large crowds, but it was up for the challenge, delivering a concise selection of its best songs, from "Fight the Power" to "Can't Truss It."

DJ Terminator X cranked the group's trademark grooves and white-noise assaults as rappers Chuck D. and Flavor Flav dropped wisdom and bounced nonstop across the stage. Overhead, a giant screen projected the cover of the group's new album, *Greatest Misses*, which reproduces an historical photo of a white crowd cheering the lynching of two black teens. At the end of the set, Public Enemy retaliated with the mock lynching of a white-cloaked Ku Klux Klan figure as Chuck D. wished the audience, "Peace."

The messages on Zoo TV were just as contradictory. The billboards flashed such alternating slogans as, "Everything you know is wrong" and "Believe everything." The other electronic highlights included an altered video of George Bush chanting, "We will rock you"; Bono's Natalie Cole–style video duet with Lou Reed on a cover of Reed's "Satellite of Love;" and a call the singer placed to White House Operator Number Two (who had obviously heard from him before) to, "Leave a message for George: Watch more TV!"

In addition to a heavy sampling of songs from *Achtung Baby*, which stands as the band's best album, the group expanded its set to include such vintage anthems as "New Year's Day" and "Sunday Bloody Sunday." But there was no nostalgia in its spirited versions of these oldies, and unlike past U2 tours, Bono didn't resort to pompous preaching, empty flag-waving, or bogus theatrics.

The singer spent a lot of time on a platform that extended far into the audience. At one point, he pulled a pair of enthusiastic female fans on stage, and they grabbed him so tight he couldn't move. Bono called to the Edge for help, and one of the fans grabbed the guitarist's ever-present cap off his head, publicly exposing his bald pate for the first time in U2 history.

It was a very human moment amid an evening of futuristic, postmodern technology—a reminder, like the music, that there is a soul somewhere in the machine—and it was funny, to boot. Which reminds me: How does U2 change a light bulb? Bono holds the bulb, and the world revolves around him.

U2: A Critical Discography
The *Chicago Sun-Times*, May 6, 2001

WITH A QUARTER-CENTURY'S history behind it, the U2 that arrives in Chicago next week to perform four sold-out shows at the United Center has actually been three or four very different bands over the course of its long and storied career. The quartet's development can be charted via its recordings, which comprise one of the most rewarding discographies in rock.

....

U2:3 EP, 1978 ☆☆ 1/2
Inspired by the Sex Pistols and the punk explosion of London's "summer of hate," the group came together in 1976 at the instigation of fourteen-year-old drummer Larry Mullen, Jr., who placed an ad on the bulletin board of Dublin's Mount Temple High School. Among those who responded were bassist Adam Clayton, guitarist Dave Evans (later the Edge), and an outspoken chap named Paul Hewson who, even though he couldn't sing particularly well at the time, brazenly rechristened himself Bono Vox (Latin for "good voice").

The name U2 was eventually chosen for its political and enigmatic qualities (referring to the famous spy plane, as well as the double meaning "you, too"), and it replaced earlier monikers like Feedback and Hype. At first, the band trampled its way through standard late '70s punk fare, including material by the Pistols and the Ramones, but its own sound was beginning to emerge on its first recording, a three-song EP that won a following in Ireland but made little or no impact in the U.S. The disc is a collector's item now, of course, but its embryonic sound isn't all that exciting.

Boy, 1980 ☆☆☆ 1/2
On the strength of its Irish success, the band signed to Island and recorded its debut album with Steve Lillywhite, a staff producer known for the

booming drums and ringing guitars that he gave to New Wave artists like Ultravox, Siouxsie and the Banshees, XTC, and the Psychedelic Furs. In retrospect, the relatively stripped-down if echo-laden sound of U2's debut has aged well: It doesn't seem nearly as dated as the work of other enigmatic guitar bands from this era—say, Echo and the Bunnymen, or Big Country, which appeared as a blatant U2 clone in 1983. The disc yielded two underground hits with "I Will Follow" and "Stories for Boys," but the track that stands as most representative of the early sound is probably "An Cat Dubh," with its massive drums, tinkling bells, minimalist Edge guitar licks, and anthemic Bono chorus. All together now: "Whoa-oh-oh! Whoa-oh-oh!"

October, 1981 ☆☆☆

More confident and self-assured, U2 opens its second Lillywhite-produced disc with the classic "Gloria," which builds on the sonic hallmarks of *Boy* while introducing the spiritual thematic so important to the musicians in their personal lives (everyone but Clayton is a devout Christian). It's a cheeky move for any rock band to pen a tune called "Gloria" in the wake of Van Morrison's classic, but U2 pulls it off with a song that's almost as great, building to a transcendent choral sing-along ending. The Christian concerns continue on "Fire," "Rejoice," and "With a Shout," but "Gloria" aside, the disc isn't quite as strong as its predecessor. (The music has aged better than the moody glamour-puss photo of the band on the cover, however. Check those floppy New Wave hairdos!)

War, 1983 ☆☆☆

Having gotten religion, the quartet from Dublin now gets political. Many fans consider this U2's first great album, but I disagree: While the Lillywhite-produced music is probably the best example of the early U2 sound, with more imaginative arrangements and Edge's stately piano coming on strong, the lyrics of tunes like "Sunday Bloody Sunday," "New Year's Day," and "Seconds" are often heavy-handed, clumsy, and strident. "Gold is the reason for the wars we wage!" *Ugh.* I saw U2 for the first time on this tour, performing at New York's Palladium. Bono lost me when he started waving a huge white flag, urging us all to fall in step and join the crusade. What crusade? Well, that wasn't quite clear, and even at the impressionable age of nineteen, I thought it was all sort of goofy. The live album *Under a Blood Red Sky* bears me out.

The Unforgettable Fire, 1984 ☆☆ 1/2

Enter U2, Mach Two. Lillywhite is out, and the "ambient atmospheres our specialty!" team of Daniel Lanois and Brian Eno is in. Unfortunately, their impact wouldn't really be felt for a while, and this remains a problematic and transitional effort. Lyrically, Bono is becoming increasingly obsessed with America—witness "4th of July," "Elvis Presley and America," and of course "Pride," a ham-fisted tribute to Martin Luther King, Jr. The singer was never more preachy, more self-righteous, or more insufferable.

The Joshua Tree, 1987 ☆☆☆ 1/2

The best example of the band's second incarnation still finds Bono crooning about America, but this time the critiques and observations in songs like "Bullet the Blue Sky" (about U.S. involvement in El Salvador) and "In God's Country" are much more artful and poetic. Meanwhile, the music on tunes such as "Where the Streets Have No Name" and "With or Without You" finds the band moving into a starker, more mysterious sound that is less easily defined (or parodied), and which rewards repeated listenings. Part of the credit is due to a heck of a support team: producers Lanois and Eno inspire the band to stretch out and experiment, Lillywhite comes back to remix several tunes, and a talented young engineer named Flood captures it all on tape.

Rattle & Hum, 1988 ☆ 1/2

Alas, it was one step forward and two steps back. U2 followed the unprecedented commercial success of *The Joshua Tree* with this mix of new material and live tracks that aspires to pay tribute to American roots music but winds up amplifying all the worst traits of *The Unforgettable Fire.* It's awkward, pretentious, ponderous—a real mess. But maybe the band had to get this out of its system before it got where it was going next.

Achtung Baby, 1991 ☆☆☆☆

The group's masterpiece, and the introduction of U2, Mach Three. Under the increasingly powerful spell of Eno, that unparalleled artistic instigator, the band finally abandons all lingering hints of its old chest-thumping and flag-waving in favor of giving a great big postmodern raspberry. But while Bono's live posturing and the whiz-bang technical assault of the subsequent Zoo TV tour were absolutely lousy with irony, the music itself is never cold or alienating. In fact, "One" is probably the most heartfelt and moving song the band has ever recorded. Overall, *Achtung Baby* stands as a disc that is both resonant of its time and absolutely timeless — the perfect soundtrack for slipping on the virtual reality helmet and flipping through three hundred channels of satellite TV while waiting for the Ecstasy to kick in.

Zooropa, 1993 ☆☆☆ 1/2

Recorded in the midst of the Zoo TV tour, these ten songs don't have quite the same impact, but they do continue the playful experimentation of *Achtung Baby*. Bono in particular has blossomed under Eno's tutelage, just as David Bowie and David Byrne did before him. In keeping with his new stage persona of a Vegas-style Satan, he adopts a darker, more sinister tone on "Daddy's Gonna Pay for Your Crashed Car," "Some Days Are Better Than Others," and the title track, while on other tunes, he successfully tackles Tony Bennett–style crooning ("Babyface") and a Smokey Robinson falsetto ("Lemon"). Bono also sits out for two songs, allowing the band to prove that its identity extends beyond its photogenic frontman. Johnny Cash sings on the wonderfully apocalyptic "The Wanderer," and the Edge does his best Lou Reed imitation on "Numb." This is far from U2's most consistent collection. But you know what they say about consistency.

Pop, 1997 ☆☆

Have you sensed a pattern here yet? U2 seems to run in cycles of one great breakthrough album, followed by a few strong discs with various refinements, followed by a real stinker. This is another stinker. Eno isn't around this time — Flood and trip-hopper Howie B. are at the helm — and the disc has a harsh digital sheen that contributes to its incorrect dismissal by some as a "techno" record. The band talked a lot about experimenting with electronic dance music, and they actually made a fairly interesting ambient album in 1995, working with Eno under the name Passengers. But *Pop* might have been better if U2 actually *did* go techno. Instead, we got tired dinosaur rock.

"Mofo" is a plodding and inferior rewrite of "One," the chiming guitar break in "Discotheque" reaches back to "Boy," and "Last Night on Earth" is just U2 circa *The Joshua Tree* tarted up with some electronics. Lyrically, Bono is still "Lookin' for to fill that God-shaped hole," but he wrongly thinks he's going to find what he's looking for in the tired cataloguing of pop-culture icons ("The Playboy Mansion"), as well as some lame synthesizers and tired drum patterns. The band seems to be running on empty.

All That You Can't Leave Behind, 2000 ☆☆☆

Which brings us to the present, but it's hard to say exactly where this effort fits in. It's a departure from *Pop*, to be sure, but as fans and critics have noted, it's a return to an "older" U2 sound—the sound of the second incarnation, more or less. It's an album that anyone who likes the band will find hard to resist, even if it's unlikely to rank as anyone's all-time favorite.

There's no heavy-lifting or serious artistic ambition here. "There's nothing you can throw at me that I haven't already heard / I'm just trying to find a decent melody / A song that I can sing in my own company," Bono sings in "Stuck in a Moment You Can't Get Out Of," and that pretty much sums things up. The band does deliver a batch of fine melodies— "Beautiful Day," "Wild Honey," "Peace on Earth," "New York"—but there's nothing as potent or memorable as "One," "Even Better Than the Real Thing," or "With or Without You."

Are Bono, the Edge, Mullen, and Clayton still capable of making another artistic leap forward à la *Achtung Baby* or *The Joshua Tree*? We'll have to wait and see where the band is going next. Right now, it has given us an apt summation of where it's been, and the perfect fodder for an onstage celebration of all that is U2.

11 HOOTIEGATE

BAR NONE, MY EIGHT MONTHS AT *Rolling Stone* maga-
zine were the worst in my working life, edging out even the summer I spent
as an assistant janitor scraping gum off the bottom of every desk at Hudson
Catholic Regional High School for Boys. As deputy music editor under my
friend, Keith Moerer, I theoretically had the power and the money to send
the best writer of my generation to Iceland for two weeks (along with a
photographer and a stylist) to do the ultimate profile of Björk. Instead I was
assigning desperate freelancers to cover the birth of Art Garfunkel's baby,
or to do a story critical of Don Henley's efforts to save Walden Woods because the magazine's infamous über-Boomer editor and founder, Jann
Wenner, had not been invited to the former Eagle's latest wedding.

Keith and I had been brought to the venerated but always overrated and
compromised magazine to update its music coverage for the alternative era.
"*Rolling Stone* needs to change or die," managing editor Sid Holt told us,
conveying Citizen Wenner's latest decree. "We need what you guys do."
Every job is in some proportion a trade-off; you may love and be fulfilled
by eighty percent of what you do, while twenty percent is strictly to pay the
rent. For Keith and me, the ratio at *Rolling Stone* was more like ten-ninety. It
was as if we had the keys to a Ferrari but we could only drive it five miles
an hour. We were desperately trying to jump from the driver's seat when,
consciously or not, I sped up our exit.

I've read a lot of different versions of what happened over the years, and
many of them are as real as Britney Spears's tits. It was like this: We had
these three shitty records—the latest by Hootie and the Blowfish, the Dave
Matthews Band, and the Spin Doctors—and Keith was looking for a way to
cover them when, as I often do, I started spouting some cockamamie theory,

that the common link between these lame jam bands was the whole vapid modern-day hippie trip, and the blame needed to be placed squarely at the feet of the Grateful Dead. For some reason Keith bought this crap, and I was off and running on a triple-header lead review. The piece you're about to read made it through three rounds of copyediting and was set in type two days before the magazine was about to go to press—a nifty little painting of Matthews, Darius Rucker, and Chris Barron sitting on a haystack had been commissioned, accepted, and positioned in place—when Wenner saw the page proof and blew a gasket.

Wenner initially said that we were slighting Hootie, lumping the band in with two other groups when he felt that it deserved a full-fledged review of its own after selling eight and a half million copies of its previous album and making the cover of *Rolling Stone* some nine months earlier. But he added, "Are you *sure* this is only a two-star record?" (A sarcastic sign about the star ratings hung in the *Rolling Stone* copy department advising that THREE STARS IS NEVER HAVING TO SAY YOU'RE SORRY. Think about that the next time you read the reviews section, though why you'd bother, I don't know.) Ignoring the hint, I separated the Hootie review from the other two, and the reworked page made it through two more rounds of copyediting.

When Wenner saw the new page, his blood pressure *really* shot skyward, and the Hootie part of my review was torn from the pasted-up layout. (The Spin Doctors and Dave Matthews critiques ran untouched, but those bands weren't selling many records at the time, so he didn't really care about them. Today a *Stone* writer could dismiss Hootie with impunity, but there's no way Matthews would be harshly critiqued while he's moving multiplatinum units.) It was only hours before the issue was set to go to press, but another Hootie review was quickly assigned, written, and plugged into the hole.

I'd been a marked man before this—*Stone* editors call it "getting in Jann's periscope," and anyone who lasts for any length of time there places the concerns of good journalism and criticism second to the pursuits of sucking up or remaining invisible—but I wasn't actually fired for the sin of daring to be a critic. I was canned because of my big mouth.

The *New York Observer,* one of the weeklies that cover the city's media industry, somehow got wind of the tale of my halted Hootie review. Columnist Carl Swanson already had the story nailed when he called me at home in Hoboken one night to ask me for a comment. "Look," I said, "I *really* can't talk to you." This ran counter to every journalistic bone in my body—I've spent my life asking tough questions, and it doesn't seem fair not to answer them—but I have yet to mention that my then-wife was six months pregnant, and I hadn't a clue about where I'd find my next place of employment. Swanson pressed on. "Just answer me one question," he said. The following exchange ran in bold as a pull quote beside Wenner's picture.

IS JANN WENNER A HOOTIE FAN? "NO, I THINK HE'S JUST A FAN OF BANDS WHICH SELL EIGHT AND A HALF MILLION COPIES."— *ROLLING STONE* WRITER JIM DeROGATIS

When I arrived at my desk the morning the paper hit the streets, two Wenner Media security guards were hovering. They proceeded to escort me first to personnel, then to the curb of Sixth Avenue, and thus ended my career at *Rolling Stone*. Keith lasted two weeks longer. The first issue he had worked on boasted Jerry Garcia's obituary on the cover; the last was JERRY GARCIA STILL DEAD, ONE YEAR LATER. Between the two lies the story of our defeat.

Rolling Stone will never change in any significant way running counter to Wenner's nostalgic, myopic, '60s-centric view of rock and the universe. Deep down we'd known that going in, but we allowed hubris to cloud our judgment. His objection to my not-really-all-that-mean pan of Hootie was, as Swanson contended, mostly about making sure his magazine greases the wheels of commerce by pandering to what's popular. This mindset has become more obvious than ever with *Stone*'s recent remake as a skin-flaunting "lad's mag" under new editor Ed Needham, but even with half-naked teen-pop phenoms on the cover, there's always room for fawning coverage of Boomer icons (or do Avril Lavigne and Keith Richards seem like a natural pairing to you?).

I think what really pissed Jann off is that in dissing the then-hot commodity of Hootie, I hit him where he lives—in San Francisco, with the Dead, in the '60s—and when it comes to viewpoints on that subject, he simply can't accept an alternative.

American Blandstand
Rolling Stone (not!), May 16, 1996

THE COMPETITION TO fill the void left by the Grateful Dead was underway long before Jerry Garcia died, but the new releases by the Spin Doctors,

Hootie and the Blowfish, and the Dave Matthews Band are the first recorded entries in the post-Garcia sweepstakes. Artists hate to be grouped by genre—just ask any grunge band—but there's no denying the similarities between these and other so-called jam bands, and most of what they have in common can indeed be traced to the Dead.

The Dead strived to explore diverse sounds such as bluegrass, jazz, and world music from a rock perspective, and the baby Dead bands attempt similar syntheses. The Dead also represented the ideal of transcending the everyday through a combination of hallucinogens, music, and community. In this regard the jam bands fall short, unless of course you consider Bud Lite a psychedelic drug.

The jam bands are devoted in varying degrees to the notion of improvisation; even Hootie stretch out their tunes live. But the single biggest factor connecting them is the lazy, elastic groove. Their loping beats are strong enough to propel you to the fridge to fight the munchies during *Letterman*, but you certainly can't dance to them. At best you just do the awkward white-person wiggle. Rock fans are quick to complain about the mechanical überrhythms of '70s disco, hip-hop, or techno, but for some reason, they can't get enough of this lame faux-Dead groove. It permeates these three albums to the extent that they merge together—just file under "Twirling Music"—but in the interest of consumers, I'll try to chart the distinctions.

New York's Spin Doctors were the first jam band to break commercially, scoring a hit in 1992 with the Stonesy pop of "Little Miss Can't Be Wrong." The group was so intimidated by success that it tried to be as annoyingly quirky and hook-free as possible on its second album, 1994's *Turn It Upside Down*. Influenced by either new guitarist Anthony Krizan (who cowrote several tunes with vocalist Chris Barron) or the prospect of being remembered as a one-hit wonder, the Spin Doctors return to more commercial terrain on *You've Got to Believe in Something*.

The title track and the single "She Used to Be Mine" follow the formula of "Little Miss Can't Be Wrong," pairing that damn shufflin' groove with arena-size hooks and lyrics that could be lifted from the men's room at Wetlands, New York's hippie rock club ("Life is a play / Sometimes you can't remember the rehearsal" is the refrain from the former). The musical experiments are limited to some ham-handed attempts at reggae, including the lumbering "I Can't Believe You're Still With Her," but the nadir is the hidden bonus track, a clunky cover of KC and the Sunshine Band's "That's the Way I Like It," with guest rapping by Biz Markie. It's not as bad as it sounds—it's worse.

South Carolina's Hootie and the Blowfish took the Spin Doctors' success to the next level. With SoundScan sales of eight and a half million for its Atlantic debut, Hootie hit that strata of hyperpopularity at which people who never buy records bought the record, though who knows what grandma would think if she knew that their last three album titles—*Kootchypop, Cracked Rear View*, and now *Fairweather Johnson*—are all sophomoric sex jokes worthy of Beavis and Butt-head.

Whether or not *Fairweather Johnson* meets the chart accomplishments of *Cracked Rear View*, it's certainly its predecessor's artistic equal, which is to say that songs such as "Be the One," "Honeyscrew," and "Tucker's Town" (which was inspired by a band vacation in Bermuda) don't vary much from the formula of Hootie hits like "Hold My Hand" and "Only Wanna Be With You." There are hints of Stax Volt soulfulness courtesy of the occasional Hammond organ and Darius Rucker's Eddie Vedder–does–Otis Redding vocals. But mostly the songs overflow with generic jangly guitars that evoke denatured versions of edgier Southern popsters like R.E.M. and the dB's, whose Peter Holsapple contributes organ, piano, and accordion.

These comfy, cozy sounds—the musical equivalent of Mom's oatmeal cookies and a big glass of milk—are paired with lyrics that reek of cheap Hallmark-card sentimentality. "I thought about you for a long, long time / I wrote about you, but the words don't seem to rhyme / Now you're lying near / But my heart still beats for you," Rucker sings in the weepy ballad "Tootie." Are these sweet nothings the heartfelt romantic declarations of a bunch of regular Joes or the trite clichés of hack songwriters? Is there really a difference?

By far the most conservative of the jam bands, Hootie's instrumental workouts are kept to a minimum on disc, and they rarely stray far from the insidious hooks. That's part of why they're so dreadfully dull. But the Dead connection is there in a recording style that reduces *American Beauty* and *Workingman's Dead* to their lowest common denominators: a down-home hippie folksiness, a lilting melodic approach, and, of course, that oh-so-mellow groove. (Remember, David Crosby, the Dead's secret weapon on those albums, also sang backing vocals on "Hold My Hand.")

Come hear Uncle Hootie's band, playing to the crowds. Eight and a half million buyers can't be wrong. Or can they?

Virginia's Dave Matthews Band takes more chances on *Crash*. The bandleader's vocals sound too much like Sting's at times, the lyrics are typically banal, and in "Proudest Monkey," the band abandons even the hint of a beat and simply plods along for nine minutes. Snappier violin-driven excursions such as "Tripping Billies" mix the progressive rock of Eddie Jobson–era Roxy Music with the earthy folk rock of Fairport Convention, at least when they aren't miring down in pretentious jazzbo wanking. This eclecticism gives Matthews a slight edge over his peers, but that's sort of like saying you prefer vanilla ice cream to vanilla frozen yogurt. Me, I dig Cherry Garcia.

(Each of these three albums was rated two stars on Rolling Stone's five-star scale.)

12 UNREPENTANT HYPES AND FABULOUS FRAUDS

THE TITLE OF THIS ONE SORTA SAYS IT ALL, doesn't it? The artists included here are those that I found most offensive, repugnant, or otherwise unjustly inflated in the '90s—the ones that really got up my ass.

N.W.A may no longer represent the nadir in hip-hop—that honor would now go to Dr. Dre's prefab protégé, Eminem—but it's amazing how *Niggaz4Life* thoroughly predicted the blueprint for Marshall Mathers a decade earlier, and it's sad how much of mainstream hip-hop continues to be fascinated with these transparent gangsta poses and unambitious sounds, especially in contrast to some of the imaginative music produced by the more significant though less successful artists chronicled in Chapter Thirteen. Fuck Dr. Dre where he lives—I maintain that he's the most over-rated producer in the history of pop music, and one of the most hateful.

I appreciate the music of the Jon Spencer Blues Explosion a lot more, but the group is included because of the thorny questions it raised (still unanswered) about appropriation and irony.

Wesley Willis presents a different dilemma—there's no more tedious pursuit among a certain substrata of rock critics than the lauding of "outsider art"—plus his music really sucks, despite its championing by the likes of Eddie Vedder, Rick Rubin, and Jello Biafra.

Bush—well, what else is there to say about Bush? It stands as representative of all of the soulless alternaclones who followed in the wakes of Nirvana and Pearl Jam, from Candlebox and early Stone Temple Pilots through Creed and Nickelback.

I never "got" Guided by Voices and I probably never will, but the notion that there is one rock critic in America who doesn't fully appreciate his efforts sent bandleader Robert Pollard into a tizzy. Shortly after the review included here was published, he delivered a long monologue on stage in Chicago about what a "fat fuck" I am. To which I reply: Can't all these damn rock stars come up with anything better than cheap slurs about someone's girth whenever their egos are bruised?

As a footnote to "Shootout at the Rage Factory," I'd like to add that I have enormous respect for Tom Morello's talents as an innovative guitarist, which continue to impress with Audioslave, the new band he formed with former Soundgarden vocalist Chris Cornell. But however well-intentioned, Morello's political agenda needs and deserves to be questioned. If he goes carrying pictures of Chairman Mao, he ain't gonna make it with anyone anyhow.

There isn't much to say about "Singer Gets an Eye for Eye" beyond the fact that I *love* Q&A interviews, especially when the subject takes the rope he's been given and fashions it into a bullwhip. This piece was earlier singled out for inclusion by Nick Hornby and Ben Schafer in *Da Capo Best Music Writing 2001*. That was an interesting litmus test: It prompted as many emails from strangers congratulating me on "winning" the debate as it did from fans who insisted that Stephan Jenkins had burned my butt. That's a point of pride—at least I was *trying* to be fair.

"Neil and Marilyn" was written as a piece of media criticism, so it's inherently inside-baseball, but I decided to include it because of the light it sheds on the pathetic process of selling pop music through carefully engineered outrage (remember, Eminem is brought to us by the same man who gave us Marilyn Manson, Universal Music Group head Jimmy Iovine), and because it illustrates that dupes willing to aid in this pursuit can be found throughout the media, even at the loftiest journalistic heights. Nothing ages faster than outrage, though, and Manson is pretty much irrelevant today (I'm thinking of a funny story in *The Onion* about him desperately trying to gross out yawning audiences at Midwestern state fairs). For his part, Neil Strauss went on to give us another classic of rock literature, *The Dirt: Confessions of the World's Most Notorious Rock Band*, the authorized biography of Motley Crüe, as well as an unpublished tell-all with Dave Navarro.

As for Britney, I could say that I'm including this piece over the objection of my saint of an editor, Ben Schafer ("It's not '90s!"), in order to make a point about how low postfeminist pop sank a mere six years after the heyday of PJ Harvey, Courtney Love, and Liz Phair. But it's really just here because I like it too much *not* to include it.

N.W.A, *Niggaz4Life*
City Pages, July 3, 1991

THIS IS AN album of hate-filled songs that glorify gang rape and beating women to death, an album so nihilistic that its lyrics brag about making money from these topics. It's the most vile, rancid, festering pile of crap I've heard in my life. It is also one of the top-selling albums in America for the third week in a row.

That alone is enough to make me consider booking one-way passage on a freighter to New Zealand, but two weeks ago, I also heard rock critic and anti-censorship zealot Dave Marsh tell a crowd at the Hungry Mind bookstore in St. Paul that *Niggaz4Life* is "great vulgar art." Marsh, the man who excluded the Rolling Stones' "Brown Sugar" from *The Heart of Rock and Soul: The 1,001 Greatest Singles Ever Made* because he considers it racist and sexist, went on to compare *Niggaz4Life* to Henry Miller's *Tropic of Capricorn*, a great book mistaken for pornography.

The fact is *Niggaz4Life* is a pathetic con designed to cash in on its transparent controversy. The most sensible response would be to ignore it, but the fact is it's impossible to avoid, sitting on top of the charts, flaunting its PARENTAL ADVISORY, EXPLICIT LYRICS sticker. Its debut at No. 2 was the highest since Michael Jackson's *Bad* in 1987; it rose to No. 1 the next week and is now at No. 3. This success flies in the face of a complete lack of play on radio or MTV and comes in the midst of *Billboard* magazine's much-ballyhooed revamping of the charts to reflect actual sales in the Musiclands and Kmarts of heartland America.

This means fifteen-year-old white kids in Edina and Eden Prairie, Chanhassen and Chaska are buying *Niggaz4Life,* and that's why it's the center of a renewed attack by the labeling and censorship crowd; last week, Florida attorney Jack Thompson announced plans to sue Musicland for selling the album, so the battle will be fought right in our backyard. No doubt kids are buying it simply because it's the most vile shit available; as our culture gets more and more jaded in the wake of Freddie Krueger and the Terminator and *American Psycho* and the beautiful fireworks over Baghdad, it gets harder and harder to shock the folks. Thompson's crew says kids need to be protected from this stuff, just like they need to be protected from the Anoka-Hennepin school district's sex and AIDS curriculum. What they always fail to realize is that the kids are rejecting *them.*

Marsh and the other critics defending *Niggaz4Life* could see the war clouds on the horizon, and that may be why they're so dogmatic: If you're not for 'em, you're agin 'em. They ask us to excuse N.W.A's hate as fantasy and accept the group as the "underground reporters" they boast about being on their 1–900–2–COMPTON phone line (a dollar forty-nine per minute). But why can't you be for the First Amendment and against misogyny? I despise any attempt to limit free expression in music and believe N.W.A had every right to make the album they wanted to make. But this is a record review, not an editorial, and I'd be betraying everything I believe is implicit in the reader-critic relationship if I didn't say you're a fool if you buy it and more than a little bit warped if you like it.

Musically the album is wack, all ultra-familiar grooves powered by whining, repetitive four- and five-note Casio riffs. It's not half as effective as Public Enemy's white-noise assaults or De La Soul's psychedelic sampling. Of course it's the words that set N.W.A apart.

The group struck a nerve even before Rodney King with "Fuck Tha Police" on its platinum-selling debut, *Straight Outta Compton*. Since then, the Geto Boys and 2 Live Crew have upped the ante on outrageous rap lyrics, and like grammar school kids at a lunchroom table, N.W.A is determined to out-gross and gross-out all comers. They even own up to the scam: "Why do I call myself a nigger you ask me? / Because my mouth is so motherfucking nasty / Bitch this, bitch that, nigger this, nigger that / In the meanwhile my pockets are getting fat / I'm getting paid to say the shit here / Making more in a week than a doctor makes in a year."

To drive the point home the album concludes with the line, "Ha, another album. The joke's on you, jack." (I wonder if they meant Thompson or Musicland's Jack Eugster?) The album's first half offers more of N.W.A's muddled politics (remember, Eazy-E's the guy who paid to attend a Republican fundraiser). Between threats to fuck former collaborator-turned-rival Ice Cube up the ass with a broomstick and skits such as N.W.A gunning down picketers outside one of its shows, the songs "Real Niggaz Don't Die," "Niggaz 4 Life," and "Real Niggaz" set a record for repetitive use of a word that's still despised by much of the African-American community. N.W.A could almost be seen as adopting Lenny Bruce's tactics on co-opting racial slurs: Claim the word as your own and it ceases to hurt (and it's hard not to laugh when the group croons jingle-style, "I'm a nigger / You're a nigger / He's a nigger / We's some niggers / Wouldn't you like to be a nigger, too?").

If this was the intention, it's ruined when Eazy-E, M.C. Ren, D.J. Yella, and Dr. Dre trot out more racial stereotypes than you'd hear at a KKK rally.

In their world, a "real nigger" is not a black human being but someone who lives by the trigger, prefers cocaine to wine or weed, and knows how to handle the bitches ("Hop in the pickup / And suck my dick up / 'til you hiccup").

In their zeal to fight the good fight, censorship's foes are too quick to put aside N.W.A's misogyny, which is overwhelming and sickening throughout the second half of the album. In the songs "To Kill a Hooker," "One Less Bitch," "Findum, Fuckum & Flee," and "She Swallowed It," the group makes its opinion of women clear: "To me all bitches are the same: money-hungry scammers, groupies, whores that's always riding on a nigger's dick, always in the nigger's pocket, and when the nigger runs out of money the bitch is gone in the wind. To me all bitches ain't shit."

When N.W.A picks up a woman and beats her to death because she's a prostitute, it's one of the most stomach-churning sound collages in the history of pop music. Marsh can dismiss this as fantasy and *Cashbox* can contend that "portrayal must not be confused with advocacy." But "To Kill a Hooker" ends with an evil laugh that's too real for comfort. It makes me want to puke, while N.W.A is laughing all the way to the bank.

The Jon Spencer Blues Explosion
Penthouse, October 1997

THE YEAR IS 2041, and while it may not be akin to probing the mystery of what really happened to Robert Johnson at the crossroads or why Madonna shifted gears from *Sex* to Broadway schmaltz, I have been pondering one of the great questions that lingers from the rock 'n' roll of the 1990s: Was the now-legendary Jon Spencer Blues Explosion genuine in its attempt to merge punk with various genres of black music, or was it all just a joke or a big "fuck you"?

Nine long, frustrating months of sorting through yellowed newspaper clippings, interviewing broken-down old men in seedy bars and skid-row soup kitchens, and stubbornly following one false trail after another has finally led to my elusive quarry. The leader of the fabled Jon Spencer Blues Explosion lives in Miami now under an assumed name, the better to avoid the documentarians who would immortalize him, the Rock and Roll Hall of Fame that would induct him, and the IRS that would indict him. Now in his early eighties, Spencer's jet-black mane and sideburns have turned a stark white, but he is still easily recognizable as the thin, wiry rocker brimming with nervous energy so often seen in vintage photos. His primary tool for distancing himself from his musical past is a stone-cold demeanor that rudely says, "Don't pry." In fact I'd been warned that he'd probably greet me with a shotgun in hand.

Instead Spencer answers the door of his town house wearing baggy plaid golf pants, a sun hat, and cleats. He postpones his afternoon on the links and politely invites me in for a chat over tuna melts and lemonade prepared by his adoring wife, Cristina. Convinced I'll keep his new identity a secret, he regales me for hours with tales of a youth spent crossing America in a rusted old van, playing a schizophrenic mixture of art-rock noise, hip-hop rhythms, and warped blues howling. I'm thrilled just to listen to him talk, but I know that I must eventually ask the question that's gone unanswered for more than five decades—the one that's on the minds of many musicologists, cultural historians, and students of those crazy postmodern nineties.

"Mr. Spencer," I hesitantly begin, "if you really loved black music as much as you said you did, how come you could never get beyond making fun of it?"

WE MAY HAVE TO WAIT fifty years for the answer, because in the present, which is to say, bad old 1997, Spencer is sitting backstage in the headliner's dressing room at First Avenue in Minneapolis—the rock club where Prince hung out in *Purple Rain*—and while he's not exactly avoiding the question, neither is he addressing it. This was early on in the tour to support *Now I Got Worry,* the fourth album by his bass-less two-guitars-and-drums trio. Since then Spencer and his band have joined Lollapalooza, serving as the token hipster act on the main stage of this year's traveling alternative-rock fest, and the critics have been more divided than ever. To some the Blues Explosion is the great white hope of indie rock. By revisiting the blues from a thoroughly postmodern perspective, its members are proving that there's still some life left in the rotting corpse of rock 'n' roll. To others the band members are a bunch of bohemian poseurs putting on a modern-day minstrel show. *Real* bluesmen could kick their asses from the Mississippi Delta all the way back to C.B.G.B.

"We're certainly getting stuck with some shit on this record," says Spencer, somewhat a master at understatement. Quiet, reflective, and notoriously shy when he isn't performing, the singer and songwriter is barely audible over the sounds of guitarist Judah Bauer, who is checking his equipment at full volume onstage. "Maybe that's something that was bound to happen if we kept working. The thing that I don't get is, it's not okay for white American kids to play blues-influenced music? I realize that there is an over-the-top element in what we do, but still . . . "

Here the boss is interrupted by drummer Russell Simins, the most boisterous, least thoughtful member of the band. "It's all because we're named the Blues Explosion," Simins bellows over the din from outside. "If we weren't called the Blues Explosion, we'd never hear this sort of crap. The only reason we get any shit is because of the name, period."

The point is debatable. Spencer's music was controversial long before he formed the Blues Explosion. The son of a chemistry professor, he grew up in upper-middle-class comfort in a small town in New Hampshire. In high school he was a self-confessed "New Wave geek" who listened to Kraftwerk and Devo, and he was elected student-council president. During his freshman year at Brown he studied semiotics and discovered avant-garde noise-rock (Test Department, the Birthday Party, Einstürzende Neubauten) and vintage punk (the Stooges, the Ramones, and the obscure '60s garage rockers collected on the *Back From the Grave* anthologies). But college didn't hold his interest for long, and in 1985 he quit and moved to Washington, D.C., to form a band with his friend Julia Cafritz. Six months later they relocated to New York's Lower East Side, and Spencer has been a fixture there ever since.

Spencer and Cafritz chose the name Pussy Galore after the James Bond villainess; it had the added appeal of being extremely offensive to feminists and other P.C. types. The band's goal was to push people's buttons with its angry, abrasive sounds (the most familiar lineup featured four guitarists who couldn't play and a drummer who pounded on a metal gas tank), confrontational lyrics (among its more popular numbers were "Cunt Tease" and "You Look Like a Jew"), and a philosophy that said, "Rock 'n' roll is dead, let's party at the wake." Unable to escape the burdens of history, Spencer didn't worry about originality. Instead he concentrated on inside jokes and sarcastic commentary. The band's most-celebrated move was releasing a song-for-song deconstruction of the Rolling Stones' epic *Exile on Main St.*

"With Pussy Galore I was certainly a lot more concerned with that kind of stuff," Spencer says. "I was frustrated, and that's what that band was about. But I sort of worked through that. I realized that I really loved listening to music, and more than anything I really love to play music."

After eight releases on five different labels, Pussy Galore broke up in 1990. Spencer did some time playing twisted roots-rock with the Gibson

Brothers and backing his wife, Cristina Martinez, in the noisy Honeymoon Killers. Simins was the Honeymoon Killers' drummer. The son of a New York City public-works commissioner, he grew up on Long Island, playing drums in his parents' basement along with records by the Ramones. A native of sleepy Appleton, Wisconsin, Bauer was Simins's roommate. He spent his high-school years practicing guitar and blasting punk rock, but his passions shifted toward the blues shortly after he moved to New York.

In 1991, Spencer, Simins, and Bauer formed the Blues Explosion. Modeled after John Mayall's Bluesbreakers, the moniker wasn't as in-your-face as Pussy Galore, but Spencer still hoped it would get a rise out of people. "The name of the band is a ridiculous name, and it's sort of a 'fuck you,'" he says. "We're not a blues band, and we're not trying to be. We're not trying to make a point about the blues, or be blues musicians. We're a rock 'n' roll band.

"It's probably most accurate to call us a punk band," he continues. "But I think what we're doing is going after a kind of ideal of rock 'n' roll. Rock 'n' roll to me is coming out of something that was going on in the '50s. I think it should be wild music, bizarre music. I also think it's alright to be funny—not like comedy and jokes, but funny because it makes you feel good. It should also be sexy. Rock 'n' roll is sex."

If Pussy Galore was devoted to pissing on rock history, the Blues Explosion is dedicated to delivering warped and usually irreverent takes on hip-hop, R&B, soul, and especially the blues. Recorded by not one but two legendary underground producers (Kramer and Steve Albini), its Caroline Records debut in 1992 featured amped-up blues-tinged stompers recorded live in all their noisy glory. Two years later, *Orange*, a much more polished affair, added lush Isaac Hayes–style strings, more hip-hop–oriented grooves, and Spencer's James Brown–inspired histrionic intros and asides. ("Thank you very much, ladies and gentlemen. Right now, I've got to tell you about the fabulous, most groovy bell bottoms!")

In 1995, the *Experimental Remixes* EP, an unexpected detour, offered Blues Explosion tracks revisited by techno avatar Moby, the Dub Narcotic Sound System, Genius of rap's Wu-Tang Clan, and Beck. The recording was intended to show that the Blues Explosion is blurring genre boundaries the same way those artists are, but it didn't quite succeed. *Experimental Remixes* was generally perceived as a novelty, and many critics continued to question the intentions of a privileged Ivy League dropout turning black music into white noise. "Does Beck get that?" Spencer grumbles. "He's somebody who's sampling this stuff. Is it cool for somebody to be doing it with a sampler, but it's not okay for a real band to be doing it?"

Any postmodernist or semiotician who knows the world is nothing but a sign factory will tell you that authenticity is an outdated concept. Rock 'n' roll was a bastardized hybrid of an art form from the beginning. The difference between Beck and Spencer is one of attitude. Beck usually seems respectful of the music, even when he's fucking with it. He takes bits and pieces of alien genres, filters them through his own strong personality, and creates a sound that is genuinely his own. Spencer never puts himself on the line. He's a commando who swoops in and grabs elements of black music, then rushes to safety behind a bunker constructed of irony. His vocals are exaggerated to the point of parody, his onstage screams of "Blues Explosion!" are repeated long after they stop being funny, and the band hired spoofmeister Weird Al Yankovic to direct a silly video for the intense tune "Wail."

Like James Brown, Mick Jagger, and the Ramones before him, Beck sometimes veers into camp. But Spencer almost always dishes out kitsch.

Throughout rock history, critics have had a difficult time dealing with any band that isn't one-hundred-percent worshipful of the black music it's incorporating. Eric Clapton and the Stones were hailed because they paid lip service to their heroes, while Led Zeppelin and Vanilla Ice were pilloried for what was branded as disrespect and wholesale theft. Spencer seems genuinely puzzled by this. In his view it's all just rock 'n' roll, and the passionate impulses that power the best blues are extremely similar if not identical to those that power the best punk rock. "Both forms are very simple," he says. "My favorite kind of punk is very individual—people just kind of teaching themselves and finding their own way. The music is really just coming straight from themselves. And that's true of the blues too. Guys like R. L. Burnside are pretty much self-taught and just kind of arriving at their own sound."

Spencer claims that Burnside, a seventy-year-old bluesman taught by the legendary Mississippi Fred McDowell, was a major influence on the Blues Explosion. The band members, who are fans of Burnside's album *Too Bad Jim*, invited him to open for them on tour. That led to a nightly jam at the end of their set—an underground version of B. B. King trading licks with U2—and eventually to the recording of the 1996 album *A Ass Pocket of Whiskey* in Burnside's hometown in Mississippi.

"The stuff we played with R. L. was very simple, straight-ahead, soulful music," Simins says. "For me, it just made me happy to be doing what I'm doing. It's not like R. L. taught us how to play the blues. But for me it was humbling, because Robert Johnson and Mississippi Fred McDowell and Howlin' Wolf are all my fucking heroes, and I never thought I would be able to have any real direct contact with them. Being in the presence of R. L. actually makes you feel connected to that world."

The plan was to record more with Burnside on *Now I Got Worry*, but Spencer was concerned the group would be accused of leaning too heavily on the bluesman. The Blues Explosion turned instead to another musical legend: Stax-Volt star Rufus Thomas came into the studio, barked and crowed on "Chicken Dog," and was paid five hundred dollars for his trouble. In both collaborations the band's distorted guitars and wailing theremin were a far cry from what Burnside and Thomas were used to. But the veterans did their best to give the younger musicians what they wanted.

Reflecting on *A Ass Pocket of Whiskey* for *Pulse!* magazine, Burnside said, "It's so much cussin' on there, man, it's like playin' the dozens with someone. That stuff tickles 'em." Rather than Burnside and Thomas adding authenticity to their sound, the Blues Explosion prodded their mentors into delivering more shtick.

"I think there was a big influence from R. L. Burnside and his band on *Now I Got Worry*," Spencer maintains. "*Orange* was like, 'We've got to make sure everything is sounding good,' and we were really trying to get a powerful sound. This one was more about, 'OK, let's just go.' We were just going after getting a performance and kind of letting it rip. I remember we were driving around Los Angeles, going back and forth from the hotel and G-Son Studio, and somebody had a cassette of *Like Flies on Sherbet* by Alex Chilton. I've heard that album before—I'm a big fan of Panther Burns and some Alex Chilton stuff—and I remember listening to that and thinking, 'This is great. It's just so messy and so out-there.'"

The ideals that Spencer espouses are indeed admirable. Too much modern rock is neat, clean, and conveniently packaged for mass consumption. It's devoid of immediacy, while at the same time it has no sense of history. As Beck, PJ Harvey, and Nick Cave have indicated, vital new sounds can be made by tracing rock's roots back to the blues. But those artists aren't afraid to betray their emotions, and even the most cathartic moments on *Now I Got Worry*—"Wail" and the raging "Fuck Shit Up"—ultimately leave you wondering, Is it real or is it Memorex?

"When I was done with this record, I thought it was such a heavy, dark record," Spencer says. "Of course there's songs like 'Chicken Dog' and

'R. L. Got Soul' that are just fun songs. But my perception of the album was shaded, because I'm aware of what's going on in some of the other songs." What kind of demons was Spencer purging? By all accounts, his home life is the picture of domestic bliss. After Thurston Moore and Kim Gordon of Sonic Youth, he and Cristina are the most loving couple in the rock underground. Spencer's vocals are usually just sputtered fragments of words and sentences, so it's impossible to tell what's bugging him from the lyrics.

"People usually ask that question and I say I'd rather not talk about it," Spencer says. "If I could talk about it in a normal way, then there probably wouldn't be troubles, and why even write a song? I'm probably not the most successful lyric writer or the most intelligible vocalist, but I think if someone can get kind of a general feeling from a song, that's all right. They don't need to get every single little bit. The thing that kind of scares me more than anything is people who think that there is no heart and soul in it—that it's emotionless music and cold and restructured and just an exercise in whatever."

Spencer may not be aware of his own contradictions. He wants to make his audience feel heart, soul, and emotion in his music, but he's reluctant to give them "every single little bit." He longs to make music as direct and visceral as that of Thomas and Burnside, but he overthinks every note. When he takes the stage in Minneapolis before a sold-out crowd of seventeen hundred, he's sweating from the very first song, bounding about the stage and hammering away at his guitar. But his tongue-in-cheek stage patter and ham-bone vocals make you think the passion may be as much of a put-on as everything else.

The question lingers: If Spencer really loves black music, why can't he get beyond making fun of it? Whether or not he ever gets around to answering it, the notion that he just doesn't feel it is as good an explanation as any other.

The Wesley Willis Fiasco
The *Chicago Reader*, May 17, 1996

HAWKING HIS DRAWINGS and CDs to anyone within shouting range, Wesley Willis has never been shy when it comes to self-promotion. But a lot of people think there are bigger bucks to be made with Willis. The self-styled singer-songwriter has always been bad; now he's nationwide. Two high-priced Los Angeles publicists are competing to see who can do a better job hyping his story, all the while insisting that they'd never exploit Willis, a diagnosed schizophrenic.

Willis's band, the Fiasco, recently released its debut album, *SpookyDisharmoniousConflictHellride*, on its own Urban Legends label. To promote it, the group hired the Mitch Schneider Organization, a public relations firm whose clients include the Black Crowes and Alanis Morissette. Fiasco guitarist Dale Meiners says that Schneider usually charges upward of three thousand dollars a month, but he really likes the Fiasco, so the band is only paying two thousand.

Schneider's press release begins by asking, "Is this Wesley Willis God or Satan? Is this madness or is it truth or is it both?" His approach to selling Fiasco albums has been to put Wesley and one of the band members on the phone to tell their story to just about any journalist willing to listen. "One of the tricks of the business is to present people as who they are," Schneider says. "If you can present somebody who does have some, you know, *liabilities*—as other people would see it—and you can present them with dignity and grace, then you're fine."

Heidi Robinson, head of publicity at American Recordings, doesn't appreciate this tactic. Willis is signed to American as a solo artist, and the label plans to release two new albums in the coming months. Robinson correctly points out that Willis is an awful phone interview—he tends to answer every question with a "Fuck, yes!" or a "Fuck, no!"—and she insists that journalists meet him in person and "really get to know him." She adds that, unlike Schneider, she "never put out a press release that said Wesley had any sort of mental problems. I put together a lot of reviews and feature interviews, letting other people talk about [the schizophrenia]."

The guys in the Fiasco say American shouldn't claim to be taking the high road. According to Meiners, the label paid Willis a ridiculously low five thousand dollars for each album. (Robinson says she's unaware of the specifics of the deal.) The only thing Schneider, Robinson, and the Fiasco agree on is that journalists who focus on the "Willis is crazy" angle are taking "the cheap and easy way out."

They're right. The celebration of the madman as speaker of the truth was an old story when Dostoyevsky told it in *The Idiot* and Faulkner wrote it up as *The Sound and the Fury*. The canonization of rockers like Syd Barrett, Roky Erickson, David Fair, and Daniel Johnston is firmly in this tradition, and it's a load of romantic rubbish. Meiners and other Willis boosters say they're helping Willis improve his lot in life and exorcise his demons. But

I'm a journalist and critic, not a social worker, and my main concern is the music.

Compiled from Wesley's DIY recordings and just released on Oglio, *Rock 'n' Roll Will Never Die* is the second widely distributed Willis solo album. Musically the twenty-four songs are all in the familiar mold of Willis appropriating one of the cheesy preprogrammed tunes in his electronic keyboard. Lyrically every song follows the same pattern: In the verses Willis raps about seeing [insert artist's name here] at [name Chicago venue here] last night, and notes that [he, she, or it] is a "rock-a-roll star" whose jams "whopped the camel's ass!" The choruses consist of Willis singing the artist's name four times in a row in a key known only to dogs. It all leads to the inevitable ending of Willis exclaiming, "Rock over London! Rock on Chicago! [Insert commercial or pop-culture slogan here]!"

The repetition is enough to drive *anyone* crazy.

At least *SpookyDisharmoniousConflictHellride* is more diverse. The band is a competent but uninspired hard-rock group with alternative leanings. Think generic Jane's Addiction. Inspired by the raunchier sounds (or goaded by his bandmates?), Willis spouts obscenities like a person with Tourette's syndrome and indulges in Beavis and Butt-head–style sexism and homophobia on tunes like "Pop That Pussy" and "Casper the Homosexual Friendly Ghost." Tellingly, Willis sounds more genuine and enthusiastic on these songs than on "Get On the Bus" or "He's Doing Time in Jail," which are rote accounts of his mental problems and the confrontation on a city bus that left him bloodied and scarred.

It's impossible for me to imagine anyone listening to either of these albums for pleasure—or listening without the knowledge that Willis is a schizophrenic. Their protestations to the contrary, that knowledge is exactly what the flacks are selling. Should you buy it? Well, as Willis himself might put it, rock over London, rock on Chicago, don't believe the hype.

Never Mind
New Times Los Angeles, November 14, 1996

FIRST GAVIN ROSSDALE stole Kurt Cobain's sound, right down to the last sad but fuzzy guitar chord and strangled vocal growl. Then he and his hired helpers rode it to a quintuple-platinum hit with *Sixteen Stone* primarily because modern-rock radio programmers were damned if they were going to let Cobain derail their gravy train by killing himself. For an encore, Rossdale made Lovey-dovey with Cobain's widow, Courtney; hired Cobain's ex-producer, Steve Albini, to record his second album, *Razorblade Suitcase*; brought in Cobain's former cello player for some sessions; started talking in interviews about Cobain's big influence (the Pixies) and favorite bodily ailment (stomach problems); and made a video for the first single, "Swallowed," that borrows the Cobain-on-a-couch-with-cross image from "Heart-Shaped Box" and the cheerleading moshers from "Smells Like Teen Spirit."

I hear the folks at Nirvana's label, Geffen Records, are keeping a list that includes a few more minor thieveries that I may be missing, but you get the point: Rossdale is the most blatant rock 'n' roll crook since Jimmy "Why credit them ol' blues guys?" Page. Mind you, as a postmodernist, I *applaud* such behavior. Authenticity is a sham invented by egghead critics who've forgotten how to rock. All's fair in the age of appropriation, and if you're gonna steal, why not steal from the best? My problem is what Bush *does* with its precious purloined wares. It's like making a toilet bowl out of gold, or robbing a homeless person to give more money to Michael Jordan because he might not have made enough on *Space Jam*.

Rossdale is a man with nothing worthwhile to say, and more often than not, he says it like Cobain. Saint Kurt didn't invent the image-laden, cut-and-paste approach to lyric writing—you can blame William S. Burroughs for that—but he had his own unique vocabulary, and Rossdale must have the words stuck up on his refrigerator like a set of Magnetic Poetry. There's a hip college drinking game involving J. G. Ballard's novel, *Crash*: You open the book and take a shot every time you find a sentence involving sex or cars. You can do the same with *Razorblade Suitcase* whenever you catch a phrase that's Cobainesque: "Deaf and dumb . . . with the lights on . . . married by signs . . . cold, contagious . . . warm sun feeds me up . . . blackened lungs . . . mouth of my father . . . say you will, never mind . . . I'm gonna find my way to the sun." Whee, I'm getting buzzed just thinking about it!

Where Cobain used such enigmatic lines to offer shards of insight into a ridiculously complicated worldview—Nirvana fans and English majors will still be trying to put it all together well into the next century—Rossdale throws this language around in a vain attempt to sound impressive while his simplistic philosophy can actually be summed up in the lyric, "Drink life as it comes / Straight no chaser." If that isn't a line from *Animal House*, surely Dean Martin said it in one of the Rat Pack movies. This too would be forgivable: Plenty of rockers have hung great music on less of a statement than *carpe diem*. But the thirteen tunes on *Razorblade Suitcase* are utterly bland, lifeless, unmemorable, and bar-code generic, though this time it's in an abrasive, skronking way as opposed to the big polished grunge way of *Sixteen Stone*. (Or *In Utero* versus *Nevermind*, but you already knew that.)

Of course Albini dialed up his patented harsh sounds—the barbed-wire guitar, rampaging drums, and a bit of that "screaming through a bullhorn" business on "Personal Holloway"—and he applied his punk-rock record-'em-live, warts-and-all techniques. Clearly Bush thought it could buy credibility with this noise, which is the only reason anyone ever puts up with Albini. As for Steve, his pals in Chicago say he's finally found a building to house the studio of his dreams, and now he has the capital to go for it. Much more amusing than this album are the interviews in which Albini, the most sanctimonious man in show business, valiantly tries to avoid the words, "I did it for the money."

Issues of originality aside, Bush has to be granted some grudging respect simply because earlier songs such as "Everything Zen" and "Glycerine" are impossible to get out of your head. But "Swallowed" is the best tune here, and it's nowhere near as indelible. The rest of the album is just pointless din delivered via needlessly serpentine arrangements with Rossdale doing his '90s romantic bit on top. Last time it was easy to dismiss the Bushmen for the many reasons cited above. This time, it's even easier, but the response that's really warranted by *Razorblade Suitcase* is simply to ignore them. If we all stop staring at Rossdale's cheekbones, they'll probably just go away.

Quantity Over Quality
The *Chicago Reader*, July 11, 1997

"EARWHIG" IS BRITISH slang for that blabbermouth at the end of the bar who fancies himself the world's greatest storyteller. There's a metaphor here for Guided by Voices' way-beyond-prolific leader, Robert Pollard. Sure, he labored admirably over his four-track down in that now-famous Dayton, Ohio, basement for ten years as the world passed him by, but ever since the indie-rock universe started kissing his ass, circa 1993's *Vampire on Titus*, he's had songwriting diarrhea of the worst sort.

Pollard has foisted ninety-nine tunes on us over four official albums since 1993, not including the twenty-one new numbers on *Mag Earwhig!*, or his solo disc, or the between-album EPs, or the '95 box set compiling the pre-fame basement tapes. The law of averages alone dictates that a fair amount of that has to be crap, or at least redundant. ("Stop me if you've heard this one before," says the earwhig.)

The best way I can think of to explain the near-universal acclaim accorded these weekend warriors is to call it NRBQ Syndrome. You know what I mean: There isn't a fortysomething white male rock critic anywhere in America who doesn't think that NRBQ is one of the greatest bands that ever walked the earth, and it's because NRBQ's music is a skillfully crafted pastiche of everything those guys grew up listening to. It pushes all their buttons, so of course they think it's genius.

Guided by Voices has a similar effect on the generation that came of age manning college-rock radio stations in the mid-'80s. The rap on 1994's breakthrough *Bee Thousand* (and for that matter most of the band's other records) was that, like Wire's *Pink Flag*, it was a collection of about twenty songs that deconstructed rock history, reordered the pieces, and served it all back up in delicious bite-size nuggets. Let us count the names dropped in the Guided by Voices entry of *The Trouser Press Guide to '90s Rock* (written by my friend, the usually reliable David Sprague): R.E.M., Postcard Records, the Who, Josef K, Blue Öyster Cult, Moody Blues, ESP Records, Beach Boys, Incredible String Band, Frank Zappa, the Soft Boys, Mersey Beat.

Not that I'm completely immune myself to the sweet nostalgia of having any of the above invoked in a catchy two-minute garage-rock ditty. Repeated listening to *Mag Earwhig!* yielded six moments I found impossible to resist: "Bulldog Skin" (Pavement meets the British Invasion), "I Am Produced" and "Now to War" (Robyn Hitchcock's *I Often Dream of Trains* meets the Kinks' "Waterloo Sunset"), "Not Behind the Fighter Jet" and "Little Lines" (glam meets Mersey Beat meets Sex Pistols), and "Jane of the Waking Universe" (Abbott and Costello meet Frankenstein).

These tunes would have made a heck of an EP—great to crank up and sing along with in the car, but certainly not original enough to warrant much further attention. As it is you have to wade through fifteen unremark-able-to-downright-awful tracks in order to get to them, and I just don't know if that's worth fifteen dollars and ninety-nine cents and forty-five minutes and forty seconds of your time. I never bought into that Deadhead argument that "every third show is brilliant." If it means you have to sit through two shitty ones to get there, forget it. And hey, tell that guy at the end of the bar to pipe down.

Shootout at the Rage Factory
Ironminds, December 1999

IN DECEMBER 1988, the mayor of Jersey City—an avuncular, grandfatherly gentleman by the name of Anthony Cucci—was visiting the town of Cuzco, Peru, at the invitation of local municipal officials who wanted to sign a sister city pact.

I was a reporter with *The Jersey Journal* at the time, and Jersey City was my beat, but this was the sort of glad-handing story that would merit a paragraph or two at best, and perhaps an Associated Press photo if the mayor was lucky. That was, until I got a call from the State Department.

Mayor Cucci, his Peruvian counterpart, their wives, and a dozen or so others had been traveling in a single-car train that was laboriously making its way up the Andes to the ancient Incan ruins of Machu Picchu when the saboteurs struck. The car hit a ten-inch steel rod strategically wedged in the tracks, derailed, and tumbled down a two-hundred-fifty-foot ravine. Mayor Cucci's wife, Anna, and Doris Mayorga de Chacon, the wife of the mayor of Cuzco, were both killed instantly, and six others were seriously injured.

To date the FBI has never formally placed the blame for the incident, but the people of Cuzco knew immediately: It was the Shining Path, the Maoist revolutionary group that has been notorious for three decades as the most vicious guerrilla organization in South America.

You may have heard of these Communist rebels before. Chart-topping rockers Rage Against the Machine posit them as heroes in interviews by guitarist Tom Morello, in comments by singer Zach de la Rocha on his recent Spitfire spoken-word college tour, and in a song called "Sendero Luminoso" from 1996's *Evil Empire*.

Rage is of course one of the founders of the rap-rock movement, a sound that has come to be a dominant force in modern rock circa 1999 thanks to lesser lights like Korn and Limp Bizkit. Rage's third album was one of the fall's most anticipated releases, and *The Battle of Los Angeles* debuted at No. 1 on the *Billboard* albums chart, selling four hundred thirty thousand copies in its first week (a hundred thousand more than the latest by Sony labelmate Mariah Carey).

Smelling a winner, the rock press cooed and applauded. *Rolling Stone* gave the band a four-star review and a cover story, while *Spin* rated the record as a nine on its ten-point scale. *Stone*'s Neil Strauss and David Fricke and *Spin*'s RJ Smith mentioned the musicians' far-left politics—

how could they not?—but after noting their many contradictions (major-label revolutionaries, underground media hounds), they maintained that the music is what matters the most. *Entertainment Weekly*'s Will Hermes went even further in his rave, thrusting a fist in the air in solidarity. The band's lyrics, he wrote, "make a case that there are still some things worth fighting for." *Viva la revolution!* But first be sure to cash Time-Warner, Inc.'s check.

If you ask me, my peers sold the band short by failing to give its politics the consideration they deserve, but then maybe these critics' understanding of politics is as shallow, simplistic, and slogan-based as Rage's. If I learned one thing during my previous life as a beat reporter, it's that the world is a complex place full of infinite shades of gray, all of which escape political demagogues. Like Lester Bangs, I've always been wary of rock bands advocating specific political agendas. "Clearly this notion of violent, total youth revolution and takeover is an idea whose time has come—which speaks not well for the idea but ill for the time," Bangs wrote in 1969 of the MC5's *Kick Out the Jams*. Yeah, what he said! And double for Rage.

To date the most celebrated example of Rage's activism has been its advocacy on behalf of Mumia Abu-Jamal, who was convicted in the December 1981 killing of a Philadelphia cop. Shades of gray: Like the O. J. Simpson case, this is a complex story with infinite twists and turns, but the best of the pieces that I've read about it appeared in August's *Vanity Fair*. Drawing on the trial transcripts and his own reporting, writer Buzz Bissinger made a convincing argument for Abu-Jamal's guilt—and his skillful manipulation of Hollywood celebs (including Rage) in his quest for a new trial.

I mentioned this piece when I interviewed Morello on the eve of the band's headlining arena tour, and the Harvard-educated guitarist started ranting about Bissinger's ties to the Philadelphia D.A.'s office and how Abu-Jamal wasn't even quoted in the story. (In response to a subsequent letter from Abu-Jamal in *Vanity Fair*, Bissinger maintained that the celebrated con was given numerous opportunities to speak, and he declined.) But I was less interested in debating the specifics of the Abu-Jamal case than in pinning down Rage's vision of rock and politics.

"In the band's lyrics, there is one obligation, which is to tell the truth as we see it," Morello said. "We are trying to get Mumia a new trial; the *specifics* matter to Rage Against the Machine. Our song 'Voice of the Voiceless' is not dissimilar from Bob Dylan's 'Hurricane.' His song created an atmosphere in which there was public demand to investigate that case further, and [Rubin] Hurricane [Carter] was freed because of the racism that infected the original trial. It was clearly an artist with conviction using the medium in which he works to effect real change in society. There's no better use of art than what Bob Dylan did in that song."

Ah, but isn't there a flip side to that, I asked? Around the same time, Dylan also wrote a song about Joey Gallo, and that encouraged some people to glorify a brutal mobster. "There are no Joey Gallo songs on Rage Against the Machine records," Morello said. I'm not so sure. What about "Sendero Luminoso"? I told Morello about Tony Cucci and his experience with the Shining Path.

"The specific story you're talking about, I don't have any knowledge of," Morello said. "If it's true, it's to be condemned. Whether it's in Peru or South Central, people have a right to fight back against oppression, but there's not an instant where I will support an atrocity like that. However, it's amazing how quickly that sort of finger-pointing is apt to happen."

Yeah, well, there's the sticky part: Who gets to decide what's righteous violence and what's just plain old violence? Perhaps that's a complex dilemma better left to God (however one chooses to define that) than a rock band. Me, I uphold many of Rage's values: racism, class biases, and the death penalty—*bad!* Free speech, individuality, socialized medicine—*good!* But I'm still wrestling with that other troublesome question.

In an effort to get my arms around it, I called the one man I know who's had first-hand experience with an actual revolutionary act. Tony Cucci is now seventy-seven years old and retired, living in Jersey City with his memories and his "old man pains" (though he stressed that he can't complain). "It's gonna be eleven years in another week or so," he said of his experience in Peru. "The Shining Path took not only Ann's life and that of the other mayor's wife, but a lot of other people, too. I just don't understand it."

Not surprisingly, the former mayor was unaware that the guerrillas had become a celebrated cause for one of the biggest rock bands in America. But he was as philosophical about that as he was about his wife's murder. "You know, liberty—how much freedom do you really need to be free?" he said. "Rock bands can go around insulting everybody and everything we stand for, drawing big crowds and so forth, at the expense of other people's feelings. But *that's* freedom."

As far as political statements go, that one is far more thoughtful and poetic than anything you'll find on *The Battle of Los Angeles*.

Singer Gets an Eye for Eye
The *Chicago Sun-Times*, July 16, 2000

I AM NOT a fan of Third Eye Blind. "Even by the standards of the decaying grunge genre, the San Francisco quartet is forgettable," I wrote the first time I saw the group perform at the Riviera Theatre in 1998.

"Early on, singer Stephan Jenkins made a great show of taking off his shoes and socks. From time to time, he sat down in a big red leather chair near the drum riser. As unexciting as these acts were, they offered welcome respite from his non-stop prancing, preening, and posing. Rarely has such a mediocre singer, uninspired songwriter, and uninvolving stage presence been lucky enough to be deigned a rock star."

I saw the quartet again a few months later when it was still riding high on its self-titled multi-platinum debut. The hit "Semi-Charmed Life" had won the band a prime spot on Q101's Twisted Christmas concert at the Allstate Arena, but my conclusion that night was that its set was the evening's nadir.

"There is simply no bigger bozo in rock today than singer Jenkins," I wrote. "He snapped a bullwhip on stage, hammed his way through the Who's 'Baba O'Reilly,' did an embarrassing rap that desperately tried to offend someone (anyone), and of course led his prefab corporate-approved band through its brainless hits."

My opinion hadn't changed when I caught the group for a third time last month at the Q101 Jamboree, touring in support of its second album *Blue*, and performing at the New World Music Theatre. This time, Jenkins decided he'd had enough. He called and asked if I'd let him have his say in the newspaper, allowing him to rebut my criticisms.

As a firm believer in the importance of discourse in the rock 'n' roll community, I happily agreed, and promised to print a transcript of our conversation (edited only for length) before the band's next Chicago show. Third Eye Blind returns on Saturday to perform as part of the Hard Rock Rockfest—and here is my conversation with Jenkins.

J.D. *So you think I've done you wrong? Give it to me.*

S.J. Indeed you have. I have a copy of your review from the Q101 Jamboree, and what you said was, "On the other side were the unrepentant boneheads, chief among them the Bloodhound Gang and Third Eye Blind." Both of my records—what we write about and the way that we play—we're not boneheaded.

J.D. *What you write about is not necessarily boneheaded, but the way you put it across on stage is, with this sort of generic, lusty hard-rock persona.*

S.J. What you wrote was, "Third Eye Blind's thoroughly generic and ham-fisted music was distinguished only by the degree of frat-boy misogyny inherent in the lyrics and stage antics."

J.D. *I maintain that that's true.*

S.J. Ham-fisted? If you listen to "Motorcycle Drive By," you can't say that I can't play. We can play! We're really good musicians. To say that we're not tight, to say that the band doesn't move as one, that we don't have dynamics . . .

J.D. *You're ham-fisted in the sense that you lack subtlety, not that you can't play.*

S.J. But if you take a song like "Narcolepsy," where we shut it down to where we're playing at like two dBs, or a song like "Motorcycle Drive By"—there are subtleties inherent in that. There are bands that are ham-fisted that make a career out of that, like, "We're gonna democratize guitar by just playing barre chords." That's not what we're about. We have really intricate voicings. The *Village Voice* wrote about this and said that, quite the opposite of ham-fisted, this band works with the intricacy and subtlety of a finely-tuned chamber-music outfit.

J.D. *Ham-fisted isn't necessarily bad. You could have said the same about Led Zeppelin or Queen; they could also be ham-fisted in the sense that they could be as subtle as a block of ice to the head. The problem with you guys—and I've seen you play three times now—is that you not only lack subtlety, but soul.*

S.J. You're saying that about the performance, not the actual songs?

J.D. *Yes; the songs are just generic. You asked me to go back and listen to* Blue *again, and I did. I listened to it three or four times before I saw you at the World, and three or four times again afterward. And my opinion is still that your music is generic and lacking anything at all that makes it distinctive.*

S.J. You are the worst example of how the media distorts things, in that what you've said about me is not really related to what I do. Generic means you can't tell one song from the other. But what does "Never Let You Go" have to do with "Jumper"? What about "Wounded"—what genre is this repeating the formula for?

J.D. *Watered-down mainstream modern rock. It's a lowest-common-denominator radio sound that's not that far off from Matchbox 20.*

S.J. That's just absurd! They're not the same chord changes or lyrics . . .

J.D. *Sure they are. You both write romantic pop trifles—manufactured music from the corporate-pop songwriting mill.*

S.J. If you go see Matchbox 20's concerts, they are coming from a very heartland-rock pose. That's their thing; that's what they do. And that has nothing to do with the chord progressions we do, the voicings that we do, the allusions that we make lyrically. And for you not to notice that, it's malicious.

J.D. *It's not malicious; I just find your music incredibly boring and ordinary and average. I admire the fact that you want to convince critics otherwise—and I've talked to a couple of peers who've gotten the same sort of phone calls from you—but I don't think you're gonna do it.*

S.J. This is what I'm talking about with the American press and why American critics are in large part a bummer, more so compared to even English critics, where there's a requirement that people have context and know what they're talking about. Next you're gonna make a comparison between us and Hootie and the Blowfish.

J.D. *That fits! Sure, you guys have a harder edge, and that's where my sexism comment comes in: You have this hard-rock edge that you flaunt that elevates your pop trifles from Hootie's pop trifles. But it's essentially the same kind of radio-friendly pap.*

S.J. Do you really think I'm a misogynist—that I hate women?

J.D. *That you are threatening to women? Yes. You walk around onstage with this strutting, cocksure persona that is the oldest rock cliché in the book. It was old when Robert Plant asked us to squeeze the lemon 'til the juice ran down his leg. Your mike stand as phallic symbol is the hoariest act in show business. There are other ways of asserting a strong male sexuality, you know.*

S.J. You have a completely warped idea about what sexuality is. I say this to people: "Walk like kings, all of you." I go strutting around on stage like a king and invite everyone to come along with me. I say in the song "Red Summer Sun," "This is my time to walk with the mighty." If I see a guy fighting, that guy gets singled out. If a girl's getting her tits grabbed when she's crowd-surfing, the guy who does it gets tossed. Our show is not a violent place; you do not see anyone being called a "bitch" or a "faggot"; there's no sense of exclusion. Do I have a cock? I sure do. It's a totally extroverted male kind of thing, but women, who make up about forty-one percent of our audience, do not feel threatened or that they're somehow being seconded.

The issues that we talk about—for example "Ten Days Late" or the song "Wounded" that talks about sexual assault—are not looking at this in some sort of P.C. way. The song "Jumper"—which is about a friend who killed himself who is gay—is not anti-gay. Our message is one of inclusion and people who are wounded becoming whole. Our atmosphere is joyous, positive, and healthy.

J.D. *Joyous, positive, and healthy? What about cracking the whip onstage at the Allstate Arena?*

S.J. What's wrong with the whip?

J.D. *It's symbolic of a sadomasochistic relationship. You're a man cracking a whip and singing about women, signifying that you are putting a woman under your control or threatening a woman. A whip is a threatening symbol.*

S.J. You know what else I do sometimes? I'll take a cowboy hat and swing it around like I'm riding a bronco. Is that subverting animals? This is what's sad: You see a guy cracking a whip as a misogynistic act and a guy who struts around with a mike stand as a misogynist. What it really is is a sort of outward sexuality. I have a cock. Am I violent? Yes, I am. Do I have violent urges? Yes, I do. Have I turned those into protective urges? Yes, I have. And that's what we talk about in the song "Wounded"—I sing, "Back down the bully to the back of the bus / 'Cause it's time for them to be afraid of us." It's about a friend of mine who got date-raped.

J.D. *So you're onstage singing lyrics like that but adopting the persona of the strutting guy with the whip—the persona of the rapist?*

S.J. Why is that the persona of the rapist? We have a lot of queer fans and a lot of female fans, and they come to our shows and they don't feel threatened, but you do. That's what this is about, me holding you accountable.

J.D. *I'm not threatened, and that's not what this is about. This is about me respecting you wanting to have your say. There's not enough meaningful dialogue in rock today; it's all about hype. I don't like your music, but I respect your desire to talk.*

S.J. Hype is something that our band has certainly eschewed. Our band has been, if not the most DIY next to Fugazi, then number two or three.

J.D. *How can you say that? Third Eye Blind is a creation of MTV and modern-rock radio and a major label. And you're taking money from the Hard Rock Cafe to play a festival that has corporate sponsorship up the wazoo.*

S.J. All of the things that go on with the making of our music come from us; we are a homegrown entity and make our own decisions. If there is a corporation out there, and we can take AOL's money or a radio or TV show and leave people with our music, then we will. You work for a newspaper that's corporate-owned; does that change anything you write?

J.D. *Nope. Anything else you wanna say before we wrap this up?*

S.J. I just want to say thank you for this, Jim, and that your take on misogyny is a comedy. I hope that comes across. That, and long live Led Zeppelin.

J.D. *Hey, I love Led Zeppelin. John Bonham was a ham-fisted drummer, and he was a god.*

S.J. The only thing ham-fisted here is your writing.

J.D. *Thanks. Subtlety is overrated anyway; I like people who say what they mean.*

Neil and Marilyn
The *Chicago Reader*, March 27, 1998

IN NOVEMBER 1996, *New York Times* reporter and rock critic Neil Strauss crawled into the hot tub at a Holiday Inn in Fort Lauderdale with desperate-to-shock rocker Marilyn Manson. Strauss was writing an article for *Rolling Stone*, and Manson was ready to take full advantage of the opportunity. "This is going to be an important piece of press," he told Strauss.

The resulting cover story did indeed change both men's lives. It legitimized Manson's emergence as one of the most notorious entertainers of the '90s and introduced him as an enthusiastic bogeyman for the right. Strauss, meanwhile, went on to become Manson's business partner, co-authoring his new autobiography, *The Long Hard Road Out of Hell*.

A hot tub isn't Robert Johnson's legendary crossroads, and despite his well-crafted image, Manson isn't Satan. But Strauss seems to have sold his soul to the self-proclaimed Antichrist Superstar. In the last fourteen months, the twenty-nine-year-old writer has served as a virtual one-man hype machine for the garish goth star. Between the first cover story and the publication of the book, he did a follow-up news piece for *Rolling Stone* and wrote seventeen articles that mentioned Manson in the *New York Times*. Seven of those portrayed the singer as a crusader for free speech.

Somewhere along the way, Manson and Strauss landed a big-money deal with Regan Books, the new Harper-Collins imprint started by Judith Regan, who was also behind Howard Stern's best-selling *Private Parts*. *The Long Hard Road Out of Hell* was excerpted as the cover story for the February 1998 edition of *Spin*, and *The New York Post* excerpted the book as well.

Sources familiar with the book deal say Strauss earned a healthy advance for his work (the exact figure has been disputed and cannot be confirmed), and presumably he gets a cut of the royalties. But Strauss has refused to grant an interview about his dealings with Manson. In a brief fax, the writer declined to say how much he earned.

Be it two dollars or two hundred thousand, what Strauss got paid isn't the issue. The issue is that he got paid anything at all by Manson and then continued to keep the artist in the headlines of the country's most influential newspaper. Why Strauss and his editors decided not to see this as a conflict of interest is a much more important question than whether the mascaraed Manson really had some ribs removed so that he can fellate himself, yet it has received much less attention.

"Entertainment writers, just like reporters who cover politics and business, ought to play by a set of ethical rules, and those rules should include not writing about anyone that you have a financial arrangement with," says Howard Kurtz, the media critic at the *Washington Post*. "This is pretty basic journalism, and the fact that you're covering rock music or baseball or some other far-flung field doesn't exempt you from those minimum nutritional requirements of journalism. To me it crosses the line when you're actually in business with the person."

A NATIVE OF Chicago, Strauss moved to Manhattan in the early '90s and began his rock-writing career as a freelancer. He became a full-time staffer at the *New York Times* about two years ago, and in mid-'97, he was named as the paper's man on the pop-music beat in Los Angeles, positioned to challenge *Los Angeles Times* music business reporter Chuck Philips. "Neil's posting to L.A. is to beef up the paper's music business coverage with an L.A. angle," Pareles says.

Strauss also contributes to both *Rolling Stone* and *Spin*. In contrast to his relatively sober newspaper work, his magazine pieces tend toward the glib, attitude-laden, and self-referential; he is often a prominent character in his own stories, hanging out with the stars. He got drunk with Soul Asylum's Dave Pirner. He busted a move onstage with Beck. Then he met the former Brian Warner of Canton, Ohio.

"It's funny because for the past two years, [guitarist] Twiggy [Ramirez] and I have listened to Dr. Hook's 'Cover of the Rolling Stone' ritualistically, as if maybe it would actually land us in the magazine," Manson writes in a tour diary included in *The Long Hard Road Out of Hell*. "And strangely enough, that interview came today. I'm not sure if the writer was gay or not, so I did most of the interview in the hot tub to either confuse or excite him. I think it did both."

Strauss was in fact extremely excited about Manson: "Never has there been a rock star quite as complex as Marilyn Manson," he gushed in the second paragraph of the *Rolling Stone* profile—a line that has the same hyperbolic qualities of Jon Landau's infamous, "I have seen rock and roll future, and its name is Bruce Springsteen." (Landau went on to become

Springsteen's manager, and there's a longstanding joke that the line should have been, "I have seen Jon Landau's future, and its name is Bruce Springsteen.")

Strauss was apparently so excited by meeting Manson that he neglected to do the same kind of reporting that would have been expected of him at the *Times*. Midway through the article he describes a Manson concert he attended: "The cops have one door barred and are videotaping the entire show, hoping for enough nudity or obscenity to justify an arrest. It wouldn't be the first time that's happened to Manson. The last time he performed in St. Petersburg, Florida, he was arrested for indecently exposing himself onstage. Before the police threw him in jail, they ridiculed him, warning him to remove his lip ring because somebody might tear it out while beating him up."

Tim Roche and Eric Deggans, two reporters at the *St. Petersburg Times*, read the *Rolling Stone* story and followed it up. They discovered that Manson was never arrested in St. Pete. What's more, the pair reported, "police had planned to take a video camera to the concerts November 13 and 14, but before the show started, the officers were called away to respond to disturbances [elsewhere] in the city."

The Long Hard Road Out of Hell changes the city of arrest to Jacksonville, and a police spokesman for that city confirms that Manson was indeed busted there in 1994. Nonetheless the book carries a disclaimer: "To protect the innocent, many of the names and identifying features of individuals in this book have been changed and several characters are composites." Strauss never steps forward in the book to clarify this blurred line between hard reality and embellishment. That may not be expected of a hired co-author, but a reporter is bound to investigate and confirm actual facts. And the line between co-writer and reporter is clouded by the book's jacket, which prominently mentions Strauss's employment at *Rolling Stone* and the *New York Times*. The Antichrist Superstar invokes the names of these journalistic institutions to lend credibility to his version of his life story.

Strauss is happy with the results. "I had the option to take my name off it if I wasn't happy with the way it came out, and it ended up so much better than I could have hoped, as suspenseful and well-structured as a novel," he posted on the "Ask Neil Strauss" message board of the *Times*'s America Online site.

In a sidebar interview accompanying the recent *Spin* excerpt and cover story, Manson (who also declined to be interviewed for this story) gives more details about the pair's working relationship. "[The book] was mostly dictated," the singer says. "I would tell Neil Strauss stories, because I don't have the patience or skill to write them down myself. I'm sure in a month or so I'll deny things I've said and attribute them to drug use or coercion by Neil."

In fact it wasn't long before Manson was denying things. On *MTV News*, the rocker claimed that *Spin* had fabricated quotes in the seemingly innocuous sidebar, which was just a small part of eight pages of free publicity for his book. "These are not the questions I was asked and not the answers I would give to those particular questions," Manson railed. A *Spin* spokesman says the magazine stands behind its story and has tapes of Manson saying exactly what was quoted.

The incident illustrates the extent to which Manson—a one-time rock writer who interviewed the Red Hot Chili Peppers, Debbie Harry, and Nine Inch Nails among others for small Florida publications—is a control freak who wants to call the shots when it comes to what is printed about him. And it raises questions about how much Strauss had to tailor what he wrote to please his subject. Which, again, a co-author has every right to do—provided he doesn't continue covering Manson as a reporter.

A NEWSPAPER BUSINESS reporter who profited from an autobiography of Bill Gates would probably not be allowed to continue covering Microsoft, and a political writer who collaborated on a book with Newt Gingrich would probably be pulled off the Gingrich beat to avoid even the appearance of conflict of interest. Pareles seems to generally agree: "Neil is now disqualified forever from writing any critical endorsements of Manson," he says.

But the senior critic has no problem with Strauss writing further news stories about Manson. Pareles notes that *Times* TV critic Bill Carter, who wrote *The Late Shift: Letterman, Leno, and the Network Battle for the Night*, continues to cover the talk-show hosts. But Carter's book was an independent work of reporting, and he was not involved in a financial relationship with his subjects. Strauss's role in *The Long Hard Road Out of Hell* was to edit and re-write Manson's anecdotes to make them more compelling. In joining with Manson in this way, he abdicates all pretense of objectivity. Given that, news stories should be doubly off-limits, since they ostensibly require a reporter to approach his topic with a blank slate.

Exactly how many times Strauss has written about Manson in the *Times* since getting the book contract depends on whose version of the contract's timetable you believe. Attempts to get Strauss's side of the story were mostly unsuccessful. When I first requested an interview with him through Regan Books, the publicist said he "doesn't want to be a spokesman for

Marilyn Manson," but that he could be reached at the *Times*'s Los Angeles bureau for questions about his role as co-author. Strauss called back the next day, sounding frantic. "Have you called my publicist?" he asked. Yes. Do you want to do the interview now? "No, I have to call my publicist, then I'll call you right back," he said. He never did.

The publicist later requested that the questions be sent via fax so she could forward them to Strauss. I sent two pages of detailed queries. He sent back a two-paragraph fax.

"As for your conflict of interest accusations, the book was first mentioned to me in August 1997 and a contract was first presented to me in October," Strauss wrote. "In the time since August, I haven't written any articles, reviews or otherwise on Marilyn Manson in any publication whatsoever. Regarding any other pieces written for the *New York Times* that touched on or involved Manson, upon submitting each story I reminded my editors about the book and they checked with their superiors for potential conflict of interest. Every instance was approved."

A source familiar with the book deal contradicts Strauss, saying that it was in the works as early as March 1997. That date appears more realistic: Strauss took several weeks off from the *Times* in August and went on the road with Manson. According to transcripts in the book, he had already made seven tapes by August 9, so it's likely that there were discussions about him being co-author well before then. But even by Strauss's own chronology, he wrote two significant Manson-related news stories for the *Times* well after he got the contract.

A November 17 "Pop Life" column addressed Kansas Senator Sam Brownback's hearings into rock lyrics, focusing on testimony from a father who blamed his son's suicide on Manson's music. The father wasn't quoted, but Manson was. "I think it's bad that they exploit parents who say that their kids have been injured because of music," Manson said in the piece. "That's far more despicable than anything I could do." And in a December 1 news story headlined "R-Rated Rock Concerts? Marilyn Manson and Mom?" Strauss reported that "in an attempt to save their businesses from complaining parents, restrictive legislation and increased police scrutiny, concert hall operators are considering a rating system for performances similar to those used for movies, television shows and recordings," and that this consideration stemmed from reaction to Manson's last tour.

In the months since the piece ran, no one has taken concrete steps to institute a rating system, and major players in the industry do not believe it will ever happen. The legislation is essentially the pipe dream of two conservative state legislators, one in Michigan and one from South Carolina. But because the story ran in the venerable *New York Times*, it (and thus Manson's involvement) was given considerable weight, with *Rolling Stone* and daily newspapers across the country following up on it.

Pareles says the *Times* has tough standards for avoiding conflict of interest, and Strauss always met them. "Basically, Neil did pretty much everything by the book," the senior critic says. "He didn't do anything endorsing Manson, really. He wrote about Manson in news stories because Manson was a newsmaker. Whenever Neil covered Manson, he asked [the paper] not to put a picture in, which would sort of pop Manson out of the story as the most important part. The concert ratings story did have a Manson picture, but he asked them not to and they overruled him."

$STORIES$ *LIKE THE* ratings piece continue to bolster Manson's controversial public image—which, in turn, bolsters the appeal of his autobiography. Pareles confesses that he hasn't read *The Long Hard Road Out of Hell*. It's unlikely that higher-ranking editors at the old gray lady have read it either, but it would be interesting to hear what they think of the behavior that Strauss chronicles, including sexual escapades that can be politely described as psychopathic.

After an opening scene in which Manson recalls watching his crossdressing grandfather masturbate to pictures of bestiality, he recounts his own exploits, including burning off a groupie's pubic hair with a cigarette lighter, playing a game with his band that involves spitting into a groupie's asshole, forcing numerous groupies to "confess their sins" while strapped to a homemade torture device, yanking on still another groupie's clit ring before shoving his thumb up her rectum, and generally mistreating one or more women per page.

The centerpiece of the book is, appropriately enough, Chapter Thirteen. Strauss presents it as a straight Q&A with Manson, who brags at length about an incident in a Miami recording studio involving a deaf groupie named Alyssa—a pseudonym that's close to her real name, according to a source who knows her. The girl likes metal because she can feel the vibrations of the music, and she is thrilled to be invited into Manson's lair. Once there she is stripped to her boots and covered in raw meat. At this point Strauss interjects, "We could call this chapter 'Meating the Fans.'"

"I was also thinking of 'Meat and Greet,'" Manson replies.

"That's good," Strauss says. "Go on."

Next Alyssa is sodomized by guitarist Twiggy Ramirez and keyboardist Madonna Wayne Gacy with their dicks taped together, fucked by Gacy, peed on by Manson and Twiggy, and joined in the shower by guitarist Daisy Berkowitz. Finally Manson throws a dead salmon in the stall as a modern analogue to the infamous shark incident in Stephen Davis's Led Zeppelin biography, *Hammer of the Gods.*

A reporter might have balanced Manson's account with the girl's side of the story. (Manson paints her as a willing participant.) A cultural critic might have ventured an opinion about what such behavior means. Strauss does neither. Instead he abets Manson in what the singer describes as a "science project" designed to "see if a white band that wasn't rap could get away with acts far more offensive and illicit than 2 Live Crew's dirty rhymes." In the midst of a six-city book tour, Manson told the *Chicago Tribune* that he'd be disappointed if government and religious officials *stopped* attacking him.

"I wouldn't know what do with myself while on tour," he said. "I'd have to start playing checkers. I expect my next tour to be just as bad as the last one, though I think people are going to have to find something new to hate eventually."

Strauss has reportedly been hanging out with Manson in Los Angeles quite a bit in recent months. He also attended Manson's New York book signing earlier this month and told gossip columnist Michael Musto of the *Village Voice,* "I definitely got a lot more than I expected [from writing the book]. I probably realized this in Marilyn's hotel one morning at four A.M. wearing a blonde wig and staring at a bottle of wine, two unidentifiable blue pills, and a nose-hair trimmer."

If Strauss's mission on the west coast is to challenge the Los Angeles *Times*'s Philips, he has so far fallen short. The west coast paper published one of the most explosive music news stories of the year on February 22, the result of a month-long investigation by Philips (who refuses even free albums and concert tickets) and *Times* staffer Michael Hiltzik. Just days before the Grammys, the story detailed charges that the National Academy of Recording Arts & Sciences, the Santa Monica organization that sponsors the awards, has given only ten percent of the money its charitable arm MusiCares has raised to the intended recipients, while organization president Michael Greene has been earning seven hundred fifty-seven thousand dollars annually and pushing major labels to release his own solo album.

Strauss had yet to write even a follow-up report on the NARAS controversy in the *New York Times.* The weekend that the L.A. paper ran its expose, he was in Hawaii covering a Pearl Jam concert for *Rolling Stone*. But even though they got scooped, Strauss's editors at the *Times* can at least find some consolation in their own pages: *The Long Hard Road Out of Hell* debuted at number twelve on the paper's bestseller list, and for the past three weeks, it's been perched at number six.

My Britney Problem—And Yours
Salon, June 2002

BECOMING A DAD is a state of mind, and it's much more complicated than becoming a father, which is a mere accident of biology. It can be traumatic for anyone, but it's especially difficult for a rock critic. Ideally, my career is based on championing music that pisses dad off and/or scares the bejesus out of him. Woe is the day I cross the line and become The Man myself, though I've been accused of doing so.

Witness the letter I received from a reader after I wrote a harsh review of *Britney*, the much-hyped third album by Britney Spears:

> Why are you constantly complaining about Britney Spears's image? Why are you so bothered by the idea that older men may desire Britney sexually? Perhaps you feel ashamed for wanting Ms. Spears yourself in some manner? Or does it have to do with the fact that you have a young daughter?

The first charge was easy enough to dismiss: I'm a healthy, red-blooded fella, and there's a long list of female pop stars who get my motor running, from Jill Scott and Angie Stone to Pink and Shakira to the fair Justine Frischmann and the risqué art-rapper Peaches. But Barbie Doll Britney? Uh-uh, no way. Sure I recognize her obvious charms, thrust out front and center from the cover of the current *Rolling Stone*. But she's too synthetic, too "perfect," and ultimately too cold in that airbrushed *Playboy* centerfold way. Hell, I'd sleep with the guy from Staind before I'd tumble for La Brit.

The daughter thing, though—that hit a nerve. Could my disdain for Spears's helium chirp and cynical, sugar-coated musical calculations be motivated by some deep-seated fear of seeing my five-year-old daughter grow up to become a sexual being? I thought I'd accepted the fact that some day, sooner rather than later, she'll become her own person, do what she wants to do, fuck who she wants to fuck. Hell, we've been singing "Mr. Suit" by Wire since she was three and a half ("I'm tired of being told what to think / I'm tired of being told what to do / I'm tired of fucking phonies / That's right I'm tired of you!"—though we change the words slightly to "*big bad* phonies").

Still, could I be falling prey to the whole paternalistic "daddy's little girl" trip, and letting it cloud my critical judgment to boot?

The question lingered for the better part of a week, until shortly after my daughter's fifth birthday party a few days before Thanksgiving. Among the presents she received from the other members of her preschool class were a tackle box–sized makeup kit (lipstick, eye shadow, nail polish—the works); a life-sized vanity-table play set with a bigger mirror than any we had in the house; and a doll from the "Diva Starz" series, a little plastic pop singer who says different things when you dress her in different outfits (all sold separately). Sample dialogue: "Let me wear my blue pants!" and "Hyper-sweet! I'm loving this purple skirt!"

The manufacturer, Mattel, says Diva Starz are intended for "Ages 6 +," though a similar, competing line called "Bratz" ("The girls with a passion for fashion!") from MGA Entertainment advises "4 +." Both collections boast a young, blonde diva who looks amazingly like You-Know-Who, complete with pneumatically inflated, Britneyesque chest, bountifully cur-vaceous hips, and a camel toe in the crotch.

I realized then and there that the most sinister thing about Spears isn't the sex, it's the selling. My objection is not dad-driven Puritanism, it's a gripe against the hyper-capitalism of America's massive, all-encompassing Teen Fashion–Beauty–Culture Machine, which has now moved the lower threshold of its target demographic from just pre-puberty to barely post-toddler. I'd like to grab hold of The Man (whoever he or she is) and choke 'em with their own marketing plan: "No, no, no, no, no, Mr. Suit!"

KIDDIE SEX IS big business today, but by no means is it restricted to obscure corners of the Internet, as some would have us believe. A friend of mine who's the head buyer at Minneapolis's largest chain of magazine stores says that *Hustler*'s faux-teen spin-off *Barely Legal* is their third best-selling sex mag; ultra-respectable businessmen invariably come in and buy it along with a copy of *Seventeen* or *Cosmo Girl*, which creeps her out to the core of her being. And more than once she's found a sticky, dog-eared copy of the Mary Kate and Ashley Olsen fan magazine in the store's bathroom.

After the horrified kiddies' voices that Michael Jackson inserted at the end of "The Lost Children" from his new album *Invincible*, there has been no creepier kiddie-porn moment in recent musical history than during

Spears's HBO concert special, when actor Jon Voight (father of the troubled Angelina Jolie) sat a young stand-in for the pop star (in fact her eight-year-old sister, Jamie Lynn) on his knee after telling her a fairy tale about how all her dreams will come true when she meets a man who will whisk her away.

Just *thinking* about it makes me want to take a shower.

But the pervs may be reaching their saturation point. Relentlessly promoted by MTV, HBO, and corporate pop radio, *Britney* sold more than seven hundred forty-five thousand copies in its first week, according to SoundScan, the company that tracks album sales. But that was considerably less than the 1.3 million units that Spears's sophomore effort *Oops! . . . I Did It Again* moved in its first seven days last year.

One reason is that, no matter how tantalizing or taboo, any act gets tired the third time you go back to the well. Another is that Spears is getting too old for the role of the coquettish nymph; she turns twenty on December 2. But mostly, I think, the horny, jaded masses have pretty much seen all that she has to offer. If she really wants to keep our attention, she's gonna have to produce that Pam 'n' Tommy–style hardcore sex tape with her boyfriend, Justin ('N Sync) Timberlake. Otherwise America will move on to its next illicit fantasy girl—and this time she may not even be flesh and blood.

While Spears has definitely benefited from modern science—if not via the surgical enhancement of her breasts, than certainly by the pitch-shifted digital tweaking of that god-awful voice, which she doesn't even pretend to really use "in concert"—the technology exists to build an even dreamier teen diva. On Halloween the Supreme Court heard the government's defense of a federal law overturned by the appeals court barring pornography using computer-generated images of children. If the top court holds that this material is legal because no harm is done to real children in producing it—and many think that it will—then the floodgates will open, and the high-tech trickery used to bring us *Monsters, Inc.* and *Shrek* could give us kiddie-porn versions of *Deep Throat* and *Debbie Does Dallas.*

Measured against that kind of competition, *Britney* is old news. "For the just under forty minutes that the albums lasts, people of all ages and genders can feel like a dirty old man," Jon Pareles harrumphed in his *New York Times* review of the album. But Spears has been working the comic-book Lolita angle since long before her first album in 1999, and *Salon* contributor Strawberry Saroyan did a fine job of dissecting it all in May 2000. "She's a Mouseketeer trafficking kiddie porn, a school-girl queen selling sex in a leathery cat suit," said the headline that ran with her essay. "Does Britney Spears have any idea what she's doing?"

Saroyan concluded that she did not, and that would seem to be confirmed by a "roundtable teleconference" that Spears's label, the teen-pop
monolith Jive Records, arranged with some two dozen journalists a week
before the new album's release. Each reporter was allowed to ask one question, with no follow-ups; you posed your query and were immediately
muted while everyone on the line listened to the diva's response.

I got to ask the first question for the *Chicago Sun-Times*. From the official
Jive transcript (which was emailed to journalists so they wouldn't have to
even tape or type up the quotes):

> **Jim DeRogatis**: Britney, this is a fairly hot and horny
> record—a lot of people are comparing it to Madonna's
> *Erotica*. Now, when I've seen you in concert before, I've gen-
> erally been surrounded by twelve- to sixteen-year-olds—
> young kids—most of them girls. I wonder if you've thought
> about the message you send to them? I see them looking at
> you, twirling around the pole in that Demi Moore sort of
> strip-tease, and I wonder if you worry about them getting
> this message of sexuality at a pre-sexualized age?

> **Britney Spears**: Well, I think it's . . . You know, first I'm
> very flattered that such young kids look up to me, be-
> cause the innocence of them is a really beautiful thing.
> But I think it's honestly up to their parents to explain to
> them that I'm a performer, and that when I'm on stage,
> that's my time to perform and express myself. I don't
> wear those clothes to the supermarket or to a ballgame.
> You know, little kids, just like when they go into their
> mom's closet and they dress up in their mom's clothes,
> it's fine and fun, and it's like their time to play at home.
> But that's not what they're supposed to wear out into re-
> ality in the real world.

A disarmingly reasonable answer, and Spears had clearly been prepped
and ready with it; the all-about-dressing-up defense even seems plausible
for a moment when you consider that she sported no fewer than thirteen
different designer outfits during her ninety-minute HBO concert special,
building to a wet and wild climax with the "caught outside in the rain in a
chain-link bra" ending. But if I hadn't been on mute, I'd have asked how

many moms have latex dominatrix outfits in their closet, much less the live python she wore to the MTV Video Music Awards.

Spears seemed less practiced later in the interview. Since she sported a white jumpsuit in the HBO ads and the special was taped in Las Vegas, someone asked if she was an Elvis Presley fan. "Yes, I am a really, really big Elvis fan," she gushed. "And I think the real reason why we did the whole Elvis thing is because, you know, he's from Vegas." (Actually, he was from Tupelo, Mississippi.)

Next she was queried about her cover of "I Love Rock and Roll." "I just love the song," she enthused. "I love Pat Benatar, and I just think she's amazing. It's like she's a rock 'n' roll chick and she's just having a good time and it's a very empowering song." (It was Joan Jett, not Pat Benatar, who recorded the most famous version of the tune.)

Finally, toward the end of the session, a reporter from Vegas (naturally) stumblingly asked if, since she's always making a point of saying that she's, you know, still a virgin, whether there are any, um, *things* that she and Justin can do to just, er, *have fun*?

The shock that Spears registered at this intrusive but not unwarranted question (she's the one making sex an issue, after all) could be felt right over the phone line; she didn't show nearly as much revulsion for the snake that was licking her ear on MTV. How could anyone even *ask* such a thing! "We can go to the next question," she snapped.

At the same time, in her latest *Rolling Stone* cover story, Spears insists that sex is wonderful and should be shared with everyone, and she maintains that she is the one who is wholly responsible for engineering her drool-worthy image. "What would you say to people who say of you, 'Oh, she's all constructed by other people, she's just selling sex'?" writer Mim Udovitch asked. Replied the singer: "If I wanna show my belly in a video or show a little bit of cleavage, I just don't see anything wrong with that. . . . I come up with the concepts for all my tour ideas, all of my videos. It's just so lame that people wouldn't understand that."

Spears has a point. Why should we assume, as Saroyan did in her essay, that some *man* designed the pedophiliac fantasy that has propelled her career thus far (and which is a heck of a lot more complicated than a glimpse of belly button in a video)? Her telechat unwittingly displayed her shallow knowledge of the musical traditions she references, but she may be completely aware of how to use sex as a sales tool. After all she was brought up to be expert at it, schooled by a stage mom since before she could walk, just like JonBenet Ramsey.

In the liner notes to *Britney*, the singer writes, "Mama—thanks for being the best role model in the world. I want to be just like you when I'm older." Natalie Merchant recently told me a revealing story about being stuck in a line of golf carts backstage at a music awards show. Someone behind her kept frantically leaning on the horn, and finally she turned around to look. There was Spears in the passenger seat, sitting beside her mom, who was pounding on the horn and shouting, "Get out of the way! Britney goes first! Britney's *got to go first!*"

Here is Lynne Spears in *Britney Spears' Heart to Heart*, the autobiography that she co-wrote with her daughter last year: "The way we saw it, our family was making an investment in Brit's future. How could we *not* help her realize her goals? It was so clear that Brit loved performing, and it would have broken my heart to get in her way. I always used to tell her, 'Don't worry about what it costs. Just do your very best.' Dreams should never have a price tag on them. I believe that if you want something bad enough, you'll find a way to do it. And we did."

Mind you, Mama Spears is discussing dance lessons for a *two-year-old* in that passage; when my daughter was two, the dreams she had for the future involved not having to pee in a diaper. Whenever it addresses the mother-daughter relationship, the Spears' book reminds me of Louis Malle's pedophiliac-prostitute fantasy, *Pretty Baby*. When Susan Sarandon turns her daughter out to trick, it's with a mixture of pride, jealousy, and self-loathing. For her part, Brooke Shields tries her damnedest at the job, partly because she doesn't want to let her mother down, and partly because she wants to prove she can be a much better lay.

There's a sort of panicked desperation to the attempted seduction of *Britney*; rarely has a coldly calculated sexual come-on been so plainly unsexy. As producers the Neptunes and Rodney Jerkins nudge the grooves away from Swedish pop perfection toward generically glossy and soulless R&B, Spears tries to update her lyrical concerns by whining about the hard life of a superstar ("Overprotected," "What It's Like to Be Me") and bemoaning the difficulties of growing up and coming of age ("I'm Not a Girl, Not Yet a Woman"). This is all a bid to stay ahead of her audience as it moves from pre-teen to puberty, of course. But for all her talk of self-empowerment, the submissive sex toy is still the role Spears plays best. She returns to it again and again ("Boys" and "I'm a Slave 4 U"), and it's certainly the pose that's being used to peddle the disc.

In Chicago, the Clear Channel Communications dance-pop station Kiss-FM celebrated the release of *Britney* with a contest offering young female listeners the chance to win Brit's tits. Engineered by the station's general manager and marketing director (both women), the tag line ran, "Wanna be like Britney? You first met her on *The Mickey Mouse Club*. You've watched her grow into every guy's fantasy slave. Now you want what she's got! Enter to win 'Boobies Like Britney' and the $5,000 grand prize!"

In defending themselves after they were criticized by local media columnist Robert Feder, the contest's architects maintained that it was all in good fun, and their listeners knew that the prize money could be used for clothes or a makeover, not necessarily new, massive mammaries. The executives were probably right; the teenyboppers who listen to their station and tune in to MTV's *Total Request Live* have been effectively programmed almost since birth. The message, as it's been paraphrased by many a feminist critic, is: You will never be smart or sexy enough as you are; the only hope of being like Barbie or Britney is to buy, buy, buy. So start spending!

Sex has always been an inextricable part of pop music; it was thus long before Elvis (wherever he was from), and it will be so long after Spears is cast off onto the slag heap of fallen idols along with Twiggy and Tiffany. And while I celebrate rock 'n' roll at its best as one of popular culture's last forums for "truth" and (only marginally commodified) rebellion, I won't deny that selling has always been a big part of the mix, too. The Beatles blew the minds of a generation and changed the music forever, but they happily moved a whole lot of boots, haircuts, and posters, too.

Spears is notable for temporarily marking a new low in the utterly shameless crassness of both the commercialism and the koochie-flaunting. But she isn't the first singer to emphasize tits over talent, or to shake her hips to move designer jeans and plastic dolls. And she won't be the last.

As for this dad's particular dilemma, my daughter has thankfully shown no interest in Spears as yet. If she ever does, I plan to follow the singer's advice and not only explain that she is playing dress up, but lay bare the whole insidious con job. Then I'll offer some alternatives.

Melody may not go right away for X-Ray Spex or Hole, Salt-N-Pepa or Angie Stone's new album, *Mahogany Soul* (which ends with the memorable declaration, "It's that time of the month, don't even mess with me!"). But I bet I could convince her that *M!ssundaztood* by Pink is a whole heckuva lot better than *Britney*. No one's submissive sex toy, the former Alicia Moore is a real and complex young woman, albeit one with artificially colored chartreuse hair. I love it when she sings, "Tired of being compared to damn Britney Spears / She's so pretty, that just ain't me."

13 FREAKS AND GEEKS

THIS CHAPTER COMES TOWARD THE END of the book and is one of the longest because it illustrates what I believe was the most encouraging aspect of the alternative era: It was a time when a truly impressive number of unique artists and dedicated individualists—my favorite kinds of rockers—crept under the barbed wire and won a chance to achieve mainstream exposure of the sort that hadn't been readily available since the heyday of the psychedelic '60s or the brief flourishing of punk and New Wave in the mid-'70s.

True, this period was short-lived, and the monolithic music industry quickly reverted to form, giving us an endless procession of grunge clones and watered-down wannabes, followed in short order by teen pop, nü metal, and lowest-common-denominator hip-hop. But while there has been endless debate in these pages among artists and observers about the ethics of "selling out" (as if the process of making music can ever be completely separated from commerce), the best of the musicians who follow benefited from the money and the recognition without compromising their distinctive visions. From the vantage point of the new millennium, it's strange to think that the Butthole Surfers and the Jesus Lizard were for a time brought to us by the same company that gave us Frank Sinatra and the Beatles. But it didn't significantly change what either group did (nor did it affect Capitol very much), and in the end the hype and the money were irrelevant: It was the music, the personalities, and their life force that mattered.

This section opens with the Flaming Lips because they remain a paradigm for a band with a sound that is unique, ambitious, and uncompromising without being elitist. They continue to thrive in the unlikely environs of Oklahoma City, using the machine but independent of it, as inspiring for the way they work as they are for music that epitomizes the central message of all great rock 'n' roll: Live in the moment and make every moment count.

Red Red Meat and Screeching Weasel (which is once again disbanded) never achieved anywhere near the acclaim they deserved, but their finest recordings live on and will almost certainly continue to be discovered and cited as inspirations by curious listeners down the road. In contrast the Jesus Lizard was always about the live experience—you really had to be there as David Yow flung himself about with more abandon than anyone since Iggy Pop, propelled by those relentless grooves—and the albums will never quite convey that.

Material Issue, Redd Kross, and Weezer illustrate that grunge wasn't the only forum during the alternative years for expressing twentysomething angst. The poignant emotions behind their mod posturing, cartoonish clowning, and defiant nerdiness made their respective brands of power pop all the more effective. And while there may not have been much emotion in the music of Ween, the Butthole Surfers, the Melvins, and Pavement, they certainly qualify as freaks, geeks, or both.

So, too, do Arrested Development and P.M. Dawn. Shunned for different reasons (too pop, too positive, too soft) by the often closed-minded hip-hop scene, these artists had as much in common sonically as philosophically with many of the alternative rockers chronicled in this chapter. It's a damn shame radio seemed incapable of recognizing that, and that hip-hop continues to marginalize similarly adventurous musical innovators and lyrical mavericks in favor of gangsta poseurs. As for Tone-Loc, he was and is a guilty pleasure. His second album sank without a trace and he has never bothered to follow it up (like Courtney Love, he's found the outlet for his sizable personality in acting), but he remains inspiring for his devotion to the philosophy of livin' large.

Armchair observers have been lamenting that "rock is dead" since the mid-1950s, but as we neared the end of the '90s, that refrain seemed to echo louder than ever. Looking back, it seems unlikely that for about ten minutes circa late 1996, the major labels thought that electronica might be "the next big thing." When it did eventually achieve a limited mainstream breakthrough a few years later via the likes of the Chemical Brothers, Fat Boy Slim, and Paul Oakenfold, it was with music of a much less challenging variety than that of the Aphex Twin, the Orb, and Trent Reznor (with the arguable exception of the always lovable Moby). Meanwhile, in the hipster underground, Tortoise was the band cited most often as leaders of some brave new "postrock revolution" that, if you actually bothered to listen to the music, was hardly anything new or revolutionary at all. To their credit, the members of Tortoise never said that it was.

Innovation lives on in rock wherever there are artists with personality and imagination, whether it's in Oklahoma City with the fabulous Flaming Lips or in another nowheresburg like Ruston, Louisiana, with the bands of the Elephant 6 collective. All you have to do is be willing to ferret it out and listen.

Psychedelic Rock from the Bible Belt
Request, July 1995

"WELCOME TO OKLAHOMA City," reads the sign at Will Rogers World Airport, "Home of Vince Gill, CMA Artist of the Year." It's early April; in two weeks, the city will be known for something dramatically different. But now, as I drive through the flat, mall-lined streets, I wonder how any rock band, let alone a really weird one, could possibly exist in a city with no rock clubs, no college- or modern-rock radio stations, and only one recording studio that caters to loud music. Then I turn my rental-car radio to KRXO–FM, "the station that brought classic rock back to Oklahoma City," and hear the strange '60s nugget, "Timothy Leary's Dead" by the Moody Blues. Maybe the Flaming Lips fit in here after all.

The Lips are the best psychedelic rock band in America today. They'd never say that themselves—"We just do what we do," they claim—and that description probably won't mean much to a new wave of fans attracted by their one hit, "She Don't Use Jelly," or their guest appearance on *Beverly Hills 90210* as the band rocking the Peach Pit After Dark. But the Lips are part of a proud creative tradition that includes the *Revolver*-era Beatles, Pink Floyd, Can, Brian Eno, and My Bloody Valentine. And to fully appreciate how impressive that accomplishment is, you have to visit them in their hometown.

The band has been hunkered down in the recording studio for six weeks. Studio 7 is a big squat building located on the wrong side of the tracks dividing Oklahoma City's north and south sides. One night two and a half years ago when the Lips were making their previous album, *Transmissions from the Satellite Heart*, they were experimenting by recording vocals in a car parked in front of the studio. Suddenly a house across the street exploded and the band watched it burn almost to the ground before the fire department arrived. The debris still sits there untouched.

The Lips have taken over every corner of the studio to record their eighth album. This isn't really a problem, since there aren't any other customers. "This place is probably gonna go bankrupt," good-humored singer Wayne Coyne says in his casual Okie drawl. "Then we'll have to buy it so we have a place to work."

As Coyne conducts a tour of the facilities, he apologizes for how neat everything looks. Guitarist Ronald Jones recently rolled up the loose cords and vacuumed the rug in the main studio, but he didn't touch the drum room. Steven Drozd's kit is set up in front of a giant tacky mural that looks like something you'd see in a hippie daycare center; two dozen broken sticks litter the floor. A monster drummer, Drozd attaches his headphones to his skull with duct tape so they won't fly off when he plays, and he has scrawled several inspirational slogans in black marker on his massive ride cymbal, including PERSONALLY, I LIKE MYSELF and PROBABLY THE COKE TALKING, BUT I LIKE YOU, TOO.

Jones didn't touch Coyne's vocal booth either. The smell of stale cigarette smoke hits you as you open the door, and there's barely room to walk without treading on Coyne's acoustic guitar, a big book of Bob Dylan lyrics, or William Joyce's children's tome, *Santa Calls.* "For inspiration," Coyne explains.

At the end of last night's session, Coyne recorded vocals and acoustic guitar for a hokey tune that sounds a little like Rick Nelson's "Garden Party." Twelve hours later the song has become a two-minute-and-seventeen-second minisymphony with a dozen guitar overdubs, and the group is preparing to do one more. "What have you got for us, Jones?" Coyne asks. The shy, lanky guitarist plays a heavily chorused riff, and Coyne recoils. "You haven't gone ELP on us, have you?" the singer asks, referring to the sometimes tedious progressive rockers. Producer-engineer Dave Fridmann defends the idea. "No, that's more 'Sound of Silence,' Wayne," he says, and the part goes down on tape.

Over and over again the band members ask, "That's not another song, is it?" or "This hasn't been done before, has it?" They don't mind borrowing from rock history, as long as it fits into something that's one-hundred-percent Flaming Lips.

Unlike most bands, the Lips don't have a set of new songs that have been perfected in rehearsal and live performance. Their tunes start with the nub of an idea and are built up in the studio. "You'll find out where this song is going as soon as we do," Coyne says of the work-in-progress. The band has been honing this method of making records for more than a decade.

THE SECOND-YOUNGEST of six children, Coyne grew up in a middle-class Catholic family surrounded by Baptists in what's often called the buckle of the Bible Belt. He didn't go to college, but he was drawn to the University of Oklahoma in nearby Norman when some enterprising rock fans began hosting hardcore-punk shows in the early '80s.

Coyne had already started the Flaming Lips with bassist Michael Ivins. They owned a practice P.A., and they'd haul it to gigs by touring groups like the Meat Puppets. In return they'd get into shows for free, and they were able to see how the DIY scene worked. They learned that a band could make its own records, tour the country in a van, and sell tapes or vinyl at shows. They decided to try it themselves.

After releasing their own self-titled EP, the Lips won a contract from the independent Restless Records. *Hear It Is* (1986), *Oh My Gawd!!! . . . The Flaming Lips* (1987), and *Telepathic Surgery* (1989) followed. The group never got much money from Restless, so making records in intense two- or three-day bursts was the only option. "We never called it punk rock, that was just all the money and all the time we had," Coyne says. He kept his day job as a fry cook at Long John Silver's and he planned tours and did phone interviews in the back of the fast-food restaurant during breaks.

On album and onstage the early Lips came across as a freakier, druggier version of the Replacements. But there were hints—like the Pink Floyd–inspired "One Million Billionth of a Millisecond on a Sunday Morning" or the lulling "Jesus Shootin' Heroin"—that they were capable of much more. When Coyne got ten thousand dollars from a song-publishing advance, he decided to spend it making a record the way he'd always wanted. "We did *In a Priest Driven Ambulance* thinking it was the last record we were ever gonna do," he says. "We really liked the idea of breaking free of that whole thing where independent bands spent fifty dollars making shitty-sounding records."

The group worked at a studio in Buffalo, New York, that was staffed by students, including their current producer, Fridmann. "These were guys who wanted to be engineers," Coyne says. "They liked us giving them challenges; it wasn't like dreading going into the recording studio. We'd wake up every day and ideas would be flying out of everybody's heads. We could set up an amp and put a mike sixty feet down the hall just to see how it sounded. After that, we didn't want to make a record ever again if we had to do it the old way."

Just as the album was released in 1990, Restless underwent a major corporate reorganization, and the Lips' finest recording to date was almost impossible to find in stores. At the same time, the band's longtime manager and booking agent, Michele Vlasimsky, threw up her hands and quit. Managing the Lips fell by default to Scott Booker, a fan who was running Oklahoma City's one cool record store. "Basically," Booker says, "the Lips liked me 'cause I had a phone." It was at the Lips' darkest hour that a surprising savior appeared.

Won over by the group's indie releases and stage shows featuring smoke, bubbles, and thousands of blinking Christmas lights, veteran A&R executive Roberta Peterson approached the band about signing to Warner Bros. The first time she called, they thought it was a friend playing a joke on them and hung up. Peterson called back. "We were like, 'We're glad you like us and all that, but we just wanna make records like the last one,'" Coyne says. "They said, 'Sure!' But we kept thinking there had to be some catch."

There was, and it came in the sort of corporate red tape that the Lips had never dealt with before. Working with Fridmann, they recorded another strong, twisted album, *Hit to Death in the Future Head.* They delivered it to Warner Bros. and then waited for six months as lawyers tried to get copyright approval from composer Michael Kamen. It seems the group had been watching a videotape of Terry Gilliam's *Brazil* during the recording and a bit of the soundtrack made its way onto the song "You Have to Be Joking (Autopsy of the Devil's Brain)." The Lips liked it too much to remove it, but getting clearance for the sample took forever.

By the time the album was released in mid-1992, the Lips had become a new band. Jonathan Donahue had hopped in the van in Buffalo, joining the group as soundman before graduating to guitar. He stayed long enough to record two albums before quitting to start his own group, Mercury Rev. Donahue was replaced by Jones, and Drozd took over the vacant drum seat.

The twenty-four-year-old Jones was born in Hawaii to African-American and Filipino parents. He wound up in Oklahoma when his father was stationed there by the Air Force, and he taught himself to play guitar, developing a swirling calliope of sounds by using racks of effects and ingenious tricks such as placing a small Realistic speaker next to his pickups to create a roar like a million electric razors. Also in his mid-twenties, Drozd started playing drums with a punk band in Texas. He attacks his kit with the bombastic ferocity of vintage John Bonham or Bill Ward, but he's also an accomplished piano and guitar player. "Those guys are both such amazing musicians, I feel sorry that they're stuck with a singer like me," Coyne says, referring to his plaintive Neil Young whine. But not only is the current lineup the Lips' strongest live incarnation yet, it recorded the band's best album.

When *Transmissions from the Satellite Heart* was released in mid-1993, Warner Bros. worked hard to promote it for the first six or eight weeks, and then—nothing. Modern-rock radio passed on the first single, "Turn It On," and only a handful of good reviews appeared. The label shifted its attention to the next piece of product in the pipeline. "This was a dead, dead, dead record," one label executive says.

Both in their mid-thirties, Coyne and Ivins knew that *Transmissions* was probably their last shot at making a major-label album. *Hit to Death* had sold only sixteen thousand copies, which is dismal by an indie's standards, let alone a major's. "I don't think anyone would say this out loud, but we knew that *Transmissions* was an important record, and if something didn't happen with it . . ." Booker says, his voice trailing off.

The Lips were determined to convert fans one gig at a time. "They just kept touring," says Tom Biery, a Midwest radio and promotions rep who was one of a handful of young Warner Bros. staffers pulling for the group. "They wouldn't go away. Even though some of the power people maybe wanted them to go away, they just wouldn't."

The band toured with Porno for Pyros, the Butthole Surfers, Stone Temple Pilots, Tool, and Lollapalooza '94. In the space of eighteen months the Lips played Chicago thirteen times. All this work started to pay off in the fall of '94, when alternative-rock radio started playing "She Don't Use Jelly," finally recognizing the potential of an irresistibly catchy ditty about tangerines, toast, and Vaseline. The video that Warner Bros. scoffed at because it was directed by Coyne for a mere twelve thousand dollars wound up in MTV's Buzz Bin. Then the group was offered two thousand five hundred dollars a show—much more than it could earn on its own—to perform sixty gigs with the wretched arena-grunge band Candlebox.

Many in the Lips camp balked, but Coyne and Booker convinced them it was worthwhile. In addition to reaching hundreds of thousands of young listeners, the Lips benefited from having the same Warner Bros. radio and promotions people working both bands. And just before the tour started, Booker was summoned to Warner Bros.' home office in Los Angeles. "Our product manager said, 'I think it's time for you to meet [high-ranking label executive] Russ Thyret,'" Booker says. "I was like, 'Who the hell's this guy?' People said, 'He's the wizard behind the curtain.' But here's this guy in front of me who looks just like Burl Ives. Our product manager does all the talking. Finally, Russ stands up, and he's getting ready to leave, and he looks at me and says, 'Scott, you didn't say a word. What do you want?'"

Booker asked for radio support, more albums in the stores, and some help getting the Lips on TV. "Russ says, 'Listen, this reminds me of the Replacements a few years back, when everyone at the label loved them and all the right opportunities were popping up, but it never clicked. We didn't follow through, and the band broke up. I don't want that to happen to this band.'"

Nine months later, *Transmissions* has sold a respectable three hundred thousand copies. The Lips have appeared on *The Late Show with David Letterman, Beverly Hills 90210,* and *MTV's Spring Break,* and the song "Bad Days" will be featured this summer on the soundtrack for *Batman III.* Their new album (which will eventually be titled *Clouds Taste Metallic*) is scheduled to be released in September, but the band would be happy to push it back if another single from *Transmissions* takes off. Either way, the group has become a priority at Warner Bros. "We're lucky in the regard that this time, if the new album flops, it's their fault," Coyne says. "We can't lose now. If we sell a million records, fine. If we sell fifty thousand, it just looks like they fucked up. But it doesn't make doing records any easier, because all that shit really doesn't matter."

True enough; at Studio 7 nobody ever mentions marketing or sales or radio or Warner Bros. The big debate is about the quality of the hand claps on "Brainville University, Tuition One Dollar," the song that grew out of the "Garden Party" chords. The lyrics sound like a swipe at people who think you can't be an intellectual unless you've gone to college, a subject that must resonate with Coyne. In typically whimsical style, he says that the song is about "these guys who put fliers up all over town saying, 'Brainville University, Tuition One Dollar,' listing this back alley as the address. Then they beat up and rob anybody dumb enough to show up."

Everyone in the studio (myself included) is pressed into service to record rhythmic claps for the end of the tune. A passionate thirty-minute debate follows about how Fridmann should make the clapping sound. Jones favors the giant hand claps that producer Roy Thomas Baker created for Queen and the Cars. Coyne prefers the loose hand claps on the first Stooges album. Finally Drozd puts David Bowie's *Hunky Dory* in the CD player and forwards to the song "Andy Warhol." Everyone agrees that *that* is the way hand claps should sound, and work moves on to backing vocals.

When the Lips mix "Brainville" the next day, the claps are barely audible—just one more element in a disorienting wall of sound—and you have to wonder why they bothered. But you can't knock a process that has created six songs out of nothing. So far these include the interstellar overdrive of "Psychiatric Exploration of the Foetus with Needles," a positively giddy *Pet Sounds*–style pop song called "This Here Giraffe," and a moody number with the working title "The Abandoned Hospital Ship" that uses the sound of a spinning movie projector as its rhythm track. "The best part about working the way we do," Coyne says, "is that you can never do anything wrong."

Some people assume that the Lips couldn't possibly make music like this without ingesting vast amounts of psychedelic drugs. Coyne himself is responsible for some of this speculation, since he named his publishing company Lovely Sorts of Death, as in L-S-D. (During the seventy-two hours I spent with the band, the only substances I saw abused were the countless packets of sugar Coyne stirred into his coffee and the prescription Percodans Ivins popped to ease the pain of five pulled teeth.) "I've done acid probably three or four times, and one of them I don't think counted because it was shitty," Coyne says with characteristic frankness. "I think that's the great misconception about our music. People think, 'The only way you could do that is to be on drugs.' If you look for the influence of drugs on our music, it's like looking for a UFO—you'll probably find it. But it has always been more about propelling the ideas away from what's boring."

More than drug use or cosmic concerns, the Lips are linked to the psychedelic legacy by their playful spirit, the willingness to experiment, and the general philosophy that you can find art everywhere. In the late '60s psychedelic rockers like England's Incredible String Band and Germany's Amon Düül II took to the countryside to create ideal communities based on music. As unlikely as it seems the Lips have done something similar in Oklahoma City.

Most of the band members live together in a big two-level brick house vaguely reminiscent of Frank Lloyd Wright. It stands out amid the ramshackle ranch houses even before you notice the gargoyles on the roof or the giant flower sculptures on the balcony. With the exception of the gun-toting rednecks next door, the Lips get along just fine with their neighbors, and the kids in the area love to come by to hang out or help mow the lawn. Most people call the house the "compound," but Coyne prefers "stately Wayne manor." He and his girlfriend, J. Michelle Martin, bought the place from the federal Department of Housing and Urban Development for twenty thousand dollars, and Coyne proudly notes that it's all paid off.

Martin is the Michelle on the "I Love Michelle" button that Coyne wears at every gig. Sitting on a funky thrift-store couch in his stone-tiled living room, he explains why. "There are some drunk women who are very nice to talk to, but I wear the button so everyone says, 'Who's Michelle?' and I can just blatantly say, 'She's my girlfriend.'"

The button is a touching romantic gesture and one of a hundred examples of how the Lips are unaffected regular guys. The only people you'll ever hear them dis are rockers who think they're better or hipper than everyone else. Maybe this attitude comes from where the band lives: There's simply no room for pretension in Oklahoma City, and the Lips don't plan on moving any time soon. "People always ask why we live here, and I say, 'Just look around,'" Coyne explains. "You really can't separate the way we work from the way we live. Success is living a good life. This is how we wanna live our lives. I don't think people have to agree with it or anything; we just do our trip. Hopefully the main thing the Flaming Lips stand for is individuality in a sea of conformity—even if conformity isn't what it used to be."

The Next Prime Cut in Rock
The *Chicago Sun-Times*, February 13, 1994

THERE IS A timeless quality to the languid head rock of Red Red Meat, and critics and industry insiders aren't the only ones who recognize it. "We were playing a show in Richmond, Virginia, to about five people," recalls guitarist Glenn Girard. "We had cleared the room of all the skate punks who were there to see the two hardcore bands before us. There was this drunk old guy at the bar, and he turned to us and asked, 'Do you guys drink whiskey? 'Cause you guys sound like *whiskey maniacs!*'"

Red Red Meat evokes a feeling of altered consciousness even if listeners haven't had the help of Jack Daniel's or any other substance. With its second album, *Jimmy Wine Majestic*, the quartet stands poised as the next band to break out of Chicago onto the national scene, though its music may be much more of an acquired taste than the Smashing Pumpkins' or Liz Phair's. The thirteen songs on *Jimmy Wine Majestic* sustain a mood that recalls the hazy burned-out vibes (though not the exact sounds) of the Rolling Stones' *Exile on Main St.*, Neil Young's *Tonight's the Night,* and the third albums by Big Star and the Velvet Underground, all influences that the band's twenty-seven-year-old leader acknowledges. "But the sound isn't conscious," Tim Rutili says. "It just kind of happens."

Red Red Meat's sound has been evolving since 1984, when Rutili moved to Chicago from west suburban Addison to study film at Columbia College. The short, quiet, blond guitarist met and fell in love with the late Glynis Johnson, a Stones fan who bore an uncanny resemblance to Brian Jones. The two formed a band called Friends of Betty that took its simple instrumental approach from punk and its laid-back grooves from West Coast psychedelia. ("Cold Rain and Snow" by the Grateful Dead was a frequent cover.) The group went through several drummers, including John Rowan, whose bombast was a poor match for the outfit.

"I was thrown out—given the boot," says Rowan, who now plays with Urge Overkill under the *nom de rock* Blackie Onasis. "I won't mention the name of the band because I have nothing good to say about it."

Friends of Betty gigged around Chicago for years and released one independent album, cheekily titled *Blind Faith II*. The group had a loyal following, but partly because of its own inertia, it never made an impact outside Chicago. In 1990 the members changed their name to Red Red Meat and started over. Girard had joined Rutili and Johnson several months earlier, and the musicians started to develop a more intricate two-guitar sound, allowing their songs to unfold slowly over six or seven minutes.

"Friends of Betty really wasn't about listening to what you were playing," Rutili says. "It was kind of like a race to the end of the song. This band is about not really wanting the song to end."

Red Red Meat released two singles and started recording its debut album in late 1991. The band was looking forward to a promising new year, but after a tour opening for the Smashing Pumpkins, Johnson quit the group. In September 1992 she died of AIDS at home in Valparaiso, Indiana. "This is her band," Rutili says of his former partner. "She's always going to be a part of the band. We still look over and expect to see her onstage." "I miss her a lot, especially at the live shows," Girard adds. "I miss the friendship. She could do things to me with a certain way she looked at me. When she'd do a rock guitar pose at me, it would completely break me away from this stiff, stoic feel and into a groove. She had this way of doing that."

Compared to the worlds of art, dance, and theater, the alternative-rock scene has been largely untouched by AIDS. Rutili and Girard grow silent when asked about the impact of the disease on their lives. "She was so much more than what she died from," Rutili finally says of Johnson in a hushed and somber voice. "This was her band, and I think she'd really like what we're doing now."

Dedicated "to Glynis forever & ever & ever love," Red Red Meat released its debut last year on its own label, Perishable. The album garnered positive reviews from the fanzine press, and the new quartet of Rutili, Girard, drummer Brian Deck, and bassist Tim Hurley started earning raves for their live performances. The group began recording the follow-up last spring at Wicker Park's Idful Studio, which was co-founded by Deck and Brad Wood. Wood has earned accolades for his work on Phair's *Exile in Guyville,* and he has recorded strong efforts by other local bands such as Seam, Trenchmouth, and Veruca Salt. He sent a tape of Red Red Meat to Jonathan Poneman, co-founder of Sub Pop, the Seattle label that launched the careers of Nirvana and Soundgarden.

Poneman was thrilled by what he heard, and he signed the band last summer. The indie icon proudly gushes about the band's qualities, calling Rutili and Girard "casual geniuses." "They have this timelessness," he says. "[Sub Pop co-founder] Bruce [Pavitt] and I always reference music geographically, and I hear Highway 61 intersecting the Rust Belt. I hear this weird migrated electric Delta blues, but I also hear this Chicago power-pop sensibility."

Like friends and tourmates the Flaming Lips, Red Red Meat are psychedelic in the sense that they use the studio to create a new world for listeners that only exists in the space between the headphones. Wood helped the band explore the alien landscapes of *Jimmy Wine Majestic,* but he says the distinctive sound wasn't calculated. "I think that they are inept enough to not be able to play any other way. I think it's all very organic. There's not an awful lot of thought that goes into it."

In the late '70s, punk poetess Patti Smith talked about "heroin consciousness"—the artist's ability to conjure a feeling like being on drugs without having had the experience. Similarly Red Red Meat evokes the druggy, decadent feel of *Exile on Main St.,* though the band members live relatively normal lives in Wicker Park, far removed from the bacchanalian vibes of the rented French villa where the Stones recorded their masterpiece. "It's not necessarily the drugs or whatever—it's the consciousness of that feeling," Girard says. "And finding the patience to trance out," Rutili adds. "It's enjoying something while you're in it, giving it the time to work itself out, and being in the music instead of being on top of it as a guitarist or vocalist."

With the focus on Chicago rock at an all-time high thanks to Phair, Urge, and the Pumpkins, Red Red Meat has already attracted the interest of the major labels. The band is amused by the attention, but content with the path it's treading. "We want to concentrate on playing the songs and making music that we like," Rutili says. "We always existed outside the music industry because we never expected anything from it. I think that if we were to change that, we'd just screw things up."

Screeching Halt
Spin, March 2001

"IT'S BEEN A long time," Ben Foster says as he takes the stage at Chicago's House of Blues. To be precise it's been almost seven years to the day since the band's last hometown performance. In its absence the pop-punk scene it helped inspire has produced platinum acts like Green Day, Blink-182, Sum 41, and the Offspring. There but for the grace of God and Foster's big mouth go Screeching Weasel.

The legendary group is still a considerable draw—here at House of Blues, they've sold out two shows running, more than two thousand five hundred tickets—but Screeching Weasel is no arena act. The band members made their name in rented VFW halls and crummy suburban bars, and they look supremely out of place under the ornate frescoes and faux outsider art decorating the House Dan Aykroyd Built. They'd probably be playing elsewhere if Foster—better known as Ben Weasel—didn't nurture ancient grudges with just about every other promoter in the Chicago area.

Glaring like a deranged preacher, the thirty-two-year-old singer leads the band through a hail of two-minute anthems spanning ten albums and fourteen years: "I'm Gonna Strangle You," "I Don't Give a Fuck," "Cindy's on Methadone," "Gotta Girlfriend." Eight songs and fifteen minutes into the set, he takes a breather and surveys the crowd, an odd mix of kids who were in diapers when the group formed and potbellied punks in cracked leather jackets screaming beery reminiscences about "the good old days."

"This is a song about getting on with your life," Foster says, and the group launches into "Acknowledge."

"I am alive! / I am here! / I am now! / I acknowledge the fact of my life!"

Many in the crowd join in, propelled by the frenetic drumming and buzz-saw guitars. It's a transcendent punk-rock moment—a celebratory declaration of joy, defiance, and triumph, made all the more poignant by the fact that six months ago, Foster was suffering from panic attacks so intense that the mere thought of leaving his apartment left him gasping for air. The four-block walk to the post office "was like storming Normandy on acid. Half the time I'd turn around halfway there and try not to run home." His therapist diagnosed it as "social anxiety disorder with agoraphobia"—in plain English, the fear of being in public. For two years he hardly left the apartment, and friends thought he'd never perform again.

The House of Blues shows are partly a celebration of Foster's recovery. If he hasn't entirely overcome his demons, he's at least beaten them into submission, chronicling the battle and finding catharsis on a pair of extraordinary albums, 1999's *Emo* and 2000's *Teen Punks in Heat*.

The gigs are also a reminder of Screeching Weasel's enduring underground popularity. Their most successful album, 1988's *Boogadaboogadaboogada!*, has sold more than one hundred thousand copies. The band runs its own aptly named Panic Button Records, and its T-shirts are ubiquitous at punk house parties as well as at corporate rock-fests like Warped. Guitarpunk.com even manufactures a "Weaselrite" six-string designed to Foster's specs. It'll set you back six hundred ninety-five dollars, but the group's cartoon logo comes stenciled on the headstock.

The persisting cult is more than just the usual cabal of fans lining up to worship the heroes of their youth. Discriminating listeners know that Screeching Weasel is the punk band that made embracing bubblegum melodies cool again. It is the missing link between the Ramones and Blink–182 or the Buzzcocks and the Offspring. As Green Day progressed from its roots on Gilman Street in Berkeley, California—recording with Lookout! and occasionally opening for Screeching Weasel—to its major-label prime headlining in stadiums, Billie Joe Armstrong frequently turned to Foster for advice. Mike Dirnt gave Foster's group a boost by playing bass on *How to Make Enemies and Irritate People* and by wearing a Screeching Weasel T-shirt onstage at Woodstock '94. That same year Blink-182 covered "The Girl Next Door" on its first album, *Buddha*.

"Screeching Weasel was probably the biggest influence on my songwriting after the Descendents," says Blink guitarist Tom DeLonge. "I absolutely *loved* that band."

Contrary to a common belief (which is perpetuated by the fact that in 1992 the band released a cover version of the Ramones' entire first album), Foster did not set out to clone da brudders from Queens. Raised in a working-class family in the Chicago suburb of Prospect Heights, he was a pot-smoking metalhead expelled from three different high schools for unruly behavior and chronic truancy. How do you get kicked out so much? "You stand up in class when the teacher asks you a question, and you say, 'Fuck you!'" he says. "So the school district and the state agreed to split the bill for my stay at this place in Portland, Maine—I use the word 'rehab' because it's too difficult to explain what it really was."

The Elan School was actually a therapeutic community modeled on a controversial California educational approach called Synanon. Foster enrolled at Elan in January 1984. For the first year of his twenty-one-month stay, he rebelled, and he was the victim of many a "shot-down"—screamed verbal reprimands from his peers that were part of the disciplinary system. In time he discovered that he could give as good as he got. "I was a very skinny kid, so it wasn't a physical thing. It was my mouth. I became very good at yelling. People told me years later, 'I was scared of you. I was afraid to be in groups with you.' At the same time, I really discovered punk rock."

The unbridled aggression of hardcore bands like Black Flag, the Dead Kennedys, and the Circle Jerks drew Foster in, their rage mirroring his own. When he finally returned home at age seventeen he got a job at the Randhurst Cinema in Mt. Prospect, and there he bonded with fellow usher John "Jughead" Pierson. The two first met years earlier on a junior-high wrestling team. "He wasn't very good," Pierson recalls. "He was always on the verge of throwing punches." In the interim Pierson had also discovered punk via the 1984 film *Repo Man*. "When we met up again we both wanted to be in a band," the guitarist says. "There was no one doing anything we wanted to be part of, so we started our own."

At first they were called All-Night Garage Sale; Screeching Weasel came later as a variation on a frat-boy T-shirt proclaiming I'VE GOT A SCREAMING OTTER IN MY PANTS! In the mid-'80s the punk underground took itself very seriously indeed. The Chicago scene was dominated by the square-jawed, broad-shouldered men of arty noise-rock bands like Naked Raygun, the Effigies, and Big Black. Along came Screeching Weasel, a bunch of giddy, longhaired geeks spewing random venom ("I Hate Old People," "I Hate Led Zeppelin") and proudly championing the culture of the strip mall ("Hey Suburbia," "Murder in the Brady House"). Their sets usually ended with "I Wanna Be Naked," and pogoing fans cheerfully followed Foster's lead by disrobing in the mosh pit.

Other band members came and went—fellow suburban doofuses given *noms de Weasel* like Steve Cheese, Brian Vermin, Dan Vapid, and Dan Panic— and the group released a string of snotcore classics including *My Brain Hurts* (1991), *Wiggle* (1992), and *Bark Like a Dog* (1996), each one a little more melodic and self-assured than the last. The audience grew as the band toured the underground circuit, found an adoptive home in San Francisco's

Gilman Street scene, and became the first act outside California to sign to Lookout! But its leader was increasingly ambivalent about success.

On the one hand Foster courted stardom and knew his band deserved it. "My friends are getting famous / Oh what can I do?" he sang in 1994. "My friends are getting famous / And I think I oughta, too!" On the other hand he was appalled by the mediocrity that often followed platinum success. He was allergic to compromise of any kind, and he derided bands that weren't, branding them hypocrites.

"People in the mainstream press who like the band always ask, 'Why is it that a band like Blink-182 or Green Day is so popular and Screeching Weasel haven't reached that level of success?'" Foster says. "It's probably ninety-five percent by choice. Not that we sat down and said, 'We don't want to be that popular,' but we made certain decisions that prohibit that. I was never willing to be on the road as much as Green Day."

Skeptics counter that Foster thwarted his band's chances of breaking big by living according to a rigid if inscrutable code of DIY conduct and serving as the self-appointed arbiter of all that was "authentically" punk. From 1990 through 1995 he penned a notorious column for the punk-rock bible *MaximumrockNRoll,* making endless pronouncements about the way things ought to be and taking to task nearly everyone in the underground. Sonic Youth reprinted one diatribe on the sleeve of a 1988 twelve-inch: "While D.R.I. & 7 Seconds may very well be the Bon Jovi & U2 of the '90s, Sonic Youth & Hüsker Dü will be the Yes & REO Speedwagon. Bleeaacchh!!" In one sentence Foster eliminated four potential allies, and he repeated this routine time after time.

"Ben's got opinions on everything, from what kind of tennis shoes you should wear to how you should wash your jeans, what records you should listen to, and how you should play your guitar," says Lookout! president Chris Appelgren, who nonetheless adds that the group's importance to the label "has been immeasurable." After fellow Chicagoan Steve Albini, Ben Weasel became the underground's most infamous grump—the punk everyone loved to hate. The Queers even penned a song in his honor: "He rants and raves, he screams and shouts / He always flips his lid / But deep down inside / He really loves you kids."

TODAY BEN FOSTER is a different man from the Ben Weasel of the early '90s. Back then he never imagined he and Pierson would be able to buy homes and cobble together careers from the band, especially at a point when they rarely perform live. Foster owns a sunny six-room condo in Oak

Park, a mannered suburb best known for its Frank Lloyd Wright architecture. His living room is dominated by a giant TV and an impressive stereo system and his new Honda is parked downstairs. Punk rock has been very, very good to him; he estimates that he and Pierson gross upward of fifty-five thousand dollars a year each from Screeching Weasel record sales and merchandise.

"At nineteen or twenty years old, I would look at a person like me now and I'm certain that I would have criticisms," Foster says. "I realize that when I was that age, I was criticizing people without having lived enough in punk rock to understand certain realities, and I've retracted some of those things through the years. I think if you're my age and you're still mired in negativity, you've got some serious problems. Frankly I'd be embarrassed if I was still acting that way."

This is a lesson learned the hard way, and one he doesn't mind showing off. His shirt—which bears the goofball Moral Crux phrase I WAS A TEENAGE TEENAGER—barely hides two new tattoos that cover earlier inkings inspired by his high school sweetheart. In 1998 a painful divorce ended their twelve-year relationship, exacerbating his agoraphobia. Foster had been plagued by occasional panic attacks since he was nineteen, but they then intensified. "A doctor described it as the worst feeling a human being can feel outside of physical pain," he says. "Your heart is racing, your palm is sweating, and you feel like somebody's got a gun to your head. The blood rushes from your head, your legs feel a little rubbery, you're hyperventilating, and you get a little bit of tunnel vision. The reason people get agoraphobic is that they associate these attacks with certain situations"—say, leaving the apartment—"and they start avoiding them at any cost."

Meditation, cognitive techniques to control his breathing, and group therapy all helped, as did the occasional use of prescription drugs such as Xanax. But Foster's best remedy was music. His drive to express himself finally overpowered his urge to live like a hermit. And just as the hardcore punk he'd discovered at Elan gave vent to his anger, his own pop-punk anthems helped him express feelings he couldn't otherwise articulate.

Screeching Weasel always mixed its more bilious ditties with outpourings of heartfelt emotion, but the latter dominate the last two albums. Tunes like "Acknowledge," "I'll Stop the Rain," and "Molecule" chronicle Foster's personal low points with a tough self-deprecating wit that evokes Charles Bukowski at his best. At the same time they emphasize that the joy of being alive outweighs the inevitable pain. "You've gotta have love in your heart / And you've gotta have pain in your life / And you've gotta have some vision and confusion for some peace of mind," Foster sings over the killer hook in "Bottom of the 9th."

"With Ben, like with a lot of creative people, when it's darkest, they take that moment to actually glance up at the sun," Pierson says. These days the two founding Weasels both have ambitions outside the band. A member of the well-regarded Neo-Futurists theater troupe, Pierson has self-published a collection of his plays, *The Incomplete Philosophy of Hope and Nonthings*, while Foster has completed a novel called *Like Hell*. Both say that Screeching Weasel's current lineup of bassist Mass Giorgini, drummer Dan Lumley, and second guitarist Phillip Hill is the most accomplished the group has ever had. But the band is not without its critics.

"The influence of Screeching Weasel on punk cannot be understated, but their insistence on staying a band long past their expiration date has only cheapened their legacy," says Dan Sinker, editor of the Chicago fanzine *Punk Planet*. "As a nostalgia act, they can still be entertaining, but their relevance to the modern punk scene has long since disappeared."

Foster draws strength from such barbs. He loves being the underdog and relishes opportunities to prove people wrong. At the House of Blues, Screeching Weasel tears through its set with precision and passion. The musicians encore with a reworked version of "What We Hate," a 1991 song about the inevitability of compromise. "You're all getting older, and you'll become what you hate," Foster sings, his gaze sweeping the crowd.

"We were on a roll, and to me, that was the exclamation point," the singer says afterward. "Like saying, 'We're back, and you can talk all the shit you want about us, but we're still around, and we're still doing this. Are you still going to have the same ideals and be doing whatever it is that's really important to you when you're our age?'"

Leapin' Lizards
The *Chicago Sun-Times*, August 5, 1994

IT'S NOT EASY being the Jesus Lizard. The Chicago quartet's sonic assaults and galvanizing live shows have earned it a reputation as the most uncompromising band in the rock underground. And that comes with a lot of baggage.

"A lot of people who meet us are disappointed that we're such moderately intelligent, well-balanced, happy guys," says bassist David Sims. "[Guitarist] Duane [Denison] and I spend a lot of time writing songs.

[Singer] David [Yow] and [drummer] Mac [McNeilly] are married. David is doing some acting and working a lot with computer graphics, and Mac has a family. That takes people back initially."

Fans can be excused for thinking of the Jesus Lizard as more than just four nice guys. Onstage Yow is possessed, spitting out his lyrics and hurling himself at the crowd while the band blasts away with machinelike precision. Denison is an inventive but economical guitarist, and McNeilly and Sims hammer away at the groove like a punk-rock version of the great James Brown rhythm sections.

The songs are sometimes built from the rhythms up, and Sims says he and McNeilly try for a soul or R&B swing. On *Down*, the group's fifth Touch and Go release in the last five years, there's also a greater use of dynamics. "The record comes a lot closer to approximating what we think the Jesus Lizard sounds like," Sims says. "The things we do musically that people like are still there, but we tried a couple of other things, too."

Down arrives only a few weeks after the release of the live album *Show*. Recorded during the twentieth anniversary celebration for New York's famed rock club, C.B.G.B., the album was released by a subsidiary of Giant Records, which is causing some to question whether the Jesus Lizard is making the leap to the majors.

"I never did buy into the whole indie-versus-major label thing," Sims says. "It's just the logo on the back of the record from the perspective of the person buying the album. The reason we've been with Touch and Go so long is just a business decision. We were looking for where we could get treated fairly and have the most hands-on control. We could stay forever, or maybe not, if we could find someone else who would do things the way we want. There is no party line."

Show is no more polished than any other Jesus Lizard release. It spans the group's five-year career and documents Yow at his crazed best. "It's a weird show for a live record because the crowd obviously doesn't give a shit," Sims says. "But I thought we played well, and the crowd made David so abusive that there was a comedic appeal."

Anyone who has seen the Jesus Lizard has a story about Yow's amazing stage antics. Sims says the most impressive thing he's seen the singer do was jump off the thirty-foot-high stage at England's Reading Festival. "If it hasn't killed him by now, he's more or less indestructible," the bassist says, laughing.

The Jesus Lizard is playing two shows this weekend in the homey confines of Lounge Ax before setting out on a tour that will run through mid-

December. The band likely will return to Chicago in October for a gig at the Vic Theatre. Despite the fact that Sims recently earned an accounting degree—he jokes that the band has the best-kept books in rock—neither he nor anyone else in the group believes that the band will end any time soon.

"Standing at the edge of the just-having-to-be-an-accountant abyss, I realize I could do this for years and years and be perfectly happy," he says. "It's a good job and I get to meet a lot of great people." And then he gets to confound their expectations.

Into the Sunset
The Chicago Reader, May 23, 1997

LONG BEFORE THELMA and Louise drove over the canyon's lip, there was *Quadrophenia.* In director Franc Roddam's 1979 film based on the Who's rock opera about the mod scene in swinging London, the hero, Jimmy (Phil Daniels), is last seen on his scooter, hurtling full-speed toward the edge of the white cliffs of Dover. The final image of the scooter smashing into the rocks far below left viewers forever wondering whether Jimmy careered over the edge to a certain death or jumped off in time to watch the scooter's destruction—a symbolic farewell to his mod persona and his troubled youth.

The ending of *Quadrophenia* was the first thing I thought of when I heard the news last June that Material Issue's thirty-one-year-old guitarist, singer, and songwriter Jim Ellison had been found slumped over a moped in the garage of his west Lakeview home. Apparently distraught over a recent breakup, he'd killed himself with carbon monoxide. But it's the movie image of Jimmy rather than that sad final scene of Ellison's real life that stays with me as I contemplate Material Issue's fourth (and by necessity, last) album.

Telecommando Americano consists of eleven new tracks that Ellison started and bassist Ted Ansani and drummer Mike Zelenko finished, plus the six songs from the trio's vinyl-only 1987 debut, thus bookending the band's career. With roots in Chicago's mid-'80s '60s revival scene, Ellison, like Jimmy, was a mod. Everyone knows he dressed the part, and the influence of mod heroes such as the Who and the Small Faces is loud and clear on driving upbeat pop songs such as "She's Going Through My Head," "A Very Good Thing," and "Chance of a Lifetime" from the original EP. But maybe more significantly, Ellison also had the strong work ethic, the self-confidence bordering on arrogance, and the love of a genuine good time that characterized the '60s mods. "We think people pay to see someone enjoy themselves on-stage," he told me during one of several interviews through the years. "We gladly admit to being full of ourselves and thinking we're great, otherwise we wouldn't be doing what we're doing."

This attitude turned out to be very much out of step with the prevailing ethos of the alternative era. Though Material Issue scored a respectable hit with *International Pop Overthrow*, its 1991 Mercury debut, it was overshadowed by that year's biggest success story, Nirvana's *Nevermind*. It quickly became evident that the Lollapalooza Nation preferred songs about rape (like "Polly") to songs about first dates (like most of Ellison's tunes), and angst and apathy got the edge over love and longing. Although they were nearly as strong as *International Pop Overthrow*, 1992's *Destination Universe* and 1994's *Freak City Soundtrack* (which included remade material from the first EP) each sold half as well as the last, and Material Issue soon found itself without a label.

Ellison was sending tapes of new songs to local writers by early '95, but I don't remember hearing any of the tunes that have now surfaced on *Telecommando Americano*. Songs such as "Satellite," "Young American Freak," and "2 Steps" boast Ellison's usual indelible hooks with big sing-along choruses and deft melodies driven home by new (to Material Issue) instruments such as piano, slide guitar, analog synthesizer, and xylophone. And they're every bit as memorable as the modern-rock radio staples "Valerie Loves Me," "Diane," and "What Girls Want."

In retrospect Ellison had a lot in common with Nirvana's Kurt Cobain. Both men were incurable romantics who bought into idealized and perhaps unobtainable standards for love and success, and both may have paid the ultimate price for that. A lot of critics dismissed Ellison's lyrics as the usual trite heartland rock crap about girls and cars, but they missed the fact that the objects of his desire were almost always poignantly out of reach. Like Lou Reed in "Satellite of Love," Ellison appeals to a distant orbiting entity in "Satellite" to help ease the pain of romantic betrayal here on earth. In "976–LOVE," he finds that phone sex is a poor substitute for a loving relationship, while in "Off the Hook" he discovers that his sweetheart is sending him a permanent busy signal.

Of course, as evidenced by the posthumous examinations of Cobain's every utterance, the temptation is almost irresistible for literature majors, armchair psychiatrists, and rock critics to seek answers about an artist's motives in his lyric sheets. But we also need to acknowledge that the mood of the music is often directly opposed to the mood of the lyrics. There's a palpable joy in every note of *Telecommando Americano*; singing and playing guitar were obviously life-affirming acts for Ellison. When I listen to his last album or Nirvana's *In Utero*, I hear the sound of talented if troubled artists drowning out the voice of nihilism with a blast of feedback or a ringing power chord. But then I've always believed that Jimmy jumped off the scooter.

Looney Tunes
Request, December 1990

THE GUYS IN Redd Kross were born to star in their own cartoon series. In each episode our long-haired, southern California heroes—the brothers Jeff and Steve McDonald, intrepid guitarist Robert Hecker, and a new drummer every week—would pursue an evil villain, capture a secret formula, or destroy the world-domination machine. In the process they'd win true love with animated heroines who look like members of Josie and the Pussycats. Of course the highlight would be the music: a loud, fast song for the battle against the forces of oppression, and an anthemic ballad at the end when they get the girls. It'd sure be more entertaining than those pizza-eating Ninja Turtles.

The innocence and enthusiasm in the music of Redd Kross also brings to mind getting drunk on cheap wine, playing electric guitar really loud in the garage, going to see *Phantasm* on your first real date, or buying your first Rolling Stones record and realizing it's every bit as cool as KISS.

At the ripe old ages of twenty-three and twenty-seven, Steve and Jeff McDonald are the grand old men of the Los Angeles underground rock scene. They've been making records for ten years, but they haven't forgotten what first made them fall in love with rock 'n' roll. "One of the reasons we play a lot of covers is because that's the stuff that got us excited in the first place," Steve says. "It's not a conscious thing, like, 'Let's write a song that sounds like this' or 'Let's pay tribute to trash culture.' We just write about what we know, and we try to have as much fun as possible at all times."

The brothers admit that they've had some real Ray and Dave Davies–style brawls ("Since we know each other so well, we really know how to piss each other off," Steve says), but they've had even more trouble getting along with other band members. About a dozen people have come and gone through Redd Kross ("We tend to chew drummers up and spit them out," Jeff says) and Hecker is the only non-relative who's been around for more than a year or two. When you talk about Redd Kross, you're really talking about the McDonalds, because in addition to playing bass and guitar and writing all the songs, their sense of humor and their unique worldview define the band.

The brothers grew up in Hawthorne, a middle-class suburb of Los Angeles that was also home to Brian, Dennis, and Carl Wilson. But if they admire any group of rock kin, it's the fictitious Partridge Family, not the Beach Boys. They inserted a photo of Susan Dey and a loving poem about Lori Partridge into one of their album packages and recorded with Danny Bonaduce on a studio side project called Tater Totz. They also speak with reverence about meeting David Cassidy while working on an unreleased B-movie called *1976*. (They wrote the film's title track, which appears on their new album, *Third Eye*.)

The McDonalds readily grant that southern California is a very strange place to grow up. "We love L.A., it's our lady, and we wouldn't want to live anywhere else," Steve says in a laid-back Valley accent. "We have a friend who's a very pretty girl, and she was shopping at this mall and sat down to have a cigarette. Cloris Leachman walked by, saw her, and came over and gave her a twenty-minute lecture about how an attractive young girl like that shouldn't be smoking cigarettes. Now where else could something like that happen besides L.A.?"

Jeff says his parents preferred jazz to rock, but older cousins turned him and his brother on to the Stones, "and that was our downfall." Steve was barely thirteen when he and Jeff formed a band with two high school buddies who'd later become members of Black Flag and the Circle Jerks. The brothers made their recorded debut in 1980 as Red Cross on a three-band sampler with such topical songs as "I Hate My School." By 1982 they had a new lineup, a new spelling of their name, and a new album, *Born Innocent*, with sloppy but enthusiastic songs such as the worshipful "Linda Blair" and a cover of Charles Manson's "Cease to Exist."

Redd Kross finally came into its own with 1984's *Teen Babes from Monsanto*, a college-radio classic consisting almost entirely of covers by the McDonalds' heroes (including the Stones, Bowie, KISS, the Stooges, and the bubblegum songwriting duo of Boyce and Hart). All in all it was a heavy dose of '70s nostalgia that prompted critic Ira Robbins to brand the group as "the ultimate bratty garage band."

"We're not really into the nostalgia aspect of it," Jeff says defensively. "We don't wish it was 1974 again." Indeed, while *Third Eye* has its share of tongue-in-cheek garage-rock gems—"1976," "Elephant Flares," and "Bubblegum Factory" among them—it also includes some of the McDonalds' most mature songs yet, such as the rousing Beatles-inspired "Love Is Not Love" and the Big Star–tinged "I Don't Know How to Be Your Friend," an eloquent, moving statement about unrequited love.

The album is the first by Redd Kross in three years. After five records on five different independent labels, the group was left in a lurch when its last label went bankrupt after the release of *Neurotica* in 1987. Subsequently no West Coast record company showed interest in the group, even though Redd Kross had the biggest draw of any unsigned band in Los Angeles. "For a while there, it seemed like everybody was getting signed except us," Jeff says. "If our mother formed a band, she would have gotten signed before we did. Everybody thought we were old news because we'd been around so long, and here we were like twenty-five years old!"

Redd Kross finally found enthusiastic ears on the other side of the country at Atlantic Records in New York. "We were finally able to make the record we wanted to make," Jeff says. "Nobody at Atlantic told us what to do in any way, but I'm sure there'll be some people who'll say we sold out just because we're on a major label. People say Sonic Youth sold out, and their new album is more abrasive than the last one, which was on an indie."

"It's kind of silly," Steve adds, "but I can understand it, because some of your fans consider you like personal property. I mean, we have fans in L.A. who were like five years old when we started."

The McDonalds look up to the B–52's as their role model for a band that has stayed true to its original vision while becoming an enormous popular success. "The B–52's are a huge inspiration to us. That was the one record all of us liked at the same time," Jeff says. "It was like, 'How did this record manage to be a hit?' And a huge hit at that! And then we saw them live and they were great."

"It's inspiring to see something like that that reminds you of why you started doing this, why you decided to go for a 'career' in rock 'n' roll," Steve says. "We've been doing this for ten years, and it's still a gas. There've been so many changes, it's never been boring. It's never been like a job. We've still got so much work ahead of us, but we just can't wait to get started."

With an attitude like that, can fame, fortune, and Redd Kross lunch boxes really be far behind?

Weening Ways
The *Chicago Sun-Times*, December 30, 1994

CERTAIN ALBUMS ARE made to be played at three A.M. when the party is over and there's no other way to get the last few stragglers to leave the house. After Lou Reed's *Metal Machine Music*, 1990's *God Ween Satan* is one of the best discs ever for this purpose. But in a pinch just about anything by the Brothers Ween will do.

Gene and Dean Ween (aka Aaron Freeman and Mickey Melchiondo) started playing at the Court Tavern in New Brunswick, New Jersey, back in 1987. Then they were two obnoxious sixteen-year-olds who performed to backing tapes, wore stockings over their heads to distort their features, and hopped around like they were possessed by demons. The act infuriated the large hippie population in New Brunswick's rock clubs, but it amused the students from nearby Rutgers and Princeton universities, and Ween began to build a following.

The duo's influence increased after a pair of independent releases, *God Ween Satan* and *The Pod* (1991). But no one at the Court Tavern would have ever predicted that Ween would wind up on a major label. The duo's third album, *Pure Guava*, was released on Elektra in 1992. After Beavis and Butt-Head started playing the single "Push th' Little Daisies," the duo had a hit, and now Ween is set to perform for some twenty-two thousand people at the Rosemont Horizon on New Year's Eve.

"I think that we've only played one show that big, and it was in Australia," Freeman says. "It was intense; we felt like the Rolling Stones. You're working that great P.A. system, and it's a power trip. But I'm down with it. If it was up to me, we'd be playing stadiums every night!"

Ween's second Elektra album, *Chocolate and Cheese*, is the first recorded in a standard twenty-four-track studio—most of the duo's earlier efforts were done on a four-track tape deck in the living room—but otherwise it isn't much of a departure. As always the duo satirizes a host of musical styles, from Prince to Mexican folk songs and from bad lounge music to the blues. The only constants are the warped sucking-on-helium vocals and an irreverent sense of humor that marks Dean and Gene as '90s successors to Frank Zappa.

The most striking track is "Spinal Meningitis (Got Me Down)," which features a childish voice asking the horrifying questions, "Why they wanna see my spine, Mommy? Am I gonna die?"

"In Seattle the last time we were there, we were soundchecking and these two guys in wheelchairs came in with all this stuff hooked up to them," Freeman says. "I'm sitting there thinking, 'This is it. I'm gonna stop making music. They've obviously got spinal meningitis and they're not amused.' But it turned out that they were just really big Ween fans. They asked for our autographs, and they gave us a drawing of a squirrel smoking a bong."

As could be expected, Ween's hardcore following is rather unique. "Most of the times, they're slacker, hippy, drugged-out people," Freeman says. "I don't take the time to know them too well, but I know that they sit around and snort Scotch-Guard. But that's our fault, so I can't dis it."

Touring to support the new album, Ween has been playing as a quartet with frequent collaborator Andrew Weiss on bass and Claude Coleman on drums. But at the Horizon, Gene and Dean will be doing an old-fashioned Court Tavern–style show, with Gene playing guitar and Dean singing over taped backing tracks.

"We're doing it solely for money purposes," Freeman says. "We would bring the band, but it would mean less money for us."

Seasoned pop veterans at the age of twenty-three, Gene and Dean are still obnoxious, still fond of wearing hosiery on their heads, and still possessed. And fans wouldn't have it any other way.

One Power-Filled Alternative
The *Chicago Sun-Times*, October 18, 1993

TWO-AND-A-HALF YEARS after the release of *Nevermind*, the rock world is still witnessing the results of the major-label feeding frenzy that followed Nirvana's startling success. The major record companies are releasing more weird, creative, and uncompromising music than at any point since the New Wave '70s. At the same time much of what's being marketed as alternative is nothing more than the same old garbage in hip new packaging.

Saturday's capacity show at the Aragon Ballroom offered one band from each camp. The Melvins are so wonderfully abrasive that it's hard to believe anyone would encourage them to make an album, much less Atlantic Records. In stark contrast, the members of Primus are just progressive-rock wankers in thrift-store clothing.

The Melvins formed in 1984 in Nirvana's hometown of Aberdeen, Washington. Kurt Cobain used to haul their equipment, and drummer Dale

Crover played with Nirvana early on. Naturally, the group was signed to a major label soon after Nirvana went platinum, and Cobain was recruited to co-produce their new album, *Houdini*.

The similarities between the bands end there. *Houdini* sounds like a Black Sabbath 45 left out in the sun then played at 33 R.P.M. In terms of its cheerful perversity, it makes Nirvana's *In Utero* sound like Blind Melon.

The trio is even more harsh onstage. Creating an ominous wall of sound with tidal waves of fuzz guitar, violent bass rumblings, and plodding dinosaur drums, the Melvins are loud and powerful in a way that listeners feel physically. This is music that makes breathing difficult, and it's probably hazardous to pregnant women and people with heart conditions.

Guitarist-vocalist Buzz Morrison took the stage with his trademark Eraserhead hair, a T-shirt bearing a word I can't use in the newspaper, and a stack of four Marshall amplifiers (one of which was decorated with "Mofo" written in the style of "Zoso," the cryptic legend on *Led Zeppelin IV*). Crover sat behind an oversized drum set, naked but for a pair of red panties, and bassist Mark Deutrom mugged it up beneath a giant cowboy hat. The air was still vibrating with the force of their forty-five-minute earthquake when roadies cleared the stage for Primus, the nominal headliners.

Primus combines the worst of aspects of Rush and Frank Zappa, playing indulgent prog-rock with a smarmy sense of humor. Tim Alexander took a solo on his massive drums only three songs into the set, Les Claypool bumbled around the stage playing lead bass, and guitarist Larry Lalonde simply bumbled.

Despite some funny background films, the San Francisco trio was even more obnoxious and boring than it was during Lollapalooza '93. At least then you could duck out for a smart drink.

Speaking of Geeks . . .
The *Chicago Sun-Times*, March 9, 2001

"GEEK ROCK LIVES!" declares the banner on Weezer Online, one of the group's many fan-run Web sites, and against all odds, indeed it does.

Weezer is probably best known to the alt-rock fan base for "Undone—The Sweater Song," a perfectly crafted power-pop gem from the Los Angeles quartet's self-titled 1994 debut. A hesitant, stuttering drum beat kicks off the tune, providing an uneasy bottom for two minimal intertwining guitars. A couple of typical Gen X slacker dudes compare notes at the bar of a rock club—"Hey, you know about the party after the show?" Then Rivers Cuomo's paranoid geek-boy enters the scene.

The Massachusetts-born guitarist-vocalist has more than a little of the ultimate nerd rocker Jonathan Richman in him, as well as plenty of the Talking Heads' David Byrne and the Feelies' Glenn Mercer. (The cover of the first album depicts the four Weezer boys standing in full geeky glory against an unsullied light blue background, an homage to the cover of the Feelies' *Crazy Rhythms*.) There are no real lyrics in the verse, just an assault of incomplete thoughts. "Oh me . . . maybe . . . God damn . . . I am," Cuomo sputters Tony Perkins–style, a man on the verge of a nervous breakdown. Then the Cheap Trick–meets–the Pixies chorus charges in, propelled by a massive fuzz guitar and an anthemic hook.

"If you want to destroy my sweater / Pull this thread as I walk away!" If the '90s produced a better depiction of adolescent romantic angst, I missed it.

It would have been easy to dismiss Weezer as just another one-hit wonder in a golden age for them if the group hadn't matched the success of that single with two more modern-rock radio hits, "Buddy Holly" and "Say It Ain't So." Still, Cuomo and his bandmates were sensitive to that charge, so they chose to produce their second album, *Pinkerton*, themselves (former Cars leader Ric Ocasek had been behind the board for the debut), and they refused to pander to MTV with flashy videos like the Spike Jonze–directed clip for "Buddy Holly" (a sly spoof on *Happy Days* that attracted as much attention as the tune itself).

You could therefore blame Weezer for its own failure with *Pinkerton*, even though it was every bit as strong as its predecessor. (The single "The Good Life" in particular was a witty and infectious indictment of alt-rock hype.) Or you could just say that 1996 was the year the alternative bubble burst, and Weezer was just one of many victims. Either way the group's sophomore album flopped, and the band disappeared from the scene. Bassist Matt Sharp quit to devote himself to his side project, the synth-pop combo the Rentals (they scored a hit with "Friends of P," and that one really *was* a one-hit wonder). Meanwhile Cuomo enrolled in the country's number-one nerd institution, Harvard. But Weezer's head geek couldn't quite shake the rock 'n' roll bug.

"I didn't graduate; I did three years," Cuomo told the online music site, CD Now. "That was one of the decisions that I made—I knew that at least I was sure I really wanted to concentrate on writing songs and facing this business. And to do that, I knew I had to get out of school and concentrate on it."

Now Weezer is back: Cuomo (now thirty), guitarist Brian Bell, drummer Pat Wilson, and new bassist Mikey Welsh. And no one is more surprised by the enthusiasm of its reception than Weezer itself.

"We were totally astonished," Cuomo told CD Now. "The first few shows we booked were just these tiny little clubs, like a hundred people or something; we were afraid no one would come or people would laugh and throw things. Those did well, so we did the Warped Tour—we were sure people were gonna throw things at us, 'cause we're not a punk band. But everyone loved us there, and the whole rest of the summer sold out. Now this Yahoo! tour is selling like crazy. We keep getting surprised."

After collecting some quick corporate sponsorship bucks on the current dot-com–sponsored tour, the band will release its long-awaited third album with Ocasek once again in the producer's chair, and more touring is expected in the late spring and early summer. Fans are raving about the new songs that the group's been playing on stage, and the business that it's been doing on tour may even be enough to make MTV and alternative-rock radio take notice. Not that Cuomo takes anything for granted; self-doubt is the geek-rock way.

"Your brain is always searching for reasons to doubt yourself," he says. "I'm pretty experienced with that."

Stone Loco
Request, January 1992

AGONIZING ABOUT THE pressures of recording a follow-up album or bragging about being one of the hardest working stars in show business is for the Hammers and Paula Abduls of the world. When you ask Tone-Loc what he's been up to since 1989, when *Loc-ed After Dark* hit No. 1 on the *Billboard* albums chart, he pauses, shoves a Cheeto in his mouth, and croaks, "I been home relaxing, man!"

Livin' large—playing a little basketball, cruising with his honey in his silver Mercedes convertible, kickin' back with his homies—is a priority for Tone-Loc, which may be why it's taken so long to record his second album, *Cool Hand Loc*. He doesn't even have a tape recorder at home to work on his rhymes. "I'm too lazy for that," he says with a laugh.

Anthony Terrell Smith, aka Tone-Loc, was an unlikely candidate for pop superstardom when he recorded his low-budget debut for a fledgling independent label, Delicious Vinyl. A husky, middle-class kid who played soccer and grew up in Texas, he moved to Los Angeles as a teen and claims to have survived some wild days as a gangbanger before stumbling onto the rap scene.

His career took off when "Wild Thing" shot to the top of the charts, propelled by a sampled Van Halen guitar lick, a grainy black-and-white video that parodied Robert Palmer's "Addicted to Love," and some horny rhymes delivered in a hoarse, four-A.M. rasp. No one was more surprised by this success than Tone-Loc, and he's taken it in stride. "I was just the average cool everyday kind of guy that I was, then the next thing you know, I was up there making records," he says. "The only way my life has really changed is that people recognize me. But myself, I'm still the same person, I do believe. I haven't changed that much. I see a lot of celebrities that I know, how they are and how they treat people, and it's kind of wack. I think you should be real happy if you've been blessed enough to have any type of success in this business."

Fans relate to Tone-Loc because there's no show-business phoniness about him; unlike, say, Hammer, it's not hard to imagine sharing a six-pack and a Lakers game with him. Some critics have portrayed him as a no-talent, giving credit for his success to producers Mike Ross and Matt Dike or Marvin Young (aka Young M.C.), coauthor of "Wild Thing" and "Funky Cold Medina." But it was Tone-Loc's inimitable delivery and laid-back persona that made those singles successful. His scowl and the sarcastic, "Hasta la vista, baby" at the end of "Wild Thing" did as much to make it a hit as the guitar riff or the lyrics. Like many an unforgettable character in rock 'n' roll, Tone-Loc is a star by the sheer force of his personality.

Cool Hand Loc is a stronger, funkier album than its predecessor, and it should dispel any lingering questions about Tone-Loc's abilities: He wrote seven of the ten tracks, cowrote the other three, and coproduced along with Ross, Dike, and Tony J. "This one has a lot more me involved in it," he says. "Before it was, 'I'll sit up there, I'll do the track, and I'm outta here,' you know what I'm saying? I don't have the patience for this shit. Mixing and all this kind of crap—I'm gone. But then sometimes I would hear something and it would be too late to change it, so I had to become more involved in my product."

The new album may disappoint fans who are only familiar with Tone-Loc's hits; there's no "Wild Thing, Part 2." Hardcore hip-hop fans who dismissed him as a novelty act who was too pop for his own good are also in for a surprise: The grooves are stronger, the rhymes are less corny, and the rock guitar samples that served as hooks on *Loc-ed After Dark* have been replaced by an R&B horn section and layers of real percussion.

"*[Cool Hand Loc] is* a lot more me. It's a lot smoother," the rapper says. "I'm into the more slower, groovier, funkier-type rhymes. I'm not into all the hype-hype-hype and shit. I like the laidback type shit. I have to establish myself with a strong R&B background, you know what I mean? Because that's my main thing in the first place. I never tried to be on the pop charts or anything like that. I'm glad it happened, it was wonderful, but I have to keep my strong R&B background as well."

Since Tone-Loc became the first California rapper to achieve mainstream success, hip-hop has split into two camps, with Afrocentric "edutainers" such as Public Enemy and Boogie Down Productions on one side and gangsta rappers such as N.W.A and Ice-T on the other. Tone-Loc says he enjoys rappers working in both styles and sees his music as the middle ground. But despite his experiences as a gang member back in the days when he earned his nickname by acting "loco," he's avoided laying down any gangsta rhymes. "I gangbanged for several years," he says. "I've been shot. I've been in fights. Man, I actually *lived* that shit, so I don't have to go out there and talk about it constantly."

Unlike Ice-T, Tone-Loc has never been too specific about his gangbanging days. He may not want his past catching up with him in the form of an overzealous rival gang member, or he may realize it's more romantic when left to the imagination. "There's a big mystery about Tone-Loc: 'Which gang is Tone-Loc from?' Nobody ever really figured out," he says. "Crips knew that I was probably one of them, but there are so many Crip gangs that Crips fight against one another, as well as fight Bloods, so I had pretty much everybody curious and wanting to know."

One subject that Tone-Loc isn't reluctant to discuss is his fondness for smoking pot. "Cheeba Cheeba" from his first album is a funny homage to the herb in which he raps about the joys of getting stoned and pigging out on junk food while watching *Late Night with David Letterman.* On *Cool Hand Loc,* "Mean Green" continues the praise of marijuana and argues against legalization because the government "would only fuck it up or chemicalize it." "Just say no" is obviously not in Loc's vocabulary, but he denies that he's encouraging kids to follow his example. "All I'm doing is just being Tone," he says. "I'm not one of these people who's afraid to speak out about what I do. I admit that I smoke bud, but I don't do any other types of drugs, you know what I mean?

"I think people are just too critical. I've never known anybody to steal a car over weed. I've never known anybody to wreck a car, or lose their whole family, or get in all kinds of debt, or all these crazy things that happen from other drugs. It's not an addictive drug. You're not gonna sit there and get the shakes if you don't have that joint. I'm just trying to let people be a little more open about it, because if they see me being more open about it, then maybe they will as well."

Tone-Loc also freely offers his opinion of Marvin Young, who's pursuing a solo career after a bitter split with Delicious Vinyl that stems in part from the lack of credit he received as coauthor of "Wild Thing" and "Funky Cold Medina." "First of all, 'Wild Thing' was like totally a Tone-Loc concept, and I wrote half of it," Loc says peevishly. "The other half was too dirty, you know what I'm saying? I couldn't really write that style that [Ross and Dike] wanted to hear because it's for a cornier type person, someone who's a little bit more nerdy, and [Young] fit the bill. He was perfect for that type of shit. The lyrics on any of these songs are not really that great. I always felt that it was the personality and the sound of the voice. He did what he did, but I think he really took a bit more credit than what he really deserved, know what I mean?"

On *Cool Hand Loc*, the rapper stretches out in several new directions, trying his hand at two slow, romantic jams ("I Adore You" and "Why?") as well as a two-part dub-reggae tribute to his Los Angeles neighborhood, "Funky Westside." But the two tunes closest in spirit to "Wild Thing" will probably get the most attention. "Fatal Attraction" borrows the title of the movie and relates Tone-Loc's comical close call with an obsessive groupie, and his unofficial theme song, "Freaky Behavior," includes a litany of his most outrageous adventures ("Since I'm from Cali, I do a little swimmin' / This one particular time, I had whole pool full of women").

How many of these lyrics are based on real experience? "Bits and pieces," the artist says with a chuckle. "You have to add a little zing to it for when you're shooting the video. I've had someone who would not leave me the hell alone. We just kind of dramatized it a little bit. And I'll always have freaky behavior; I just can't help myself."

Despite his bragging, Tone-Loc says he doesn't consider himself a sexy guy. "I used to before I made records—all my life I thought I was—but once you make records you can't think that anymore, otherwise you're big-headed and a snob. I think I'm a cool individual. I think I'm real cool, and I think I'm a nice person, and man, that's the biggest compliment I can give myself."

Loc's attitude toward women isn't exactly enlightened ("I keep a steady girlfriend, but it's hard," he says. "It's a rough business because you see a lot of beautiful women and they know that you know"). Coming from another rapper, some of his macho boasts would be tired and offensive, but it's hard to take anything Tone-Loc says too seriously. A strong sense of humor runs through everything he does, and he's often the butt of his own jokes, whether he's discovering that he picked up a man in "Funky Cold Medina" or being chased out of his house at knife-point by a woman who caught him cheating in "Fatal Attraction."

"I'm silly, man. I'm a silly motherfucker," he says. "If there's one thing I like to do in life it's just laugh, and I can never get enough laughter. I think everybody in this world takes everything too seriously. Me, myself, I can't be around uptight people. I like people just to relax and chill. I'm that type of person, and I always have been."

....

THE CONNECTION

Tone-Loc	**Reg Presley**
Unlikely, overweight, marginally talented rapper-comedian.	Unlikely, overweight, marginally talented singer-comedian with the garage band the Troggs.

Breakthrough Hit

"Wild Thing"	"Wild Thing"

Favorite Lyrical Topic

Sex	Sex

Best Sexy Lyric

"That's what happens when bodies start slappin' 'n' doin' the wild thing!"	"Your slacks are low and your hips are showin'."

Criticisms

Didn't write his own hits; not a "real" rapper.	Didn't write his own hits; not a "real" rocker.

Motto

"I can't help myself!"	"I can't control myself!"

....

An Arresting Development in Hip-Hop
The *Chicago Sun-Times*, June 12, 1994

IF ARRESTED DEVELOPMENT'S much-lauded multiplatinum debut, 1991's *3 Years, 5 Months and 2 Days in the Life of . . .*, was largely about rediscovering the family traditions of the South, the follow-up, *Zingalamaduni*, is about drawing inspiration from the rich legacy of the last four decades of African-American music.

The opening track features senior-citizen percussionist Baba Oje reading the playlist for an ideal radio station with the call letters WMFW ("We Must Fight and Win"). "This hour we've got Bob Marley, the sound of Miriam Makeba and Mutabaruka," Oje announces. "Public Enemy's brand-new sounds, Curtis Mayfield, an old one from Isaac Hayes, a brand-new one from Tracy Chapman . . . and, last but not least . . . brand-new sounds by Arrested Development!"

"WMFW" is intended to make a point about the depressing state of radio: No one station would play such a broad collection of music today, let alone mix Arrested Development's brand of "alternative rap" with alternative rock. But the more subtle message is that the group is the '90s offspring of a rich and varied collection of musical greats. The disc takes its name from a Swahili term that means "beehive of culture." "We thought that was a good way to describe the album—the direction it was going in," says the group's primary rapper, Speech.

Speech is Arrested Development's founder and leader, but even he can't tell you exactly how the "beehive" works. "Your guess is as good as mine," he says with a chuckle. He writes most of the music and lyrics but he gives DJ Headliner, drummer Rasa Don, dancers Montsho Eshe and Aerle Taree, and dancer, vocalist, percussionist, and spiritual adviser Baba Oje equal billing as part of what he calls "the Arrested Development extended family."

A former student at the Art Institute of Atlanta, Speech grew up in a middle-class neighborhood in Milwaukee, where his parents owned the *Milwaukee Community Journal.* He co-wrote a regular column for the twice-weekly paper called "20th Century African" until Arrested Development's career began to take off. "I was writing music before I ever wrote the column," he says. "My parents owned the paper, and I realized it could be an outlet to get things across to people who I felt really needed to hear another perspective. To me, it was just an extension of what I'm doing with music."

On both of Arrested Development's albums, Speech's raps address such pressing issues as prejudice, the need for African-American unity, safe sex, and the role of religion in bringing about social change. The group's break-through hit, "Tennessee," is a sentimental call for the sense of family he experienced as a teenager visiting his grandparents in the small town of Henning. But while most of his lyrics are uplifting and positive to the extent that some have called him a hippie, he doesn't hesitate to get tough, and he famously attacked gangsta rappers in the song "Give a Man a Fish."

"Arrested Development is really trying to make social change and economic change, and gangsters don't play a part in change because they don't control their own lives," Speech says. "They're being pimped by oppression like most people are being pimped, but the gangsters are allowing it to happen. I think music motivates people, it inspires people positively or negatively, depending on the music."

Arrested Development's outspoken criticism of the gangster mentality, its devotion to melody, and its musical genre-hopping have prompted some to peg the group as the leading light of a genre called alternative rap. It began with the Jungle Brothers, De La Soul, A Tribe Called Quest, and Digital Underground and continues today with other groups such as P.M. Dawn, Me Phi Mi, and the Disposable Heroes of Hiphoprosy. But the tag doesn't sit well with Speech. "What that implies is that this is not rap, this is an alternative to rap, and I think that limits what rap is," he says. "We're just an extension of hip-hop. People who say they don't like hip-hop, but they like us, well, they *do* like hip-hop."

The first impression of *Zingalamaduni* is that the fifteen tunes are mellower and groovier than out-of-the-box hits such as "Tennessee" and "People Everyday" from the band's debut (which was named for the length of time it took the group to secure a recording contract). But songs such as "United Minds" and "Achen' for Acres" pack subtle keyboard and horn hooks that keep you coming back. The drums and percussion were recorded live, and Arrested Development makes better use of backing vocals, including the soaring gospel-style singing of Nadirah, who joined the group before its appearance on MTV's *Unplugged*.

Performing a rare club gig at Chicago's Park West in May, the new material came to life during an enthusiastic and uplifting two-hour party. (The band plans to return on an arena tour in late summer, possibly as part of

Peter Gabriel's WOMAD Festival.) "We're calling our show a celebration, and that's what we do," Speech says. But even the group's catchiest melodies carry a hard-hitting message.

"You're just a shell until you learn to rebel," is the chorus of one song. As on the first album, Arrested Development calls for a positive social revolution, but this time, it also offers some advice for dealing with the status quo. "Achen' for Acres" encourages African-Americans to control their neighborhoods by buying land and building housing, "United Minds" calls for global concern for human rights, and "Warm Sentiments" is an anti-abortion song that argues for a more responsible—and old-fashioned—approach to sex.

"Maybe we'll get married and then we'll be intimate / And from then on we'll share and bare our warm sentiments," Speech raps in his distinctive nasal style. These lines are a sharp contrast to the view of male-female relationships offered by Snoop Doggy Dogg and other gangsta rappers. The rap magazine *The Source* has dubbed Arrested Development "the anti-gangstas," and many hardcore hip-hoppers have attacked the group for selling out by performing on Lollapalooza '93. Speech still bristles over the charges.

"We made that record three years ago, and we didn't know where it was going to go or who it was going to reach," he says. "If you want to say that we sold out or crossed over, it's ridiculous, 'cause it ain't like we remixed the album and put some Eric Clapton on it or something to try to sell more records. As far as on tour, we toured wherever people asked us to tour. We did small club tours, and we did Lollapalooza. We did charity gigs at Malcolm X Park in Washington, D.C., and we did a gig at Penn State University. Our message was never diluted, whether we were performing at Penn State or Malcolm X Park. And every time, before every celebration, we prayed to life, death, and the struggle of our ancestors."

Arrested Development's fascination with African-American history, its intense environmentalism, and its campaign against gangsta misogyny have also resulted in criticisms that the group is too preachy, but those are charges that Speech can live with. "The powers that be have such a grip on popular culture that they can just reign supreme and do whatever they want to do to the masses," he says. "When somebody speaks up against it, then you're being too preachy. Well, we the people, the masses that are being affected by these problems, we don't need to let it happen. Power to the preacher! Power to the person who gives a damn! Hopefully, he or she can help somebody else."

The P.M. Dawn of a New Day in Hip-Hop
The *Chicago Sun-Times*, June 13, 1993

TO APPRECIATE THE philosophy of P.M. Dawn, you have to know a bit about the place the hip-hop duo calls home. Just across the Hudson River from Manhattan, their hometown of Jersey City, New Jersey, has all the problems of its larger neighbor and none of the charm. The state took control of the city's public schools after decades of political patronage and neglect. The last elected mayor is serving time in federal prison for extortion. And drugs, racism, and street crime are pervasive forces that few people manage to avoid.

Attrel Cordes, Jr., grew up in these gray surroundings as an introverted, overweight misfit. But instead of letting reality drag him down, he chose to ignore it, creating an alternative universe through music. "Reality used to be a friend of mine," he sang, and reincarnated as Prince Be, he and his brother Jarrett (aka DJ Minutemix) became the pop success story of 1991.

P.M. Dawn's debut, *Of the Heart, of the Soul, of the Cross: The Utopian Experience*, sold eight hundred fifty thousand copies and spawned four hits. The follow-up, *The Bliss Album . . . ? (Vibrations of Love and Anger and the Ponderance of Life and Existence)*, peaked at No. 30 on Billboard's pop albums chart, but it's climbing again, spurred by the success of the single "Looking Through Patient Eyes."

The particulars of Prince Be's philosophy—a cross between Catholicism, Zen mysticism, and the teachings of Edgar Cayce—are difficult for the most patient listener to grasp. But his broader message of self-reliance and spiritual transcendence is obviously inspiring. "I just sort of live a fantasy," he says. "I can understand things in a surrealistic way. I don't like dealing with reality, and I can change all of it, if I think hard enough or have faith in myself and in spirituality."

Comments like this have earned P.M. Dawn a reputation as hip-hop hippies, but the group isn't that easy to pigeonhole. Prince Be, twenty-two, and DJ Minutemix, twenty-one, claim they've never tried hallucinogens or any other drug. But their second album places them in a tradition of psychedelic visionaries that includes artists as diverse as Prince, Stevie Wonder, and their heroes, the Beatles. "To me, psychedelia is finding something tangible that you can hold on to in the unusual, and that's what any innovator does," Prince Be says. "That happened with the Beatles. They were trying to find something new because they were tired of just guitars and drums, so they started using sitars and xylophones and all kinds of stuff. It's just finding innovative ways of making music, to make it different, to make it sound more and more fresh."

With its funky, laid-back beats, sweet pop hooks, ambient mixes, fluid rapping, and soulful singing, P.M. Dawn has expanded hip-hop's horizons and paved the way for a wave of "alternative rappers" that includes Arrested Development, Digable Planets, and Basehead. But the group's success also has prompted a backlash from hardcore hip-hoppers who consider the group soft. Prince Be has been criticized for refusing to call himself a rapper; in one well-publicized incident, KRS-One of Boogie Down Productions bum rushed a P.M. Dawn performance in the spring of '92 and pushed Prince Be off the stage. The singer was angry, but he waited until the new album to strike back.

Over a driving groove on the song "Plastic," Prince Be asks, "What's hard at first, but melts in the heat? They call that plastic." "If there's a real culprit in the hip-hop community, it's the person who made up the terms 'hardcore' and 'alternative,'" Prince Be says. "We were trying to be innovative, and the definition of hardcore is being traditional. If you do that continuously, it's like water: Water that doesn't move goes stagnant, and I couldn't see that happening to myself or hip-hop. I am a songwriter and I write whatever comes out, which is predominantly rap. I refuse to call it that because when people hear the word 'rapper,' they think, 'half a songwriter.' I wasn't saying it as a negative energy toward rappers; it was to provoke a positive statement."

Hardcore rappers aside, P.M. Dawn's peers have been quick to recognize the duo's talent. Prince and Paul McCartney have praised the group and volunteered samples, and Prince Be and his brother are producing and writing songs for new albums by Aretha Franklin, Paula Abdul, and supermodel Naomi Campbell. DJ Minutemix sums up the pair's simple production technique: "We fit their style, but we do it in a P.M. Dawn sort of way."

Prince Be prefers studio work to touring and says he would be happy if the group played live only at occasional benefits. But this is one of the rare topics that prompts disagreement from his soft-spoken brother. "The only reason why we didn't tour last time is because our stage performance was nowhere near how new and different our music was," DJ Minutemix says. "We had to wait until everything was correct, but now the band is kickin' and the show is really good."

A recent appearance on *The Tonight Show* proved he wasn't exaggerating. The Cordes brothers fronted a thirteen-member band that pushed their grooves to new heights. Unfortunately, the band's only other recent performances have been as part of a monthlong gig at Disney World. "I fucking hate it," says the usually mild-mannered Prince Be, growing irate. "Mickey is a fucking fascist! It's hell."

The band took the gig, he says, "because we did a whole bunch of benefits, didn't make any money, and had to use Disney to come out of the hole."

Like "Plastic," this outburst is refreshing because it shows another side of P.M. Dawn. Prince Be is no New Age prophet dishing out readymade platitudes, but a genuine, multilayered talent who shows every indication of being a force in the music world for quite some time. These days, he's mobbed by children who run up to hug him and teenage fans who ask for his autograph every time he walks the streets of Jersey City. But he isn't looking to be anyone's hero.

"I don't really want to take responsibility for being a role model, because I'm not actually a complete person," he says. "When I look at a role model, they have to be totally into it; they have to be flawless, basically. And the only person to me who was flawless was Jesus Christ. I only say, 'These are my emotions, this is how I feel,' and I can't really go past that because I don't know anything.

"All my records are questions," he adds. "Sometimes, I find things out because some questions can cancel others out. And some questions can answer other questions. The thing is, I'm constantly learning. That's what it's like to be alive."

The Aphex Twin, *Richard D. James*
Request, February 1997

ALTERNATIVE ROCK'S DEATH rattle has prompted more than a few big-time media players to bet that techno will be the next "next big thing." Danny Goldberg, who had a thing or three to do with the rise of Nirvana and modern rock, is investing heavily in dance music as president of Mercury Records. MTV executives recently trumpeted a move to air more nonalternative, nonrap videos. And network–TV news shows ranging from *Hard Copy* to *20/20* have been weighing in with alarmist rave-scene exposes, recalling the moshing panic of a few years back. But if techno *does* become the sound of young America, don't expect Richard D. James to be its poster boy, deserving though he may be.

A native of Cornwall, England, James is obsessed with the mechanics of music-making: As a kid, he took apart and reassembled the living-room piano. Under the names the Aphex Twin, Polygon Window, AFX, and numerous other aliases, he showed that he could make entire tracks with, say, the sounds produced by tapping on a Coke can. James is to techno what Hüsker Dü and the Minutemen are to alternative rock: He's a founding father and a ubiquitous influence, but he's too damn iconoclastic and inspired to be marketed for mass consumption à la the lowest-common-denominator Chemical Brothers or the Prodigy. Like the indie rockers of yore, he revels in his marginality because of the creative freedom it gives him. He's dedicated to blurring genre boundaries, moving from quiet ambient house to frantic jungle, and from regal synth rock to grating *musique concrète*, often in the space of one song.

James's 1994 American major-label debut, *Selected Ambient Works Volume II*, includes some of the most serene sounds this side of the Orb, but his hobby is the not-too-blissful pastime of driving a vintage Daimler Ferret Mark 3 tank through the Cornwall countryside. None of his recordings has captured those competing impulses to lull you to sleep and blast out your eardrums as well as *Richard D. James*, the third and best album by the Aphex Twin. James has turned inward for inspiration, painting aural pictures of real and imagined scenes from his childhood. "Goongumpas" is a fanciful tune that wouldn't sound out of place on the soundtrack to *Willy Wonka and the Chocolate Factory*; the dominant instrument on "Logan Rock Witch" is a kid's pennywhistle; the chugga-chugga rhythm and synthesized steel drums on "Fore Street" evoke a wild ride on a toy train; and a stern call of "Richard!" interrupts the proceedings on the percussion-crazed "4," bringing to mind a parent intruding on an overly enthusiastic bedroom recording session.

As his adventures with the family piano indicate, James was a bit of a devil as a child. "Beetles" brings to mind the sound of a boy frying bugs on the sidewalk with a magnifying glass, and "To Cure a Weakling Child" shows flashes of the sort of sadism found only on elementary school playgrounds. "Milkman" is a nursery-rhyme sing-along that sounds as wholesome as a glass of Vitamin-D–fortified, until you realize that James is chanting, "I would like some milk from the milkman's wife's tits." If you doubt that young Richard's sexual urges developed early on, the romantic Nino Rota–style strings on "Girl/Boy Song" are made for passionate seductions, and the tune appears in three mixes, each one hotter and hornier than the one before.

The raucous undercurrents of even his calmest tunes and the sources of many of his most common sounds are what link James to the rock tradition. The background burbles on "Milkman" bring to mind "Alan's Psychedelic Breakfast" from Pink Floyd's *Atom Heart Mother*, the sleek analog synthesizers on "Peek 824542,01" could have been lifted from Kraftwerk's "Neon Lights," and the springy, bargain-basement electronic drums throughout the album recall Brian Eno's primitive drum machines on *Another Green World*. With *Richard D. James*, the Aphex Twin solidifies his position as an electronic-music mastermind who has earned a spot beside these revered innovators.

The Orb, Orblivion
Audio, March 1997

IT'S THE END OF THE WORLD as we know it and Dr. Alex Patterson is feeling just fine. Returning with his seventh release under the moniker of the Orb, the grandfather of ambient house and the master of transcendental techno has made the cheeriest album about millennial tension and apocalyptic craziness that you're likely to hear. Not since Prince's *1999* has the beginning of the end sounded like so much fun.

With music industry institutions from MTV to *Billboard* rushing to proclaim that electronica is the next "next big thing," the contributions of veterans like Patterson and Richard James (aka the Aphex Twin) are being overlooked while relatively slight talents such as the Prodigy and the Chemical Brothers are being lauded. The same thing happened when grunge took off and no one had the time of day for pioneers such as Hüsker Dü, the Replacements, and Mudhoney. Such is life. Meanwhile, Patterson is at his turntables leading a new version of the Orb with Andy Hughes and Thomas Fehlmann, and the group is making some of the best music of its career.

On 1991's *The Orb's Adventures Beyond the Ultraworld* and 1992's *U.F.Orb*, Patterson merged the sounds of Brian Eno's ambient efforts, Pink Floyd's interstellar overdrives, a bit of Hawkwind's space rock, and cutting-edge electronic dance music. But the DJ seemed to lose his way with the bleak industrial tones of 1994's *Pomme Fritz* and the bland, almost–New Age Muzak of 1995's *Orbus Terrarum*. Part of the problem was that those recordings lacked a coherent narrative, but Patterson has returned to the conceptual shenanigans of older songs like "Little Fluffy Clouds" and "The Blue Room" for *Orblivion*, using well-chosen samples to tell the story and set the scenes for his imaginative and hypnotic soundscapes.

Over the ominous sounds of "S.A.L.T.," a paranoid Scottish preacher predicts that the number of the Beast described in The Book of Revelations is showing up on our credit cards. Elsewhere, a solemn voice intones, "The rocket is waiting," and a perplexed weather girl stumbles when she reads that temperatures tomorrow will be sub-zero, "continued mild." Throw in a snippet from Joe McCarthy's red-baiting Senate hearings and a hysterical commercial jingle with a bouncy chorus about "the youth of America on LSD" and you may find yourself rushing in a panic to the bomb shelter.

Once you get there, *Orblivion* will certainly keep you entertained. Considering the subject matter, it's ironic that "Delta MKII," "DJ Asylum," and "Toxygene" contain some of the Orb's happiest hooks ever, as well as the uniquely fluid and jazzy mid-tempo grooves that have come to characterize the combo's live performances. Like the ravers who throw roof-top parties to greet the aliens in the blockbuster film *Independence Day*, Patterson is going out dancing, and judging from the pleasantly disorienting swirl of sounds in his patented Orb mixes, he's probably high as a kite. And why not? In his warped but wonderful vision, the end of the world is just one more groovy trip.

Nine Inch Nails, *The Fragile*
New Times Los Angeles, September 17, 1999

NOW THAT THE dust has settled on that relatively brief but well-hyped era known as alternative rock, it's fairly obvious that the Lollapalooza Nation produced only one artist whose particular brand of rock excelled at every level: musical intensity, emotional content, and intellectual core. (How's the heroin up in heaven, Kurt?) Of course, the class of '92 also gave us a number of amusing clowns—hello, Courtney!—and two significant if flawed sonic innovators—if not the Pink Floyds of our generation, then at least the Steely Dans.

On 1989's *Pretty Hate Machine* and especially 1994's *The Downward Spiral*, Trent Reznor created a language all his own—a unique musical Esperanto—hand-crafting each verb and adjective electronically out of discarded mechanical noises and unrecognizable shards of "real" instrumental sounds.

He built on the industrial foundation of genre architects like Ministry, Big Black, and Throbbing Gristle the way the Beatles built on the rock 'n' roll rudiments of Carl Perkins and Little Richard, in the process paving the way for the music's crass commercialization and ultimate trivialization by the likes of former buddy Marilyn Manson, Filter, and Stabbing Westward.

Blaming Reznor for the angst-ridden automatons that followed in his wake is like denigrating Little Richard for giving us Pat Boone, but there's no denying that the leeches changed the landscape. Five years in the making, *The Fragile* is the most anticipated album of 1999. Business-wise, it may prove to be a bust: The program director of one of the country's largest alternative-rock radio stations confided to me that he thinks it's "a piece of crap," and this is a man who plays "Nookie" once an hour. But the little Goths still understand, and they're likely to embrace this sprawling mess of a double album the way Lestat goes for a juicy jugular.

On tunes such as "Where Is Everybody?" and "The Mark Has Been Made," His Trentness marries the metal machine music to soulful, funky grooves, resulting in a sort of jam that's fluid and entrancing without ever being pothead-indulgent. Elsewhere, on ditties like "The Day the World Went Away," he proves he's equally adept playing with conventional rock sounds, fashioning dare-I-say beautiful soundscapes out of grand pianos that sound like grand pianos and electric guitars that sound like electric guitars. In contrast there are also alien, mind-melting sounds like the synthesized gamelan and bassoon on the intro of "Into the Void" and the marching insects of "Pilgrimage."

Nine Inch Nails devotees and recording engineers alike will be listening to *The Fragile* for years to come, on Walkmen, on fancy home stereos, and in their cars, and still discovering tasty licks and killer riffs, just as they might on another sprawling rock epic, *The Wall.* Toward that end Reznor has certainly bettered all attempts by his fellow alternative-era sonic scientist, Billy Corgan. But like the Great Pumpkin, he still falls far short of Roger Waters in giving us anything to *think about* while comfortably numbing ourselves in his noisy spew.

Despite his millionaire status and a creative freedom that other artists would kill for (he spent *five years* on this album!), poor, pitiful Trent remains mired in shallow self-pity, cheap nihilism, and plain old bad poetry. "Do you know how far this has gone? / Just how damaged have I become?" he moans in "Just Like You Imagined." Sure I do, buddy: You tell me on every tune! Aren't you able to write a lyric without the words "decay," "debris," or "defeat"?

The only time the artistry of the lyrics matches that of the music is in "Starfuckers, Inc.," a hard-rocking, vitriolic rant that's seemingly inspired by the corporate rockers who've betrayed Herr Reznor (hello, Courtney and Marilyn). Hey, Trent, let me save you a couple of grand a year on therapy and simultaneously elevate your music from merely nifty to truly magnificent: Go with that anger, work with it, and stop dragging us all down.

The End of Rock
Option, October 1997

"DID YOU SEE that PBS rockumentary thing, the twelve-part series?" asks Tortoise's Doug McCombs. "There's this quote in one of the last episodes where Laetitia from Stereolab says, 'Rock is dead; there is nothing more you can do with rock.' And then a person from L7 says, 'That's the most ridiculous thing I've ever heard!' And I guess I would have to side with the person from L7, even though our music has much more in common with Stereolab."

Four of the six members of Tortoise are seated around a makeshift plywood table in the living and working loft that they share in the industrial no man's land west of Chicago's Loop. In between fielding calls (the phone never stops ringing), mainlining extra-large coffees, and playing with Billy, the resident pooch, John Herndon, Doug McCombs, John McEntire, and Jeff Parker are listening intently to a CD of rough mixes from *TNT*, the working title of their third full-length album for Thrill Jockey Records. Two giant paintings of John Coltrane look down on the area where the instrumental combo's gear would normally be set up; right now, there are only a few stray congas, snare drums, and floor toms, as well as a vibraphone that sits below a shelf holding an impressive collection of old thermoses of the kind that Ralph Kramden used to carry to work on the bus.

It's difficult to describe this scene without giving it an air of serious self-importance that doesn't really exist. Most of the journalists who visit the Tortoise loft play up the industrial setting and the musicians' shy, soft-spoken demeanors, working some grand metaphor about a group that intellectuallizes its every move, forging a distinctive brand of "postrock" from elements of dub reggae, jazz, Krautrock, the Canterbury sound, hip-hop, and electronica. But the quickest way to see some evidence of the band members' sense of humor is to mention that phrase "postrock."

"I was just on tour with Eleventh Dream Day in Germany, and there were actually posters at one club advertising us as 'Chicago's pre-postrock legends,'" says McCombs. "Doesn't that mean we're just 'rock'?"

The musicians crack up. It's clear that journalists' failed attempts to hang a label on them is a big inside joke, and they're quick to respond when asked about the biggest misconceptions about Tortoise. "There's this idea that has been propagated that we are all very serious and we spend hours and hours in the studio," says McEntire. "And that when we're on stage, we all just stare at our instruments." He pauses for a beat. "Well, we *do* do that. But there's a big misconception about us being super-serious, because we have a lot of fun with what we do."

"I don't think there's anything I'd rather do than play in this band," Parker adds when the laughter dies down. "I think it can still be serious *and* be fun."

There was no master plan when neighbors McCombs and Herndon conceived of the band back in 1990, inspired in part by a shared passion for David Byrne and Brian Eno's *My Life in the Bush of Ghosts.* McCombs was the bassist for Eleventh Dream Day, and Herndon was the drummer in Precious Wax Drippings. Looking for a pleasant diversion from their regular gigs, they took as their role models the reggae rhythm section of Sly and Robbie, planning to record on their own as well as sitting in with other groups.

One by one other members joined the fold—not because there was a blueprint for a sound that required their services, but because they were friends who stopped by to jam and never left. The group changed its name from Mosquito after it discovered that that moniker was taken; Tortoise was chosen from the name of John Fahey's publishing company. No one had a pre-defined role—everyone in the band is best described as a multi-instrumentalist—and they all traded off on bass, guitar, Farfisa organ, Moog synthesizer, vibes, marimba, melodica, timbales, percussion, lap steel, and whatever other instruments happened to be lying around.

When the group's self-titled and rather static debut was released in 1994, the band consisted of McCombs, Herndon, McEntire, Dan Bitney, and Bundy K. Brown. Brown left shortly thereafter—his own Thrill Jockey album, *Directions in Music,* is well worth investigating—and he was replaced by Dave Pajo of Slint. Tortoise Mach 2 recorded the 1996 album, *Millions Now Living Will Never Die*. It was a significant step forward, with an extraordinary twenty-one-minute opening suite called "Djed" and five other multi-layered tracks comprising a sort of "ambient with attitude"—invigorating hipster party music somewhere between the kitsch of space-age bachelor pad exotica, the sometimes joyless precision of progressive rock, and the snoozy quality of New Age aural wallpaper.

Tortoise rarely gets credit for writing catchy tunes, but that's exactly what "The Taut and the Tame," "Along the Banks of Rivers," and even "Djed" are. "In the most general sense, I tend to think of things in a verse-chorus-bridge way, even if it's only a slight difference in texture," McCombs says. "It's there just in terms of the way I build a song. But it's kind of a weird area for me to think about, because while I think most of our stuff is 'crowd rock,' the melodies aren't always super-recognizable."

"A lot of dance or hip-hop music doesn't have melodies that are typical of whatever your standard song structure is, but it does have hooks," Herndon interjects.

"That's true," McCombs says. "But my mom tells me she likes Tortoise and listens to it a lot, and I always wonder what she's responding to."

No doubt Mrs. McCombs is grooving on the same things that excite many listeners: a certain visceral power inherent in the music (it moves you) and a sense of fun that comes through even in the more dense and complicated pieces. These are the factors that keep Tortoise firmly in the rock tradition, and which make the group kindred spirits with the best of the droning "intuitive music" bands.

Although band members say that the second album only sold about twenty-six thousand copies in the United States and twenty-five thousand in the U.K., it created a major buzz, and Tortoise became the hip name to drop, even among people who never listen to indie rock. *Rhythms, Resolutions and Clusters*, a 1995 album of remixes by Steve Albini, Brad Wood, Jim O'Rourke, and others, won admirers from the cutting-edge dance and electronic avant garde, and it cemented the band's reputation for blurring boundaries, exploring new sounds, and confounding simple genre classifications.

That's a lot of baggage to carry into a recording studio, but the musicians insist that the only pressure they felt when starting *TNT* was internal. "There *is* pressure on ourselves to push our own abilities and make music that we find interesting," McEntire says. "But that's it."

Before starting work on the new album, the band was joined by Parker, a talented jazz guitarist who plays with the New Horizons Ensemble and is a member of the prestigious Association for the Advancement of Creative Musicians. As evidenced by the rough mixes coming from the boom box at the end of the table—percolating grooves that display the influence of drum 'n' bass while maintaining the familiar fluid feel of *Millions Now Living Will Never Die*—the group is stronger than it's ever been. But the band's modest success has already put a strain on its members, particularly McEntire. His production skills are much in demand by groups such as Stereolab, Trans Am, and Come, and the sixteen-track ADAT studio that he named Soma occupies part of the Tortoise loft. He's also busy with his own band, the Sea and Cake.

"I can't think of a time in the last two years where John *didn't* have anything to do," McCombs says. But Tortoise found a new way to work. Where earlier pieces had come together in rehearsals and were recorded in relatively short periods, the new album took shape over a longer time as band members laid down instrumental lines on their own and their mates came in and built upon them, constructing the songs on tape one layer at a time.

"There was a certain point about a month ago where we thought about taking the few things that seemed most complete and making another forty-minute record out of those," Herndon says. "We could have made a really good album, but at the same time I would have been slightly disappointed that there were things that would have fallen by the wayside. We decided to take the challenge and push back the release date and finish everything—we have fifteen to twenty songs in varying stages of completion—and put out a really long double record."

"What we decided is that we didn't want to play this game of making a record every year and touring behind it, following all those rules that are imposed on everyone," McEntire says. "There is no reason to do that. We aren't competing with anyone. We are going to be doing this for a long time, so there is no reason to force this stuff out really quickly."

McEntire stops, and the band members lean back in their chairs and listen in silence to the music for a while. None of the tracks have names yet, and they're likely to change before the album's release. But from the hypnotizing sounds that fill the loft, there's every indication that Tortoise has topped itself again. Look around the table and you see the somber poker faces that the group almost always displays in photographs. But I swear I saw them trying to hide some smiles.

Psychedelic Radio Shack
City Pages, September 15, 1996

IF RUSTON, LOUISIANA, isn't officially the middle of nowhere, it's the first exit before it. Five or six hours north of New Orleans, the only reason Ruston even made my AAA guidebook is because it's home to Louisiana Tech University—an engineering school, not exactly an artistic hotbed or a center of cultural thought. But Louisiana Tech has a college radio station, and wherever there's a college radio station, there's a group of curious music fans plotting to take over.

Jeff Mangum, Robert Schneider, William Cullen Hart, and Bill Doss started infiltrating Louisiana Tech's radio station as volunteer DJs when they were all still in high school. (I don't believe any of them ever bothered to actually enroll in the college.) There they had access to all the hippest indie rock—Guided by Voices and Pavement and Sebadoh—but they also discovered Krautrock, the trippy sounds of '70s German art-rock bands like Neu! and Amon Düül II, Brian Eno's pop efforts, and albums such as *Revolver*, *Pet Sounds*, and *The Piper at the Gates of Dawn*, relics of the first era of psychedelic rock and shining testaments to what can be accomplished in the recording studio when folks are fueled by the potent drug of rampant imagination.

The Ruston boys started making music themselves in various combinations in various parents' basements and garages. They traded four-track cassettes with each other and—with a teenage sense of drama amplified in those who live one exit before the middle of nowhere—they marked all of their recordings as products of something called "the Elephant 6 Recording Company." They had time on their hands to dream up stuff like that, but time passed, the gang split up, and everyone moved out of Ruston. The guerrilla DJs of Louisiana Tech kept making music, though, and now lo and behold, we have three startlingly unique albums from three bands with four auteurs in three different cities—all of them marked somewhere in the fine print as products of Elephant 6.

Despite the ties of friendship and history (not to mention the same master record collection down at the station), the full-length debuts by Neutral Milk Hotel (Mangum), the Apples in Stereo (Schneider), and the Olivia Tremor Control (Hart and Doss) are surprisingly diverse except for two general similarities: They are all essentially home recordings, and they are all remarkably ambitious. In the past too many of the leading lights of the four-track movement have been lo-fi as a sort of political statement; bedroom albums don't have to sound as if they were recorded through the wall from the apartment next door. The Elephant 6'ers could care less about being hip if it means they have to sound like crap. They're emulating the musical heroes whose fanciful soundscapes transported them out of Ruston via their headphones and late-night radio shows.

Neutral Milk Hotel's *On Avery Island* kicks off with the rollicking "Song Against Sex," a driving ditty punctuated by off-kilter trombone lines and boasting torrents of words that paint an impressionistic picture of what may or may not be the weird rush of feelings following a virgin same-sex experience. ("And the first one tore a picture of a dead and hanging man / Who was kissing foreign fishes that flew right out from his hands / And when I put my arms around him I felt the blushing blood run through my cheeks / And an eeriness surrounded when his tongue began to speak.")

Now based in New York, Mangum sang and played just about everything on the album—guitar, drums, xylophone, organ, and tape loops—though he did get a little help from Schneider on extra keyboards. *On Avery Island* never comes up with another melody as indelible as "Song Against Sex," but "You've Passed" is an effective drone in the mold of "Tomorrow Never Knows," "Three Peaches" is a somber and scary mood piece, and the funhouse-mirror instrumentals sprinkled throughout make for a listening experience that keeps you wondering, "How did he *do* that?"

Schneider offers a clue to his working methods with liner notes that thank Mark Lewisohn, author of *The Beatles Recording Sessions*, a tome that lovingly details every backwards guitar and tape loop on *Revolver* and *Sergeant Pepper's Lonely Hearts Club Band* (which, after all, were the first really wacky four-track recordings). The aptly titled *Fun Trick Noisemaker* is the slickest and most consistent of the Elephant 6 albums, and Schneider seems to be the master technician of the crowd. He is also the least interested in visual wordplay.

From their new home in Denver, the Apples in Stereo play fairly conventional songs of love and loneliness ("Love You Alice/D," "Pine Away"), with a sprinkling of science-fiction fun thrown in. ("Step inside the rocket ride / You're leaving on a race through outer space," Schneider sings with childlike enthusiasm in the giddy "Dots 1–2–3" as drummer Hilarie Sidney, the most prominent female voice in the collective, provides gorgeous backing vocals.) Like the fabulous Flaming Lips, the Apples contort their old-fashioned pop songs into something new and different by injecting weird synthesizer sounds and odd vocal effects, or contrasting chaotic guitar noise with crisp, jangling acoustic guitars. It's a heady and winning mix.

Best of all is the Olivia Tremor Control's *Dusk at Cubist Castle,* a debut double album plus bonus ambient disc. In the manner of Eno's *Music for Films, Dusk at Cubist Castle* consists of songs that Hart and Doss conceived for a movie that doesn't exist; it's billed as "music from the unrealized film script." But the album creates plenty of pictures on its own.

Now residents of Athens, Georgia (once home to some monsters of rock who haven't made music this inventive since *Murmur*), Hart and Doss offer up a ridiculously generous twenty-seven tracks, not counting the extra ambient cuts. They visit landscapes ranging from the fanciful and sweetly nostalgic town of a child's imagination—as on *Pet Sounds*–styled pop songs such as "No Growing (Exegesis)" and "Courtyard"—to the icy Antarctic and the dark side of the moon (as on the creepily static and mostly untitled instrumentals).

Like all of the Elephant 6 efforts, it's a trip you shouldn't miss taking if you're at all interested in rock music that uses the studio as a portal to brave new worlds. That the studio can be just a four-track cassette deck in a place like Ruston is the sort of thing that gives me the faith to keep listening, even in the age of Hootie and the Macarena.

14

MAKES NO SENSE AT ALL

"THINK PIECES," WE CALL THEM in the biz, though I heard from plenty of readers who complained that the thinking in these essays was absolutely wrong-headed—that is when they granted that there'd been any thought at all.

"Mud, Moshing, Mayhem, and Money" was the traditional year-end overview for *BAM* written at the request of its editor and my pal, Bill Holdship. In retrospect it serves as a pretty solid overview of the alternative era at its mid-point, just before the beginning of the end.

"Postmark Cleveland" was penned shortly after I arrived in Minneapolis the second time—I had visited the Rock and Roll Hall of Fame and Museum en route from New Jersey to Minnesota while trying to leave *Rolling Stone* in the dust as quickly as possible—but I don't think that my objections to the institution stem from any bitterness about my experiences at the magazine.

"Heavy Hitters" speaks for itself, though I'll have you know that in the last four years I've shrunk from a peak of three hundred fifty-eight pounds to a still-not-svelte-but-at-least-more-manageable two hundred twenty—thank you, Dr. Atkins.

While it was written as a reaction to the most significant event of the new century, "What's Up with Generation Y?" is still relevant to a book that looks back on the music of the '90s because of its musings about the shift in attitudes about rock from one generation to the next, and because the questions it raises continue to loom large on the cultural landscape.

The final piece in this section was also assigned by Holdship and written for *BAM*. Part of a package of articles addressing the question "Is Rock Dead?," I'd forgotten that it existed. When I rediscovered it while rummaging through the clip files in compiling this book, I was struck by how time-less and relevant it still seemed, and I realized at once that there could be no better way for this book to end.

Mud, Moshing, Mayhem, and Money: The Best and Worst of '94
BAM, December 16, 1994

DID YOU EVER have one of those days when the alarm clock doesn't go off and you wake up an hour later than you were supposed to? You wind up wearing mismatched socks and you rush out the door without brushing your teeth. For the rest of the day everything seems blurry and nothing you do helps bring it into focus. Well, in terms of popular music, 1994 was an entire year like that.

The bleary-eyed hangover that was '94 probably won't make sense as far as "what it all means" until twenty years down the line. Pop music has al-ways been a wonderfully chaotic mess, but evolving technology, fracturing musical cliques, and our remote-control attention spans have made it messier than ever. The channels are changing way too fast. From the van-tage point of mid-December, the best we can do to sum up the preceding eleven and a half months is to put the familiar names in bold, search for shared experiences, and move on, leaving the questions to be answered in 2014 (if ever).

Questions? Perhaps the biggest is: Alternative to what? Three years after the breakthrough success of Nirvana's *Nevermind*, alternative is the main-stream. Lollapalooza draws thirty thousand fans per tour stop and the Smashing Pumpkins approach quadruple platinum sales. Another band from Chicago, Veruca Salt, gets some airplay for an indie single and Geffen snatches it up for a reported half-million dollars. In many cities what *Billboard* magazine calls the "modern-rock" outlet is really just the top-rated rock station and the closest thing in town to Top 40 radio (minus, unfortu-nately, any hint of hip-hop, R&B, or music made before something called "the MTV years").

"Indie rock" and "college rock" were once the code words for an exclu-sive group of bands that almost no one (but us) liked. Clearly alternative means something else. Indie rock was partly about doing things differently than the way everybody else did them, but the veterans of college radio and frat-party punk hands are running things now—former Caroline Records publicist and Hole manager Janet Billing is vice-president at Atlantic Records!—and they're doing things pretty much the way they've always been done. For chrissakes, Veruca Salt hired Metallica's managers, and Hole employed high-priced flack-to-the-stars Pat Kingsley to get a puff piece printed in *Entertainment Weekly*. Nothing alternative there.

Maybe what alternative really means is "alternative to the music of our parents." Of course Counting Crows are a bogus Van Morrison rip, but, dammit, they're *our* bogus Van Morrison rip! For a decade classic-rock radio underestimated people's willingness to hear new sounds while overestimating their fondness for Baby Boomer heroes. Now even pathetic crap is being embraced, just as long as it's fresh *new* pathetic crap. Gimme Sheryl Crow (Rickie Lee Jones)! Gimme the Crash Test Dummies (bad Tom Waits)! Gimme Blind Melon (the Grateful Allman Brothers)! I'm on the cutting edge!

Questions: Could that really be all it means? Despite their annoying classic-rock fixation, Pearl Jam's energy is infectious, and the band is fighting the good fight. In '94 the group took on the tyrants at Ticketmaster in an effort to keep fans from getting raped at the box office. The fact that it stood up for consumers at a Congressional hearing and the only thing that made the papers was how funny the band members looked in their shorts and baseball caps only underscores how alternative their actions really were. (Yes, Stone Temple Pilots and Candlebox are the Journeys and REO Speedwagons of a new generation, but we shouldn't necessarily blame Pearl Jam for them any more than we should blame Led Zeppelin for giving us Kingdom Come.)

Other artists also sent inspiring messages. L7, Liz Phair, Courtney Love, Tori Amos, and Sinéad O'Connor are brilliant rockers first and inspiring role models second. But please don't call them "riot grrrls," and please don't marginalize them by putting them on the cover of another "Women in Rock" issue. In a similar slight, boneheaded journalists lumped Green Day with the Offspring and Bad Religion together in a dozen "Punk Revival" stories. More important than selling records and making a racket, Green Day is teaching a new and very young audience that punk is about four things: doing away with rock-star posing, supporting a do-it-yourself ideal (even if the bookmobile they used to tour in is now long gone), turning just about everything into a joke, and playing catchy, hard-hitting rock 'n' roll in the style of Chuck Berry at the tempo of the Ramones. The band also provided one of the few inspiring moments during three sorry, soggy days in Saugerties, New York.

Who ever thought that Woodstock '94 was a good idea? The fabled '60s shindig came together largely by chance, but the greedy bastards who organized the twenty-fifth anniversary fiasco essentially planned a disaster. The three hundred fifty thousand (half paid, half uninvited) mud people were conned into being extras in a really bad movie while being treated like crap the whole time (bad food, no toilets, rotten sound, overpriced everything), all for the benefit of those who paid per view.

While Woodstock '94 was actually going down, I couldn't wait for the movie to see what it was I was supposed to be experiencing. Now I've caught the video and listened to the double CD, and guess what? They stink as bad as the actual event.

Related queries: How come no one aside from *BAM*'s Mick Farren celebrated the anniversary of Altamont? That meant as much to the development of rock in the '70s as Woodstock, if not more. And while we're on the subject of '69 plus twenty-five, why are people still so fascinated with Charles Manson? Maybe Trent Reznor answered that one for us: Bad taste is timeless.

Questions: Is the Las Vegasization of rock inevitable? The Summer of Dinosaurs made it seem that way. The top-dollar ticket prices, whiz-bang gimmickry, and polished but empty nostalgia of Pink Floyd, the Eagles, Traffic, and "Daltrey Sings Townshend" had more in common with glitzy Broadway stage shows than real rock 'n' roll. And a new trend emerged as dozens of concertgoers held up their cell phones and said to the people on the other end, "Guess where I am?" They bought tickets to a status symbol rather than a communal celebration, and the music was irrelevant. They had to act like it was great even if it sucked or admit that they were fools for shelling out an astounding one hundred eighteen bucks per ticket (plus Ticketmaster service charge, of course).

Always in a league of their own, those sly old buzzards the Rolling Stones provided the press with the designated theme for their '94 tour: Are the Stones too old to rock? Saying yes made you an ageist and played right into their hands. The great bluesmen all made wonderful music until their dying days, so why should the Stones be any different? The band floated this nonsense to keep people from asking the really important question, which was: Why do the Stones suck so bad? The band hasn't made a good album since *Some Girls* in 1978, and *Cocktail*—er, *Voodoo—Lounge* certainly wasn't an exception.

Can a group of musicians be considered an honest-to-goodness band when it hasn't created anything but tired retreads of past glories two decades old? In the face of this dilemma Led Zeppelin had been a shining example of a group that quit before pissing on its legacy. But in an astounding reversal of good judgment, Jimmy Page and Robert Plant reunited for a tepid performance of hashed-over classics and pointless new grooves stolen from Moroccan natives. John Bonham would have puked even more than usual at the very thought.

Sadly the number of geezers with functioning shit detectors continues to shrink. In fact, in '94 there were only three: Neil Young, who made a sorta disappointing but not horribly embarrassing album called *Sleeps With Angels*; Brian Eno, who threw a spanner into the works for James and his old buddy Bryan Ferry; and former Zep bassist John Paul Jones, who collects his royalty checks, then does cool things like scoring R.E.M. albums, producing the Butthole Surfers, and touring and recording with Diamanda Galas. I don't care what anyone says, their album *The Sporting Life* blows *Unledded* away.

Questions: How the hell did Michael Jackson get away with it, and will anyone ever hear his music the same way again? Fans who believe that the self-proclaimed "King of Pop" was innocent of having sex with an under-age boy will hear the protestations of a man who was wrongly accused. Cynics will hear the sounds of a multimillionaire who bought justice then solved his public-relations problems by marrying a hunka hunka burnin' love named Lisa Marie Presley. At this point it certainly looks as if the Gloved One walked away from one of the most heinous crimes a pop star has ever been accused of committing—providing, of course, that Snoop Doggy Dogg isn't convicted in 1995.

An element of lawlessness has always been part of rock's appeal, but there's a big difference between trashing a hotel room or marrying your cousin and molesting a fourteen-year-old boy or serving as an accessory to murder. Early in the year sales of Snoop's mediocre solo debut seemed to benefit from what police say are bona fide criminal actions. What does it say about us when we champion a video celebrating how bad an accused bad guy is in real life? I mean, we wouldn't applaud if Quentin Tarantino went around actually shooting people and stabbing needles in their hearts, would we?

As the year progressed gangsta rap seemed increasingly played out. In fact hip-hop in general failed to come up with anything fresh in '94. The sophomore efforts by alternative rappers Arrested Development and Digable Planets were disappointing flops. Public Enemy continued to dilute its message with self-serving whining and pointless attacks on the press. And emerging artists were novelty acts at best (Coolio and Lucas) and more of the same old shit at worst (Warren G.).

R&B wasn't much better. The Man Who Once Was Prince showed that he has well and truly lost his marbles, accusing Warner Bros. of institutional- ized slavery at the same time that he was pulling the insulting scam of rid- ing out his contract with the label by cleaning out his closet. R. Kelly bumped and grinded with all the sexy subtlety of *Hustler* magazine, and Boyz II Men continued their sorry sub-doo-wop vocalizing while dressing up the way Urkell might when going to junior prom. It took that seasoned old pro Barry White to remind us what a sexy groove and a sly lover's rap is really all about. Who'd have thought the Round Mound of Sound still had it in him?

Questions, questions, questions! After a while, they all run into one an- other, and some don't even need elaboration. For example: Lisa Loeb? Aerosmith? Sebadoh? The Cranberries? Evan Dando? Chantmania? Enhanced CDs? Internet interviews? The Cocktail Nation? Puck? Rachel? Kennedy? Hank "Powerbook" Rollins? Madonna (remember her)? British rock (what about that)? What are the words to that damn Beck song? Does Nine Inch Nails really say what I think it says in that modern-rock hit? Who the hell reads *Rolling Stone*? Or *Spin*? Or *BAM*? Is rock 'n' roll dead? Is there anybody out there? How many licks does it take to get to the center of a Tootsie Roll Tootsie Pop???

But there is one more question that's a lot more substantive. Simply put: Kurt Cobain—why?

Check out the Nirvana shelf in your local bookstore's rock section. The explanations were quick to come, and one thing I'm sure of is that they're going to keep coming over the next three hundred sixty five, as well as in the years to come. Another thing I know for certain is that nobody is ever going to know exactly why one of the most important voices of his (our) (my) (your) generation took his own life at the age of twenty-seven when there was a wife and a baby and an awful lot of listeners who really cared about him.

That "why" will linger along with all the other mysteries, and people who care about music will always associate 1994, at least in part, with that particular awful question mark. Rather than fixating on it, we have Nirvana's legacy to explore and listen to and draw inspiration from. Thankfully, with the passage of time, the questions fade, but the music gets louder and louder.

Postmark: Cleveland
The *New York Press,* September 20, 1996

PERCHED ON THE banks of Lake Erie, its angular glass surfaces reflecting the sun and the waves and looking prettier than anything in Cleveland has a right to, the Rock and Roll Hall of Fame and Museum beckons to tourists more forcefully than any scenic view, rest stop, or roadside fireworks stand ever could. Driving west from New York to Minneapolis, I had heard it calling to me from as far away as the New Jersey–Pennsylvania border. Like King Arthur's knights to the Holy Grail or Clark Griswald to Wally World, I felt like I was being drawn to I.M. Pei's Pyramid of Rock 'n' Roll Past as if it were my destiny to visit it.

I knew better, of course. I have spent my career as a rock critic railing against nostalgia and the monolithic version of rock history presented by Baby Boom critics, and the ninety-two-million-dollar "House That Rock Built" is the epitome of both. Still burned out by the grueling ordeal of covering Woodstock '94 for the *Chicago Sun-Times,* I had successfully avoided the opening of the museum the following summer and cheerfully missed such dubious highlights as Sheryl Crow belting out "Let It Bleed" and Slash jamming on "Red House." (These are now preserved on an album called *The Concert for the Rock and Roll Hall of Fame,* which was released in late August on Columbia.)

But the breathless prose in my AAA guidebook finally reeled me in. My wife Kim read aloud about how we could see the Sun Studio gear used by Elvis Presley, the psychedelic Porsche driven by Janis Joplin, the cub scout uniform worn by Jim Morrison—these are as close as we get to the relics of saints in these godless times!—and suddenly I felt like Ebenezer Scrooge on Christmas Eve. Was my heart really so hard that I could just say, "Bah, humbug!" and keep doing seventy down Route 90? I turned to Kim and told her to load the Instamatic. "Honey, we're goin' in!"

We called for tickets in advance from a Perkins an hour outside of Cleveland. Dial the number listed on information and in the tourist books—1–800–493–ROLL—and you're connected directly to Ticketmaster, which proceeds to charge you five dollars and thirty cents more in service costs than the twenty-five dollars and ninety cents you would pay for two tickets if you just walked right in. Maybe the Hall of Fame honchos haven't heard of the Ticketmaster controversy; more likely, they don't care, and are almost certainly getting a portion of the service fees kicked back. Come to think of it, there's precious little Pearl Jam inside.

There are, however, lots of sharp angles, big white expanses, and tons of chrome and glass. The museum looks like all of those newer airports and shopping malls that were going for a sleek, futuristic design but ended up with the same old sterile public-place vibe. Except that *this* sterile public place is darker than most, it smells better, and it's louder. Music plays throughout the building, but there are different tunes at every exhibit, so the effect is like visiting an appliance store with a wall of TVs, each of them tuned to a different station. Raucous it is; rocking it's not.

You enter on the plaza level—the only free part of the museum, so it's devoid of attractions—and are directed down to the ground level before being led upward in ever-tightening circles until reaching the tip of the pyramid. The biases of the founders are obvious almost immediately. The ground level is named after one of them—"The Ahmet M. Ertegun Exhibition Hall"—and there are large displays devoted to Atlantic Records (the label he founded) and his close personal friends, the Rolling Stones. A few floors above there's an entire wall paying tribute to *Rolling Stone* magazine, whose founder, Jann Wenner, is the Hall of Fame's biggest booster. "*Rolling Stone* has always incited its writers to take risks," I read in the accompanying placard, and I couldn't help laughing: I had just been fired by Wenner because I dared to write a negative review of Atlantic superstars Hootie and the Blowfish and complain publicly when he killed it.

"Rock 'n' roll is a force unlike any other," the museum's promotional brochure declares, "and there's only one place on earth where you can *touch* its uncontrollable power." This isn't entirely true. While the Ahmet M. Ertegun Exhibition Hall is full of many *things*—Alice Cooper's prop guillotine! Madonna's conical bustier! Run–DMC's Adidas sneakers! ZZ Top's furry drum set!—you aren't allowed to *touch* any of them, or even photograph them. Museum spokesman Tim Moore said that some of the people who have loaned memorabilia to the joint have requested that it not be photographed. I'm sure the ban also boosts sales of the official souvenir book at the end of the tour and prevents dissatisfied customers from showing off their evidence.

This isn't to say that I was instantly turned off by the museum. On the contrary, there was plenty to fire my enthusiasm and appeal to my jaded postpunk sensibilities. I found myself rushing gleefully between displays of John Cipollina's oversized amplifiers and primitive guitar effects, Roger McGuinn's prototype 1968 Moog synthesizer, and some of the bricks and stage props from Pink Floyd's legendary Wall. The insidiousness of it all only struck me as I stared at a dummy of George Clinton wearing one of Parliament-Funkadelic's outlandish '70s stage costumes, full of fur and colorful feathers, and complete with "Atomic Dog"–shaped platform shoes.

Robert Christgau once wrote that the theme of all of Clinton's prodigious output is that "the forces of life—autonomous intelligence, a childlike openness, sexual energy, and humor—defeat those of death," which, when you think about it, is a pretty workable definition of good rock 'n' roll in general. But the museum is most comfortable with *dead* musicians: Jim, Jimi, Janis, and a lot of Kurt, too, since he's no longer around to sport a CORPORATE MUSEUMS STILL SUCK T-shirt. Clinton is one of the most alive people I've ever met. His statue, like all of those in the museum, is roughly the quality of a cheap showroom dummy, but even if it had been made by Madame Tussaud herself, it would convey none of his energy and passion.

The values of our All-American consumer culture aside, clothes, cars, guitars, and amplifiers don't make the man or woman, let alone the music. If I wanted to get close to the life force—the essence—of Clinton or any of the other artists I cared about, I'd have been better off going back out to my car and popping a tape in the cassette deck. Because the music, unlike the old guitars and Salvation Army cast-offs on display in the museum, is still alive. Everything else is irrelevant, but this isn't even the museum's biggest problem.

Writing in *Spin*, Elizabeth Gilbert recently poked some well-deserved fun at the Hard Rock Hotel and Casino in Las Vegas. The Hall of Fame likes to think it's better, purer, and nobler than the Hard Rock chain—the emphasis is on *education*, it screams. But the curators have chosen the cold medium of video to teach rock's history, even though it may have done more to kill the music than anything else. The constant barrage of images is disorienting and overwhelming. Documentaries in the style of those PBS and Time-Life history-of-rock specials run nonstop in the museum's theaters, and "interactive" exhibits allow visitors to call up images and information by smearing their fingerprints on touch-sensitive video screens. That none of these systems work very well adds a sort of unintended Zen to the experience: I tried to call up Lou Reed's discography, for example, and was rewarded with Randy Newman's.

Even when things are working correctly, the version of rock history that's presented is simplistic and '60s-centric. The reductionist aspect of it all came rushing home in a display called "The Beat Goes On," which purports to connect the dots between key influences and modern rock groups. I touched the screen to find out where Nirvana came from and learned that the Pixies plus the Melvins gave us "Smells Like Teen Spirit." Similarly the Stooges plus Glenn Branca equals Sonic Youth, Phil Spector plus the Beach Boys equals the Ramones, and the Velvet Underground plus Al Green equals the Talking Heads. And here I thought innovation was complicated business.

Hidden agendas abound, and history is contorted to fulfill them. The museum needs to maintain the illusion that Cleveland was chosen as the host city because of its contributions to rock 'n' roll, and not just because it was willing to come up with the municipal funding. The curators bend over backwards to include anything with a local angle, whether or not it fits in. Notorious heterosexual and former Clevelandite Trent Reznor is featured in an exhibit of gender-benders influenced by Iggy Pop and David Bowie, and the local fanzine *Alternative Press* is included among the "magazines that changed rock history" (a showcase which, in any event, is only a quarter of the size of the *Rolling Stone* display). Unfortunately, Cleveland natives Pere Ubu, universally recognized as one of the first and most influential punk bands, don't turn up anywhere.

Touchy but pervasive issues like drug abuse, racism, and misogyny are also given short shrift. A wall is devoted to a display called "Don't Knock the Rock," and Frank Zappa is depicted as single-handedly saving the music in the '80s from evil right-wing censors (never mind that Tipper Gore was and is an allegedly moderate Democrat). No one seems to have caught the sad irony of the official Hall of Fame maps and brochures issuing a parental alert that states, "Because some films and exhibits contain mature themes and images, please ask Visitor Services for information regarding suitability of exhibit content."

Just for kicks Kim called Visitor Services to find out what was considered unsuitable in the temple of the Devil's music. A peppy-voiced employee named Elise advised us to avoid the *Mystery Train* video—she didn't say why—and added, "There's a picture near the men's rest room of Janis Joplin. She's just covered with beads, so it's kind of provocative."

In addition to a few more breasts and some cuss words, *Mystery Train* features Plato's famous quote, "When the mode of the music changes, the walls of the city shake." It was odd to ponder this while sitting in a plush, air-conditioned theater surrounded by people who associate revolution with Nike. Moore said that the museum hosted its one-millionth visitor in August, a year after its opening. On the afternoon I dropped in it was almost exclusively a white, middle-aged crowd, full of chubby moms and dads in shorts and T-shirts, many of them pushing baby strollers. These are not the people your parents warned you about; these *are* your parents.

Mind you, I have no problem with this; I'm about to become a chubby dad myself. But if I ever become as humorless and lifeless as the folks at the Rock and Roll Hall of Fame and Museum, I sincerely hope my kid pulls a Lyle and Eric Menendez on me. In the same video with the Plato quote, token punk-rocker John Lydon defines rock 'n' roll as "giving money to talentless assholes." Not only was I the only person who laughed out loud at that, I actually got nasty stares from the Kmart shoppers sitting around me.

My irritation at this lack of irreverence only grew as I climbed higher in the pyramid, past the Museum Cafe ("where light, healthy refreshments are served"), past the broadcast studio underwritten by Radio Shack, and up to the top floor, which is devoted to those artists who have formally been inducted into the Hall of Fame, which as a foundation predates the museum by eleven years. The induction ceremony takes place every January at New York's Waldorf-Astoria—why would Wenner and Ertegun want to travel to Cleveland?—and the tuxedoed fat cats pay two-hundred fifty dollars a plate for rubber-chicken dinners. They listen to command performances by those they have chosen to honor, and the artists do their best to be gracious right up to the end, when they all join in for a big closing jam that always seems to feature Bruce Springsteen front and center.

The Boss hasn't been inducted yet, but he's a shoo-in for 1998. To make the list for the twelfth annual inductions in 1997, an artist has to have recorded by 1971 or earlier. A small, select, and secretive panel met this spring in New York, presumably in a smoke-filled room located—surprise!—in the suites of *Rolling Stone* magazine to select seventeen eligible names, including the Bee Gees, Black Sabbath, Buffalo Springfield, Solomon Burke, Crosby, Stills & Nash, the Dominoes, the Jackson 5, Lynyrd Skynyrd, the Mamas and the Papas, the Meters, Joni Mitchell, the Moonglows, Parliament-Funkadelic, Gene Pitney, Lloyd Price, the (Young) Rascals, and Iggy and the Stooges. Ballots were then sent to a larger voting body of some two hundred writers, DJs, and industry types, who were directed to choose nine honorees out of the seventeen. The Hall of Fame Foundation will mysteriously winnow the list further, to five to seven artists, before announcing the inductees in the fall.

Wenner added my name to the list of voters shortly before he canned my ass. The ballot was forwarded in the mail to Minneapolis too late for me to vote, but it arrived with a nifty little "Voter Information Booklet" chock full of useful history. "The Bee Gees have three calling cards when it comes to Hall of Fame consideration: popularity, artistry, and impact," it stated. "Nothing will ever come close to the magic of the Mamas and the Papas when they were the Sight and Sound of the Summer of Love," and so on. There was also a handy cassette featuring one song by each nominee (Skynyrd's "Sweet Home Alabama," Sabbath's "Paranoid," the Mamas and the Papas' "California Dreaming"). Such is the grasp one must have on rock history when trusted with the task of determining Hall-of-Famer from non-Hall-of-Famer.

Not surprisingly there is no mention of this selection process in Cleveland; indeed the curators would have you think that the honorees are chosen by some Higher Force. The escalators stop just below the tip of the pyramid, and you must climb the final steps to the *sancto sanctorum* under your own power. It is the only place in the museum where speakers and video monitors aren't blaring, and the only light comes from the thin spots that illuminate the glass walls into which the names of the chosen have been carved: Buddy Holly. Otis Redding. John Lennon. Bob Marley. As I stood in the darkness, enveloped by the silence and solemnity, I could sense the spirits of the greats as they were when they made the music that earned our admiration, and it prompted in me a deep and moving revelation.

The Rock and Roll Hall of Fame is a mighty mountain of crap.

I turned and started trudging back down to earth. The museum is designed so that before you get to the exits, you must fight your way through the giant HMV chain record store that is the climax and final stop of the tour. CDs of all of the artists in the Hall of Fame are featured at top list price, as well as racks of T-shirts, jackets, and baseball caps and shelves of shot glasses, ashtrays, pins, pennants, coasters, coffee mugs, refrigerator magnets, and fountain pens, all adorned with the official pyramid logo.

I cannot tell a lie—I did not escape without shelling out eleven dollars and ninety-nine cents plus tax for an official Hall of Fame souvenir snow globe. As the cashier reached over a rack of *Rolling Stone* magazines to take my hard-earned lucre, the ATM in the corner caught my eye: It's a *rock 'n' roll* cash machine, shaped like a giant jukebox. I was mulling over the symbolism of this as Kim and I headed to the parking lot, and suddenly the sound of a dozen clanging cash registers filled the air, followed by a bass riff you've heard a hundred times if you've heard it once. Pink Floyd's "Money" was being piped into the concrete plaza, and I knew then and there that I couldn't invent a better ending if I tried.

Heavy Hitters
The *Chicago Sun-Times*, January 31, 1993

EVER SINCE ELVIS started fans screaming when he wiggled his skinny butt, the stereotypical rocker has been svelte to the point of anorexia, and that is nothing short of a big fat shame. Because throughout rock history, some of the best music has been made by folks with more aggression, more volume, more imagination, and just plain *more*, period.

When it comes to rock 'n' roll, fat is where it's at.

Not that you could tell from the ministers of popular culture. When a chunkier Stevie Nicks resurfaced with Fleetwood Mac for the Clinton inauguration, Baby Boomer pundits were quick to laugh at her expansion. MTV continues to discriminate against fat performers, bluntly rejecting Tad's "Woodgoblins" video because the singer is "too ugly." Fans vetoed the fat Elvis stamp, even though the singer spent less of his life as a skinny teenager than as a peanut-butter-and-banana-munching lounge lizard. But worst of all is Madonna, who lashes out with surprising vitriol in her coffee-table book, *Sex*.

"I had sex with someone who wasn't grossly obese, but he was pretty overweight," she writes. "If I see someone who's not necessarily conventionally beautiful, I can still be attracted based on their intellect or whatever. But fat is a big problem for me. It sets off something in my head that says, 'overindulgent pig.'"

Enough's enough! It's time fat rockers and fat rock fans started getting some respect.

Anyone who watches daytime TV knows that the fat pride movement is under way. The first step is getting rid of the euphemisms and reclaiming the right adjective. Me, I'm fat and I'm proud. Or, in twelve-step lingo, "My name is Jim, I'm a two-hundred-eighty-pound rock writer, and I'm fat."

Now maybe this gives me an insider's perspective, or maybe I have a big chip on my shoulder. But with all of the tributes in recent years to English rockers, African-American rockers, women rockers, Southern rockers, West Coast rockers, and even rockers from New Jersey, rotund rockers still haven't gotten their due.

From the music's inception fat folks have been among the greats. Down in New Orleans a man they called Fats recorded a string of timeless hits starting in 1956. "They call me the Fat Man," the former Antoine Domino sang, "because I weigh two hundred pounds." That never stopped him from scaling the charts, or from climbing up Blueberry Hill with the ladies.

Perhaps inspired by Fats, a Texas disc jockey named J. P. Richardson made his size a trademark, calling himself the Big Bopper and scoring a hit in 1958 with "Chantilly Lace." (In an injustice rivaling the non-Asian casting of the lead in Broadway's *Miss Saigon*, slim 'n' trim Brian Ruf was cast as the Bopper in the recent production of *Buddy: The Buddy Holly Story* at Chicago's Shubert Theatre. This is revisionist history of the worst sort!)

Unfortunately fat went out of fashion at the start of the British Invasion, when Twiggy and fitted mod trousers were all the rage. Reg Presley of the Troggs looked like he was shoehorned into that striped uniform, and Mark Volman of the Turtles clearly wasn't a marathoner. But they were rare exceptions.

As the decade wore on, the few fat hippies in the Woodstock Nation came to ignominious ends: Prototypical earth mother Cass Elliot of the Mamas and the Papas died of a heart attack in 1974 (she didn't choke to death on a ham sandwich, as is often reported). After some modest but fleeting fame early on, Mountain guitarist Leslie West faded into obscurity. And Canned Heat singer Bob "the Bear" Hite's career was on a long downhill slide well before his death in 1981.

Tipping the scales at well over three hundred pounds, Marvin Lee Aday of Dallas, Texas, made pop-music history as the powerhouse voice behind one of the best-selling albums of all time, 1977's *Bat Out of Hell*, but that didn't earn him any respect. Becoming famous with a name like Meat Loaf is a mixed blessing (especially when publications such as the *New York Times* refer to you as "Mr. Loaf"), and the number of jokes that have been made in rock mags at his expense through the years is right up there with the number of albums that he's sold.

Things were a bit better for the first and only fat black superstar of the '70s, Barry White. He had a brief career as a boxer in Los Angeles before he struck gold with his silky smooth grooves and honey bass voice. Hits such as "I'm Gonna Love You Just a Little More, Baby" and "Love's Theme" helped White sell more than a hundred million albums. "Please don't take off your panties," he would croon. "Let me take them off for you . . . *slo-o-o-o-wly*." As comical as it sounds, this pillow talk was a hit with the ladies and an inspiration to men, and the "Round Mound of Sound" became one of pop music's biggest sex symbols—literally.

Back in the rock world it took punk to bring fat back into vogue. From its beginning in the mid-'70s punk rock's nonconformist stance attracted anyone who deviated from the sound and look of reigning lightweights such as the Eagles and the aforementioned Fleetwood Mac. Predating Sex Pistols singer Johnny Rotten and just behind Joey Ramone was fellow punk pioneer David Thomas (the leader of Pere Ubu, not the guy who sells Wendy's hamburgers). Calling himself Crocus Behemoth he provided bizarre wailing vocals and ran the band's record label, creating a model for the many do-it-yourself releases that followed. Like the Big Bopper, Thomas made his size a trademark, wearing vintage suits, bow ties, and suspenders that exaggerated his resemblance to Oliver Hardy. But fat rockers made their biggest splash in the early '80s.

In San Francisco, singer Debora Iyall exuded a smart 'n' sassy sex appeal while fronting Romeo Void. Led by the mighty D. Boon, the Minutemen from San Pedro, California, were the first and most successful group to mix funk, jazz, and myriad other influences with hardcore punk rhythms and song structures. And the Minneapolis trio Hüsker Dü was driven by the songwriting tag team of Bob Mould and Grant Hart, two sumo-shaped fellows known to relax after shows by pinning each other in a half-nelson.

Today the fat-rock influence is strongest in the grunge-rock capitals of Seattle and Portland. The fish-eye lens that Epic Records employed for promo photos couldn't hide the fact that the Screaming Trees are led by bountiful brothers Gary Lee and Van Conner. There is no such trickery for Tad, who fronts the band of the same name. The former butcher lets it all hang out, and he's fast becoming a star of song and screen: As the surprised recipient of Bridget Fonda's amorous phone call in *Singles*, he scores the film's biggest laugh. But the heaviest of all, musically and physically, is Poison Idea.

Based in Portland, Poison Idea has been turning out revved-up garage-punk for more than a decade, and it ranks among Nirvana leader Kurt Cobain's favorite groups. "I think we might be the heaviest rock band in the world," says bandleader Tom Roberts, aka Pig Champion. "I've actually lost some weight lately 'cause I quit drinking, but I was probably up over the five-hundred-pound mark. Now I'm down at a svelte four-fifty."

Two of Pig's current bandmates weigh in at three hundred seventy and three hundred pounds. The band has never required its members to be large, but Pig maintains that the fat people he's played with have always been the most creative. In fact he doesn't have much tolerance for anyone else. "It's been my experience that the few good people out there—I only consider about two percent of the human race worth shit—they're fat," he

says. "Because they're good people and they're big, they've got just that little bit more *oomph*. Call it soul, life-force, whatever."

Many rappers would agree. Since its earliest days, hip-hop has been especially accepting of fat musicians. The Fat Boys, B. Fats, and Biz Markie all
scored big hits as the music established itself in the '80s. But they were co-
medians who traded on clichéd images of jolly fat jesters. The new heavy
hip-hop stars demand to be taken seriously.

Prince Be of P.M. Dawn delivers wisdom like a black Buddha, both on album and in his Nike commercials. The sizable Samoans in the Boo-Yaa
T.R.I.B.E. are making inroads into the alternative-rock world since touring
with Lollapalooza '92. Chubb Rock is known as a "rapper's rapper" because of his hardcore rhymes and agile tongue. And with songs such as
"The Overweight Lover's in the House" and "Mr. Big Stuff," Heavy D. is a
hip-hop link back to good ol' Barry White.

As in society in general, fat women have had a harder time with prejudice and stereotyping than fat men. They're rarely seen as sexy, and even
the most talented female musicians are shunned by the star-making machinery if they're fat.

Martha Wash's voice powered the sounds of C+C Music Factory, but she
was replaced because producers thought she didn't look good in the
videos. "Everything with companies now is from the standpoint of marketing; it's all visual," she says. "It's, 'We'll deal with the visuals first and figure out later if she can sing.' But you can look wonderful in a bikini and not
be able to sing worth anything!"

Trained in the gospel and opera traditions, both of which embrace fat di-
vas, Wash has always had a healthy attitude about her size. She experienced her initial success as half of the un-selfconsciously named duo Two
Tons o' Fun. The San Francisco native went on to sing with the Weather
Girls (best remembered for the hit "It's Raining Men") and Black Box before
recording with C+C Music Factory. Now she's striking out on her own.
Wash's self-titled RCA debut was recently released, and like the woman
herself, the album is bouncy, optimistic, and life-affirming.

"I have my bad days, but I would say I'm basically a very happy person," she says. "I'm large and I still think I need to lose weight, and I probably will. But I don't think I'll ever be very, very thin. I deal with it the best
way I can. I'm just who I am."

But a positive attitude isn't necessarily enough to overcome inherent biases. The futile efforts to disguise the size of singer Ann Wilson in Heart's

recent videos are well-known: After trying to shroud her in fog and hide her behind silk curtains, directors finally resorted to showing only her eyes. The size discrimination is only a little less obvious in Wilson Phillips's videos. While her bandmates frolic on the beach in halter tops, Carnie Wilson sweats it out in a long frock coat. She gets less screen time, although she's the best singer and most talented member of the group.

Wilson has had the last laugh, however. Because of her riotous personality and irreverent wit, she has become a hero in the gay and underground rock communities. She's a favorite among drag performers, and there's even a new grunge band called the Fat Chick in Wilson Phillips.

Wilson, Wash, and other fat performers are also lauded by fat rights groups such as the Sacramento-based National Association to Advance Fat Acceptance. NAAFA has branches throughout the United States, and its activities range from lobbying for bigger airplane seats to protesting TV sitcom fat jokes. "What we're trying to do is change the stereotypes about fat people," said Laura Eljaiek, the group's program director. "Our basic message is that any body is a good body. We can all dance, all sing, and all have fun, and those things have nothing to do with size. The media is too concerned in promoting one particular look as acceptable, and that's not healthy for any of us."

Well, most of the media, anyway. And, of course, Madonna.

Miss Ciccone, you owe us an apology, and you'd better hurry. There's a man named Pig I'd like you to meet. *In a big way.*

....

Cool Fat Songs
Willie Dixon, "300 Pounds of Joy"
Root Boy Slim, "Dare To Be Fat"
Queen, "Fat Bottom Girls"
Spinal Tap, "Big Bottom"
Six Mix-A-Lot, "Baby Got Back"

Big Flops (Fat Rockers Who Weren't So Cool)
Randy Bachman of Bachman Turner Overdrive
David Crosby
Christopher Cross
Robert "Fat Bob" Smith of the Cure
Anyone in Molly Hatchett

**The Oprah Syndrome (Pop Stars Denying
Their True Fat Selves)**
Paula Abdul
Belinda Carlisle
Wynonna Judd
Bob Mould
Ozzy Osbourne
Luther Vandross

....

What's Up with Generation Y?
Salon, September 25, 2001

AS AMERICA STRUGGLES both literally and metaphorically to climb out
from under the bloody wreckage of September 11, many a pundit has taken
to quoting the famous line often attributed to Japanese Admiral Isoruku
Yamamoto in the wake of the attack on Pearl Harbor: "We have woken a
sleeping giant, and filled him with a terrible resolve."

Never mind that, as World War II scholars have pointed out, Yamamoto
never uttered those words. (To quote the moderators of the Pearl Harbor
Attacked online message board, "Nobody can provide a source for this
quote prior to the release of the movie *Tora! Tora! Tora!*") There is a potential
sleeping giant here, but it isn't the military-industrial complex that
Hollywood's Yamamoto or the current crop of talking heads mean to evoke.
It is Generation Y, and it has just gotten a big bucket of ice water in the face.

Encompassing more than seventy million people born between 1980 and
1996, Generation Y is, at its core, the largest group of teenagers in American
history, dwarfing even its parents, the Baby Boomers who came of age in
the '60s. In the next decade it will come to represent forty-one percent of
the U.S. population, according to the Census Bureau. Until recently its entire existence has been spent in a period of unprecedented prosperity and
a cocoon of creature comforts the likes of which we've never seen before—or at least not since Camelot, which, after all, was quickly interrupted by the unfortunate ugliness of assassinations, the war in Vietnam,
and riots in the streets.

For the business press and many sociologists, the defining characteristics
of this generation to date have been its buying power (two hundred seventy-five billion spent annually, according to some estimates) and—despite

an astounding degree of media savvy thanks to being raised with cable and the Net (and literacy be damned)—its cheerfully compliant consumerism and gleeful malleability at the hands of the shrewd and ubiquitous über-brands and lifestyle firms. (From a piece published in the *Washington Business Journal* last spring: "Smarter marketers such as Tommy Hilfiger and Old Navy have understood that coolness is an important ingredient in cultivating Y's. Abercrombie & Fitch has done it best. What was once a conservative, white-male sporting goods store is now the coolest spot in the mall. . . . Codifying what today's teenager cool is all about.")

If there could possibly be a bright side to the obscene events of two weeks past, it's that Britney Spears and the Backstreet Boys, *Total Request Live* and Limp Bizkit, *Survivor*, Sony PlayStation, 'N Sync, and their ilk will never be enough again. Everything changed on September 11—it's a cliché but it's true—and that includes the sudden realization for many that their current opiates were nothing but placebos.

For Generation Y, nothing much has ever been at stake, even during our most galvanizing and engrossing national news events. (Did O.J.–Clinton–Condit really "just do it," in the words of Nike? Who cares!) Hence even the "edgiest" of its music (Rage Against the Machine? Brought to you by Sony! Eminem? Vanilla Ice as hate-filled slasher-movie obsessive!) has just been another piece of empty but well-hyped product meant to be purchased on credit, displayed along with one's hundred-fifty-dollar sneakers as irrefutable evidence of hepness, then consumed and shit out (just like the news), to be replaced the minute a new and improved model is sent hurtling down the corporate pipeline.

As the celebrated Gen X eggheads of the Chicago culture zine *The Baffler* have theorized, perhaps any form of genuine protest or real community (post–Seattle grunge, they favored the word "scene") is impossible in an era when Madison Avenue has perfected its ability to transform everything into a marketing pose, "turning rebellion into money," as the Clash once sang.

Nevertheless a revolution is a-brewin'. A small but passionate vanguard of Generation Y has been galvanized by the issue of globalization. They see as their enemy the mega-corporations that are trying to spread consumerism to every corner of the globe, killing Western culture and turning us all into the equivalent of those cannibalistic zombies traipsing through the shopping mall in *Dawn of the Dead*. In addition to our souls, they believe that corporatization is claiming the blood of the Third World, as child laborers from Beijing to Jakarta and sweatshop workers from Tijuana to the

Philippines manufacture the overpriced jeans and useless sunglasses that American companies brand with their copyrighted logos and spend billions to market to us as indispensable accoutrements of our hip, modern lifestyles.

Who are these contrarian anti-consumerists? They're the computer hackers who live to torment Bill Gates and Microsoft. They count among their numbers some of the legions of college students who use their dorms' T3 lines to distribute and download vast libraries of MP3 files—the marketing of music through relentless tour sponsorships, saturation airplay via the monopolistic mediums of corporate radio and MTV, and overpriced major-label CDs ranking among the corporate byproducts that they hate most of all. Rare is the twentysomething who is unaware of *No Logo* ("The book that became part of a movement," to quote the banner on the book's Web site)— regardless of whether they've actually read Naomi Klein's phenomenally successful screed against globalization or just seen it name-checked in interviews with Radiohead.

Some of these Y's have been motivated to more serious action. They disrupted the meeting of the World Trade Organization in Seattle in 1999, and rioted again at the Group of Eight summit in Genoa, Italy, in July. (The last event even produced a martyr, twenty-three-year-old Carlo Giuliani—and how's that for an ironic name right now?—who was shot dead by a police officer as he tried to rush a jeep with a fire extinguisher.) Maybe all dissent is instantly commodified these days, as the *Baffler* boys say. But what's to stop youth from rebelling against the act of commodification itself? To bite the hand of anyone who tries to sell it anything—including (or especially) music? Here is the battlefield of the real "new war."

So far the activists' advance guard has been limited to the smallest fraction of Generation Y, but it has had an impact nonetheless. The movement is certainly being monitored in high places: On September 13, just two days after the attacks on the World Trade Center and the Pentagon, the *Wall Street Journal* published a prominent analysis of how the outbreak of terrorism in the United States might result in a crackdown against "America's homegrown radicals . . . members of the burgeoning antiglobalization movement." The hopeful tone of the article was unmistakable, though the writer never bothered to spell out how tree-hugging environmentalists and Starbucks-defacing graffiti artists equate with murderous, suicidal hijackers.

Two questions will loom large in the coming weeks. The first: Whither Generation Y now?

Rudely awoken, will this now-alert giant listen to the beating of the war drums; parrot the ubiquitous television commentators' jingoism; applaud the bloodlust of the hawks; buy the benefit single that's being planned by the pathetically lapsed King of Pop, Michael Jackson; and be conned once more by Viacom-owned MTV? (Speaking of logos, the cable music giant has turned its symbol into a waving flag, which appears in the corner of the screen through all its programming, including regular showings of "Overcome," a video by the ridiculous fourth-generation grunge band Live that, according to its spokesperson, "is dedicated to the tragedies' victims." It also helps hype an album that's due out on Tuesday.)

Alternately, will the masses of young America start thinking about the political movement that has been embraced by some of their peers? Will they begin to seriously question the substantive problems facing America and the world, challenging the unilateral foreign policies and the global corporatization that are clearly a part of what provoked the reprehensible actions of September 11? (There's a third possibility, too, and that's that absolutely nothing will change and everybody will go right back to ringing up credit-card debt—which in some ways would be even more awful than the warmonger option.)

Make no mistake, as our president is so fond of saying: Only an idealist who's even more hopelessly naive than the hardest hardcore holdover from the Age of Aquarius could think that Generation Y will actually affect what is about to go down. How Bush's "war on terrorism" plays out will be determined by the top-level power struggle that's currently being waged between the old-line military-industrial hawks that Ike famously warned us about and the new forces of globalization, epitomized by the split between Cheney-Rumsfeld on one side and Colin Powell on the other. (I'm betting on Powell and the corporations—war is very bad for business, and in the new millennium, business is everything. You'll notice that W. hasn't started bombing anyone yet, and that can't possibly be because of Christian restraint.)

So no, Generation Y won't control world events—at least not yet. But that brings us to our second question: What sort of an impact can we expect the indelible images of September 11 to have on popular culture, especially rock 'n' roll, which, four generations of commodifiers be damned, is still the last great bastion of "truth" in popular culture?

At its best, rock has always given the finger to the self-important forces of the reigning hegemony. The music first sprouted as a race-mixing juvenile delinquent scourge on the otherwise picture-perfect '50s. It blossomed at the height of an unjust war in the '60s; was rejuvenated by punk during the recession of the mid-'70s; and flowered again with indie rock and hip-hop during the cultural conservatism ushered in by Reagan, trickle-down economics, and AIDS in the mid- to late '80s. That wonderful fuck-you spark has been missing for some time now—it was muted at best during the alternative era of the early '90s, as Gen X's antiheroes struggled with an irresistible penchant for irony and their own ambivalence toward stardom (cf. Nirvana and Pearl Jam). Some would have us believe that it was buried for good along with the generation gap at the dawn of this new century—that it is now safe enough to permanently enshrine in a Rock and Roll Hall of Fame and Museum in Cleveland and chart through VH1's *Behind the Music* in neat thirty-minute segments that all seem to have identical plot lines.

But if we accept that at least some of the enduring music of the Woodstock Nation was inspired by the anger of young women who saw babies being killed in their mothers' arms and the fears of young men reluctant to get their butts blown off in Southeast Asia for a cause that no one could explain, what kind of soundtrack will be produced by the sudden awareness that—regardless of age, sex, race, or class—random annihilation at the hands of an unseen enemy can arrive almost anywhere and at any time? And that the enemy, partly produced by American arrogance in the first place, is being fought with nothing more than another dose of that same arrogance, a whole lot of brute strength, and bushels of money?

Which side will Generation Y be on? All we have to do to find out is listen. As Bertolt Brecht said, "In the dark times, will there still be singing? Yes, there will be singing. There will be singing about the dark times."

Rock 'n' Roll Is Alive and Well and Living at (Address Unlisted at the Customer's Request)
BAM, October 7, 1994

THE CORRECT—INDEED, the only—response to that hoariest of hoary old questions, "Is rock 'n' roll dead?" is, of course, *fuck you*. ("I don't care" is also acceptable, but "fuck you" has a much nicer ring.) If you don't understand why, well, you probably don't understand rock 'n' roll. So let's start there.

One can only answer the question of whether rock 'n' roll is dead after defining what the hell rock 'n' roll *is*. Even after five decades it's still such a slippery beast that each and every one of us has a different definition.

Someone who defines the music by the narrow stylistic parameters of its early practitioners—Chuck Berry, Bo Diddley, Little Richard, or Eddie Cochran—is perfectly correct in saying that rock was dead and buried by 1959. The Beatles, the Stones, Jimi Hendrix, the Troggs, Lothar and the Hand People, and everything else that followed was a pale imitation or a useless elaboration.

My friend, *Chicago Reader* rock critic Bill Wyman, defines rock 'n' roll as "the sound of a generation speaking to itself." Not bad. That allows for the Monkees, the Sex Pistols, Public Enemy, Madonna, and Nirvana to all be considered rock 'n' roll. But it doesn't explain why *Exile on Main St.* is so fascinating to twentysomething Liz Phair, or why the Wayne and Garths cruising through middle America on Friday night still believe that "Stairway to Heaven" (twenty-three years old) or "Walk This Way" (nineteen years old) are as good as it gets. And while Barney or Boyz II Men could also be described as examples of generations talking to themselves, they sure ain't rock 'n' roll.

Me, I have a definition that's expansive on the one hand and completely Jim-o-centric on the other. Rock 'n' roll is a spontaneous explosion of personality, and it is an attitude. What exactly *is* that attitude? Hard to say, but I know it when I see it. Mostly, it's *fuck you*, but that's a *fuck you* delivered with a sneer and a smirk and a defiant gleam in the eye that says, "I am here, I am alive, I am me, and I am unique!," and maybe also a nervous laugh that masks myriad other emotions that may or may not be well-articulated. As much as it negates, rock 'n' roll is also something that makes you feel alive, and from that feeling comes a sense of community. However short-lived, people on either side of you are having the same feeling at the same time. We are stupid and contagious, a-wop-bop-a-loo-bop, a wop-bam-boom.

My hero, the late rock critic Lester Bangs, once wrote a letter to the late *Soho Weekly News* to settle a long-forgotten argument about who invented punk. I'm paraphrasing here, but it went along the lines of Lester invented it, but he stole it from Dave Marsh (who actually saw ? & the Mysterians live once), and he stole it from Iggy, who stole it from Lou Reed, who stole it from Brando, who stole it from Robert Mitchum (that look on his face in the photo when he was busted for grass), who stole it a few times removed from Mike Fink, who stole it from Stonewall Jackson, who stole it from Napoleon, who stole it from Voltaire, and so on—and on and on, as was Lester's wont—until it gets to Lady Godiva, who stole it from her horse, who stole it from some toothless wino lying in a Parisian gutter, and there it ends, but not really, 'cause it trails off with an ellipsis . . .

Lester was great at reshaping history to serve his own purposes, but all of us do that. These days it's even encouraged and called postmodernism. So what if Lester said John Coltrane was a punk, or I say that the Doors were a lousy cocktail band fronted by a fat, sophomoric, sub–Robert Bly poet? Who's to say that either of us is right or wrong? Every single listener brings different criteria for what rock 'n' roll is to his or her stereo, Walkman, or neighborhood rock club. Today's Lollapaloser may be blissfully unaware that the explosions of feedback in Hendrix's version of "The Star-Spangled Banner" were meant to evoke the very real explosions on the battlefields of Vietnam. The song either speaks to his or her reality here and now or it doesn't. Unlike Elvis, Hendrix is irrefutably dead. But his music may or may not be alive for listeners today, and it may or may not be rock 'n' roll.

Indie-über-alles ethicist Steve Albini defines rock by the package it comes in, going so far as to say he may like a band on the Touch and Go label but dislike another group that sounds exactly the same on [name your favorite major label here]. *Yawn.* That the business part of the music business is a rancid sludge pit filled with vile poison-spewing slugs is such old news that even the slugs get a laugh outta this rap. Over time music stands on its own merits or it doesn't. A good song isn't forever tainted by its major-label promotion, the fact that the artist was screwed by his or her manager, or the possibility that the tune may be sandwiched between crap like Candlebox and Lisa Loeb on computer-programmed modern-rock radio. The music industry sold its soul to the devil long before Robert Johnson sold his, and that doesn't have any bearing on rock 'n' roll's vital signs.

For a time it seemed as if the factor most likely to kill the patient off was the bogus promotion of the pantheon as defined by Boomer rock critics and classic-rock radio: All Beatles-Stones-Who, all the time. The aging of the Baby Boom's heroes is not a pretty sight, and the notion that they are still relevant is even more repugnant. This is not simply ageism. Paul McCartney, *Voodoo Lounge,* and "Daltrey Sings Townshend" suck because they are soulless, vapid, mercenary, and mechanical, not because the perpetrators are all fiftysomething. Neil Young's a geezer, too, but he hasn't burned out, faded away, or lost his attitude. You can rock until you croak, so long as the attitude remains.

The question ultimately comes down to whether there are still genuine rock 'n' roll experiences to be had in 1994, and we all have to answer that one for ourselves. Me, I've found 'em over the preceding three hundred sixty-five courtesy of shiny plastic discs by Ride, Red Red Meat, L7,

Eugenius, Arrested Development, Wake Ooloo, Material Issue, the Jesus Lizard, Hole, Pavement, the Orb, Low, the Brand New Heavies, Smog, Blur, Luna, Sinéad O'Connor, R.E.M., Liz Phair, Weezer, Stereolab, Green Day, Public Enemy, Julian Cope, the new Hawkwind, and Neil Young, and that's just my Top Ten on this particular day (and yeah, I know I can't count). I've had 'em at an early morning rave on a remote hilltop in Hixton, Wisconsin; at a four-hour show by the inimitable George Clinton; with the Flaming Lips in the mosh pit at Lollapalooza; and while witnessing Courtney Love take a swan dive into the crowd after a heartbreaking version of "Where Did You Sleep Last Night." I've even had 'em (very briefly) in that hellish shithole called Woodstock '94 (copyright by Pepsi).

Hell, if rock 'n' roll was any *more* alive, I might be dead.

But I'm not. I'm writing this piece, and that brings up one more point: It's tempting to say that rock *writing* is dead, but technically even that's not true. *BAM* is paying me one hundred fifty bucks just to write this stupid rebuttal. There are, however, a lot of rock writers who should be dead—or at least forced to retire—and first and foremost is anyone who insists on maintaining that rock 'n' roll is R.I.P.

Appendix:
The Ninety Best Albums of the '90s

Nirvana	*In Utero*
My Bloody Valentine	*Loveless*
The Flaming Lips	*Transmissions from the Satellite Heart*
Public Enemy	*Fear of a Black Planet*
Sinéad O'Connor	*I Do Not Want What I Haven't Got*
U2	*Achtung Baby*
R.E.M.	*Automatic for the People*
Hole	*Live Through This*
P.M. Dawn	*Jesus Wept*
Blur	*Parklife*
PJ Harvey	*To Bring You My Love*
Mudhoney	*Superfuzz Bigmuff*
Urge Overkill	*Saturation*
The Smashing Pumpkins	*Adore*
Liz Phair	*Exile in Guyville*
Nirvana	*Nevermind*
R.E.M.	*Out of Time*
Teenage Fanclub	*Bandwagonesque*
Spiritualized	*Lazer Guided Melodies*
Red Red Meat	*Jimmywine Majestic*
Neil Young	*Ragged Glory*
Brian Eno and John Cale	*Wrong Way Up*
Redd Kross	*Third Eye*
Galaxie 500	*This Is Our Music*
Ride	*Carnival of Light*
Julian Cope	*Peggy Suicide*

Nirvana	*MTV Unplugged in New York*
P.M. Dawn	*Of the Heart, of the Soul and of the Cross: The Utopian Experience*
Elastica	*Elastica*
Björk	*Post*
Blur	*Modern Life is Rubbish*
Arrested Development	*3 Years, 5 Months and 2 Days in the Life of . . .*
Stereolab	*Switched On*
The Orb	*Orblivion*
Los Lobos	*Kiko*
L7	*Bricks Are Heavy*
Sinéad O'Connor	*Universal Mother*
PJ Harvey	*Rid of Me*
Matthew Sweet	*Girlfriend*
Pearl Jam	*Vs.*
The Smashing Pumpkins	*MACHINA / The Machines of God*
Madonna	*Erotica*
Nine Inch Nails	*The Downward Spiral*
The Orb	*Live 93*
Beck	*Odelay*
The Screaming Trees	*Dust*
Stereolab	*Transient Random-Noise Bursts with Announcements*
Luscious Jackson	*Fever In Fever Out*
Spiritualized	*Ladies and Gentlemen We Are Floating in Space*
P.M. Dawn	*The Bliss Album . . . ? (Vibrations of Love and Anger and the Ponderance of Life and Existence)*
The Muffs	*The Muffs*
Yo La Tengo	*Painful*
Pearl Jam	*Vitalogy*
Cardinal	*Cardinal*
Ride	*Nowhere*
Liz Phair	*Whip-smart*
Eugenius	*Mary Queen of Scots*
Green Day	*Dookie*
The Flaming Lips	*In a Priest Driven Ambulance*
The Olivia Tremor Control	*Music from the Unrealized Film Script "Dusk at Cubist Castle"*
The Jesus and Mary Chain	*Psychocandy*
Soundgarden	*Superunknown*
Alice In Chains	*Jar of Flies*

Material Issue	*Freak City Soundtrack*
Foo Fighters	*Foo Fighters*
Oasis	*(What's the Story) Morning Glory?*
The Smoking Popes	*Destination Failure*
Pulp	*Different Class*
The Boo Radleys	*C'Mon Kids*
Julian Cope	*The Interpreter*
Yum-Yum	*Dan Loves Patti*
Blur	*Blur*
Helium	*The Magic City*
Monster Magnet	*Dopes to Infinity*
Pearl Jam	*Ten*
The Smashing Pumpkins	*Mellon Collie and the Infinite Sadness*
Urge Overkill	*The SuperSonic Storybook*
Veruca Salt	*American Thighs*
The Breeders	*Last Splash*
Tori Amos	*Little Earthquakes*
PJ Harvey and John Parrish	*Dance Hall at Louse Point*
Lush	*Gala*
Urge Overkill	*Exit the Dragon*
Babes In Toyland	*Spanking Machine*
Wake Ooloo	*Stop the Ride*
Sonic Youth	*Goo*
Pere Ubu	*Worlds in Collision*
Robyn Hitchcock	*Perspex Island*
Neutral Milk Hotel	*On Avery Island*
Tone-Loc	*Cool Hand Loc*

Index

About the Author

Born in Jersey City, New Jersey, the year the Beatles arrived in America, Jim DeRogatis began voicing his opinions about rock 'n' roll shortly thereafter. As a high school senior, he spent a long and fascinating day interviewing Lester Bangs two weeks before that legendary rock writer's untimely death. Thus was born a lifelong obsession with rock criticism, though DeRogatis spent the first five years of his career as a beat and in-

PHOTO BY MARTY PEREZ

vestigative reporter at *The Jersey Journal*. In 1990 he moved to Minneapolis and began working as the assistant editor at *Request*; in 1992 he became the pop music critic at the *Chicago Sun-Times*. Together with Greg Kot, the rock critic at the *Chicago Tribune*, he is the host of *Sound Opinions*, "the world's only rock 'n' roll talk show," now in its fifth year on Chicago radio. (Check it out on the Net at www.soundopinions.net.) A televised version of *Sound Opinions* recently debuted on WTTW, Chicago's PBS–TV affiliate. DeRogatis is also a regular contributor to *Spin, Modern Drummer, Guitar World, Harp*, and Playboy.com. His first book, *Kaleidoscope Eyes: Psychedelic Rock from the '60s to the '90s*, was published in the summer of 1996 (a new edition is forthcoming from Hal Leonard under the title *Turn On Your Mind: Four Decades of Great Psychedelic Rock*). He is also the author of *Let It Blurt: The Life and Times of Lester Bangs, America's Greatest Rock Critic*, published in the spring of 2000. He jokes that he is not a musician, but he *is* a drummer (he was a member of the semi-legendary Wire cover band, the Ex-Lion Tamers; the Feelies offshoot, Speed the Plough; and Airlines, among many other bands), and a book about his adventures in various groups over the last two decades is in the works. His current band, Vortis, has released two albums on the independent Thick Records. He can be reached through the Web at www.jimdero.com.